# The Running Centaur

This book surveys the practice of horse racing from antiquity to the modern period, and in this way offers a selective global history.

Unlike previous histories of horse racing, which generally make claims about the exclusiveness of modern sport and therefore diminish the importance of premodern physical contests, the contributors to this book approach racing as a deep history of diachronically comparable practices, discourses, and perceptions centered around the competitive staging of equine speed. In order to compare horse racing cultures from completely different epochs and regions, the authors respond to a series of core issues which serve as structural comparative parameters. These key issues include the spatial and architectural framework of races; their organization; victory prizes; symbolic representations of victories and victors; and the social range and identities of the participants. The evidence of these competitions is interpreted in its distinct historical contexts and with regard to specific cultural conditions that shaped the respective relationship between owners, riders, and horses on the global racetracks of pre-modernity and modernity.

The chapters in this book were originally published as a special issue of *The International Journal of the History of Sport*.

**Sinclair W. Bell** is Professor of Art History and Presidential Teaching Professor at Northern Illinois University. One of his primary areas of research is sport and spectacle in the Roman period, about which he has published numerous articles and books and which he discusses in a recent documentary, 'Rome's Chariot Superstar.'

**Christian Jaser** is Professor of Medieval History and Historical Auxiliary Sciences at the University of Klagenfurt. His research interests encompass the history of premodern sport cultures in the context of urban and courtly settings. His book on urban horse racing in fifteenth- and early sixteenth-century Italy and Germany is forthcoming.

**Christian Mann** is Professor of Ancient History at the University of Mannheim. His research interests include sport and spectacle in antiquity, Greek athletes as well as Roman gladiators. He is co-editor of the journals *Klio* and *Nikephoros*.

**Sport in the Global Society: Historical Perspectives**
*Series Editors: Mark Dyreson, Thierry Terret and Rob Hess*

**A Half Century of Super Bowls**
National and Global Perspectives on America's Grandest Spectacle
*Edited by Mark Dyreson and Peter Hopsicker*

**Sport in Socialist Yugoslavia**
*Edited by Dario Brentin and Dejan Zec*

**The Olympic Movement and the Middle East and North African Region**
*Edited by Mahfoud Amara*

**Sport Development and Olympic Studies**
Past, Present, and Future
*Edited by Stephan Wassong, Michael Heine and Rob Hess*

**Match Fixing and Sport**
Historical Perspectives
*Edited by Mike Huggins and Rob Hess*

**New Dimensions of Sport in Modern Europe**
Perspectives from the 'Long Twentieth Century'
*Edited by Heather L. Dichter, Robert J. Lake and Mark Dyreson*

**Asian Sport Celebrity**
*Edited by Koji Kobayashi and Younghan Cho*

**Indigenous Sports History and Culture in Asia**
*Edited by Fan Hong and Liu Li*

**Sport and Apartheid South Africa**
Histories of Politics, Power, and Protest
*Edited by Michelle M. Sikes, Toby C. Rider and Matthew P. Llewellyn*

**The Running Centaur**
Horse-Racing in Global-Historical Perspective
*Edited by Sinclair W. Bell, Christian Jaser and Christian Mann*

For more information about this series, please visit: www.routledge.com/Sport-in-the-Global-Society—Historical-perspectives/book-series/SGSH

# The Running Centaur
Horse-Racing in Global-Historical Perspective

*Edited by*
Sinclair W. Bell, Christian Jaser
and Christian Mann

LONDON AND NEW YORK

First published 2022
by Routledge
2 Park Square, Milton Park, Abingdon, Oxon, OX14 4RN

and by Routledge
605 Third Avenue, New York, NY 10158

*Routledge is an imprint of the Taylor & Francis Group, an informa business*

Chapters 1-5 and 7-10 © 2022 Taylor & Francis
Chapter 6 © 2020 Christian Jaser. Originally published as Open Access.

With the exception of Chapter 6, no part of this book may be reprinted or reproduced or utilised in any form or by any electronic, mechanical, or other means, now known or hereafter invented, including photocopying and recording, or in any information storage or retrieval system, without permission in writing from the publishers. For details on the rights for Chapter 6, please see the chapter's Open Access footnote.

*Trademark notice*: Product or corporate names may be trademarks or registered trademarks, and are used only for identification and explanation without intent to infringe.

*British Library Cataloguing-in-Publication Data*
A catalogue record for this book is available from the British Library

ISBN13: 978-1-032-16233-1 (hbk)
ISBN13: 978-1-032-16234-8 (pbk)
ISBN13: 978-1-003-24765-4 (ebk)

DOI: 10.4324/9781003247654

Typeset in Minion Pro
by codeMantra

**Publisher's Note**
The publisher accepts responsibility for any inconsistencies that may have arisen during the conversion of this book from journal articles to book chapters, namely the inclusion of journal terminology.

**Disclaimer**
Every effort has been made to contact copyright holders for their permission to reprint material in this book. The publishers would be grateful to hear from any copyright holder who is not here acknowledged and will undertake to rectify any errors or omissions in future editions of this book.

# Contents

|   | | |
|---|---|---|
| | *Citation Information* | vi |
| | *Notes on Contributors* | viii |
| | *Series Editors' Foreword* | x |
| 1 | Introduction: Towards a Global History of Horse Racing<br>Sinclair W. Bell, Christian Jaser and Christian Mann | 1 |
| 2 | Horse Races and Chariot Races in Ancient Greece: Struggling for Eternal Glory<br>Christian Mann and Sebastian Scharff | 8 |
| 3 | Horse Racing in Imperial Rome: Athletic Competition, Equine Performance, and Urban Spectacle<br>Sinclair W. Bell | 28 |
| 4 | The Emperor and His People at the Chariot Races in Byzantium<br>David Alan Parnell | 78 |
| 5 | Horse Racing at the Ottoman Court, 1524–1728<br>Tülay Artan | 91 |
| 6 | Urban *Palio* and *Scharlach* Races in Fifteenth- and Early Sixteenth-Century Italy and Germany<br>Christian Jaser | 117 |
| 7 | Spectacular Spanish Horses in New Spain<br>Isabelle Schürch | 133 |
| 8 | The Sport of Kingmakers: Horse Racing in Late Stuart England<br>Richard Nash | 149 |
| 9 | Capitalist Horse Sense: Sports Betting and Option Trading during the English Financial Revolution, 1690–1740<br>Christiane Eisenberg | 168 |
| 10 | 'A Horse-Race is the Same All the World Over': The Cultural Context of Horse Racing in Native North America<br>Peter Mitchell | 182 |
| | *Index* | 203 |

# Citation Information

The chapters in this book were originally published in *The International Journal of the History of Sport*, volume 37, issue 3-4 (2020). When citing this material, please use the original page numbering for each article, as follows:

**Chapter 1**
*Towards a Global History of Horse Racing*
Sinclair Bell, Christian Jaser and Christian Mann
*The International Journal of the History of Sport*, volume 37, issue 3-4 (2020) pp. 520–528

**Chapter 2**
*Horse Races and Chariot Races in Ancient Greece: Struggling for Eternal Glory*
Christian Mann und Sebastian Scharff
*The International Journal of the History of Sport*, volume 37, issue 3-4 (2020) pp. 163–182

**Chapter 3**
*Horse Racing in Imperial Rome: Athletic Competition, Equine Performance, and Urban Spectacle*
Sinclair W. Bell
*The International Journal of the History of Sport*, volume 37, issue 3-4 (2020) pp. 183–232

**Chapter 4**
*The Emperor and His People at the Chariot Races in Byzantium*
David Alan Parnell
*The International Journal of the History of Sport*, volume 37, issue 3-4 (2020) pp. 233–245

**Chapter 5**
*Horse Racing at the Ottoman Court, 1524–1728*
Tülay Artan
*The International Journal of the History of Sport*, volume 37, issue 3-4 (2020) pp. 246–271

**Chapter 6**
*Urban Palio and Scharlach Races in Fifteenth- and Early Sixteenth-Century Italy and Germany*
Christian Jaser
*The International Journal of the History of Sport*, volume 37, issue 3-4 (2020) pp. 272–287

**Chapter 7**
*Spectacular Spanish Horses in New Spain*
Isabelle Schürch
*The International Journal of the History of Sport*, volume 37, issue 3-4 (2020) pp. 288–303

**Chapter 8**
*The Sport of Kingmakers: Horse Racing in Late Stuart England*
Richard Nash
*The International Journal of the History of Sport*, volume 37, issue 3-4 (2020) pp. 304–322

**Chapter 9**
*Capitalist Horse Sense: Sports Betting and Option Trading during the English Financial Revolution, 1690–1740*
Christiane Eisenberg
*The International Journal of the History of Sport*, volume 37, issue 3-4 (2020) pp. 323–336

**Chapter 10**
*'A Horse-Race is the Same All the World Over': The Cultural Context of Horse Racing in Native North America*
Peter Mitchell
*The International Journal of the History of Sport*, volume 37, issue 3-4 (2020) pp. 337–356

For any permission-related enquiries please visit:
http://www.tandfonline.com/page/help/permissions

# Notes on Contributors

**Tülay Artan** is Professor in the History Program, Sabancı University, Istanbul. She works on prosopographical networks of the Ottoman elite and their households; material culture, consumption history and standards of living; and seventeenth and eighteenth century Ottoman arts, architecture, and literature in comparative perspective.

**Sinclair W. Bell** is Professor of Art History at Northern Illinois University, DeKalb, USA, and is currently the Richard D. Cohen Fellow at the Hutchins Center for African and African American Research at Harvard University, Cambridge, USA. One of his primary areas of research is sport and spectacle in the Roman imperial period, about which he has published numerous articles, reviews, and books.

**Christiane Eisenberg** is Professor of British History and Society and Director of the Centre for British Studies, Humboldt-Universitat zu Berlin, Germany. Before joining Humboldt-Universitat in 1998, she worked as a Research Associate at the Centre for Interdisciplinary Research, Bielefeld and then as Assistant Professor at the University of Hamburg, Germany. She held a fellowship at the Institute for Advanced Study in Princeton. Her main research foci are the history of modern sport and the history of modern market society.

**Christian Jaser** is Professor of Medieval History and Historical Auxiliary Sciences at the University of Klagenfurt. His current research focuses on sport Cultures in late medieval cities, in particular in Italy and Germany. His recent publications include the chapter *Rules and Order* in *Bloomsbury's Cultural History of Sport in the Renaissance* (2021). His book *Palio und Scharlach. Städtische Sportkulturen des 15. und frühen 16. Jahrhunderts am Beispiel italienischer und oberdeutscher Pferderennen* is forthcoming (Hiersemann Verlag, Stuttgart, Monographien zur Geschichte des Mittelalters).

**Christian Mann** is Professor of Ancient History at the University of Mannheim, Germany. He has authored and edited many publications on ancient sport, including Athletics in the Hellenistic World, co-edited with Sofie Remijsen and Sebastian Scharff (2016), and is also co-editor of the journal *Nikephoros: Zeitschrift fur Sport und Kultur im Altertum*.

**Peter Mitchell** is Professor of African Archaeology at the University of Oxford, Tutor and Fellow in Archaeology at St Hugh's College, Oxford, and an Honorary Research Fellow, GAES, University of the Witwatersrand. In addition to numerous papers and several books and edited volumes in the field of African prehistory, he is author of *Horse Nations: The Worldwide Impact of the Horse on Indigenous Societies Post-1492* (2015) and has previously published on a Native American topic in Ethnohistory (2016).

**Richard Nash** is Professor Emeritus of English at Indiana University Bloomington, USA. He is interested in British Literature and Culture in the 'long' eighteenth century, with a special interest in Literature and Science, concentrating on the Restoration and early eighteenth century. His current project focuses on the origins of the thoroughbred racehorse and what it means to invent an animal.

**David Alan Parnell** is Associate Professor of History at Indiana University Northwest, Gary, USA. He is the author of *Justinian's Men: Careers and Relationships of Byzantine Army Officers* (2017) and many articles about the military and social life of the Byzantine Empire in the Age of Justinian.

**Sebastian Scharff** is Assistant Professor of Ancient History at the Westfälische Wilhelms-Universität Münster, Germany. He was a Fellow at the Center for Hellenic Studies in Washington, DC, and held a scholarship from Gerda Henkel Stiftung. One of his main research interests is ancient sport, on which he has published widely, including the volume *Athletics in the Hellenistic World* (co-edited with Christian Mann, 2016) and his forthcoming book *Hellenistic Athletes. Agonistic Cultures and Self-Presentation*.

**Isabelle Schürch** is Senior Lecturer in Medieval History at the University of Bern, Switzerland. From 2015 to 2017, she was Senior Researcher in the DFG-funded Reinhart Koselleck project *'Societalisation among Participants and Their Transformation. A History of Society and Theory of the European Early Modern Period'*. Her main research interests include historical human and non-human interactions, the history of horse riding, practice theory, and the history of mediality and materiality.

# Series Editors' Foreword

*Sport in the Global Society: Historical Perspectives* explores the role of sport in cultures both around the world and across the timeframes of human history. In the world we currently inhabit, sport spans the globe. It captivates vast audiences. It defines, alters, and reinforces identities for individuals, communities, nations, empires, and the world. Sport organizes memories and perceptions, arouses passions and tensions, and reveals harmonies and cleavages. It builds and blurs social boundaries--animating discourses about class, gender, race, and ethnicity. Sport opens new vistas on the history of human cultures, intersecting with politics and economics, ideologies and theologies. It reveals aesthetic tastes and energizes consumer markets.

Our challenge is to explain how sport has developed into a global phenomenon. The series continues the tradition established by the original incarnation of *Sport in the Global Society* (and in 2010 divided into *Historical Perspectives* and *Contemporary Perspectives*) by promoting the academic study of one of the most significant and dynamic forces in shaping the historical landscapes of human cultures.

In the twenty-first century, a critical mass of scholars recognizes the importance of sport in their analyses of human experiences. *Sport in the Global Society: Historical Perspectives* provides an international outlet for the leading investigators on these subjects. Building on previous work and excavating new terrain, our series remains a consistent and coherent response to the attention the academic community demands for the serious study of sport.

Mark Dyreson
Thierry Terret
Rob Hess

# Towards a Global History of Horse Racing

Sinclair W. Bell, Christian Jaser and Christian Mann

**ABSTRACT**
By investigating the global history of horse racing from antiquity to the modern period, it is likewise possible to overcome the traditional pitfalls in the periodization of sport history. Instead of claiming an exclusiveness of modern sport and downgrading premodern physical contests as pure phenomena of alterity, this special issue discusses racing in the horse age as a deep history of diachronically comparable practices, discourses, and perceptions centered around the competitive staging of equine speed.

In his acceptance speech for the historian's prize of the city of Münster in 2003, the famous German historian Reinhart Koselleck proposed a new periodization of global history. Bearing in mind that the horse belonged to the most important, but rather neglected protagonists in the depths of history, he argued for three historical epochs: the pre-horse age, the horse age and the post-horse age.[1] During Koselleck's horse age (ranging from 4000 BC to circa 1950 AD), the equine species played an indispensable role in every aspect of social, religious and political life – from cultic rituals and war to agriculture and trade – thereby reflecting a millenia-long experience of human-animal dependence.[2]

This macro-historical approach was recently updated and refined by Ulrich Raulff in his bestselling book *Farewell to the Horse*, which focused on the 'separation between man and horse' in the long nineteenth century and, in consequence, explored the historical significance of the horse in the age before (i.e. in the premodern era).[3] In particular, Raulff stressed the performance capacities of the horse as an 'animal vector' and 'supplier of kinetic energy' without which one would have to write the history of human civilizations in a very different way.[4] During the horse age, horse races became a key competitive stage and representational space of equine speed that pervaded nearly every social practice of premodern societies as a whole – at least in the fields of mobility, communication, and the economy.

By investigating the global history of horse racing from antiquity to the modern period, it is likewise possible to overcome the traditional pitfalls in the periodization of sport history. Instead of claiming an exclusiveness of modern sport and downgrading premodern physical contests as pure phenomena of alterity,[5] this special issue discusses racing in the horse age as a deep history of diachronically comparable practices, discourses, and perceptions centered around the competitive staging of equine speed.

The assessment of differences and similarities with regard to this worldwide longue durée phenomenon represents both an analytical challenge and a cooperative research opportunity. The essence of the subject seems at first to be very simple, even not sufficient compared to the degree of abstraction of other historical topics: a speed contest between two or more horses to determine a winner over a previously agreed distance, which is carried out with riders or carts and is subject to varying degrees of regulation. Nevertheless, from a global historical perspective, the phenomenology of horse racing consists of a broad spectrum of historical variants[6]: Is it simply a pragmatic performance test of the 'speed machine'[7] horse, which helps to assess individual prices and breeding preferences? Is it elsewhere a ludic phenomenon, a form of entertainment, a mere stage in the protocol of secular or religious celebrations? Is it a specific human-animal physical exercise that demanded certain historically and anthropologically comprehensible body techniques from all participants, horses and riders? Or is it – as ipso facto assumed for the English horse races of modern times – a 'sport': a physical, rule-bound form of competition with specific social and cultural ramifications?

Even this brief outline of historical interpretations reveals the range of organizational, performative, and representational manifestations that characterize the global history of horse racing and constitute the core topic of this special issue: from informal and less institutionalized races in the surroundings of horse markets, inns and amusement parks to serial, spatially- and exclusively-installed horse races, which imply social competition and political significance. Historically, horse races have had a comparatively large spectator appeal, which not only results in condensed face-to-face communication, but also in reporting via distance-media, be it in the form of handwritten letters, print media or live coverage on radio, TV and streaming platforms. By this interplay of praxeological variability and different ranges of perception, global horse races reveal themselves as 'total social facts' (following Marcel Mauss), which at the same time raise social, political, religious, economic, legal, moral and media dimensions.

In order to compare horse racing cultures from completely different epochs and regions, this special issue is based on a catalogue of questions which will serve as structural comparative parameters. Certainly, the evidence has to be interpreted in its historical contexts and with regard to specific cultural conditions which shaped the respective 'centaurian pact'[8] between owners, riders, and horses on the global racetracks of pre-modernity and modernity.

The main aspects of this catalogue of questions are the following:

*(I) The Spatial and Architectural Framework*: In this respect, one has to deal with a wide range of venues and spatial arrangements that conditioned the performance of horse racing. In some cases, such as the ancient Olympic Games, open spaces without any architectural structures were used. With the Roman circus or the

modern hippodrome in mind, elaborately designed horse racing tracks existed for the sole purpose of staging fast horses. For the palio races of Renaissance Italy and modern Siena, urban streets and squares were temporarily rededicated for equine speed contests. In each case, the spatial setting of the racetrack – a circuit with narrow or wide bends or a straight route – rebounds on the competitive practice and the structural tension between performance and contingency. Another key issue was the placing of numerous spectators along the racetrack – for example, in the form of temporary or stable structures or grandstands or a specially-secured zones. At the same time, the organizers of racing events also had to take into account the requirements of a fair competition to ensure equal opportunities for all participants – for example, by removing possible obstacles, by preparing the surface of the racetrack and by creating proper starting and finish areas.

*(II) Race Organization*: In addition to the frequency of the race events (a race series or an individual event), one has to examine the organizational responsibilities as well as the rights and obligations deriving from them. Which person or institution organizes and finances the horse races to be discussed and who pays and awards the corresponding prizes? At the same time, this raises the question of regulatory authority: Who decides on and issues binding regulations, who acts as arbitrator and before which institutions or persons and in what way are disputes dealt with? How and with what degree of literacy does the contest administration take place in detail? And finally: What do we know about the people who provided the horses or teams and selected jockeys or charioteers? In historical retrospect, different models are at work here. In Classical Antiquity, for example, private individuals took part in the Greek competitions at their own expense, while in the Roman circus, professional racing stables organized like clubs provided horses and charioteers. During the Italian Renaissance, princes, nobles, and townspeople acted as racing patrons in the urban palio races, while later in the early modern era, urban neighborhood associations such as the Sienese *contrade* took over. Even later in the early modern age, the notion of 'sport of kings' indicates a heavy presence of royal and noble patrons in the starting fields.

*(III) Prizes*: The competitive momentum of horse racing has often been increased by the offer of prizes. Their quantity, quality, and symbolic significance vary greatly from one period to another. In addition to the type of prizes, the scope of the awarding of prizes must always be clarified: Did only the winner receive a prize or also in the case of certain placements, for example the second- and third-placed horses? Did there exist consolation prizes for the slowest horses? Did the prizes go to the jockeys or charioteers or to the owners of the race horses? In which ceremonial framework did the awards ceremony take place and what symbolic forms of communication were used (stage arrangements, acclamations, ceremonial props)? How can the relationship between the economic and symbolic value of the prizes be qualified?

*(IV) Symbolic Representations of Victories and Victors*: This aspect deals with the question how competitive successes were commemorated and which media forms were used in doing so. On the part of the organizers, publicly accessible lists and portraits of winners were produced, on the part of the winners themselves, for example, there existed funerary monuments or a textual-visual memory of victories in book format. Behind these symbolic representations lies the fundamental question to

whom the performative agency was attributed: Were horses, riders, or owners perceived as decisive players in the field? What role did the racehorses actually play as performing and symbolic animals? There is a need for explanation why in some historical cultures, such as ancient Greece, winners and losers were differentiated in a striking way, while elsewhere pictorial representations tended to depict the participants in a more homogeneous way.

*(V) Social Range and Identities*: For each of the case studies to be discussed, one has to consider the social range of participants and aspects of identity building through competitive participation. In order to take an active part in this resource-intensive 'sport of kings', it is usually required to belong to the social and financial elites of the respective societies. In this respect, horse races provided a stage for public demonstrations of status and reputation. Conversely, the exclusion or non-participation of certain groups reveals ethnic, political, and social boundaries. Likewise, the behavior of participants and spectators alike reveals competitive constellations (between families/cities/city districts or neighborhoods/nations etc.). Horse racing could also be culturally charged, such as through 'national styles' of riding or through specific group formations of participants and supporters. In this context, the betting practices along the racetracks should also be taken into account: Clifford Geertz's classic essay on Balinese cockfights has clearly shown that betting did not exhaust itself in economic profit interests but was also practiced in order to demonstrate social affiliation.[9]

These questions are meant to serve as guidelines for the individual contributions of this special issue that is based on the papers given in 2017 at a conference held at the University of Mannheim and organized by Christian Mann (Mannheim) and Christian Jaser (Berlin). However, it is clear that not every question included in this catalogue can be answered by each author, due to the different types and degrees of sources from each horse-racing culture. Nevertheless, the findings present the first comparative perspectives on global horse racing across a wide temporal and geographical range – from Greek and Roman antiquity to the Native American mid-1800s.

Christian Mann and Sebastian Scharff investigate horse and chariot races in ancient Greece. More precisely, their essay deals with the Greek *agones*, i.e. a specific format of organizing competitions linked to religious festivals that flourished in the whole Greek world, from the Iberian Peninsula to Afghanistan. These *agones* contained a variety of hippic disciplines that could be studied with a view to race organization, spatial structures, prizes, and the self-representation of equestrian victors in the form of monuments, poems, and coinage.

Sinclair Bell discusses perhaps the best-known form of horse racing, one immortalized in the novel *Ben-Hur* and its later cinematic representations: chariot races in imperial Rome. The earliest, most popular, and longest-lived of all forms of mass entertainment or 'spectacles' in the Roman world, chariot races were held in circuses, the oldest and largest of which was the Circus Maximus in Rome. Bell's chapter surveys this practice in imperial Rome and beyond by surveying the history, setting, and operation of the races, the athletes who competed in the arenas, the horses that were bred for racing, and the spectators and fans for whom the sport served as a socially-binding religion.

David Alan Parnell focuses the Byzantine Hippodrome as one of the most important public spaces in Constantinople and a central space for the negotiation of the relationship between the emperor and his people. As a spectator sport, Byzantine chariot races evoked direct dialogues between emperor and people in the hippodrome. More than pure shoptalk about the performances of charioteers, chariot racing provided an occasion to express complaints and requests so that the Hippodrome became a political arena and an important stage for the legitimization of imperial power.

Tülay Artan explores post-Byzantine traditions of horse racing in Constantinople during the Ottoman Era, from 1524 to 1728. In the new Ottoman capital, the Byzantine Hippodrome (renamed Atmeydanı) hosted public festivities like royal weddings and princes' circumcision ceremonies and various equestrian games, but horse races only relatively rarely. However, long-distance endurance races were held during the 1524, 1530, 1539, and 1582 imperial festivals in the Kağıdhane and Alibeyköy valleys at the upper end of the Golden Horn. After the 1720s, track-based flat racing was introduced at the Sa'adabad Palace where a permanent racetrack was erected. Insofar, Artan discusses courtly organizational practices and spatial arrangements from the sixteenth to the eighteenth and nineteenth centuries.

The contribution of Christian Jaser shifts the focus from imperial to communal horse racing cultures. In fifteenth- and early sixteenth-century Italy and Upper Germany, flat races for the prize of a precious piece of cloth called *palio* or *scharlach* were organized and financed by city councils, mostly during annual fairs, patronal feast days, and shooting contests. Despite many organisational similarities, Italian *palio* and German *scharlach* races attracted different levels and depths. In order to trace some key comparative aspects of the transalpine field of urban horse racing, Jaser deals with the practices of race organization, spatial arrangements, the social ranges of participants, the perceptions of equine agency, and the different medial representations of victories.

On the late medieval Iberian peninsula as well as during the early modern Spanish transatlantic expansion, horse races did not play a major role, quite unlike various other equestrian displays (game of canes, running of the ring, lange games, bull runs). As Isabelle Schürch's contribution clearly shows, this variety of competitive and martial displays of speed, competition, and power gained a new cultural and social significance in colonial contexts of the West Indies and New Spain. They inspired claims of cultural specificity as well as social distinction and manifested the commemoration of the martial 'reconquista' period.

Richard Nash seeks to revise the common assumption that King Charles II of England is to be regarded as the founding father of the modern sport of thoroughbred horse racing. More than being just a 'sport of kings', the emergence of horse racing as a national sport must be seen in the context of national political change, first and foremost with regard to the conflict between Protestants and Catholics and the anxieties about succession and rebellion. Based on a particular organization of the sport that would later lead to the 'Jockey Club', horse racing became an ideological platform to mobilize popular support through sporting spectacle during a time of tension over the relationship between church and state.

**Figure 1.** Participants in the international conference 'Pferderennen in globalhistorischer Perspektive / Global History of Horse Races' held at the University of Mannheim from June 15–17, 2017.

Nash's findings from archival sources indicate that horse racing was less the sport of kings than of protestant kingmakers, thereby turning it into a form of popular political theater.

Christiane Eisenberg brings together two historical processes that were regularly discussed separately in previous research: the emergence of horse racing as a modern sport in England and the concomitant betting practices on the one hand, and the English Financial Revolution (1690–1740) on the other hand. In particular, option trading was perceived as a form of time trade and shared structural affinities with the betting on horses. Hence, there developed a telling reciprocity between these two speculative practices: Firstly, there were sporting impulses on the financial markets because by betting on horses, actors on the financial markets became more willing to take risks. Secondly, and vice versa, there were also impulses for sport from the financial markets, as the experience in option business resulted in a preparedness to take greater risks on betting on horse races.

Peter Mitchell addresses the hitherto rather neglected field of Native American horse racing, particularly on the Great Plains and in the Southwest of North America. As a competitive arena for male status and prestige, Native American horse races belonged to a wider field of agonistic activities, including warfare. Each race and its result had a significant impact on the standing of individuals, men's societies, and tribal groups. By invoking supernatural powers, horse racing was both secular and sacred. As in other temporal and spatial settings, betting was a fundamental part of Native American horse races. Despite the strong opposition from Euro-American authorities during the reservation era, Native American horse racing traditions persisted in the form of rodeo and Indian Relay racing.

The volume is based on a conference titled 'Global History of Horse Races', which was held at Mannheim, Germany, in June 2017 (Figure 1). The editors would like to express thanks to Judith Schönholz, Max-Quentin Bischoff, Jennifer Goetz, and Melanie Meaker for their efficient help in running the conference. We are extremely grateful to Peter Hofmann, whose generous support made the conference possible. Isabelle von Neumann-Cosel, Reiter-Verein Mannheim e.V., gave us an unforgettable introduction into the behavior of horses, and she offered us the opportunity to sit on a horse – for some of us for the first time in life! Stephan Buchner, Natascha Buchner, and Marco Klein, Badischer Rennverein Mannheim-Seckenheim e.V., were generous to welcome us at the racecourse in Mannheim-Seckenheim and to offer insights into the training of modern racehorses. Last but not least, we are grateful to Wray Vamplew and the board of editors (especially Mark Dyreson) of the *IJHS* for accepting the essays for publication as a single volume and for shepherding them through production.

## Notes

1. Reinhart Koselleck, 'Der Aufbruch in die Moderne oder das Ende des Pferdezeitalters', in *Historikerpreis der Stadt Münster 2003: Prof. Reinhart Koselleck. Dokumentation zur Feierstunde zur Verleihung am 18. Juli 2003 im Festsaal des Rathauses zu Münster* (Münster: Presse- und Informationsamt, 2003), 23–39, here 25. See also, Simone Derix, 'Das Rennpferd. Historische Perspektiven auf Zucht und Führung seit dem 18. Jahrhundert', *Body Politics* 2, no. 4 (2014): 397–429, here 398.
2. Koselleck, 'Aufbruch', 25, 28.
3. Ulrich Raulff, *Farewell to the Horse: The Final Century of Our Relationship* (London: Allen Lane, 2017), chapter 'A Long Farewell'.
4. Ibid., chapter 'Connoisseurs and Conmen'.
5. See Allen Guttmann, *From Ritual to Record. The Nature of Modern Sports* (New York: Columbia University Press, 1978); John Carter and Arnd Krüger, eds., *Ritual and Record: Sports Records and Quantification in Pre-Modern Societies* (New York: Greenwood Press, 1990); Arnd Krüger and John McClelland, eds., *Die Anfänge des modernen Sports in der Renaissance* (London: Arena Publishers, 1984).
6. See for a first assessment of global horse racing cultures in the early modern era Christian Jaser, 'Pferderennen', in *Enzyklopädie der Neuzeit Online*, ed. Friedrich Jäger (Leiden 2018), http://dx.doi.org/10.1163/2352-0248_edn_COM_058059 (accessed March 1, 2020).
7. Raulff, *Farewell to the Horse*, chapter 'A Long Farewell'.
8. Ibid.
9. Clifford Geertz, 'Deep Play: Notes on the Balinese Cockfight', *Daedalus* 101, no. 1 (1972): 1–37.

## Disclosure Statement

No potential conflict of interest was reported by the author(s).

# Horse Races and Chariot Races in Ancient Greece: Struggling for Eternal Glory

Christian Mann and Sebastian Scharff

**ABSTRACT**
The essay is about ancient Greek horse and chariot races. The architecture of Greek hippodromes was very rudimentary, but—at least at Olympia—the organizers put much effort in constructing a starting mechanism which was meant to guarantee all starters equal chances for winning. Concerning the prizes, symbolic prizes were common as well as valuable prizes. In ancient Greece, it was the owner of the horses who counted as the participant. The jockeys' and charioteers' strength and skill obviously had a strong impact on the outcome of the race, but they are very rarely mentioned in the ancient texts. Equestrian victors had two means of representation at their disposal: the erection of agonistic victor monuments or the commission of *epinikia*. It is equally true for both forms of representation that the way the victor was showcased was not up to the artistic license of the poets, but was controlled by the victors. Victory poetry was poetry on commission for which the victors reached deeply into their pockets. The poems dealt with important political implications. This is why *epinikia* and victory monuments constitute amazing pieces of evidence for the ancient historian, since they allow him to reconstruct the protagonist's view.

The title of this chapter needs some explanation: the subject of our analysis is neither limited to the territory of the modern Greek state nor restricted to the period of the 'free' Greeks, i.e. before the Romans came to dominate the eastern Mediterranean in the second century BC. Rather, it is the specific Greek format of organizing competitions, the *agon*, that determines the scope of this investigation. The most frequent (and most important) *agones* were connected to recurrent religious festivals (e.g. the Olympics), but there were also funeral contests and *agones* on military campaigns.[1] From about 700 BC to the fourth century AD, *agones* flourished in the Greek world, which extended from Spain in the west to Afghanistan in the east and from the Black Sea in the north to Egypt in the south. For many centuries, Greek *agones* and Roman circus races existed side-by-side.[2]

Due to the importance of the ancient Olympic Games for the history of modern sport, many scholars have published on the hippic competitions in Olympia and other Greek hippodromes. A comprehensive study of the topic, however, is still missing.[3]

## Organization

*Agones* could be part of a burial ceremony, as in the famous funeral games for Patroclus in Homer's *Iliad*,[4] and sometimes generals organized *agones* during military campaigns.[5] But the most important *agones* were connected to religious festivals and organized in a cycle of one, two, or four years. *Agones* of this kind were named after the patrons of the respective sanctuaries, for example *Olympia* (i.e. Olympic Games) after Zeus Olympios or *Pythia* after Apollo Pythios, and they had a fixed set of disciplines, prizes and rules. The disciplines of the *agones* were divided into three classes: musical competitions (like singing, lyre-playing and flute-playing), gymnic contests (combat sports, track and field), and hippic disciplines, which means equestrian sport (*hippos* = horse). In the fifth century BC, the 'guestimated' number of *agones* was 155,[6] while in the second and third centuries AD, when the Greek agonistic system reached its peak, no less than 500 are attested in the numismatic and epigraphic evidence,[7] and there might have been even more that have not left any traces in the sources.

Not every *agon*, however, comprised all three classes of disciplines; musical competitions, for example, were missing in the program of the *Olympia*, the most important *agon* of the ancient world. Hippic disciplines, on the contrary, were included in the ancient Olympics, which featured a variety of races with driven chariots and ridden horses:

- Four-horse chariot race (*tethrippon*), introduced in 680 BC (?)[8]
- Horseback race (*keles*), introduced in 648 BC (?)
- Mule-cart race (*apene*), introduced in 500 BC, abolished in 444 BC
- Horseback race for mares (*kalpe*), introduced in 496 BC, abolished in 444 BC
- Two-horse chariot race (*synoris*), introduced in 408 BC
- Four-colt chariot race (*tethrippon polikon*), introduced in 384 BC
- Two-colt chariot race (*synoris polike*), introduced in 268 BC
- Horseback race for colts (*keles polikos*), introduced in 256 BC

These races were embedded in a set of competitions and rituals: on the first day of the great festival that took place at Olympia every fourth year, the authorities divided the participating horses and athletes into age-classes.[9] Due to the absence of officially recognized criteria, the referees evaluated their physical development. Their visual appearance was the basis for the decision on who was allowed to start in the races for colts and who had to compete with the full-grown horses. The classification of athletes as boys or men was made in a similar fashion. On the second day, the boys' contests took place, and on the third day the crowd moved to the hippodrome to watch the horse and chariot races. These competitions were considered the most magnificent and most spectacular part of the festival. After several processions and sacrifices and the men's gymnic competitions, the festival ended with the victory ceremony on the sixth day: all winners were announced by the heralds and received their prize, a crown made of a branch of the sacred olive tree.

The distances of the hippic races differed significantly: The horses in the *tethrippon* had to run more than ten times longer than the colts in the *keles polikos*. Yet the exact distances remain unclear as there are no traces left of the Olympic hippodrome (see below).[10] Most of what we know about the hippic disciplines in Olympia comes from Pausanias, a Greek writer of the second century AD. His work offers not only a detailed description of the architecture and statues in the sanctuary, but also details of the rituals of his time and stories from the past.[11] He gives the following information on the *apene* and *kalpe*:

> The trotting-race (*kalpe*) was for mares, and in the last part of the course the riders jumped off and ran beside the mares, holding on to the bridle, just as at the present day those do who are called "mounters." The mounters, however, differ from the riders in the trotting-race by having different badges, and by riding horses instead of mares. The cart-race (*apene*) was neither of venerable antiquity nor yet a graceful performance. Moreover, each cart was drawn by a pair of mules, not horses, and there is an ancient curse on the Eleans if this animal is even born in Elis.[12]

Riders jumping off their horses and running a part of the distance would make a strange impression on modern spectators, but races like this were quite common in ancient Greece.[13] The *agon* called *apobates*, which was popular in Athens and Boiotia, started as a chariot race, but at some point the drivers had to dismount and run a portion of the course.[14] This action can be explained as a remembrance of the Homeric heroes, who drove to the battlefields with their chariots, jumped off and fought as foot soldiers. Parallels like this have led some scholars to consider warfare as the root of ancient Greek equestrian sport,[15] but one should be very careful with this hypothesis: in the seventh and sixth centuries BC, when the system of hippic disciplines at Olympia and other *agones* evolved, there were no war chariots at all in the Greek armies, and the cavalry had only a minor role on the battlefield.[16] It is more likely that hippic competitions evolved out of the social elites' desire to represent their superior status, using the horse as a symbol of wealth and luxury.[17]

A list of prizes of the Great Panathenaia at Athens reveals the hierarchy of the disciplines. While the winner of the four-horse chariot race received 140 amphoras filled with olive oil (the runner-up 40), the winner of the chariot race with four colts got only 40 (the runner up 8) and the winner of the horseback race 30 (the runner-up 6).[18] For comparison, the winner of the wrestling competition received 60 amphoras. These numbers confirm the impression given by ancient authors that the four-horse chariot race was the highlight of an *agon*. The 'Olympic' hippic disciplines flourished in festivals throughout the Greek world, but there were also many local and regional specialties. In Thessaly the *aphippolampas*, a kind of mounted torch race, was popular together with mounted bull-hunting.[19] A victory list from Egypt includes a winner with a "shining horse" (ἵππωι λαμπρῶι), which is interpreted as a kind of dressage.[20]

The organization of the *agones* was in the hands of the Greek *poleis* (city-states). In the case of Olympia, the *polis* of Elis, situated about 25 miles from the famous sanctuary of Zeus, was responsible for the games: Elis made the decisions about the building program of Olympia, the officials and umpires of the Olympic Games were magistrates of Elis, and reputable men from Elis formed the Olympic council, which had to settle cases of dispute. For the Panathenaia, it was the city of Athens that was responsible for the organization, in case of the Isthmia, it was the city of Corinth, and so on. The financial burden also was the city's, but since the Hellenistic period, kings or rich private citizens could step in with their own money.[21] An inscription from Delphi reveals the considerable costs for the construction works (like digging and levelling the athletic facilities) that had to be done before the competitions started,[22] and the organizing *polis* had to pay for the prizes as well. But these expenses were more than compensated for by the fame *agones* brought to the sanctuary and to the organizing *polis*.

This is especially the case for Elis, a city far away from the powerful centers of the Greek world. Elis' reputation was tightly connected to the Olympic Games,[23] and although Eleians were often successful in Olympia, they had a reputation of being impartial umpires.[24] When Troilus of Elis won two of the hippic disciplines in 372 BC while being umpire at the same time, the Eleians passed a law that in the future no umpire would be allowed to participate.[25] The Eleians were less scrupulous when using their control of the Olympic Games as a political weapon: in 420 BC, in a time of increased tensions on the Peloponnese, they banned the Spartans from the Olympic Games. The historian Thucydides relates an incident that followed this ban:

> Great fears were felt in the assembly of the Lacedaemonians coming in arms, especially after Lichas, son of Arcesilaus, a Lacedaemonian, had been scourged on the course by the umpires; because, upon his horses being the winners, and the Boeotian people being proclaimed the victor on account of his having no right to enter, he came forward on the course and crowned the charioteer, in order to show that the chariot was his. After this incident all were more afraid than ever, and firmly looked for a disturbance: the Lacedaemonians, however, kept quiet, and let the feast pass by, as we have seen.[26]

Texts like this reveal the differences between the Greek and the Roman systems of provisioning horses and chariots. In Olympia and other Greek hippodromes, unlike in the Roman circuses, there were no factions, no "blues", "greens", "reds" or "whites".[27] Instead, wealthy aristocrats had racehorses bred and trained, and they paid for the transport and the maintenance of the horses.[28] The amount of money needed to have a realistic chance of winning an Olympic victory were enormous, but aristocrats from all parts of the Greek world were willing to make this effort as they could expect prestige and immortal fame in return for their investment. In the eyes of a Greek, winning the four-horse chariot race in Olympia was among the greatest accomplishments a man could achieve in his life. It is no wonder, then, that we find the crème de la crème of Greek society in the victor lists: the mighty tyrant Hieron of Syracuse at the beginning of the fifth century BC, the Macedonian king Philip II in 356 BC, Ptolemaic kings in the third century BC, and members of the family of the Roman emperor Augustus in the early first century AD.

Victories in horse or chariot races were considered a sign of wealth and power and fostered the legitimation of monarchs, and they could also be used by politicians in democracies. When the famous Alcibiades claimed the command of an Athenian fleet to Sicily, he referred to his success in the hippodrome in Olympia (416 BC):

> The Hellenes, after expecting to see our city ruined by the war, concluded it to be even greater than it really is, by reason of the magnificence with which I represented it at the Olympic games, when I sent into the lists seven chariots, a number never before entered by any private person, and won the first prize, and was second and fourth, and took care to have everything else in a style worthy of my victory. Custom regards such displays as honorable, and they cannot be made without leaving behind them an impression of power.[29]

The Greek custom to honor the owner of the horses, and not the driver or charioteer, also had an important gender-related impact. Women were not allowed to watch the Olympic Games,[30] but they could have horses and chariots compete in their name. The first woman to win an Olympic victory was the Spartan Cynisca, and she found some successors, especially among the women of the Ptolemaic court at Alexandria.[31]

Vary rarely did the owners themselves ride the horses or drive the chariots. Those who successfully did so laid great emphasis on their action, claiming to be successors of the Homeric heroes like Diomedes or Menelaos, who competed in the chariot race in *Iliad* 23. The Spartan Damonon owned swift horses and, being a skillful charioteer himself, won some races, but only in minor events on the Peloponnese.[32] The chariot of king Arcesilaus from Cyrene that triumphed in the Pythian Games in 462 BC was driven by his relative Carrhotus.[33] The normal procedure, however, was to train a slave or to rent a specialized wage earner.[34] Vase paintings and statues show very young riders on horseback, but adults as charioteers (Figures 1 and 2). The skills of riders and charioteers were decisive for the outcome of the races—especially the handling of the chariots with four horses was difficult and risky!—but their social status was low, and we do not even know their names. This is a further contrast to Roman circus races.[35]

Characteristic is the following anecdote reported by Pausanias:

> The mare of the Corinthian Pheidolas was called, the Corinthians relate, Aura, and at the beginning of the race she chanced to throw her rider. But nevertheless she went on running properly, turned round the post, and, when she heard the trumpet, quickened her pace, reached the umpires first, realized that she had won and stopped running. The Eleans proclaimed Pheidolas the winner and allowed him to dedicate a statue of this mare.[36]

What in modern horse races is unthinkable—that a horse crossing the finish line without a jockey wins the race—is taken for granted by Pausanias. The authenticity of the anecdote, however, remains uncertain; either it is a true story that demonstrates the low reputation of the riders, or it was invented (and believed) due to the low reputation of the riders.[37]

## Architecture

Hardly any traces of ancient Greek hippodromes have been preserved. In 2008 'sensational news' spread that archaeologists had found the hippodrome of Olympia,[38] but it turned out to be a false report: the structures that had been detected in geophysical prospections were not remains of human building activity, but geological formations in the riverbed of the Alpheios.[39] In other agonistic centers of the Greek world, archaeological activity in search of hippodromes has been very vivid in recent years, and new insights are to be expected in the near future.[40] But so far the only traces that have survived from Greek hippodromes are some remains of the sanctuary on Mount Lykaion in Arkadia.[41] The reason for the scarcity is the archaeological habit of Greek horse races. In contrast to the monumental architecture of Roman circuses in Rome, Constantinople, Thessaloniki, and other places, Greek hippodromes were 'built' in a very simple way: the Greeks just chose a plain terrain, removed any plants, set the turning posts, and fenced it off before the races began; the spectators sat or stood on the ground behind the ropes. But in Olympia, one spectacular construction was built, a starting mechanism that is (again) described by Pausanias:

> Passing out of and over the stadium at the point where the umpires sit, you come to the place set apart for the horse-races, and to the starting-place of the horses. The starting-place is shaped like the prow of a ship, the beak being turned towards the course, and the broad end abutting on the colonnade of Agnaptos. At the very tip of the beak is a bronze dolphin on a rod. Each side of the starting-place is more than four hundred feet long, and in each of the sides stalls are built. These are assigned to the competitors by lot. In front of the chariots or race-horses stretches a rope as a barrier. An altar of unburnt brick, plastered over on the outside, is made every Olympiad as nearly as may be at the middle of the prow. On the altar is a bronze eagle, with its wings spread to the full. The starter sets the machinery in the altar going, whereupon up jumps the eagle in the sight of the spectators, and down falls the dolphin to the ground. The first ropes to be let go on each side of the prow are those next to the colonnade of Agnaptos, and the horses stationed here are the first off. Away they go until they come opposite the chariots that have drawn the second stalls. Then the ropes at the second stalls are let go. And so it runs on down the whole of the chariots till they are all abreast of each other at the beak of the prow. After that it is for the charioteers to display their skill and the horses their speed.[42]

The whole construction was swept away by the Alpheios river in the course of the centuries, and there is much debate about its exact appearance.[43] Yet the intent of this starting mechanism, an elaborate technological innovation, is obvious: it should guarantee a fair race with an equal chance of winning for all competitors, regardless of their starting place.

## Prizes

It is well known that Olympic victors received an olive crown, a prize of huge symbolic value, but worthless in respect of its material. The Pythian, Nemean and Isthmian Games—together with Olympia they formed an ancient 'Grand Slam' of the four most important *agones*—also awarded crowns from sacred trees to the champions. But there were also festivals where winners received valuable items: amphoras filled with olive oil at the Panathenaia at Athens, bronze shields at the Heraia at Argos, as well as tripods, living animals, and even cash prizes.[44] Moreover, victors at important *agones* were rewarded by their hometown with honors in the form of victory ceremonies, statues or honorary seats in the theater, but also with a sum of money that was fixed by the city's laws, or with exemption from certain taxes. In the Roman Imperial period, we even have evidence of monthly pensions paid by the *poleis'* treasurers to citizens who had won agonistic victories.[45] But these recompenses for the efforts undertaken by the horse-owners should not mislead us: breeding horses and sending them to the hippodromes of the Greek world was *not* a business. Nobody saw the expenses as a kind of investment that could be profitable in economic respect. Participation in horse and chariot races was always seen as a kind of largesse, characterized by the loss of money. If it was an investment, the return was not measured in financial terms, but was situated in the world of fame and glory.

## The Self-Representation of Equestrian Victors

The second part of this essay is dedicated to the self-representation of equestrian victors and the question of how different victor identities came into play. Its organizing principle is given by the media in which this representation was carried out. In general, victors had two common forms of representation at their disposal. The most costly form was the erection of an elaborate victor monument including the figural display of the victorious horses and a victor inscription attached in verse or prose.[46] The second (also expensive) form was constituted by the so-called epinician, comparatively long poems with a fixed meter that were performed at the place of victory or in the hometown of the victor and that consisted of a combination of singing, dancing and instrumental music.[47] A third and less common possibility was to celebrate the victory by means of coinage—a medium, however, which obviously was not at every victor's disposal.[48]

## Agonistic Victor Monuments

In their most common form, agonistic victor monuments were statuary dedications by victorious athletes or horse owners erected at the place of victory or in the hometown of the victor (or both) at the occasion of a sporting success.[49] Compared to smaller dedications such as statuettes and reliefs, these monuments simply differed in size. According to the remaining evidence, the custom of erecting agonistic victor monuments set in in the sixth century BC.[50] At the beginning, some victor statues were made of wood,[51] but since the fifth century BC nearly all victor statues were bronzes. Sometimes also marble was used, but this seems to have been restricted to a rather limited amount of cases. Victors in the single horse race usually erected statues of a horse with jockey (Figure 1), victors in chariot races depicted a team of horses with a charioteer (Figure 2). For the erection of monuments at the most important Greek sanctuaries a permission of the respective cult authority was necessary.[52] Yet this constituted a mere formality[53] since we even hear of an athlete who was as self-confident as to bring his victor statue to the games in advance.[54] Victor monuments actually were among the most important statuary groups which can be demonstrated by the mere amount of chapters which the second century AD traveler Pausanias dedicated to the description of this type of evidence. They flourished from the sixth century BC until the 'end of athletics' in Late Antiquity.[55]

**Figure 1.** So-called Artemision-jockey. Bronze, circa 140 BC. Athens, National Archaeological Museum, inv. no. X 15177. Photo © Gary Todd, Wikimedia Commons, licensed under the Creative Commons Attribution 1.0 Universal Public Domain Dedication (URL: https://creativecommons.org/publicdomain/zero/1.0/deed.en).

What is problematic, however, is the fragmentary state of the evidence. Even our best-preserved example—the famous 'Charioteer of Delphi' (Figure 2) shows this very clearly: although this life-size bronze itself is more or less complete—even the inlaid glass eyes of the statue are intact and only the left arm is missing—the rest of the monument is fragmentary at best.[56] It is important to note that the statue was originally part of a larger victor monument. The charioteer was standing on a chariot drawn by horses whose manes are partly preserved. What also survived is the arm of a boy, maybe a groom, also in bronze. The exact reconstruction of the monument is up to debate.[57] What art historians and archaeologists agree upon is that there are no indications that the owner of the horses was also part of the sculpture group.[58] Therefore, the focus of the figural display was on the prestigious horses and the charioteer, as it was usually the case in Greek antiquity. Yet, we should not interpret this as a sign for a certain modesty of horse owners. To the contrary, these wealthy aristocrats displayed their fame and glory by setting up statues of horses because these horses were luxurious objects of prestige. That jockeys, charioteers, even grooms, became part of the picture was only to indicate the agonistic occasion of the dedication.[59]

It is not the place here to dwell on the archaeological details of the statue. It should be emphasized, however, that we are lucky to have this fine work of art since most bronze statues from antiquity were melted down for their raw materials or

**Figure 2.** Charioteer of Delphi. Bronze, 478 or 474 BC. Delphi, Archeological Museum, inv. no. 3484. Photo © Raminus Falcon, Wikimedia Commons, licensed under the Creative Commons Attribution 3.0 Universal Public Domain Dedication (URL: https://creativecommons.org/licenses/by/3.0/deed.en).

corroded naturally. Another even bigger problem concerning victor statues is that a lot of them only survived in the form of Roman copies.[60] These copies can be studied as works of art, but they are of no use with reference to agonistic self-representation because nothing is known about the concrete historical circumstances of their dedication.

Due to the current state of the evidence, the most important part of the victor monument—at least for the reconstruction and interpretation of agonistic self-representation—is a rather unspectacular one: the victor inscription, which could be set in verse or prose.[61] In the case of the Charioteer of Delphi, there is a verse inscription of two lines which is also not unproblematic.[62] This is due to the fact that the first line of the epigraph was erased and re-written afterwards. The earlier inscription reads as follows:

Gela's ruler dedicated me. ( … ) make him prosper, glorious Apollo.

The second epigraph which only differs in line one and which can be better read today goes:

Polyzalos dedicated me. ( … ) make him prosper, glorious Apollo.

The mentioning of Gela in the earlier version of the inscription (I) and of Polyzalos in the later one (II) makes it clear that the monument was dedicated by the homonymous tyrant of Gela, a Greek *polis* in Sicily.[63] Since a lot of Pythian victors in the four-horse chariot race are known for the lifetime of Polyzalos, his victory can be safely dated to either 478 or 474 BC. It is not entirely clear why the first line of the inscription was erased, but political reasons seem more plausible than agonistic motives (like a second victory of Polyzalos) because this would have resulted in a second epigram at least, if not in a second victor monument.[64] We must also bear in mind that it was precisely the denomination as 'Gela's ruler' that was erased.[65] Therefore, this term must have been understood as inappropriate at least by some people at a certain point in time. So it seems rather probable that people took offense at the political implications of the first line. Despite all the uncertainties that remain in the details (one epigraphist even read a third inscription),[66] the monument shows that victor representation was a sensitive area in which a political discourse took place that mattered to people.

Luckily, the evidence for victor epigrams is better in other cases. Such epigrams are known from the sixth century BC to the third century AD,[67] but the genre reached its peak probably no earlier than in the Hellenistic period.[68] It is for the first half of the third century BC that we are able to identify, for instance, the way members of the Ptolemaic dynasty wanted their victories to be understood. This is mainly thanks to the discovery of 18 new victor epigrams, compiled under the title *Hippika*, which were part of a larger epigram collection that was recovered from the wrappings of an Egyptian mummy and first published in 2001.[69] Of these 18 new poems attributed to the poet Posidippus of Pella whose prime was between 280 and 240 BC, at least five were dedicated to victors of the Ptolemaic family.[70] As one of these epigrams demonstrates, an important aspect of the agonistic representation of the dynasty was to be of Macedonian origin:

When we were still horses, people of Pisa,

we gained the Olympian crown of Berenike the Macedonian,

the crown that has the glory much spoken of,

with which we took away Cynisca's long-lasting kydos.[71]

Such a focus on being of Macedonian descent is striking because Macedonia was not part of the Ptolemaic kingdom which included above all Egypt. It can be explained by the desire of the members of the family to show their belonging to the Greek world. Since participation in horse races was considered a typically Greek activity, equestrian competition was a promising field for showing such an affiliation. This is why the Ptolemies did not present themselves as kings of Egypt in the agonistic context, but as the legitimate successors of Alexander who just happened to be residing in Egypt.[72]

Another Ptolemaic epigram in the collection of Posidippus makes it clear that the dynastic element was another important aspect of this family's agonistic self-representation:

> We alone were the first three kings to win at Olympia
>
> in chariot-racing, my parents and I.
>
> I am one, of the same name as Ptolemy, and son of Berenice
>
> of Eordean descent—my parents (the other) two.
>
> I have added to the great glory of my father, but my mother,
>
> a woman, won a victory in the chariot races—this, a great feat.[73]

Again, the Macedonian identity is referred to since the 'Eordean descent'[74] in line four refers to Eordaia which was part of the Macedonian homeland of the Ptolemaic dynasty. In addition to the ethnic as well as to the dynastic aspect of the family's agonistic representation, a third main element is about gender: the Ptolemaic women were integrated into an image of power, an aspect that shines through in both epigrams cited above. The female members of the Ptolemaic dynasty competed at Olympia and won victories and fame, but they also took part in a virtual competition that crossed the borders of space and time: Berenice I is even said to have overshadowed the fame of Cynisca of Sparta,[75] the first female Olympic victor ever.[76]

In sum, Ptolemaic self-presentation was about being a successful Macedonian dynasty. Yet this was only one possible way of presenting equestrian success. Other dynasties like the Attalids prioritized different aspects in their self-representation—and this was all the more the case when it came to successful horse owners who were not of royal origin: Greek aristocrats from a region like Thessaly or from so different *poleis* like Elis or Sidon in Phoenicia stressed other features when it came to their agonistic self-representation.[77] Hellenistic horse owners from Thessaly, for instance, strongly emphasized their regional identity to the almost total neglect of their polis identity.[78] There can be no doubt that the basic socio-political parameters of the polity the victor stemmed from had an impact on the way equestrian victors presented their successes to their fellow citizens. All these political entities did not only dispose of unique 'political cultures', but also of unique 'agonistic cultures'[79] that widely influenced the self-representation of successful horse owners.

## Epinician

Another key medium for the representation of agonistic success is constituted by the genre of the epinician. Like victory monuments, those long poems had the function of permanently securing the fame of their commissioner since they were not composed for a one-time recital only but for multiple performances.[80] Whereas victory monuments flourished throughout antiquity, the heyday of the epinician is limited to a rather short period in time (from the late sixth century to the middle of the fifth century BC). The bulk of the remaining evidence stems from the work of two poets: Pindar and Bacchylides.[81] As in victor epigrams, the most important point of reference for the victor's self-presentation was usually constituted by his hometown which was proclaimed in the award ceremony (for instance the herald's announcement in Olympia)[82] together with the name of the successful horse owner.

As Leslie Kurke has demonstrated, the relation between a sporting victor and his hometown was regulated according to an 'economy of praise'[83] in ancient Greece. The performance of epinician odes served to re-integrate the victor into his *polis* community. Such a re-integration was necessary since a victory was interpreted as a sign of divine support and temporarily made the victorious athlete rise above his aristocratic peers.[84] By emphasizing not only the personal *arete* of the victor, but also highlighting the notion that the victory crowned the entire city, epinician odes stressed that the victory should be understood as an achievement for the entire community, a civic good. According to this interpretation, the epinicia always served to make sure that sporting victors did not get too politically ambitious.

However, when the victor originated from a polity with a monarchic rule, the *polis* community necessarily played a less decisive role since the focus was rather on the personal achievements of the victor or his family.[85] Therefore, epinicia differed greatly in their political message (like they did in their form and structure): whereas the long *Olympian* 1 is dedicated to Hieron, 'the king of Syracuse who delights in horses',[86] the very short *Pythian* 7 programmatically sets in with 'the great city of Athens'.[87] Whereas *Olympian* 1 says that 'the peak of the farthest limit is for kings',[88] *Pythian* 7 asks: 'What fatherland, what family will you name that is more illustrious in Greece?'[89] Hence, although in both odes the relation between the victor and his hometown plays a decisive role, the focus is very different, as was the political context to which the odes refer. In Hieron's Syracuse the tyrant constituted the center of the community,[90] whereas in Athens the *polis* itself was this center.[91] Therefore, Pindar may cautiously remind Hieron that there is a limit even for a tyrant ('do not look beyond that', Pindar recommends),[92] but the emphasis of the passage is rather on the aspect that the victor's limit goes far beyond that of every ordinary citizen, a message not advisable to deliver for any successful horse owner in democratic Athens.[93] Sicilian tyrants used equestrian competition for the public display of the legitimacy of their ruling;[94] a re-integration into the civic body was not part of their agenda.

So it must be emphasized that epinician odes (like victor epigrams) did not all serve the same purpose (a re-integration of the victor into the polis community) nor did they simply follow the rules of the genre: agonistic self-presentation of sixth- and fifth-century BC victors varied according to the political constellations the successful horse owners faced in their hometowns. Moreover, such agonistic self-representation was not up to the artistic license of the poets, but was supervised by the victors.[95] Victory poetry was poetry on commission for which the victors had to reach deeply into their pockets.

## Coinage

A third possibility for successful horse owners consisted in displaying their victories on coins in order to have them commemorated. This ancient "mass medium" had the advantage of being widespread. Yet not every victorious horse owner had the possibility of minting his own coins. For a powerful king like Philipp II of Macedon, however, coinage was an available means of representation and he made good use of it. Since the Macedonians were considered to be semi-Greek at best in his time,[96] he had a great interest in presenting himself as a Greek ruler in order to legitimize his 'extension of power over Greece'.[97] In his coinage he proudly displayed his equestrian victories.[98] The imposing gold staters with a two-horse chariot on the back side of the coin are likely to have made some impression on the intended Greek audience; and the same is true for his silver tetradrachmae which commemorated an Olympic victory in the single horse race. Like his presidency over the Amphictyonic Council in Delphi, these Olympic victories won in the years 356, 352 and 348 BC[99] constituted an important part of his political agenda which aimed at legitimizing his expansion of power over Greece.[100] In doing so, Philipp showed his good connections with the two most important Greek sanctuaries. With regard to equestrian success, coins had become the key medium for his display of wealth, power, and Greekness. The message was so strong that it did not matter that he probably was not even present in Olympia when his horses won victory.

## The Importance of Being Praised

To put it in a nutshell, agonistic poetry focused on the owners of the horses. So it is somewhat ironic that the most famous victory statue is that of a charioteer. In any case, agonistic poetry was poetry on commission and not up to the artistic license of the poets. Since equestrian success could be used to achieve and secure political power or to enforce political arguments, agonistic poetry did not just reflect an innocent desire to remember a past event, but was political poetry. Victor epigrams, epinicia, and 'commemorative cash'[101] were, for instance, media of dynastic representation or served as a means of re-integrating equestrian victors into their home communities. To conclude, all these media for the presentation of agonistic fame constitute wonderful pieces of evidence for the ancient historian because they allow him to reconstruct in detail a protagonists' view.

## Notes

1. For an overview of the *agones* in the Archaic and Classical periods, see Thomas Heine Nielsen, *Two Studies in the History of Ancient Greek Athletics* (Copenhagen: Det Kongelige Danske Videnskabernes Selskab, 2018), 11–167.
2. On Roman horse races, see Sinclair Bell's contribution in this volume.
3. For a brief overview, see Wolfgang Decker, *Sport in der griechischen Antike. Vom minoischen Wettkampf bis zu den Olympischen Spielen*, 2nd ed. (Hildesheim: Arete Verlag, 2012), 86–94, and Carolyn Willekes, *The Horse in the Ancient World: From Bucephalus to the Hippodrome* (London: I.B. Tauris, 2016), 191–211; for collections of sources, see Werner Petermandl, *Olympischer Pferdesport im Altertum. Die schriftlichen Quellen* (Kassel: Agon, 2013), and Filippo Canali De Rossi, *Hippiká: Corse di cavalli e di carri in Grecia, Etruria e Roma*, 2 vols. (Hildesheim: Weidmann, 2011 [vol. 1]; 2016 [vol. 2]). For hippic competitions in Greek art, see Erika Maul-Mandelartz, *Griechische Reiterdarstellungen in agonistischem Zusammenhang* (Frankfurt am Main: Peter Lang, 1990), Frank Jünger, *Gespann und Herrschaft. Form und Intention großformatiger Gespanndenkmäler im griechischen Kulturraum von der archaischen bis in die*

4. Homer, *Iliad* 23. 262–897. This funeral contest is fictitious, but there are well-attested historical examples: see Lynn E. Roller, 'Funeral Games for Historical Persons', *Stadion* 7 (1981): 1–18.
5. Christian Mann, 'Campaign *agones*: Towards a Classification of Greek Athletic Competitions', *Classica et Mediaevalia* 68 (2020): 71–89.
6. Thomas Heine Nielsen, 'Reflections on the Number of Athletic Festivals in Pre-Hellenistic Greece', in *Athletics in the Hellenistic World*, ed. Christian Mann, Sofie Remijsen and Sebastian Scharff (Stuttgart: Franz Steiner, 2016), 31–41, here 38. See also, Nielsen, *Two Studies*, 108–55).
7. Wolfgang Leschhorn, 'Die Verbreitung von Agonen in den östlichen Provinzen des Römischen Reiches', in *Agonistik in der römischen Kaiserzeit*, ed. Manfred Lämmer (St. Augustin: Academia Verlag, 1998), 31–57, here 31.
8. There is no precise Olympic chronology before the sixth century BC, but there is solid evidence that the *tethrippon* and the *keles* were the first hippic disciplines in Olympia. Paul Christesen, *Olympic Victor Lists and Ancient Greek History* (Cambridge: Cambridge University Press, 2007), 45–160.
9. Nigel B. Crowther, 'The Age-Category of Boys at Olympia', *Phoenix* 42, no. 4 (1988): 304–8.
10. For a reconstruction of the distances on the basis of literary evidence, see Joachim Ebert, 'Neues zum Hippodrom und zu den hippischen Konkurrenzen in Olympia', *Nikephoros* 2 (1989): 89–107.
11. For an introduction to Pausanias' methods, see Christian Habicht, *Pausanias und seine 'Beschreibung Griechenlands'* (Munich: Beck, 1985).
12. Pausanias, *Description of Greece* 5.9.2; trans. W.H.S. Jones and H.A. Ormerod.
13. See the *aphippodrome* in Thessaly (*Inscriptiones Graecae* IX 2, 527); for the *kalpe* in Sparta, see Paul Christesen, *A New Reading of the Damonon Stele* (Newcastle upon Tyne: Histos, 2019), 51–100.
14. Nigel B. Crowther, 'The *Apobates* Reconsidered (Demosthenes LXI 23–9)', *Journal of Hellenic Studies* 111 (1991): 174–6; Hubert Szemethy, *Der Apobatenagon. Eine philologisch-epigraphisch-archäologische Studie* (Diplomarbeit, Universität Wien, 1991).
15. David Bell, 'The Horse Race in Ancient Greece from the Pre-Classical Period to the First Century B.C.', *Stadion* 15 (1989): 167–90, here 187–8; Willekes, *The Horse in the Ancient World*, 193–4.
16. For the development of the cavalry in ancient Greece, see Ian G. Spence, *The Cavalry of Classical Greece* (Oxford: Oxford University Press, 1993), and Alexandre Blaineau, *Le cheval de guerre en Grèce ancienne* (Rennes: Presses universitaires de Rennes, 2015).
17. Zinon Papakonstantinou, *Sport and Identity in Ancient Greece* (London and New York: Routledge, 2019), 36–42.
18. *Inscriptiones Graecae* II² 2311 (early fourth century BC).
19. *Inscriptiones Graecae* IX 2, 531.
20. *Supplementum Epigraphicum Graecum* XXVII 1114; Hans Langenfeld, 'Der Hellenismus als Epoche der Sportgeschichte', in *Geschehen und Gedächtnis. Die hellenistische Welt und ihre Wirkung (Festschrift Wolfgang Orth)*, ed. Jens-Frederik Eckholdt, Marcus Sigismund and Susanne Sigismund (Berlin: LIT Verlag, 2009), 177–99, here 181.
21. Léopold Migeotte, 'Le financement des concours dans les cités hellénistiques: essai de typologie', in *L'argent dans les concours du monde grec*, ed. Brigitte Le Guen (Saint-Denis: Presses Universitaires Vincennes, 2010), 127–43.
22. *Corpus des inscriptions de Delphes* II 139 (246 BC).
23. Sebastian Scharff, *'The Very First of the Citizens'. Agonistic Cultures and the Self-Presentation of Hellenistic Athletes* (Habilitationsschrift, Universität Mannheim, 2019), 125–38.
24. Plutarch, *Life of Lycurgus* 20.3.

25. Pausanias, *Description of Greece* 6.1.4–5.
26. Thucydides, *History of the Peloponnesian War* 5.50, trans. J.M. Dent.
27. Bell, this volume.
28. For the difficult logistic problems in shipping horses for hundreds of miles, See Sandra Zipprich, 'Logistics and Requirements for Overseas Participants in the Olympic Games: The Example of Sicily', in *Les hippodromes et les concours hippiques dans la Grèce antique*, ed. Jean-Charles Moretti and Panos Valavanis (Paris: École française d'Athènes, forthcoming).
29. Thucydides, *History of the Peloponnesian War* 6.16.2, trans. J.M. Dent. This argument was risky, however, because many Athenians disliked elitist behavior: Christian Mann, *Athlet und Polis im archaischen und frühklassischen Griechenland* (Göttingen: Vandenhoeck & Ruprecht, 2001), 86–113.
30. Pausanias, *Description of Greece* 6.20.9 with Donald G. Kyle, 'Fabulous Females and Ancient Olympia', in *Onward to the Olympics: Historical Perspectives on the Olympic Games*, ed. Gerald P. Schaus and Stephen R. Wenn (Waterloo, Ontario: Wilfrid Laurier University Press, 2007), 131–52, here 138–41.
31. The most recent treatment is Scharff, *'The Very First of the Citizens'*, 211–29, with further bibliography.
32. *Inscriptiones Graecae* V 1, 213; See also, Massimo Nafissi, 'La stele di Damonon (IG V 1, 213 = Moretti, IAG 16), gli Hekatombaia (Strabo 8.4.11) e il sistema festivo della Laconia d'epoca classica', *Aristonothos* 8 (2013): 105–74, and Paul Christesen, *A New Reading of the Damonon Stele*.
33. Pindar, Pythian 5.20-33. See also, Mark Golden, *Greek Sport and Social Status* (Austin: University of Texas Press, 2008), 12–3.
34. Ibid., 44–5.
35. Bell, this volume.
36. *Description of Greece* 6.12.9; trans. W.H.S. Jones and H.A. Ormerod.
37. Nigel J. Nicholson, *Aristocracy and Athletics in Archaic and Classical Greece* (Cambridge: Cambridge University Press, 2005), 95–6. On charioteers and riders, see Henry John Walker, 'Horse Riders and Chariot Drivers', in *Animals in Greek and Roman Religion and Myth*, ed. Patricia A. Johnston, Attilio Mastrocinque and Sophia Papaioannou (Newcastle upon Tyne: Cambridge Scholars, 2016), 309–33.
38. E.g., 'Pferderennbahn im antiken Olympia entdeckt', *Welt*, July 4, 2008, https://www.welt.de/wissenschaft/article2178989/Pferderennbahn-im-antiken-Olympia-entdeckt.html (accessed September 6, 2019).
39. https://www.dainst.org/projekt/-/project-display/33190?p_r_p_redirectURL=%2Fsuchen%3Fp_p_id% (accessed September 6, 2019).
40. For the current state of research, see Moretti and Valavanis, *Les hippodromes*.
41. David Gilman Romano, 'The Hippodrome and the Equestrian Contests at the Sanctuary of Zeus on Mt. Lykaion, Arcadia', in Moretti and Valavanis, *Les hippodromes*.
42. *Description of Greece* 6.20.7, trans. J. Frazer.
43. Barbara Dimde and Catharina Flämig, 'The *Aphesis* of the Olympic Hippodrome: Dimensions, Design, Technology', in Moretti and Valavanis, *Les hippodromes*; Werner Petermandl, 'On the Length of the Greek Hippodrome' (ibid.).
44. Donald G. Kyle, 'Gifts and Glory. Panathenaic and Other Greek Athletic Prizes', in *Worshipping Athena: Panathenaia and Parthenon*, ed. Jennifer Neils (Madison: University of Wisconsin Press, 1996), 106–36; Christian Mann, 'Cash and Crowns: A Network Approach to Greek Athletic Prizes', in *Ancient Greek History and Contemporary Social Science*, ed. Mirko Canevaro et al. (Edinburgh: Edinburgh University Press, 2018), 293–312, with further bibliography.
45. William J. Slater, 'Victory and Bureaucracy: The Process of Agonistic Rewards', *Phoenix* 69, nos. 1–2 (2015): 147–69.
46. On equestrian victor monuments, see Patrick Schollmeyer, *Antike Gespanndenkmäler* (Hamburg: Kovač, 2001), and Jünger, *Gespann und Herrschaft*, 7–222; on victor

inscriptions in general, Luigi Moretti, *Iscrizioni agonistiche greche* (Rome: Signorelli, 1953); for poetic victor inscriptions, Joachim Ebert, *Griechische Epigramme auf Sieger an gymnischen und hippischen Agonen* (Berlin: Akademie-Verlag, 1972).

47. On the study of epinician, Leslie Kurke, *The Traffic in Praise: Pindar and the Poetics of Social Economy* (Ithaca, NY: Cornell University Press, 1991), is indispensable reading; see also Leslie Kurke, 'The Economy of Kudos', in *Cultural Poetics in Archaic Greece. Cult, Performance, Politics*, eds. Carol Dougherty and Leslie Kurke (Cambridge: Cambridge University Press, 1993), 131–63, but note Mann, *Athlet und Polis*, 50–9.

48. On numismatic evidence as a means of commemorating agonistic fame, see Robert Weir, 'Commemorative Cash: The Coins of the Ancient and Modern Olympics', in *Onward to the Olympics: Historical Perspectives on the Olympic Games*, eds. Gerald P. Schaus and Stephen R. Wenn (Waterloo, ON: Wilfrid Laurier University Press, 2007), 179–92. For an exciting case study with regard to a less well-known example from Chalcis on Euboea, Denis Knoepfler, 'Contributions à l'épigraphie de Chalcis', *Bulletin de Correspondance Hellénique* 103 (1979): 165–88.

49. Agonistic victor monuments, as understood here, are methodologically different from statuary groups that include sporting motifs, but for which the original circumstances of their creation are not entirely clear (which is unfortunately the case for most of the remaining agonistic statues and statue groups). See Mann, *Athlet und Polis*, 52–3.

50. Pausanias, *Description of Greece* 6.18.7: 'The first athletes to have their statues dedicated at Olympia were Praxidamas of Aegina, victorious at boxing at the fifty-ninth Festival [sc. 544 BC], and Rexibius the Opuntian, a successful pancratiast at the sixty-first Festival [sc. 536 BC].' (trans. W.H.S. Jones and H.A. Ormerod). For the epigraphic evidence, Ebert, *Griechische Epigramme*, no. 1–11 (including some agonistic dedications as well). See also Mann, *Athlet und Polis*, 49–50.

51. Pausanias, *Description of Greece* 6.18.7.

52. In the victors' hometown the citizen body had to agree on the erection of such a monument. It was in the course of the second century BC that the epigraphic habit changed in many Greek *poleis* so that civic authorities now proudly emphasized that they gave their permission for the erection of the monuments, a process than can be best observed for Hellenistic Messene (Scharff, 'The Very First of the Citizens', 154–7).

53. For Olympia: Pausanias, *Description of Greece* 5.21.1, 6.1.1.

54. Pausanias, *Description of Greece* 6.8.3.

55. On the "end of Greek athletics" in Late Antiquity, Sofie Remijsen, *The End of Greek Athletics in Late Antiquity* (Cambridge: Cambridge University Press, 2015). See also Andreas Gutsfeld and Stephan Lehmann, eds., *Der gymnische Agon in der Spätantike* (Gutenberg: Computus 2013), and Alexander Puk, *Das römische Spielewesen in der Spätantike* (Berlin and Boston, MA: de Gruyter 2014).

56. From the extensive archaeological literature on the Charioteer of Delphi, see esp. François Chamoux, *L'Aurige. Fouilles de Delphes, IV: Monuments figurés: Sculpture, V* (Paris: Boccard, 1955). See Schollmeyer, *Antike Gespanndenkmäler*, and Jünger, *Gespann und Herrschaft*, 150–68.

57. For a possible reconstruction of the entire monument, see Chamoux, *L'Aurige*.

58. Mann, *Athlet und Polis*, 289 note 939.

59. Nigel J. Nicholson, *Aristocracy and Athletics in Archaic and Classical Greece* (Cambridge: Cambridge University Press, 2005) has pointed out with good reason that, like athletic coaches, jockeys and charioteers played no role at all when it came to the agonistic self-representation of sporting victors. The reason for this has to be seen in the lower social statuses of these groups (see above).

60. Mann, *Athlet und Polis*, 50–1.

61. In other cases, a victor epigram is accompanied by an additional prose inscription that outlines the "technical details" of the victory (like the event, the "age class" of the horses, and the place of victory).

62. A drawing of the surviving remains of the epigram is given by Ebert, *Griechische Epigramme*, 60.
63. On the historical context, see Nino Luraghi, *Tirannidi arcaiche in Sicilia e Magna Grecia da Panezio di Leontini alla caduta dei Dinomenidi* (Florence: Leo S. Olschki, 1994), 323-4. See also Daniela Bonanno, *Ierone il Dinomenide: storia e rappresentazione* (Pisa: Fabrizio Serra, 2010), and Nigel J. Nicholson, *The Poetics of Victory in the Greek West. Epinician, Oral Tradition, and Deinomenid Empire* (Oxford: Oxford University Press, 2016), 94-6. On the representation of Sicilian tyrants at Panhellenic sanctuaries, see also Sarah E. Harrell, 'King or Private Citizen: Fifth-Century Sicilian Tyrants at Olympia and Delphi', *Mnemosyne* 55 (2002): 439-64.
64. Mann, *Athlet und Polis*, 290-1.
65. On this "title", Gianfranco Adornato, 'Delphic Enigmas? The "Gelas anasson", Polyzalos, and the Charioteer Statue', *American Journal of Archaeology* 112, no. 1 (2008): 29–55.
66. Claude Vatin, 'Das Viergespann des Polyzalos in Delphi. Weihinschrift und Künstlersignatur', *Boreas* 14-5 (1991-2): 33-44, esp. 40-4.
67. See the impressive compilation of Ebert, *Griechische Epigramme*. For an overview on the additional evidence from the Hellenistic period discovered after Ebert's book has been published, see Scharff, 'The Very First of the Citizens', 10-1.
68. See Ebert, *Griechische Epigramme*, 19: 'Eine Blüte erlebte das Siegerepigramm in hellenistischer Zeit.'
69. On these epigrams, see e.g. Benjamin Acosta-Hughes, Elizabeth Kosmetatou, and Manuel Baumbach, eds., *Labored in Papyrus Leaves. Perspectives on an Epigram Collection Attributed to Posidippus (P.Mil.Vogl. VIII 309)* (Cambridge, MA: Harvard University Press, 2004), and Kathryn J. Gutzwiller, ed., *The New Posidippus. A Hellenistic Poetry Book* (Oxford: Oxford University Press, 2005). The best text (as well as several useful English translations of the poems) can be found online as *New Poems Attributed to Posidippus: An Electronic Text-in progress, Version 13.0* published as part 1 of the classics@ series of the Center for Hellenic Studies (https://chs.harvard.edu/CHS/article/display/1343 [accessed September 14, 2019]). Helpful commentaries on the section *Hippika* include Matthew W. Dickie, 'The ἱππικά of Posidippus', in *Papers of the Langford Latin Seminar, XII: Greek and Roman Poetry, Greek and Roman Historiography*, ed. Francis Cairns (Cambridge: Cambridge University Press, 2008), 19–51, and Martin Hose, 'Hippika (71–88)', in *Der Neue Poseidipp. Text – Übersetzung – Kommentar*, eds. Bernd Seidensticker, Adrian Stähli, and Antje Wessels (Darmstadt: Wissenschaftliche Buchgesellschaft, 2015), 283–318.
70. The 'royal' poems include Posidippus, *Epigrams* 78, 79, 82, 87, and 88. In addition, there are two epigrams which are very fragmentary but which could possibly also be attributed to Ptolemaic victors (*Epigrams* 80 and 81), and another one for a Ptolemaic courtier (*Epigram* 74). There is a vast amount of literature on the equestrian activities of the Ptolemaic family. Important contributions include Dorothy J. Thompson, 'Posidippus, Poet of the Ptolemies', in *The New Posidippus. A Hellenistic Poetry Book*, ed. Kathryn J. Gutzwiller (Oxford: Oxford University Press, 2005), 269–83; Sofie Remijsen, 'Challenged by Egyptians: Greek Sports in the Third Century BC', in *Sport in the Cultures of the Ancient World*, ed. Zinon Papakonstantinou (London: Routledge, 2009), 98–123; and Christian Mann, 'Könige, Poleis und Athleten in hellenistischer Zeit', *Klio* 100 (2018): 447–79, esp. 450-60 (with further references).
71. Posidippus, *Epigram* 87 (trans. M. Lefkowitz).
72. On the concrete historical situation in which equestrian successes became important for the dynasty, see Lukas Kainz, '"We are the Best, We are One, and We are Greeks!" Reflections on the Ptolemies' Participation in the agones', in *Athletics in the Hellenistic World*, eds. Christian Mann, Sofie Remijsen, and Sebastian Scharff (Stuttgart: Steiner, 2016), 331–53.
73. Posidippus, *Epigram* 88 (trans. E. Kosmetatou and B. Acosta-Hughes).
74. See Hose, 'Hippika', 317.

75. Posidippus, *Epigram* 87.4.
76. Her victories are usually dated to 396 and 392 BC (Luigi Moretti, *Olympionikai, i vincitori negli antichi agoni olimpici* (Rome: Accademia Nazionale dei Lincei, 1957), no. 373, 381. The literature on Cynisca is "something of an industry unto itself" (Christesen, *A New Reading of the Damonon Stele*, 189 note 246). See e.g. Donald G. Kyle, 'The Only Woman in All Greece: Kyniska, Agesilaos, Alcibiades and Olympia', *Journal of Sport History* 30, no. 2 (2003): 183–203. It is striking that Cynisca appears as a point of reference here because her victories date at least 100 years earlier than the Ptolemaic successes. This shows that her victories were remembered by people living as far away as Egypt more than a century later. The text of Berenice's epigram even shows some knowledge of Cynisca's victor epigram that has also survived from antiquity (in an epigram collection *Greek Anthology* 13.16, as well as on stone: *Inschriften von Olympia* 160. See Ebert, *Griechische Epigramme*, no. 33). In this epigram Cynisca is called the only woman in Greece who won an Olympic victory (l. 3–4: 'of the women of all Hellas, I am the only one to have won this crown'). Such a statement could be no longer valid after Berenice's success.
77. On Elean horse owners, see Sebastian Scharff, 'In Olympia siegen: Elische Athleten des 1. Jahrhunderts v. Chr. und die Frage nach der Attraktivität der Olympischen Spiele im späten Hellenismus', in *Griechische Heiligtümer als Handlungsorte. Zur Multifunktionalität supralokaler Heiligtümer von der frühen Archaik bis in die römische Kaiserzeit. Erweiterter Tagungsband einer internationalen Konferenz, Villa Vigoni, 15.–18. April 2015*, eds. Matthias Haake and Klaus Freitag (Stuttgart: Steiner, 2019), 227–49, esp. 241–4. On Sidon: Corinne Bonnet, *Les enfants de Cadmos: le paysage religieux de la Phénicie hellénistique. De l'archéologie à l'histoire* (Paris: Boccard, 2015), 260–5. On the self-representation of Hellenistic victors in general, see Riet van Bremen, 'The Entire House is Full of Crowns. Hellenistic Agōnes and the Commemoration of Victory', in *Pindar's Poetry, Patrons and Festivals. From Archaic Greece to the Roman Empire*, eds. Simon Hornblower and Catherine Morgan (Oxford: Oxford University Press, 2007), 345–75.
78. Sebastian Scharff, 'Das Pferd Aithon, die Skopaden und die πατρὶς Θεσσαλία. Zur Selbstdarstellung hippischer Sieger aus Thessalien im Hellenismus', in *Athletics in the Hellenistic World*, eds. Christian Mann, Sofie Remijsen, and Sebastian Scharff (Stuttgart: Steiner, 2016), 209–29. On Archaic and Classical horse owners from Thessaly, see Maria Stamatopoulou, 'Thessalian Aristocracy and Society in the Age of Epinikian', in *Pindar's Poetry, Patrons, and Festivals. From Archaic Greece to the Roman Empire*, eds. Simon Hornblower and Catherine Morgan (Oxford: Oxford University Press, 2007), 308–41.
79. Stephen Hodkinson, 'An Agonistic Culture? Athletic Competition in Archaic and Classical Spartan Society', in *Sparta. New Perspectives*, eds. Stephen Hodkinson and Anton Powell (London: Duckworth, 1999), 147–87, was the first to use the term "agonistic culture" with regard to a particular Greek city state. On "agonistic cultures" as a research tool for the understanding of athletic self-representation in ancient Greece, Scharff, *'The Very First of the Citizens'*, 12–15.
80. See e.g. Bruno Currie, 'Reperformance Scenarios for Pindar's Odes', in *Oral Performance and Its Context*, ed. Christopher Mackie (Leiden: Brill, 2004), 49–69, and Arlette Neumann-Hartmann, *Epinikien und Aufführungsrahmen* (Hildesheim: Weidmann, 2009). On the places of performance, Christopher Eckerman, 'Was Epinician performed at Panhellenic Sanctuaries?', *Greek, Roman, and Byzantine Studies* 52, no. 3 (2012): 338–60, where he challenges the traditional view that some of the extant odes were performed at Panhellenic sanctuaries immediately after the victory. On Pindar's poetry being configured for multiple performances, see also Carey's identification of Pindar's "oral subterfuge", whereby the poet pretends to compose for the occasion (see Christopher Carey, *A Commentary on Five Odes of Pindar. Pythian 2, Pythian 9, Nemean 1, Nemean 7, Isthmian 8* [Salem: Ayer, 1981], 5).

81. There are also some fragmentary odes of Simonides and other poets; on Simonides, see Orlando Poltera, *Simonides lyricus. Testimonia und Fragmente. Einleitung, kritische Ausgabe, Übersetzung und Kommentar* (Basel: Schwabe 2008) and Richard Rawles, *Simonides the Poet. Intertextuality and Reception* (Cambridge: Cambridge University Press, 2018). After the middle of the fifth century BC, then, the genre fell out of use; and when Euripides composed his epinician on Alcibiades' famous victory in the Olympic four-horse chariot race of 416 BC, where the dazzling Athenian nobleman had competed with seven (!) *quadrigae* (Moretti, *Olympionikai*, no. 345), the poem appeared to be already out of step by the time of its appearance. In the third century BC, the great Hellenistic poet Callimachus tried to revitalize the genre (not surprisingly by composing odes, now in a different meter, on victors from Egypt), but he did not succeed. On the 'end of epinician', see Mark Golden, *Sport and Society in Ancient Greece* (Cambridge: Cambridge University Press, 1998), 84–88.
82. On the herald's announcement, all of the evidence, and its contents, see Aleksander Wolicki, 'The Heralds and the Games in Archaic and Classical Greece', *Nikephoros* 15 (2002): 69–97.
83. Kurke, *The Traffic in Praise*, Kurke, 'The Economy of Kudos', 131–63.
84. Kurke, 'The Economy of Kudos', 136 speaks of 'talismanic potency' or power.
85. This is one of the main observations of the study of Mann, *Athlet und Polis*; see e.g. 292–3.
86. Pindar, *Olympian* 1.23 (trans. D. Arnson Svarlien). On Olympian 1, see Kathryn A. Morgan, *Pindar and the Construction of Syracusan Monarchy in the Fifth Century B.C.* (Oxford: Oxford University Press), 209–59.
87. Pindar, *Pythian* 7.1 (trans. D. Arnson Svarlien).
88. Pindar, *Olympian* 1.113–4 (trans. D. Arnson Svarlien).
89. Pindar, *Pythian* 7.5–8 (trans. D. Arnson Svarlien).
90. On Hieron's agonistic self-representation, Christian Mann, 'The Victorious Tyrant: Hieron of Syracuse in the Epinicia of Pindar and Bacchylides', in *The Splendors and Miseries of Ruling Alone. Encounters with Monarchy from Archaic Greece to the Hellenistic Mediterranean*, ed. Nino Luraghi (Stuttgart: Steiner, 2013), 25–48. See also Nicholson, *The Poetics of Victory in the Greek West*, 237–76.
91. On 'civic athletics' in Athens, Donald G. Kyle, *Athletics in Ancient Athens*, 2nd edn. (Leiden: Brill, 1993). It is not the place here to elaborate on the political differences between different *poleis* like Sparta, Athens, or Croton, to name just some of the most successful *poleis* in terms of athletics in the age of the epinician. But we should bear in mind that these differences had a clear impact on the way victors presented their successes to their fellow citizens.
92. Pindar, *Olympian* 1.114 (trans. D. Arnson Svarlien).
93. Pindar, *Pythian* 7.19 clearly expresses the fact that there was sometimes 'envy' on sporting victors among the fellow citizens (see also note 22 of this chapter).
94. This was especially necessary due to the type of their ruling. As tyrants, their rule was extremely precarious which was not similarly the case for a dynasty like the kings of Cyrene who "could point to the fact that their ancestors had ruled since the founding of the city" (Mann, 'The Victorious Tyrant', 26).
95. See Mann, 'The Victorious Tyrant', 41: 'Epinicia do not ( … ) carry a message from the poet to the patron, but a message from the patron to the audience.'
96. See, for instance, Demosthenes, *Third Philippic* 31 which is, however, highly polemic in tone.
97. Donald G. Kyle, *Sport and Spectacle in the Ancient World*, 2nd edn. (Malden, MA: Blackwell, 2015), 225.
98. On Philipp's coinage, Stefan Ritter, *Bildkontakte. Götter und Heroen in der Bildsprache griechischer Münzen des 4. Jahrhunderts v. Chr.* (Berlin: Reimer, 2002), 137–8, 142, 144, 230; Manuela Mari, *Al di là dell'Olimpo. Macedoni e grandi santuari della Grecia dall'età Arcaica al primo ellenismo* (Athens: Boccard, 2002), 80–1.

99. According to Moretti, *Olympionikai*, no. 434, 439, 445, the victories were won in the Olympic single-horse race in 356, probably in the four-horse chariot race of 352, and in the two-horse chariot race of 348. The victory in the four-horse chariot race left no traces in the numismatic evidence, but Plutarch, *Life of Alexander* 4.9 records victories of Philipp in this event and additionally points out 'Philipp's attention to having his victories depicted on coins', as Kyle, *Sport and Spectacle*, 225 put it.
100. On the role of Philipp's equestrian activities for his political agenda, see e.g. Golden, *Greek Sport and Social Status*, 16–7, and Kyle, *Sport and Spectacle*, 224–7 ("Proclaiming Greekness through Games").
101. Weir, 'Commemorative Cash', 179.

## Acknowledgements

We would like to thank the two anonymous reviewers of this essay for their useful comments and Melanie Meaker who improved the English of the first half of this essay and helped with some formal aspects.

## Disclosure Statement

No potential conflict of interest was reported by the authors.

# Horse Racing in Imperial Rome: Athletic Competition, Equine Performance, and Urban Spectacle

Sinclair W. Bell

**ABSTRACT**
Chariot races were the earliest, most popular, and longest-lived of all forms of 'spectacles' in the Roman world. This essay surveys the spatial and architectural framework of the Circus Maximus, the primary chariot racing venue at Rome, and circuses around the empire; the organization of the races, including the role of the factions; the symbolic representations of victories and athletic victors, as well as the charioteers' actual prizes; and the horses that were bred for racing. Throughout I also briefly discuss the sport's spectators and fans, for whom the sport was a socially binding religion.
The essay focuses on the first through the fourth centuries A.D., with the bulk of the evidence (literary, epigraphic, artistic, and archaeological) drawn from the first two centuries. In keeping with current directions in the study of ancient sport and spectacle, the approach adopted here places less emphasis on the legal and technical aspects of the chariot races ('event-oriented sport history') and more on these competitions as 'part of a broader social canvas' (the 'social history of sport and spectacle').

[T]heir temple, their dwelling, their assembly, and the height of all their hopes is the Circus Maximus.[1]

The horse we most admire is the one that romps home a winner, cheered on by the seething roar of the crowd.[2]

We, steadfast and devoted supporters, have from our own resources set up an altar-tomb for Fuscus of the Blue team, so that all might know the record and token of devotion. Your reputation is unsullied, you won for speed, you contended with many, though not rich you feared nobody, though you experienced envy you always bravely maintained silence, you lived a fine life, being mortal you died, but a natural death. Whatever sort of man you may be, you will miss such a one as Fuscus; halt, traveler, read, if you remember and know who the man was. Let men all fear Fortune, yet you will make one remark: "Fuscus has the epitaph and tomb that belong to death. The stone covers his bones. All is well with him. Away with you, Fortune. We poured our tears for this good man, now (we pour out) wine. We pray that you rest in peace. No one is like you."

The ages will talk of your conquests.[3]

*In memoriam Mark Golden (August 6, 1948–April 9, 2020)*

From the ancient Olympics to the modern film *Ben-Hur*, horse racing has proven a potent and enduring symbol of the agonistic culture of Classical Antiquity. Similarities did exist between the two cultures, where equestrianism of all forms, due to the expense involved, had aristocratic overtones for Romans as it did for Greeks.[4] But in contrast to the Greeks' equal passion for mounted horse races and chariot racing[5], Romans strongly favored the latter. Indeed, chariot races were the earliest, most popular, and longest-lived of all forms of 'spectacles' (*spectacula*) in the Roman world.[6]

Like other essays in this collection, the present contribution situates its topic within the context of a longstanding, world-wide agonistic tradition of horse racing while also still subject to its own distinct historical evolution and culturally specific meanings. To that end and in keeping with the thematic approach outlined in the introductory essay to the anthology, this essay surveys (1) the spatial and architectural framework of the Circus Maximus at Rome and beyond; (2) the organization of the chariot races, including the role of the factions; (3) the symbolic representations of victories and the athletic victors, as well as their material prizes; and (4) the horses that were bred for racing. Throughout I also briefly make reference to the sport's spectators and fans—a subject too large and rich for full discussion here, but fortuitously the focus of a landmark new study.[7] The remit of this essay is the first through the fourth centuries A.D., with the bulk of the evidence (literary, epigraphic, artistic, and archaeological) drawn from the first two centuries.

In keeping with current directions in the study of ancient sport and spectacle[8] and sport history more generally[9], the approach adopted to the evidence here places less emphasis on the legal and technical aspects of the chariot races, which an earlier scholarly tradition tended to treat as if they were isolated phenomena ('event-oriented sport history'), and more on these competitions as 'part of a broader social canvas' (the 'social history of sport and spectacle'). As a consequence, I attempt to paint the long history of the Roman circus and its chariot races with broad brushstrokes, while still giving that narrative form and detail by situating it within the social-historical context of individual emperors, athletes, equines, and spectators.

## 1. The Spatial and Architectural Framework of Chariot Racing[10]

### 1.1. The Circus Maximus at Rome and Circuses across the Empire

Chariot races were customarily held in a circus, a monumental arena that took the form of an elongated horseshoe.[11] The Circus Maximus in Rome (Figures 1–3, 6) was the oldest, largest, and most famous of all circus arenas.[12] As the site of the legendary Rape of the Sabines[13], the Circus Maximus—unlike any other building for Roman spectacles (i.e., the theater, amphitheater, or stadium)[14]—was intertwined with the legendary foundation of Rome itself. At its most fully developed stage under the

**Figure 1.** Sestertius of Trajan. Circa 103–11 A.D. Orichalcum. 26.26 g, 6:00, 33 mm. Image: © Yale University Art Gallery, Gift of Ben Lee Damsky, inv. no. 2018.65.1.

**Figure 2.** Visualization of the opening procession (*pompa circensis*) in the Circus Maximus during the Roman imperial period for the documentary film "The Greatest Race: Rome's Chariot Superstar." Image © Faber Courtial / Lion TV, Smithsonian Channel, Channel 4, ZDF, ARTE.

emperor Trajan (Figure 1),[15] the structure measured circa 580 m. long and 140 m. wide. The venue could have accommodated approximately 150,000 spectators, though it may have been as many as 250,000.[16] While its architectural remains are poorly preserved today, a recent program of excavation and restoration by the Sovrintendenza Capitolina ai Beni Culturali has done much to clarify our understanding of its building history and operation, including the geology of the Murcia valley (the depression between the Palatine and Aventine hills where the Circus Maximus sat)[17]; the position, orientation, and length of the central barrier or *euripus*[18]; the hemicycles with their bars and latrines[19]; and the now-lost Arch of Titus (compare Figure 1, where the Arch looks down from the upper left).[20]

The architectural form of the Circus Maximus served as the prototype for satellite arenas elsewhere in Italy and around the Mediterranean, with most (but not all) built after its Trajanic remodeling. Among these, more than 50 other circuses are now known[21], the majority being found in the regions where horse-breeding was already well-established: Italy[22], North Africa[23] (16 known, eight confirmed archaeologically), and Spain[24] (19 known, 12 archaeologically confirmed). The evidence from other parts of the Roman empire remains patchier, although circuses are found in most of the major cities (especially the capitals) of the provinces, including the east (e.g. Antioch, Bostra, Tyre), west (e.g. Lyon, Vienne, Trier), and northwest (e.g. Colchester). The sizes of these venues vary considerably across the empire, from more than 500 m. (at Antioch and El Djem/*Thysdrus*) to 269 m. (at Jerash/*Gerasa*). However, the majority fall into the middle size, so that a 'canonical' circus measures c. 420–485 m. long. In addition, there were surely many other venues that were never monumentalized (for instance, held in flat fields), and that were constructed of perishable materials, such as earth and wood, which are now permanently lost to the archaeological record.

Recent topographical surveys, geophysical prospections, and archaeological excavations are steadily filling in the picture of structures both known and suspected, especially at Colchester,[25] Segobriga,[26] Sagunto,[27] Milan,[28] Assisi,[29] Lyon,[30] Trier,[31] Corinth,[32] Carthage,[33] Caesarea Maritima,[34] and Berytos.[35] In addition, the study of new and old finds (including sculptures, mosaics, and inscriptions) and fresh syntheses are improving our understanding of the races and their venues in regional perspective, especially in Britain,[36] Spain[37] Egypt,[38] North Africa,[39] Palestine and Israel,[40] Lebanon,[41] and Syria.[42] The creation of three-dimensional, archaeological reconstructions—especially of the Circus Maximus[43] (Figure 2)—have done much to test hypotheses and consequently enrich our perspectives on the ancient appearance and experience of these venues as well (for instance, about viewer sightlines). This recent exploration and research has given further texture to the larger picture of how the circus design was translated across the provinces, where it was mapped onto local landscapes and pre-existing cultural traditions.[44]

The circus at Tarragona (*Tarraco*), for example, was constructed in the first century A.D. in the heart of the city where it sat beneath and was joined to the sanctuary of the imperial cult as part of a monumental, three-terraced complex. The decision to locate the structure intramurally, to construct it on such a massive scale (the circus-terrace complex consumed *nearly twenty percent* of the urban area), and to integrate it with the imperial cult clearly signaled the city's deep-seated fidelity to Rome as well as its regional ambitions vis-à-vis rival Iberian cities.[45] By contrast, many circuses were constructed as stand-alone buildings on the urban periphery (including extramurally), where they lacked a direct connection to the core infrastructure (as at Carthage and Trier). Some also leave less of an impression today because they were subsequently quarried or because less enduring building materials were employed in their construction, such as the earthen *cavea* and gravel perimeter at Colchester. Thus, where the mortared rubble substructures of the Tarragona circus have endured in the lower levels of later buildings, approximately 25,000 now-lost pines and oaks were employed in the foundation system of the circus at Arles.[46] The latter remarkable discovery calls attention to the significant investments of capital that would have been leveraged locally for the construction of circuses all across the empire, and explains (at least in part) why they are the least common form of spectacle building to have been built by the Romans. The discovery also sheds light on the tremendous material and ecological resources harnessed in their construction, not to mention those expended for their routine maintenance (such as repairs from storm damage,[47] water for cleaning, and so forth) as well as on game days (for instance, fielding hundreds of horses, some of which would have died in the races; see below). Indeed, the environmental impact of Roman spectacles generally has only recently been given consideration, and a comprehensive and innovative new study is certain to inspire future work in this area.[48]

As in so much of Roman culture, the success of the circus as a mechanism for 'becoming Roman' lay in the transferability and adaptability of its monumental form across diverse ecosystems, both cultural and environmental.[49] On the one hand, all provincial circuses owed their inspiration, morphologically as well as ideologically, to the Circus Maximus, and the faithful replication of its form bound urban centers across the Mediterranean into a collective *imperial* culture of spectacle. On the other hand, the local settings of these buildings gave them special charge throughout the empire, where audiences of diverse backgrounds thronged to them and translated a distant-born custom into a shared passion.[50] And if the circus was the vessel, the races themselves were the catalyzing agent that bound Rome's subjects together.

## 1.2. The History and Functions of the Chariot Races

The Circus Maximus and circus arenas generally were not only venues for horseracing but also sites of performance because of the different functions they served and the diverse programs they hosted in connection with the Roman religious calendar.[51] Some circus games (*ludi circenses*) were held annually as celebrations of the seven festivals central to state religion (*ludi publici*)[52], including the *Ludi Megalenses* (April 4–9), *Ludi Cereales* (April 12–18), *Ludi Florales* (April 28–May 2), *Ludi Apollinares* (July 6–12), *Ludi Romani* (September 4–12), *Ludi Victoriae* (October 26–31), and *Ludi Plebei* (November 4–12).[53] Other games (*ludi votivi*) were held in association with major state events, such as military triumphs, temple dedications, imperial birthdays and funerals, and government jubilees.[54] The games held in the circus included chariot races as well as other types of spectacles, including equestrian maneuvers by aristocratic youth (the *lusus Troiae*),[55] animal hunts (*venationes*)[56], mock battles[57], public executions[58], and other one-off events.[59]

While the exact origins of the chariot races at Rome remain subject to speculation, Italic influences (Etruscan in particular) are rightly attributed a greater (if not exclusive) role over Greek in the most recent studies.[60] The first races at Rome were said to have been organized by Romulus in the context of religious ritual and to have taken place in the *Vallis Murcia*.[61] There the Circus served as a cult site for the worship of Murcia;[62] the agrarian deity Consus[63], whose cult was celebrated with a festival (the *Consualia*) and whose shrine sat along the *euripus* (see Figures 3.10, and Figure 4, where at least 14 monuments are visible on the barrier, including that of

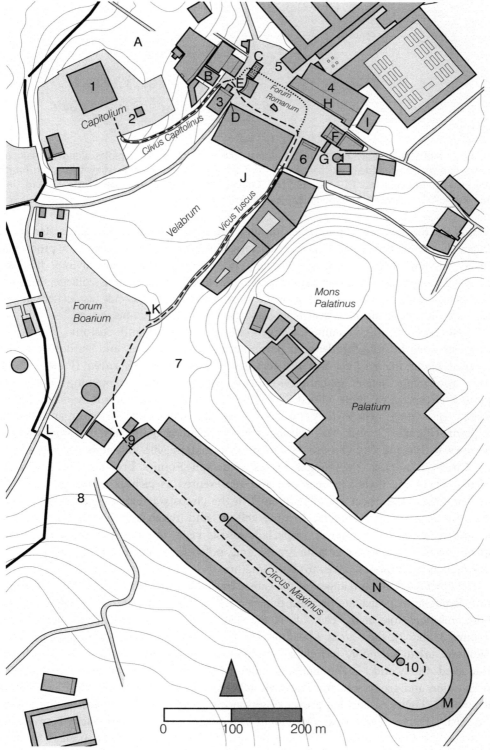

**Figure 3.** The itinerary of the *pompa circensis* in the imperial period (ca. 44 B.C. to 235 A.D.). Image: from Latham, *Performance, Memory, and Processions*, 135 Map 2; drawn by Marie Saldaña; reproduced with permission.

**Figure 4.** Mid-16th century drawing of a Roman relief depicting the temples along the *euripus*, a *praeses ludorum* (president of the games), and the spectators. Original relief: second to fourth century A.D. Drawing: H. 13.2 × L. 43.5 cm; Coburg, Kunstsammlungen der Veste Coburg, inv. no. Hz.2.Nr.75.b. Image © Kunstsammlungen des Veste Coburg.

Consus on the far right)[64]; and the sun-god Sol, among others.[65] On the sestertius of Trajan illustrated here (Figure 1), for instance, the bust of Sol surmounts a prominent gabled building (the *aedes Solis*), reflecting his status as the major divinity honored there.[66] Through such state-sanctioned, widely-dispersed media such as coinage, 'imperial architectural foundations, veneration of the emperor, and religious cult (associated, in this instance, with the games) are thus insistently visualized for the coin's viewer'.[67]

These competitions remained forever cloaked in ritual and custom. The circus itself was a world full of gods, with monumental altars, shrines, and statues of deities installed along the *euripus* and the temples within the circus *cavea* (Figures 2–5). They also made *active* appearances in the games, from the opening procession (*pompa circensis*) of their gilded likenesses to their deposition in a monumental skybox (*pulvinar*), where they presided over the games in the company of the emperor (Figures 2 and 3).[68] Because of its winding path past various sites of memory within the city (Figure 3) and its culmination with the gods' installation in the Circus Maximus, the *pompa* represented well Rome's broader '"processional" culture where the gods are imagined and represented as *viewers of the games*'.[69] At the same time, the 'spectacle of religion'[70] in the circus was experienced in still other ways by Romans: astrologers, fortune tellers, and magicians peddled hopes and dreams to everyday racegoers (especially those keen to alter the outcome of an upcoming race[71]), while erudite poets and polemicists explored the idea of the racetrack as a temple or a cosmos-in-miniature.[72]

The function, scale, and appeal of the games expanded over time, so that '[t]he transition from Republic to principate invested the spectacle of the circus with an even larger and more ambitious role in the civic life of the state'.[73] In its fully developed imperial form (Figures 1 and 2), the Circus Maximus was the grand showpiece for Rome's hallowed traditions, urban splendor, and global ambitions—'a fitting place for a nation which has conquered the world'.[74] The building came to serve as an instrument of collective socialization and group solidarity, through adherence to a public dress code[75] and seating hierarchy[76] (Figure 4) and the proper observance of repetitive rituals (such as the *pompa circensis*)[77] (Figures 2 and 3); as a symbol of the emperor's role as intermediary between the gods and the Roman people,[78] through his seat in the *pulvinar* and his palace's location directly above on the Palatine hill (*Mons Palatinus*)[79] (Figures 2 and 3); as an arena for

**Figure 5.** Relief (funerary?) with scene of the circus races. Late third (?) century A.D. Marble. H. 55 cm. x L. 1.30 m. Foligno, Palazzo Trinci, Museo Archeologico. Image: author; reproduced with permission of the Comune di Foligno.

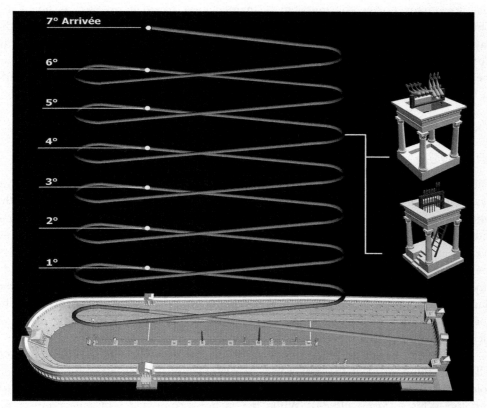

**Figure 6.** Reconstruction of the seven laps around the Circus Maximus. Image: after Fauquet, *Le cirque romain*, 268 fig. 7; reproduced with permission of the author.

collective action and political negotiation, where the Roman people publicly petitioned the emperor (such as for tax relief);[80] as an advertisement for imperial munificence (*liberalitas*) through the provision of jaw-dropping spectacles and state-of-the-art amenities[81] that made it 'one of the most beautiful and most admirable structures in Rome';[82] as a megaphone for Rome's military muscle and superpower greatness, through both temporary and permanent exhibitions of exotic captive cultures (for instance, the dedication of an Egyptian obelisk along the *euripus*[83], visible in Figures 1, 2, 4, 5); and as a mechanism for euergetism, through which elite benefactors vied with their peers to underwrite the physical magnificence (*magnificentia*) of their communities, competed with other urban centers for regional prominence, and advanced the imperial project far and wide.[84]

Chariot races continued to thrive in and evolve throughout the western empire into late antiquity[85], with the rise of Christianity marking out the sacred spaces[86], performative rituals[87], and performers' bodies[88] in new and often highly contested ways. The nature and extent of that transformation is still being understood: for instance, whether or not the Roman circus form directly inspired the six 'circiform' or U-shaped basilicas in Rome's *suburbium* remains a topic of vigorous debate.[89] What is clear is that for many Romans, even those living under the influence of Christianity in the fourth century, chariot races were still tantamount to a religion, the Circus Maximus their 'temple,' and charioteers and race horses their gods.[90] For instance, circus horses continued to be named after pagan gods even as one Early Church Father lamented that the people of Rome could name the star horses of the day but not the number of the apostles.[91] That kind of devotion found fertile soil in Constantinople as well, where the races endured for many centuries after the fall of the western empire.[92] As a consequence of their early origins and prolonged afterlife in the east, chariot races were the longest lived form of Roman spectacle.

## 2. The Organization of the Chariot Races[93]

### 2.1. Factions

The number of races on any given day would have varied over time and location based upon a number of factors, including the occasion for the games and the wherewithal of the game sponsor. However, a record from mid-fourth century Rome indicates that there were approximately 24 chariot races on a game day (among other events) and some 66 days of games in a calendar year. While the exact frequency of the games across the duration of the empire cannot be established (a figure that in any case would fail to take into account special, one-off events), it is clear that staging the chariot races required the support of a complex infrastructure. The enormous burden of their cost and organization fell upon the four racing teams or factions (*factiones*) that served as contractors.

The factions began as independent agents in the Republic and early empire and fell under the control of the emperor in the later empire. They were known by their colors: the Blues (*factio veneta*), the Greens (*factio prasina*), the Reds (*factio russata*), and the Whites (*factio albata*). While the factions competed with one another for resources (especially charioteers) as well as victories, from the early imperial period onward the Greens were allied with the Reds while the Blues and the Whites cooperated with one another.[94] Each of the factions attracted their respective adherents or 'fan clubs', but the Greens and Blues enjoyed the greatest popularity overall as well as imperial favor.[95]

These factions or clubhouses were responsible for procuring the race horses, maintaining stables with animals and staff (sometimes in the hundreds), training the athletes, and providing the necessary equipment (such as chariots). They were richly rewarded for these services by the sponsor of the games (*editor ludi*), who had to underwrite a race day.[96] Because the factions were able to demand ever-higher prices for their services until their eventual takeover by the imperial administration, they functioned as powerful business concerns with international reach (on provincial stud farms, for instance, see below). At Rome the faction stables (*stabula factionum*) sat about 1–2 km. away in the lower Campus Martius[97], where they could take advantage of the nearby *Trigarium* for equestrian riding.[98]

Each of the four factions had a large support staff that was overseen by the faction manager (*dominus factionis*) who supervised several hundred employees with specialized roles. A well-known inscription from the reign of Domitian details the structure of the *familia quadrigaria* of the Red team which was managed by Titus Ateius Capito, an elite Roman citizen.[99] In addition to the charioteers themselves (six of whom are mentioned by name), the staff included professionals who managed the stables (*sutor*, cobbler; *sellarius*, stablehand), who assisted in the operation of the racecourse (*tentor*, who operated the starting gates; *morator*, who held the horses at the starting gate; *sparsor*, who threw water on the horses to keep them cool), and who directly assisted the athletes and horses (*medicus*, doctor; *conditor*, groom [Figure 11]), and still others.[100] Thus, where '[i]n the Greek world the horses, charioteers and jockeys were simply a symbol of the owner's prestige, in the Roman world the charioteers and their horses were the very public face of the business that was a racing faction.'[101]

## 2.2. A Day at the Races

While the vestiges of the Circus Maximus itself offer little direct evidence of the chariot races that once thrilled its hundreds of thousands of spectators on a given day, the totality of the surviving sources allows us to reconstruct their key characteristics with confidence. That evidence includes recent archaeological excavations of some better-preserved circuses (mentioned above); literary descriptions of the races[102]; written documents such as papyri (three circus programs)[103] and inscriptions (especially victory and funerary monuments for charioteers, such as Figure 8; see further below); and a wealth of iconographic representations[104], which appear in every conceivable artistic medium and from a variety of viewpoints (for instance, Figures 1, 4, 5). While the precise contours of the chariot races saw significant variations over space and time—for instance, the length of the racecourses, the number of starting gates, and more—generally speaking a 'typical day' at the Circus Maximus can be thoroughly re-imagined.[105]

On race days, the animals, performers, and staff would have travelled from their faction houses to the Circus Maximus. There the races were preceded by the sacred procession (*pompa circensis*) (Figure 3) that paraded through the city streets and terminated in the Circus Maximus, where it lapped around the track.[106] The procession was led by the president of the games (*praeses ludorum*) (Figure 4) and included both images of the gods (the 12 Olympians and others) and their symbols, which were conveyed to their shrine and house (the *pulvinar*) where they were accompanied by the emperor. Trailing the images of the gods in the procession were magistrates, young nobles, temple attendants, dancers, musicians, athletes, and chariot drivers.[107] In this way, 'public architecture, images, and living participants amounted to a visual experience of unique character, combining the effects of stability and movement, ritual dignity and spectacular surprise'.[108] This visual parade of gleaming statues and colorful faction jerseys was further enhanced for certain races under the emperor Caligula (if not others) by the sprinkling of powdered lead and copper all over the arena floor to make it red and green (the faction colors).[109]

With the conclusion of the procession, the crowd's attention shifted to the 12 starting gates (*carceres*) (see Figures 2, 3.9, 5 (far left), **6** (far right)). There the different factions' teams of two- (*bigae*), three- (*trigae*), or (more commonly) four-horse (*quadrigae*) chariots sat ready, having been assigned their places by lot. (In some rare cases, exceptional charioteers were tasked with commanding teams of six or even seven horses, which held concomitantly greater prize value). One or more trumpets sounded to gather the crowd's attention and then the game magistrate or sponsor (*editor ludorum*),[110] who sat in the loggia over the *carceres* (Figures 3.9 and 5 (upper left-hand corner)), dropped a white handkerchief (*mappa*) onto the track.[111] The gates then unlocked, probably opening simultaneously by a springing mechanism operated by the ground attendants, and the teams exploded forward. While we assume that many races featured three teams from each of the four factions, there were many events with smaller numbers of competitors, as discussed below.[112]

The start of the race was a moment of intense adrenaline release not only for the athletes who had been waiting inside the *carceres* with their teams of anxious horses, but also for the hundreds of thousands of audience members. Ammianus Marcellinus writes of the idle plebs who 'swear by their hoary hair and wrinkles that the state cannot exist if in the coming race the charioteer whom each favors is not first to rush forth from the barriers, and fails to round the turning-point closely with his ill-omened horses.'[113] The spectators' anticipation would have been built up from seeing advertisements for the games around the city and from reading programs at the games listing the participating athletes[114], some of whom they would have financial stake in through betting. The audience monitored the progress of the race by checking the lap-counting devices (one of seven eggs, the other seven dolphins) installed at either end of the *euripus* (see Figures 2, 4 (center and right side), 5, and 6 (right side)).[115] However, the lack of a *velarium* (fabric canopy), in contrast to the Colosseum[116], exposed spectators to the sun's blinding glare and sweltering heat. While the glare would have made it hard to see, the 'seething roar' of the crowd would have made it hard to hear[117]—problems that the signaling system of trumpets and the lap counters at either ends of the *euripus* were intended to alleviate.

The first stage of the race allowed chariots to accelerate into position. That stage extended from the *carceres* to the white break line (*alba linea*) between the lower, conical turning post (*meta secunda*) and the right-hand wall of the stadium seating (Figure 6).[118] Because the *carceres* were designed on a curve (visible in Figures 2, 3, and 6), this first stage had the effect of a staggered start. The chariots sprinted in straight lines, not allowed to cross each other's path. In the second stage, the course narrowed, and the chariots raced in parallel lanes from the break line to the line before the judges' tribunal. From this point onward, the seven laps of the races were

**Figure 7.** Money box with representation of a victorious charioteer. Late first to early second century A.D. Ceramic. H. 16.6 × 9 cm. Gotha, Stiftung Schloss Friedenstein, inv. no. Ahv.A.K. 97. Image: © Stiftung Schloss Friedenstein Gotha.

counted and the teams crossed lanes. The teams raced counterclockwise and circled the *euripus* seven times (Figure 6) for a distance of approximately 5 km. in about 8-9 minutes total at an average speed of around 35 kph.[119]

Victory in the races depended upon a number of factors. First, a charioteer drove a chariot (*currus circensis*) that was optimized for speed and maneuverability, especially in its lightweight materials and in the design of its wheels, but that was also easy to overturn.[120] Second, a charioteer needed to exert special command over the horses that raced on the inside of the track as they were key for tight cornering (these horses often garner special mention in their honorific and funerary inscriptions; see further below). Third, a charioteer was assisted by his respective factions' auxiliary rider on horseback (*hortator*), who appears to have communicated orders from the stable to the racetrack from a position behind or alongside the charioteer (Figure 5). In this way, a charioteer strategized how to avoid the threats of the hairpin turns or too-close competitors as well as to ensure the victory by a member of his faction, if not himself.[121] Every winning charioteer's victory would have been signaled by a trumpet as he crossed the finish line, which was located two-thirds down the right side of the track and sat parallel to the *pulvinar* (on the left) and the judges' tribunal (see Figures 2 and 6). The victor performed a commemorative lap in celebration, ascended to the judges' box to claim his prize of a palm branch, wreath, and purse[122] (Figure 7), and likely offered a libation in honor of the gods.[123]

Because the charioteers veered as close as possible to the central barrier to shorten their paths, racing accidents occurred most often by the turning posts (*metae*), which they had to tightly round 13 times. Other accidents could have been due to the competitors employing devious tactics to ensure a lead, such as whipping another driver's team (eye injuries from whips are mentioned in the veterinary texts; see below).[124] Whatever their cause, these accidents must have made for memorable, if grisly, public spectacle: Suetonius, for instance, mentions a charioteer for the Green faction who was dragged to his death by his team.[125] The fact that crash scenes appear routinely in visual representations (Figure 5, bottom left) suggests that these so-called 'shipwrecks' (*naufragia*) were not only frequent events but also that they held widespread appeal to their spectators (much as in today's NASCAR races). Given the pace of the race, ground attendants would have had only about a minute to clear away any victims and wreckage from these accidents before the racing teams returned.

If spectacular crashes were a frequent feature and appealing draw of the races, so too were the different ways in which the race might be run or the victory clinched. For instance, if a charioteer held the lead from the beginning to end (*occupavit et vicit*), intentionally fell behind then won (*praemist et vicit*), came from behind to win (*successit et vicit*), or snatched the lead at the end (*eripuit et vicit*), he would be certain to call attention to such distinctions on an inscription, as the Lusitanian-born *agitator* Gaius Appuleius Diocles did in the early second century A.D.[126] The type of race also mattered: there were standard team races with groups of two (*certamina binarum*), three (*certamina ternarum*), or four (*certamina quaternarum*) teams of chariots as well as higher-status races in which a single charioteer represented his faction (*certamina singularum*), a major crowd-pleaser because of its narrow pooling of talent. Similar to the latter in featuring the 'best of the best', the *diversium* was a race that involved the participation of only two teams: the victor of the previous race switched *quadrigae* with his recently-defeated rival, challenging each driver with gaining command over unfamiliar horses and getting them to perform at their peak immediately after competing.[127] Such special events and unforeseen finishes clearly held greater value for the crowd as well, whose interest in the race would have been held in breathless suspension until the final seconds. Such come-from-behind victories are a staple of the literary accounts, from the commoner who fainted in the stands when the horse he bet on unexpectedly won[128] to the blow-by-blow account of the charioteer Consentius's race, complete with surprise finish.[129]

## 3. The Symbolic Representations of Victories and the Athletic Victors: Roman Charioteers[130]

Because most charioteers were of lower social status (slaves especially), like public performers in imperial Rome generally, they occupied an unusual place within its society, at once famous and infamous. But even though charioteers' low birth and humble profession provoked the elite's contempt of them as servile upstarts and déclassé entertainers, their skill, bravery, and victories earned them widespread acclaim as the people's heroes—such as the legendary Flavius Scorpus (Figure 10 below), 'darling of the noisy circus, the talk of the town, and your short-lived darling, Rome'.[131]

**Figure 8.** Victory tablet of the two-horse charioteer (*bigarius*) Menander. Circa 15 A.D. White marble (iron nails original). H. 10 x W. 20 cm. Rome, American Academy in Rome, inv. no. 9451. Image: American Academy in Rome; reproduced with permission.

### 3.1. The Elite Critique and the Modern Myth of Infamia

Upper-class authors such as Tacitus, Suteonius, and Cassius Dio consistently characterize the reputation of charioteers and their supporters in hostile terms, employing such adjectives as *sordida* ('vulgar'), *flagitiosa* ('disgraceful'), *infima* ('the lowest'), and *vilissimi* ('most vile').[132] While it is sometimes but not always explicitly stated, these authors' outrage is provoked by the fact that most charioteers were slaves or freedmen[133] (like other categories of Roman entertainers, especially gladiators[134]), and that their success in their professions enabled them to attain wealth and to exercise public influence disproportionate to their ingrained social position.[135] Charioteers are consequently criticized for competing publicly for money and for the astronomical sums that they win, as when Martial decries how Flavius Scorpus (Figure 10) could win 15 bags of gold in a single race[136]; for their large entourages, which rivaled even those of the elite[137]; for their lionization as public heroes with life-size portrait images[138], a much-coveted distinction within the Roman civic economy of honors (Figure 9); and for their special access to and allegedly corrupting influence on emperors, some of whom were said to keep their company at the faction houses and reward them with material gifts and even appointments to political office.[139] Some emperors, such as Nero, are said not only to have idolized these charioteers, but to have raced themselves—an ambition that Suetonius labelled a 'disgraceful desire' (*foedum studium*) and diagnosed as symptomatic of his defective character.[140] At the same time, the inherent riskiness of their profession, combined with their slave (or former slave) status and reputation for hooliganism, associated charioteers in legal codes and the popular imagination with the dark arts[141], especially in Christian sources.[142]

While the 'dangerous reputations' of charioteers were distinct from other performers, their social marginalization was not, for they were often lumped together with other public performers in the elite authors' attacks.[143] This was due to 'the fact that spectacles to a fair degree eluded control by the elites [which] helped to inspire those same elites to marginalize entertainers.'[144] By drawing a sharp contrast between their own alleged disinterest in the chariot races and the vulgar masses such spectacles were said to attract, elite authors framed their deep anxieties about the games in *moralistic terms*: as popular culture ('bread and circuses', *panem et circenses*) rather than 'classical' culture ('leisure', *otium*), and by extension their public performers as degraded.[145] (The paradoxical position of charioteers in Roman society and their hypocritical treatment as gods by the people *and* as monsters by the elite are fortunately not lost upon all literary observers, however.[146])

Due to their overwhelmingly negative literary portrayal, their public competition for money (vs. the selfless pursuit of athletic glory), and the lack of any *explicit* statement of their status in the legal sources, charioteers have been widely understood by scholars as tainted by *infamia*: that is, as socially and legally dishonorable.[147] This view has been championed in particular by the ancient historian Gerhard Horsmann, who influentially argued that where Greek athletes competed in sacred competitions (*certamina sacra*) and thus enjoyed an exception to any stigma for their public performance, Roman charioteers were affected by *infamia* on account of their participation in the circus games, which he classified as *ars ludicra* (like actors).[148] However, Horsmann's thesis on the legal infamy of charioteers has now been thoroughly disproven on the basis of a reexamination of several key passages in the *Digest* by two Roman legal historians, Andreas Wacke and Richard Gamauf.[149] These historians separately demonstrate that participation in the races was *virtutis causa* and thus, contrary to Horsmann's view, charioteers were not subject to legal restrictions.[150] This reversal of the longstanding *communis opinio* holds important implications for our understanding of their epigraphic (Figure 8) and visual (Figure 9) self-representation through honorific dedications[151], not to mention their wider perception by the Roman people.

### 3.2. Athletic Abilities and Professional Careers

Although charioteers' honorific and funerary inscriptions vary in length, detail, and preservation, they collectively provide a highly valuable snapshot of their social backgrounds, abilities, and achievements. Standard information includes their names (where preserved), some of which were nicknames or stage names[152] and which can provide information about their social and legal status[153]; their status within their factions (*auriga, agitator, bigarius, quadrigarius*); their movement between the four factions; the number and categories of their races (for instance, *a pompa* or '[direct] from the procession', the most prestigious race since it directly followed the opening procession and after which the horses were most nervous); the number and, in many cases, manner of the victories (discussed above); the value of their prizes (in sesterces); and the names, origins, and numbers of horses with which they competed (that is, with a *biga* or *quadriga*, of which the latter was standard; see further below); and other details (such as the consular names affiliated with the games). For instance, the victory tablet for Menander (Figure 8),[154] which dates to the reign of Tiberius and thus is one of the earliest inscriptions of its kind, documents that he was a slave (he still belonged

**Figure 9.** Portrait herm of an unknown charioteer. Trajanic (?). Lunesian marble (bust); *bardiglio* marble (herm). H: 41 cm. (bust); 1.36 m. (herm). Discovered in Rome, Trastevere (Porta Portese). Rome, Museo Nazionale Romano-Palazzo Massimo, inv. no. 317. Image: author; reproduced with the permission of the Ministero per i beni e le attività culturali e per il Turismo – Museo Nazionale Romano.

to his two masters), records his modest victories at Rome (together with the names of his race horses), and specifies that he was a *bigarius* (possibly for the Greens).[155]

The term *bigarius* is of particular interest here because it points to the way in which charioteers were ranked according to experience.[156] The two words most often used in Latin to describe a charioteer—*auriga* and *agitator*—are not synonymous. An *auriga* was a less experienced and thus lower-ranking figure who drove a two-horse chariot (a *bigarius*). An *agitator* was a well-tested and higher-ranking driver who commanded a four-horse chariot (a *quadrigarius*) and might also have responsibility for managing his faction (as a *dominus et agitator factionis*), especially in the later empire.[157] A charioteer's categorization as a *bigarius* or *quadrigarius* was not age-contingent, however. One might graduate to being a *quadrigarius* at an early age, or a driver might still be classified a *bigarius* at a relatively older age: Eutyches *died* at age 22 while still an 'untested junior charioteer' (*rudis auriga*), having just graduated from racing as a *bigarius* but not yet realized his transition to a full charioteer (*quadrigarius* or *agitator*), while M. Nutius Aquilius *began* his racing career at age 23, dying 12 years later.[158]

Despite its brevity, the recently published funerary inscription of the *auriga* Sex. Vistilius Helenus provides a surprising wealth of information about a driver-in-the-making whose promising career was tragically cut short, even sooner than Eutyches'.[159] The nine-line text states that prior to his death at the age of 13, Helenus

**Figure 10.** Grave altar of T. Flavius Abascantus. Flavian (circa 95 or 98 A.D.). Marble. H. 78.5 x W. 37.5 cm. Urbino, Palazzo Ducale (Museo Lapidario), inv. no. 41117. Image: author; reproduced with the permission of the Soprintendenza per i Beni Archeologici delle Marche.

had recently been transferred from the Green faction, where he was under the tutelage of a coach named Orpheus, to the Blues, where he was coached by Datileus. Helenus is referred to as an *auriga* under the care of an apprentice (*doctor*). The Blues likely had managers or talent scouts who spotted the promise of this *florens puer* ('budding lad') and poached him from the rival faction. This inscription confirms that athletes moved between factions like free agents (even though some were still slaves and bought) and that the competition for rising stars such as himself must have been great. In addition, it supports the belief that many charioteers started their training at a very young age: Helenus had to have been racing for several years already before his transfer. Similarly, the charioteer Crescens' won his first race with a *quadriga* at age 13 and thus his professional racing career must have begun around age 10, making him 'the youngest known charioteer' to have raced in the Circus Maximus, and indeed anywhere in the Roman Empire.[160] Thus, 'there seems to be nothing to prevent boys in Rome from competing with adults, if they were experienced and skilled enough'.[161]

The premature deaths of Crescens and Helenus, among others, is also a reminder of the riskiness of their profession. In similarity to Etruscan practice (but in contrast to Greek), Roman charioteers tied the heavy reins around their waists.[162] This technique increased not only their maneuverability but also the risk of dragging, injury, and death in the event of a crash (they were equipped with a knife to cut themselves free).[163] They wore special clothing as protection in the event of crashes: padded helmets[164] and thick tunics with horizontal leather bands around their chests and trunk (*fasciae pectoralis*) and leggings (*fasciae crurales*) (see Figures 5, 7, 8, 10).[165] While racing accidents are almost never explicitly stated in their funerary inscriptions as the cause of death,[166] the dangers of the racetrack are nonetheless clearly indicated by their frequently young ages at death (most in their 20 s),[167] by medical remedies prescribed for race-related injuries,[168] and by gruesome literary similes: 'as an ill-trained charioteer is thrown from his chariot, ground, lacerated and dashed to pieces'.[169]

And yet even if often premature and grisly, a death while racing in the circus was still seen by some (perhaps even most) charioteers as an ideal, glory-tinged ending. The funerary inscription for Eutyches, the 22 year-old *rudis auriga* who died in Tarragona in 104 A.D., explicitly voices the charioteer's regret at perishing from an intestinal illness that deprived him of 'the glory (*gloria*) of dying in the circus, lest the faithful crowd honored me with tears.'[170] Given our knowledge of the massive complex at Tarragona (discussed above) and the descriptions of the 'seething roar of the crowd' at Rome, modern readers can well imagine the kind of impassioned spectators—and thus *gloria*—that Eutyches (and the commissioners of his tomb) had in mind.[171] For as the funerary inscription for Fuscus (see the start of this essay) bears direct witness, a good death for a charioteer was one secure in the knowledge that '[t]he ages will talk of your conquests.'

The good fortune (and not just skill) that charioteers appeared to possess in navigating their chariots at breakneck speed, especially around the treacherous turns of the *metae*, contributed to their 'dangerous reputations' as both sorcerers and good-luck bringers.[172] Romans sought to harness charioteers' seeming good fortune, invincibility, and wealth by wearing their images on their person with finger rings or amulets, some of which were embedded with a gem the same color as their prized faction[173] and/or inscribed with commands that echoed the emphatic chants of the crowd, such as AVE ('hail') or NICA ('win'; for instance, NICA PRASINE or 'Win Green Faction!').[174] Others commissioned curse tablets (*defixiones*) against them, which were inscribed by magicians with texts, sometimes accompanied by visceral images, that summoned demons to maim or kill competitors and/or their horses (most surviving examples come from North Africa).[175] Many of these curses were likely commissioned by hardened partisans of other factions, especially those with a financial investment in seeing competitors fail.[176] These were activated through burial at the starting gates or on the race track, which were seen as liminal junctions to the netherworld because of the dangerous technical challenges they presented to the teams.

For charioteers who survived the racetrack's dangers and kept winning races until retirement, like Fuscus at Tarragona, they might continue to leverage their skills by taking up a position within their own or another faction as a trainer (*doctor*)[177] or even as head of the faction (*dominus factionis*). For a still more select few, their profession could bring fame and wealth on a scale unthinkable to most Romans—making their likenesses highly appropriate as decoration on household objects such as moneyboxes[178] (Figure 6). Juvenal reports that Lacerta of the Red team made 100 times what lawyers bequeath their sons, while elsewhere he jests that, in a twelve-month period, a teacher would make 'the same amount that a chariot driver earns in one race.'[179] While Juvenal is undoubtedly prone to exaggeration, the career of Gaius Appuleius Diocles, the self-styled 'most outstanding of all drivers' (*omnium agitatorum eminentissimus*), provides a concrete example of this kind of wealth. A lengthy honorific inscription set up for him, the longest document of its kind, states that he raced for all four factions over the course of his 24-year career (though it is the Red faction, with whom he raced the longest and last, that appears prominently in its first line).[180] This inscription states that he competed in 4,257 races (an average of 170 per year), placed 2,900 times, and won a total of 1,462.[181] Of these wins, 1,064 were in single races (*certamina singularum*), 347 for teams of two chariots from each faction (*certamina binarum*), and 51 for teams of three chariots (*certamina ternarum*). These victories were clinched with teams of two, three, four, and even six or seven-horse teams; for *quadrigae* races the standard first prize (*pura*) seems to have been 20,000 sesterces, while (presumably rarer) wins with teams of six horses were worth 30,000-40,000 and seven horses were worth 50,000. Upon his retirement at the age of 42, Diocles had accumulated more than 35 million sesterces in winnings, making him richer than even most senators (a standard legionary earned c. 1,400 sesterces *per year*). By contemporary standards, he was the Tiger Woods of his day, maybe even 'the best paid athlete of all time.'[182]

Diocles' victories place him in an exclusive class of charioteers or *miliarii* (winners of a thousand victories or more) which also included P. Aelius Gutta Calpurnianus[183], Flavius Scorpus (Figure 10), and Pompeius Musclosus.[184] In these inscriptions the charioteers categorized their races according to their priority and uniqueness, such as the ways in which a race was won (i.e. leading from the outset, snatched victory at the end, came from behind). Not surprisingly, they are keen to call attention to 'firsts'[185] that they achieved or to their performance in special events that had greater prestige than the standard chariot races, whether held at Rome (such as the Capitoline Games, a Roman version of the Olympic games)[186], regionally, or internationally. The exhaustive, meticulous catalogues of these races and self-conscious references to rivals' records in these texts reflect a sense of professional pride that finds parallels in the funerary monuments of gladiators.[187] Not unlike baseball players today, their personas and status were defined through their performance records. The public documentation and display of these career statistics not only ensured their social memory but also perpetuated the fame and luster of their factions.

These seemingly dry facts and figures in turn seeped into the Roman popular consciousness through conversations about charioteers' technical abilities and tactical choices[188]. Lucian, for instance, writes of 'the uproar of the city, the crowding, the theatres, the races, the statues of the drivers, the names of the horses, and the conversations in the streets about these matters.'[189] The vocabulary of the circus and its stars insinuated itself across literary genres, from epic and bucolic poetry[190] to medical texts.[191] True to Martial's words, the careers of charioteers like Scorpus were 'the talk of the town': dissected by the riffraff on street corners,[192] replayed by children in classrooms,[193] scratched into the surfaces of their buildings,[194] and toasted by guests at dinner tables,[195] who invoked their names on glass cups[196] and translated their triumphs into metaphors of sexual conquest.[197]

Indeed, given the seemingly endless menu of visual[198] and material culture[199] that the races and their heroes inspired, '[i]t is difficult to think of anything more mass-consumed than Roman circus games'.[200] Lowborn charioteers and bloody racing accidents were tastefully commodified for every imaginable income, style, and setting—from ceramic souvenirs (Figure 7) and household bronzes to sprawling dining mosaics. Even the architectural form of the circus was transplanted to countryside villas where it was reimagined as a stadium-shaped garden (*hippodromus*) for the élite, the very social class whose members so vociferously protested their disinterest in the games.[201]

The 'passion for the circus' (*furor circensis*) thus extended far beyond the arena's walls, penetrating deep into the lifeways of *all* Romans, regardless of age, gender, or social status, and even following them into death.[202] Hundreds, if not thousands, of Romans across the empire who have no known connection to the world of the circus commissioned funerary monuments with charioteer-themed imagery or were buried with circus-related artefacts in their tombs. The costumes of at least one faction spawned imitation clothing for children, whose parents outfitted them with 'little green jackets',[203] and who buried them in tombs with circus-themed wall paintings and sarcophagi.[204] Adults partook in the custom as well, as witnessed most quixotically by the grave altar of Titus Flavius Abascantus (Figure 10), which commemorates an imperial freedman who worked as clerk of the courts in the late first century A.D.[205] While the depiction of the deceased in a 'funerary banquet' scene at the top makes it largely indistinguishable from hundreds of similar representations from around the Roman world, the relief panel that decorates the altar's base is without parallel: a charioteer racing his *quadriga* with an inscription overhead that identifies the figures as the legendary (Flavius) Scorpus and his four horses Ingenuus, Admetus, Passerinus, and Atmetus.[206] Abacscantus's (or his wife's) motivation for selecting this imagery for his grave goes unexplained.[207] However, since Romans invoked charioteers in a wide range of visual media—presumably on account of their popularity, winning records, and/or reputed magical powers—the tomb's commissioner may have sought to capitalize on the fame and success of Scorpus for similar reasons here: as a talisman to protect him and as a vehicle to perpetuate his memory, the 'darling of the noisy circus' seducing viewers to his tomb in perpetuity.[208]

The extreme example of a fan appealing to his favorite charioteer for salvation and immortality in this way is provided by Pliny the Elder's anecdote about the funeral for the charioteer Felix from the Red faction. According to his account, a fan leapt onto the deceased athlete's funeral bier and immolated himself together with his favorite.[209] In this way, 'by at last 'realizing' the many earlier potential deaths shared vicariously with his idol, the dead man had brought what the games represented directly into life.'[210] Such ephemeral incidents—especially when seen together with graffiti, curse tablets, and funerary monuments—attest not only to the financial but also the *psychological investment* that many Romans placed in these heroes. In this sense, they reflect how central *victory* was to the Roman culture of spectacle—not just to the game givers and factions who organized the races or to the athletes and horses who competed in them, but also to the spectators for whom they were a socially binding religion, 'the height of all their hopes'.

**Figure 11.** Grave altar of L. Avillius Dionysius. Late first to early second century A.D. Pentelic marble. H. 66.5 x W. 41.5 x D. 34.5 cm. H. portrait 20 cm. Rome, Musei Capitolini, Palazzo Nuovo, Galleria Lapidaria AH XXVI, inv. no. 1826. Image: FAP Köln Neg. no. MAL 146-04; © Roma, Sovrintendenza Capitolina ai Beni Culturali.

## 4. Equine Performance: Race Horses[211]

Like the charioteers with whom they competed, race horses became popular idols and their breeding, training, medical treatment, names, and alleged magical properties are well-documented by diverse sources, including literary texts, inscriptions (Figures 9, 10, 11), and visual representations (Figures 5, 10, 11).[212]

Modern estimates suggest that a single day of games required on the order of 700–800 horses[213] and this demand, combined with need to supply horses to the Roman cavalry, contributed toward the rise of an extensive animal trade across the Mediterranean.[214] Both wealthy private and imperial stud farms raised and trained stock for the track in Spain, Sicily, Thessaly, North Africa, and Cappadocia, and their brand marks were clearly visible on horses' flanks, including the names and perhaps also icons of the stable (as seen on mosaics[215] and various inscribed objects[216]). However, horses bred on an estate did not necessarily originate from that region's stock.[217] Roman authors appear to document a preference for African (Libyan) bloodlines in the early empire and Spanish and Cappadocian[218] as well as Sicilian[219] in the late empire. The preference in the early empire for African horses, which are widely singled out for their speed and endurance, is further suggested by the inscriptions of the charioteers who raced with them: in the mid-second century Diocles explicitly states that he was the best driver of African horses while one of his contemporaries, Avilius Teres, raced with the Africans Callidromus and Hilarus to 100 and 1,000 wins, respectively.[220]

Race horses were also selected according to age, sex and physique, disposition, stamina and dexterity. The majority were stallions, though the names of a few mares do exist.[221] Skeletal evidence suggests that the average horse was of stocky build and stood approximately 135–55 cm high.[222] While this makes them comparable to a large pony in modern terms (147 cm. being the dividing line between a pony and horse today), they would have been considered large animals during this period. Pliny notes that 'a different build is required for the Circus, and consequently though horses may be broken as two-year-olds to other service, racing in the Circus does not claim them before five.'[223] These horses underwent thorough programs of exercise and training, since 'racers and chargers are both a job to breed: for either it is youth, mettle and pace that trainers first demand.'[224] This training took place first on the stud farms and later at facilities near the tracks themselves (for instance, the *Trigarium* in the Campus Martius in Rome). The best horses might race until 20 years old.[225]

Depending on its suitability, a horse bred for racing would assume one of two positions within a chariot team: either harnessed on the inside (*iugales*) or attached to the center pair by rein, not yoked (*funales*). The experienced lead horse on the inside left side (*introiugus*) of the chariot was the most important in the team, since it guided them around the sharp, treacherous turns of the *metae*. Because of their pivotal role in the races, the names of the *introiugi* survive not only on inscriptions for charioteers[226] and other faction personnel (such as Figure 11), but also surface in the wider material culture of the empire—from their praise in graffiti and the poet Martial's *Epigrams*, to their commemoration on mosaic pavements and funerary monuments[227], to their condemnation in curse tablets.[228] In addition to the stress of the turns, horses' stamina was tested by the length of the course (which at around 5 km. was considerably longer than those of the most significant modern flat races, such as the Kentucky Derby at 2 km.) and by repeated races on the same day.

Race horses thus endured remarkable trauma and stress over their careers and literary sources provide insights into their ailments and care. The most important of these that survives is Pelagonius' *The Veterinary Art*, commentaries written in the fourth century that were probably intended for wealthy Roman horse-owners or breeders.[229] Some of the topics that he discusses include leg injuries, such as concussions sustained from the constant pounding on the hardpacked track or calcified growths caused by blows from axles or wheels to the hooves; joint and tendon stress in the legs and back and shoulder injuries resulting from sudden, high-speed turns; and also eye injuries such as blows or scarring from whips or inflammation, probably from the sandy racecourse.[230] The analysis of horse bones from contexts associated with circus tracks confirms some of these maladies, such as the osteopathological trauma detectable in equine remains from Sirmium in Pannonia (modern Serbia).[231] Beyond the wealth of technical information that these commentaries provide about medical practice, they exhibit a genuine appreciation and sympathy for their subject that is consistent with the tone and approach of other veterinarian treatises.[232]

The Romans' devotion to horses can also be seen in their appellatives, which evoke them as living personalities.[233] Nearly 600 horses' names survive from disparate sources, including literary texts, inscriptions for charioteers, and a wide variety of inscribed objects and monuments (for instance, knife-handles, curse tablets, mosaics). These names can be organized into six categories, ranked in decreasing order of frequency: (1) skill, with sub-categories of speed (*Celer*, swift), strength (*Adamus*, cast-iron), agility (*Passerinus*, sparrow); (2) appearance, with an emphasis on color (*Aureus*, golden) or markings (*Maculosus*, speckled), beauty (*Elegans*), size (*Adauctus*, bulky), movement or other physical traits (such as their manes); (3) origin, including divine descent (*Pegasus*), owners' names, sire, ethnic extraction (*Aegyptus*); (4) expectations, such as victory (*Victor*) or good fortune (*Felix*); (5) behavior, ranging from docility (*Volens*, willing) to impetuousness (*Temerarius*, hothead); and (6) expressions of affection (for example, *Adamatus*, much-beloved). Some names overlap categories: *Pyrobolus* (flamethrower), for example, could refer to the horse's manner or its speed, as fire is at once ravaging and fast.

Unlike the harsh treatment that some animals endured in other spectacles, many horses became beloved celebrities in their own right, immortalized in artistic representations[234] and literature. The poet Martial noted dryly that, 'Martial is known to the nations and to the people. Why do you envy me? I'm no more famous than Andraemo the horse.'[235] The legendary Apulian stallion Hirpinus (Figure 11) stood celebrated—some 20 years apart—by both Martial and Juvenal.[236] Such *hippomania* could be found at all levels of Roman society, from commoners to its political pinnacle: the emperors Caligula and Lucius Verus allegedly spoiled their favorite race horses, Incitatus and Volucer, with lavish stables, blankets, and foodstuffs.[237] While some high-minded Romans claimed disinterest in the races, Lucian noted that many had succumbed: 'the craze for horses is really great, you know, and men with a name for earnestness have caught it in great numbers.'[238] For the urban mob (*plebs urbana*), horse-racing was said to be an all-consuming passion in which racegoers reveled in their mastery of its trivia: 'the favorite among all amusements, from sunrise until evening, in sunshine and in rain, they stand open-mouthed, examining minutely the good points or the defects of charioteers and their horses.'[239] Ovid even counseled his male readers to pick up attractive female spectators at the races, since the circus held out the promise of a chance romantic encounter that sexually segregated seating at the amphitheater prevented: 'nor let the contest of noble steeds escape you; the spacious Circus holds many opportunities.'[240]

Fans were knowledgeable of horses' bloodlines, ethnic provenance and much else, but all that seemingly mattered in the end was their thirst for victory:

> The horse we most admire is the one that romps home a winner, cheered on by the seething roar of the crowd. Good breeding doesn't depend upon a fancy pasturage; the thoroughbred earns his title by getting ahead of the field, by making them eat his dust. But lack of victories means that the auction-ring will claim him, even the one from the flock of Coryphaeus and the posterity of Hirpinus.[241]

Superstition hung heavily over the races, and spectators went to extremes to secure victory for their chosen horses. The physician Galen relates how some enthusiasts smelled the dung of their favorite horses to evaluate their health and forecast the outcome of their races.[242] Some horses were decked out with ornaments thought to aid their performance: 'wolf teeth hung around a horse's neck make it race faster.'[243] Other items, such as crescent-shaped amulets (*lunulae*) and bronze bells (inscribed with the names of the driver and the lead horse), were used as amulets against the threat of envy and the Evil Eye.[244] Such *bullae* and other neckwear were therefore not merely decorative,[245] but were employed as talismans against witchcraft attacks, since some spectators attempted to influence the outcome of the races by casting spells on drivers or, in some cases, exclusively on their 'ill-omened horses.'[246]

Some race horses met a kinder fate than the 'auction-ring' or accidents on the racetrack and were put out to pasture. Their lives and deaths might even be commemorated through tombstones, especially those which were famous. For instance, Lucius Avillius Dionysius, a *conditor* (a groom) for the Red faction in Rome in the late first or early second century A.D., was remembered by his wife with a grave altar that includes his image (a staff in his right hand and fodder for the horses in his left hand), and inscribed name (Figure 11).[247] But just as prominently featured on either side of him are the images of two legendary race horses, Aquilo and Hirpinus, together with lists of their names, bloodlines, and winning records: (left) 'Aquilo N(iger) K(anus), son of Aquilo, won 130 times, came second 88 times, and third 37 times' and (right) 'Hirpinus Niger, son of Aquilo, won 114 times, came second 56 times, and third 36 times.'[248] Like the grave altar of Abascantus, these images and victory lists demonstrate how the calculus of Dionysius' monument depended as much, if not more, on the fame of the race horses that he managed than the humble accomplishments of the deceased man himself.

Other funerary monuments are dedicated to race horses themselves and can include affecting epitaphs, such as a relief from Brescia: '[Such a horse neither ...] and Coporus would have produced, nor the Tuscan valleys nor the Sicilian pastures. You who were accustomed to outrunning the roaming birds and defeating the blasts of the North-Easterlies now have your stable in this tomb.'[249] The desire to humanize race horses in this way—commemorating at once their personal qualities and agonistic achievements through words and stone—is a reminder that Romans' engagement with animals could be more complex, even humane, than is often appreciated.[250] Race horses impacted human lives in diverse ways, and thus—together with other animals—are as central to the history of human culture as humans are. They accordingly deserve a distinct place of their own in the history of Rome's oldest and most venerable form of athletic competition.[251]

## 5. Reflections on Horse Racing in Imperial Rome and Future Directions for Research[252]

This essay has sought to provide an up-to-date survey of our understanding of chariot races in imperial Rome, encompassing the venues, factions, athletes, horses, and their spectators. As discussed above, that understanding has long been distorted by the Roman elite's moral opposition to the races and their hostile view of charioteers. Such views have proven difficult to retire even in modern scholarship, especially where Roman practices are compared to Greek. As Mark Golden has argued in a related context, 'the popularity of gladiatorial spectacles in the Greek east calls into question our standard stereotypes of the Greeks and Romans—cultured and crude—and *the gladiators' ambitions to be seen as athletes invite us to examine our very definition of sport*.'[253]

The ancient historian Sophie Remijsen, for instance, has recently argued that charioteers, together with 'gladiators, and the like', should be categorized as 'performers' and 'entertainers' in contrast to athletes competing in the Greek *agones*.[254] To be sure, there were often pronounced differences between the social and legal status of these athletes and charioteers, who were mostly slaves or freedmen. Furthermore, some (if not most) of the latter would have sought to cultivate the favor of the crowd, from flamboyant displays of their technical mastery during competitions to cultivating their own cults of personality through 'stage names', urban entourages, and more. But as discussed above, the long-standing categorization of charioteers as *infames* has been shown to hinge on a modern misunderstanding and demands our reconsideration of charioteers' social position, athletic performance, and public perception.

In point of fact, charioteers possessed hard-won skills as athletes, and the many different kinds of races in which they participated tested their mettle, *even if* these events had a crowd-pleasing element. Furthermore, since most charioteers were slaves, they would have relied on demonstrations of their athletic prowess in order to win races and ultimately gain their freedom, making the stakes of the competition far greater than for freeborn athletes. Finally, those who competed in the races risked serious injury or death (especially at a young age, like Helenus or Scorpus)—much less of a hazard in most forms of athletic competition. In sum, it is only by turning to charioteers' own texts (and images) that we can reconstruct their lived reality as historical actors as well as their self-understanding as 'athletes'—and *not* as mere 'performers'.

Remijsen has also contended that in contrast to the Greek games, the 'Roman games belonged to a spectacle culture. The main goal was not winning, but entertaining the public'.[255] To be sure, a chief attraction of attending the games must have been their edge-of-your-seat, high-speed spectacle: the opportunity to witness a favorite faction, charioteer, or horse prevail while risking life and limb and, at the same time, to watch rivals suffer spectacular crashes in defeat. Nor can we discount the power and appeal of the other kinds of events staged there, from the wild animal displays that transformed spectators into vicarious tourists of Rome's far-flung empire to the religious processions that encouraged the communal reenactment of the city's numinous origins in the deep past. However, to dismiss the games as merely 'entertaining the public' is to uncritically reproduce the Roman literary elite's moralizing rhetoric that they were the regressive, infantile pleasure of the restless masses who preferred 'bread and circuses' over their own burnished 'classical' culture.[256]

And yet ironically some of these elite critiques hit on a central truth: that from the perspective of the *invested* spectator, *everything* was at stake in the race arena. Not unlike certain NASCAR fans today, for whom the races are 'a religious experience and [an event that] represents a lifestyle around which their lives revolve'[257], so for some Romans 'their temple, their dwelling, their assembly, and the height of all their hopes is the Circus Maximus.'[258] The fact that the real target of many of these authors' attacks (such as Lucian's) is the 'men with a name for earnestness', who appear to forget their proper social station in attending the races alongside the frenzied masses, points to a larger reality: that this allegedly 'childish passion'[259] attracted young and old, male and female, slave and free, native and foreign, and poor and elite alike. In other words, '[t]he Roman circus was a monumental miniature of Roman society'[260] and *that society was consumed with the idea and image of victory*: from depositing curse tablets at the arena's starting gates to favor certain teams to everyday conversations in the streets and debates at dinner tables about the victories and defeats of favorite horses and charioteers to their depiction on domestic mosaics and tomb monuments.[261] The challenge for the historian of ancient sport then—like that for the historian of popular culture in antiquity—is to view this highly-diverse audience 'beyond the confines of the ancient mob, and instead to *restore a degree of agency to this group*'.[262]

As I have argued throughout, actor/audience-centered readings of the literary and epigraphic sources and visual and material artefacts promise rich, if still largely untapped, resources for recuperating Romans' individual experiences of the chariot races and, with them, aspects of this now-obscured group agency. Recent work on the sensory experience of Roman life,[263] including the olfactory landscape ('smell-scape') of the spectacles[264] as well as crowd's experience of the games more broadly[265], has also done much to map out strategies and sources for recovering non-elite perspectives and experiences. In a similar vein, some new research on monumental buildings is shifting focus from their taxonomic study as structures to their as role as 'modes of collective existence'[266], such as the bodily sensation of their very materiality.[267] For as Thomas Markus has written, '[b]uildings are treated as art, technical or investment objects. Rarely as social objects.'[268] Sylvain Forichon's research promises the most significant intervention in this direction.[269]

In conclusion: ancient Roman culture was a performance culture and the Circus Maximus was its grandest stage. But the chariot races that filled that stage in imperial Rome, like the equine competitions in other cultures discussed in this collection, were much more than mere ceremonial events or spectacular diversions for 'entertaining the public.' They were events that could play a highly significant role in the way that Romans *at all levels of society* structured their private experiences, both inside and outside the arena. The races brought fame and glory to Rome's political leaders, from urban magistrates to emperors, through which they sedimented their authority and reproduced state power; they granted lowborn charioteers the winnings to transform themselves from slaves into citizens or, by a sudden false turn, immortalized them with 'the glory of dying in the circus' before adoring audiences; they transported horses from 'the Sicilian pastures', North Africa, and Cappadocia to the capital, where their fame rivaled court poets and apostles; and they lured hundreds of thousands of spectators to arenas with the promise of exhilarating moments of personal revelation—of winning a bet on a horse, of finding romance in the stands, of seeing a curse fulfilled, of finding salvation in a hero or losing all hope witnessing his death. Romans came to the circus not only to live in the hyper-charged present, to see and to be seen within the collective hive, but also to imagine an escape from their own mundane lives—perhaps even to alter their very fates. The potential for such moments of individual revelation, set against the backdrop of the 'seething roar of the crowd', undoubtedly explains why—hundreds of years after he wrote them—Juvenal's words still rang true: 'all Rome today is in the Circus.'[270]

## Notes

1. Ammianus Marcellinus, 28.4.29; transl. John C. Rolfe.
2. Juvenal, *Satires* 8.57; transl. Peter Green.
3. *CIL* 2.4315 = *ILS* 5301. D(IS) M(ANIBVS). / FACTIONIS VENETAE FVSCO SACRA / VIMUS ARAM DE NOSTRO, CERTI STV / DIOSI ET BENE AMANTES; VT SCI / RENT CVNCTI MONIMENTVM / ET PIGNVS AMORIS. INTEG[RA] / FAMA TIBI, LAVDEM CVR / SVS MERVISTI; CERTASTI / MVLTIS, NVLLVM PAVPER TI[MV] / ISTI; I[NVIDIAM PASSVS SEM] / [PER FORTIS TACVISTI]; PVL / CHRE VIXISTI, FATO MORTA / LIS OBISTI. QVISQVIS HOMO / ES, QVAERES TALEM. SVBSISTE / VIATOR, PERLEGE, SI MEMOR / ES. SI NOSTI, QVIS FVERIT VIR, / FORTVNAM METVANT OMNES / DICES TAMEN VNVM: 'FVS / CVS HABET TITVLOS MOR / TIS, HABET TVMVLVM. CON / TEGIT OSSA LAPIS, BENE HABET / FORTVNA, VALEBIS. FVDIMVS / INSONTI LACRIMAS, NVNC VI / NA. PRECAMVR, VT IACEAS PLA / CIDE. NEMO TVI SIMILIS.' / ΤΟΥΣ ΣΟΥΣ ΑΓΩΝΑΣ ΑΙΩΝ ΛΑΛΗΣΕΙ. Transl. Edward Courtney, Musa Lapidaria: *A Selection of Late Verse Inscriptions*, American Classical Studies 36 (Atlanta: Scholars Press, 1995), 321–22, no. 112.
4. See further the essay by Mann and Scharff in this collection. For comparisons between Greek and Roman sport, see Donald G. Kyle, 'Ancient Greek and Roman Sport', in *The Oxford Handbook of Sports History*, ed. Robert Edelman and Wayne Wilson (Oxford: Oxford University Press, 2017), 79–99; Paul Christesen, 'Theories of Greek and Roman Sport', in *The Oxford Handbook of Sport and Spectacle in the Ancient World*, ed. Alison Futrell and Thomas Scanlon (Oxford: Oxford University Press, 2020/forthcoming); and contributions in Paul Christesen and Charles Stocking, ed., *A Cultural History of Sport in Greco-Roman Antiquity (c. 800 BCE–600 CE)* (London: Bloomsbury, forthcoming).
5. There has been an explosion of interest in the Roman circus of late; I make no claims to comprehensiveness here. Rather, I seek to offer here a snapshot of scholarship over the last decade or so since around 2008, when Jocelyne Nelis-Clément and Jean-Michel Roddaz published their volume on the circus. At the same time, I draw upon, update, and synthesize some of my own earlier research on this topic, especially 'Roman Chariot-Racing: Charioteers, Factions, Spectators', in *Wiley-Blackwell Companion to Sport and Spectacle in Greek and Roman Antiquity*, ed. Paul Christesen and Donald Kyle (Malden, MA: Wiley-Blackwell, 2014), 492–504, and 'Horse Racing and Chariot Racing', in *The Oxford Handbook of Animals in Classical Thought and Life*, ed. Gordon Lindsay Campbell (Oxford: Oxford University Press, 2014), 478–90. In addition, I keep references to ancient sources to a minimum since most are already well-known to readers and are thoroughly cited in the scholarly literature below.
6. On Roman sport and spectacles generally, there are now many different resources which include material relevant to about the Roman circus, including: (1) traditional sourcebooks, such as Allison Futrell, *The Roman Games. A Sourcebook* (Malden, MA: Blackwell, 2006); (2) thematic surveys, including Hazel Dodge, *Spectacle in the Roman World* (London: Bristol Classical Press, 2011); David Potter, *The Victor's Crown: A History of Ancient Sport from Homer to Byzantium* (Oxford: Oxford University Press, 2011); and Donald Kyle, *Sport and Spectacle in the Ancient World*. 2nd ed. (Malden, MA: John Wiley & Sons, 2015); (3) readers/companions/handbooks, such as Christesen and Kyle, *A Companion to Sport*; Thomas F. Scanlon, ed., *Sport in the Greek and Roman Worlds. Volume 1: Early Greece, the Olympics, and Contests; Volume 2: Greek Athletic Identities and Roman Sports and Spectacle*, Oxford Readings in Classical Studies (Oxford: Oxford University Press, 2014); and Scanlon and Futrell, *The Oxford Handbook of Sport*; and (4)

conference volumes, *Giochi e spettacoli nel mondo antico. Problematiche e nuove scoperte. Atti del Convegno internazionale, 24 Marzo 2018*, ed. Paolo Storchi and Gianluca Mete (Rome: Scienze e Lettere, 2019).
7. See Sylvain Forichon, '*Furor circensis*: étude des émotions et des expressions corporelles des spectateurs lors d'une course de chars', *Nikephoros* 25 (2012): 159–203, and now Idem, *Les spectateurs des jeux du cirque à Rome (du I$^{er}$ siècle a.C. au VI$^{e}$ siècle p.C.): passion, émotions et manifestations*, Ausonius Éditions Scripta Antiqua 133 (Bordeaux: Ausonius, 2020).
8. Christesen and Kyle, 'General Introduction', in Christesen and Kyle, *A Companion to Sport*, 1–15, at 1. In a similar vein, Sinclair Bell, 'Introduction', in *Sport and Social Identity in Classical Antiquity: Papers in Honor of Mark Golden, Bulletin of the Institute of Classical Studies* 61-1, ed. Sinclair Bell and Pauline Ripat (Oxford; Malden, MA: Wiley, 2018), 1–4.
9. For an overview of this methodology beyond classical antiquity, see Dave Day and Wray Vamplew, 'Sports History Methodology: Old and New', *The International Journal of the History of Sport* 32, no. 15 (2015): 1715–24.
10. This section updates, corrects, and expands on my discussion of the circus structures in Bell, 'Roman Chariot Racing' and 'Horse Racing and Chariot Racing.'
11. John H. Humphrey, *Roman Circuses: Arenas for Chariot-Racing* (Berkeley: University of California Press, 1986), remains the core text for the study of Roman circuses. The most important research on the circus and chariot racing to appear in (approximately) the last decade includes: Jocelyne Nelis-Clément and Jean-Michel Roddaz, ed., *Le cirque romain et son image: Actes du colloque tenu à l'Institut Ausonius, Bordeaux, 2006*, Mémoires 20 (Bordeaux: Ausonius Éditions, 2008); Francesco Marcattili, *Circo Massimo: architetture, funzioni, culti, ideologia* (Rome: "L'Erma" di Bretschneider, 2009); Pierre Cattelain, *Des jeux du stade aux jeux du cirque: Exposition créée au Musée du Malgré-Tout de Treignes (Belgique) du 28 mars au 14 novembre 2010* (Treignes: Éditions du CEDARC, 2010); Jacob A. Latham, *Performance, Memory, and Processions in Ancient Rome: The* Pompa Circensis *from the Late Republic to Late Antiquity* (New York: Cambridge University Press, 2016); Jean-Paul Thuillier, *Allez les rouges! Les jeux du cirque en Étrurie et à Rome*, Études de littérature ancienne, 26 (Paris: Éditions Rue d'Ulm, 2018). Note also three forthcoming works: Forichon, *Les spectateurs des jeux du cirque à Rome*; Frederik Grosser, *Darstellungen von Wagenlenkern in der römischen Kaiserzeit und frühen Spätantike*; and Sinclair W. Bell, *Chariot Racing in Roman Imperial Art and Culture: Athletic Competition, Social Practice, and Urban Spectacle*.

Three reviews of Nelis-Clément and Roddaz's *Le cirque romain* also function as states-of-the-field: Pierre Aupert, '"De Circensibus": notes de lecture', *Revue des études anciennes* 111, no. 1 (2009): 257–70; Joseph Patrich, 'A Major Conference on the Roman Circus', *Journal of Roman Archaeology* 24, no. 2 (2011): 627–34; and Jean-Paul Thuillier, 'Vingt ans au cirque. Des "Roman circuses" au "Cirque romain"', in *Theatra et spectacula. Les grands monuments des jeux dans l'Antiquité*, Études de lettres 288 (Lausanne: Université de Lausanne, 2011), 325–40.

In addition to these works and various specialized studies cited below, a significant number of works written by scholars for general audiences has also appeared during this time: Adriano La Regina, ed., *Circhi e Ippodromi: Le corse dei cavalli nel mondo antico* (Rome: Cosmopoli, 2007); Wolfram Letzner, *Der Römische Circus: Massenunterhaltung im römischen Reich* (Mainz: Philipp von Zabern, 2009); Fijk Meijer, *Chariot Racing in the Roman Empire: Spectacles in Rome and Constantinople*, transl. Liz Waters (Baltimore, MD: Johns Hopkins University Press, 2010); and Karl-Wilhelm Weeber, *Circus Maximus: Wagenrennen im antiken Rom* (Darmstadt: Primus, 2010). There is also the recent documentary 'Rome's Chariot Superstar' (https://www.smithsonianchannel.com/shows/romes-chariot-superstar/1005773), which is based on the most recent scholarship

12. For the latest archaeological work on the structure of the Circus Maximus, consult the regular reports appearing in the *Bullettino della Commissione Archeologica Communale di Roma* (and publications in the various notes below). In addition, see the recent collections of the different forms of evidence (literary, artistic, epigraphic, and archaeological) in Paola Zanovello, 'Il ruolo storico dei circhi e degli stadi', in *Gli edifici per spettacoli nell'Italia romana*, 2 vols., ed. Giovanna Tosi (Rome: Quasar, 2003) 835-99, esp. 846-64 on the Circus Maximus; Chiara Bariviera, 'Region XI. Circus Maximus', in *The Atlas of Ancient Rome: Biography and Portraits of the City. Vol. 1: Text and Images*, ed. Andrea Carandini and Paolo Carafa, transl. Andrew Campbell Halavais, 2 vols. (Princeton, NJ: Princeton University Press, 2017), 421-45.

13. Antonia Holden, 'The Abduction of the Sabine Women in Context: The Iconography on Late Antique Contorniate Medallions', *American Journal of Archaeology* 112, no. 1 (2008), 121-42, with earlier bibliography.

14. See *inter alia* (with earlier bibliography) Filippo Coarelli, 'Gli edifici per i giochi', in *Storia dell'architettura italiana. Architettura romana i grandi monumenti di Roma*, ed. Henner von Hesberg and Paul Zanker (Milan: Electa, 2009), 224-35; Paul Zanker, 'By the Emperor, for the People: "Popular" Architecture in Rome', in *The Emperor and Rome: Space, Representation, and Ritual*, Yale Classical Studies 35, ed. Björn Ewald and Carlos Noreña (Cambridge: Cambridge University Press, 2010), 45-88; Kathleen M. Coleman, 'Public Entertainments', in *The Oxford Handbook of Social Relations in the Roman World*, ed. Michael Peachin (Oxford: Oxford University Press, 2011), 335-57; Nicholas Purcell, 'Romans, Play on! City of Games,' in *The Cambridge Companion to Ancient Rome*, ed. Paul Erdkamp (Cambridge: Cambridge University Press, 2013), 441-58; Mantha Zarmakoupi, 'Entertainment and Public Buildings', in *A Companion to Roman Republican Archaeology*, ed. Janet DeRose Evans (Oxford: Blackwell, 2013), 33-49; Hazel Dodge, 'Building for an Audience: The Architecture of Roman Spectacle', in *A Companion to Roman Architecture*, ed. Roger B. Ulrich and Caroline K. Quenemoen (Malden, MA: Wiley Blackwell, 2014), 281-98; Mantha Zarmakoupi, 'Spectacle Buildings: Theaters, Odea, Amphitheaters, Circuses, Stadia', in *De Gruyter Handbook: Roman Architecture*, ed. Monika Trümper (Berlin and New York: de Gruyter, forthcoming). And note also the recent discussion of the theory of entertainment buildings (especially as related by Vitruvius): Paola Pasquino, Paola Pasquino, 'Gli edifici per spettacoli in Roma antica quali "res publicae"', in *I beni di interesse pubblico nell'esperienza giuridica romana*, 2 vols., ed. Luigi Garofalo (Naples: Jovene, 2016), 81-120.

15. Marialetizia Buonfiglio, 'Traiano e la ricostruzione del Circo Massimo', in *Traiano. Costruire l'Impero, creare l'Europa. Catalogo della mostra Mercati di Traiano – Museo dei Fori Imperiali (Roma, 29 novembre 2017– 16 settembre 2018)* (Rome: De Luca, 2017), 227-31.

16. The ancient sources disagree: from 150,000 (Dionysius of Halicarnassus 3.68.3) to 250,000 (Pliny the Elder, *Natural History* 36.102). See now Forichon, *Les spectateurs des jeux du cirque à Rome*, 135, with earlier literature.

17. Elena Carpentieri et al., 'The Smart Use of the Valle Murcia Geology in the Construction of Circus Maximus', *Rendiconti Online della Società Geologica Italiana* 33 (2015), 16-19.

18. Valeria Eulilli and Luca Maria Puzzilli, 'Indagini geofisiche per l'individuazione della spina del Circo Massimo', *Bullettino della Commissione Archeologica Comunale di Roma* 119 (2018), 167-78.

19. Marialetizia Buonfiglio, Stefania Pergola, and Gian Luca Zanzi, with an Appendix by Domenica Dininno and Alessandro Vecchione, 'Hemicycle of the Circus Maximus: Synthesis of the Late Antique Phases revealed by Recent Investigations', *Memoirs of the*

*American Academy in Rome* 61 (2016), 278–303; Marialetizia Buonfiglio, 'Relazione preliminare sulle nuove acquisizioni sul Circo Massimo: Indagini Archeologiche 2009–2016', in *La Glòria del Circ. Curses de Carros i Competicions Circenses. Actes del 3r Congrés internacional d'Arqueologia i Mòn Antic, Tarraco Biennal (Tarraco 16–19 Nov. 2016)*, ed. Jordi López Vilar (Tarragona: Fundació Privada Mútua Catalana, 2017), 119–26.

20. Mauro Saccone, Giorgia Romito, Marco Canciani, and Marialetizia Buonfiglio, 'Virtual Anastylosis of the Arch of Titus at Circus Maximus in Rome', *International Journal of Heritage in the Digital Era* 3, no. 2 (2014): 393–411; see also Tommaso Leoni, 'The *Sylloge Einsidlensis*, Poggio Bracciolini's *De Varietate Fortunae*, the Turris de Arcu, and the Disappearance of the Arch of Titus in the Circus Maximus', *The Memoirs of the American Academy in Rome* 63–64 (2018–2019): 253–89; Idem, 'The Arch (*Fornix*) of Lucius Stertinius in the Circus Maximus (Livy 33.27.3–5): Some Reflections on Its Significance and Its Likeliest Topographical Location', *Bullettino della Commissione Archeologica Comunale di Roma* 121 (2020/forthcoming); and Idem, Urbem Hierusolymam delevit: *The Arch of Titus in the Circus Maximus in Antiquity and the Middle Ages* (forthcoming).

21. The most up-to-date and thorough treatment of the archaeological evidence of circuses across the empire appears in the first section of Nelis-Clément and Roddaz, *Le cirque romain*. In addition, various site reports and synthetic chapters have appeared since (see below).

22. Giuseppina Pisani Sartorio, 'Le cirque de Maxence et les cirques de l'Italie antique', in Nelis-Clément and Roddaz, *Le cirque romain*, 47–78.

23. Louis Maurin, 'Les édifices de cirque en Afrique: bilan archéologique,' in Nelis-Clément and Roddaz, *Le cirque romain*, 91–108; Ridha Ghaddhab, 'Les édifices de spectacle en Afrique: prospérité et continuité de la cité classique pendant l'Antiquité tardive?', in Nelis-Clément and Roddaz, *Le cirque romain*, 109–32.

24. Trinidad Nogales Basarrate, 'Circos romanos de Hispania. Novedades y perspectivas arqueológicas', in Nelis-Clément and Roddaz, *Le cirque romain*, 161–202; Raymond L. Capra, 'Chariot Racing in Hispania Tarraconensis: Urban Romanization and Provincial Identity', in *Urban Dreams and Realities in Antiquity: Remains and Representations of the Ancient City*, ed. Adam M. Kemezis (Leiden: Brill, 2015), 370–92; numerous chapters in López Vilar, *La Glòria del Circ*, especially Trinidad Nogales Basarrate, '"Ludi circenses" en "Hispania": tipologías monumentales y testimonios iconográficos'; and Alejandro Jiménez Hernández, Inmaculada Carrasco, and José Antonio Peña Ruano, 'The Intramural Chariot Racing Stone Barrier at Carteia (Spain): Geophysical Survey and Verification by Archaeological Test Excavation', *Mediterranean Archaeology and Archaeometry* 19, no. 3 (2019): 139–56.

25. Philip Crummy, 'The Roman Circus at Colchester', *Britannia* 39 (2008): 15–32; Philip Crummy, 'The Roman Circus at Colchester, England,' in Nelis-Clément and Roddaz, *Le cirque romain*, 213–34.

26. *El circo romano de* Segobriga *(Saelices, Cuenca). Arquitectura, estratigrafía y función* (Cuenca: Consorcio del Parque Arqueológico de Segobriga, 2009).

27. María Engracia Muñoz-Santos, 'Roma como muestra, Sagunto como ejemplo: espectáculos en el circo (carreras de carros, *munera gladiatoria* y *venationes*). Supuestos probables', *Arse:* Boletín *anual del* Centro Arqueológico Saguntino 51 (2017): 123–34.

28. Paul Blockley, Nicoletta Cecchini, and Carla Pagini, 'L'area archeologica del Monastero Maggiore di Milano: una nuova lettura alla luce delle recenti indagini', Quaderni del civico museo archeologico e del civico gabinetto numismatico di Milano fasc. 4 (2012); Paul Blockley and Donatella Caporusso, *L'area del Monastero Maggiore in epoca romana* (Milan: Civico Museo Archeologico, 2013).

29. Francesco Marcattili, '"*Agrum qui appellatur circus* (*ILAfr*, 527): Postilla sul circo di Assisi', *Ostraka* 16 (2007): 311–17.

30. Michèle Monin and Djamila Fellague, 'Le cirque de *Lugdunum*. Données anciennes et récentes', *Gallia* 67, no. 2 (2010): 41–68.

31. Joachim Hupe, 'Das neue Grabungsschutzgebiet "Archäologisches Trier". Erläuterungen der Landesarchäologie', *Funde und Ausgrabungen im Bezirk Trier: Aus der Arbeit des Rheinischen Landesmuseums Trier* 43 (2011): 97–131, at 106 with fig. 6 (my thanks to Franziska Dövener for this reference). See also Ulrike Wulf-Rheidt, *"Den Sternen und dem Himmel würdig": kaiserliche Palastbauten in Rom und Trier*, Trierer Winckelmannsprogramm 24 (Wiesbaden: Harrassowitz, 2014).
32. David Gilman Romano, 'A Roman Circus in Corinth', *Hesperia: The Journal of the American School of Classical Studies at Athens* 74, no. 4 (2005): 585–611.
33. Ralf Bockmann, 'Karthago, Tunesien: Der Circus – Ein Monument und sein Quartier', *E-Forschungsberichte des Deutschen Archäologischen Instituts* Fasc. 3 (2015): 130–34; Ralf Bockmann, Hamden Ben Romdhane, and Manuela Broisch, 'Le cirque romain de Carthage: une nouvelle analyse géophysique en coopération tuniso-allemande', *CEDAC Carthage Bulletin* 23 (2016): 43–46; Ralf Bockmann et al., 'The Roman Circus and Southwestern City Quarter of Carthage: First Results of a New International Research Project', *Libyan Studies* 49 (2018): 177–86.
34. Peter Gendelman 'A Chronological Revision of the Date of the Pottery Finds from the Eastern Circus at Caesarea Maritima', *Atiqot* 92 (2018): 106–35; Rivka Gersht, 'Statues from the Eastern Circus at Caesarea Maritima', *Atiqot* 92 (2018): 141–58.
35. Hans Curvers et al., 'The Hippodrome of Berytos. Preliminary Report', *Bulletin d'archéologie et d'architecture libanaises* 17 (2017): 7–78.
36. Jeremy J. Rossiter, 'Chariot Racing in Roman Britain. The Horkstow Circus Mosaic Reconsidered', in *O mosaico romano nos centros e nas periferias: originalidades, influências e identidades: Actas do X colóquio internacional da Associação internacional para o estudo do mosaico antigo (AIEMA), Museo Monográfico de Conimbriga (Portugal), 29 de outubro a 3 de novembro de 2005* (Conimbriga: Instituto dos Museus e Conservação; Museu Monográfico de Conimbriga, 2011), 609–16. See also the brief comments about the circus of Martin Henig, '"The Race that is Set before Us": The Athletic Ideal in the Aesthetics and Culture of Early Roman Britain', in *Communities and Connections: Essays in Honour of Barry Cunliffe*, ed. Chris Gosden, Helena Hamerow, Gary Lock, Philip de Jersey, and Gary Lock (Oxford: Oxford University Press, 2007), 449–64, esp. 455–56.
37. Laurent Brassous, 'Les édifices de spectacles d'Hispanie entre les IIe et IVe siècles', in *Urbanisme civique en temps de crise. Les espaces civiques d'Hispanie et de l'Occident romain entre les IIe et IVe siècle*, ed. Laurent Brassous and Alejandro Quevedo (Madrid: Casa de Velazquez, 2015), 273–88.
38. Wolfgang Decker, 'Wagenrennen im römischen Ägypten', in Nelis-Clément and Roddaz, *Le cirque romain*, 347–59.
39. Renate Lafer, 'What can the Inscriptions tell Us about Spectacles? The Example of the Provinces of *Africa Proconsularis* and *Numidia*', in *Roman Amphitheatres and Spectacula: A 21st-Century Perspective. Papers from an International Conference held at Chester, 16th–18th February, 2007*, ed. Tony Wilmott (Oxford: Archaeopress, 2009), 179–83; Adeline Pichot, *Les édifices de spectacle des Maurétanies romaines* (Montagnac: M. Mergoil, 2012).
40. Joseph Patrich, 'Herodian Entertainment Structures', in *Herod and Augustus*, ed. David Jacobson and Nikos Kokkinos (Leiden: Brill, 2009), 181–213; Zeev Weiss, *Public Spectacles in Roman and Late Antique Palestine*, Revealing Antiquity 21 (Cambridge, MA: Harvard University Press, 2014).
41. Hany Kahwagi-Janho, *L'hippodrome romain de Tyr. Étude d'architecture et d'archéologie*, Mémoires 30 (Bordeaux: Ausonius, 2012).
42. Marek Titien Olszewski and Houmam Saad, 'Pella-Apamée sur l'Oronte et ses héros fondateurs à la lumière d'une source historique inconnue: une mosaïque d'Apamée,' in *Héros fondateurs et identités communautaires dans l'Antiquité, entre mythe, rite et politique*, ed. Maria Paola Castiglioni, Romina Carboni, Marco Giuman, and Hélène

Bernier-Farella, Quaderni di Otium 2 (Perugia: Morlacchi Editore, 2018), 365–416 (my thanks to Tommaso Leoni for this reference).

43. Robert Vergnieux, 'Origine de l'usage de la Réalité Virtuelle à l'Institut Ausonius et les premiers travaux sur le Circus Maximus', in Nelis-Clément and Roddaz, *Le cirque romain*, 235–41; Saccone et al., 'Virtual Anastylosis'; and the recent documentary 'Rome's Chariot Superstar' (Smithsonian Channel).
44. Such as the long tradition of horsemanship in the Iberian peninsula: Capra, 'Chariot Racing', 374–76. On Spanish equestrianism in a later context, see Isabelle Schürch's essay in this collection.
45. See most recently Capra, 'Chariot Racing', esp. 383.
46. See Claude Sintes, 'Le cirque d'Arles: l'apport des fouilles depuis 1986', in Nelis-Clément and Roddaz, *Le cirque romain*, 203–11.
47. Such as Livy 40.2, where he mentions destruction in the Circus Maximus caused by a storm in 182 B.C.
48. Jocelyne Nelis-Clément, 'Roman Spectacles: Exploring their Environmental Implications', in *Pollution and the Environment in Ancient Life and Thought*, ed. Orietta Dora Corodovana and Gian Franco Chiai, Geographica Historia 36 (Stuttgart: Franz Steiner, 2017), 217–81.
49. See further the scholarship of Greg Woolf, most recently his *Rome. An Empire's Story* (Oxford: Oxford University Press, 2012), esp. 222–6 on baths and food as mechanisms of 'enfranchisement, loyalty, and acculturation' (222).
50. For instance, as reflected in the emphasis (e.g. prominence of Cybele) or absence (e.g. Augustan obelisk) of certain architectural features of the Circus Maximus on mosaic pavements from across the provinces (Humphrey, *Roman Circuses*, 208 ff.) or the naming of charioteers who may have been participants and heroes in local games, such as those recently discovered at Philippi: see further Emmanouela Gounari, 'The Roman Mosaics from Philippi. Evidence of the Presence of Romans in the City', *Bollettino di Archeologia on line* 1 (Volume speciale C / C9 / 3) (2010), 27–38, esp. 35–6; Katherine M. D. Dunbabin, *Theater and Spectacle in the Art of the Roman Empire* (Ithaca, NY: Cornell University Press, 2016), chapter six.
51. This multi-functionality is particularly evident in the Near East, where buildings such as the so-called 'hippo-stadium' at Caesarea admits ambiguity in their classification (as amphitheater, circus, or stadium) and literary attestations document the different events to which such buildings might play host; see Hazel Dodge, 'Circuses in the Roman East: A Reappraisal', in Nelis-Clément and Roddaz, *Le cirque romain*, 133–46; Weiss, *Public Spectacles*.
52. See further Frank Bernstein, *Ludi publici: Untersuchungen zur Entstehung und Entwicklung der öffentlichen Spiele im republikanischen Rom*, Historia Einzelschriften 119 (Stuttgart: Franz Steiner Verlag, 1998).
53. See recently Werner Eck, 'Einladung zum Fest in der Stadt', in *Urbanitas – Urbane Qualitäten. Die antike Stadt als kulturelle Selbstverwirklichung. Kolloquium 19.-21. Dezember 2012 in München*, ed. Alexandra W. Busch, Jochen Griesbach, and Johannes Lipps (Mainz: Verlag des Römisch-Germanischen Zentralmuseums, 2017), 53–66.
54. Paul Zanker, *Die Apotheose der römischen Kaiser. Ritual und städtische Bühne* (Munich: Carl Friedrich von Siemens Stiftung, 2004), esp. 40ff., figs. 15–17; Matthew Gisborne, '*Pompae* and Circumstances: Triumphs, Funerals and Circus Processions as Spectacles in the Roman Republic', D.Phil. diss., University of Oxford, 2005; Frank Bernstein, 'Complex Rituals: Games and Processions in Republican Rome', in *A Companion to Roman Religion*, ed. Jorg Rüpke (Malden, MA: Wiley-Blackwell, 2007), 222–34; Maggie L. Popkin, *The Architecture of the Roman Triumph: Monuments, Memory, and Identity* (New York: Cambridge University Press, 2016); Fabian Goldbeck and Johannes Wienand, ed., *Der römische Triumph in Prinzipat und Spätantike* (Berlin: de Gruyter, 2017); and Gian Luca Gregori and Giovanni Almagno, *Roman Calendars: Imperial Birthdays, Victories, and Triumphs* (Mauritius: Lambert Publishing, 2019).

55. Sinclair Bell, 'Lusus Troiae,' in *The Blackwell Encyclopedia of Ancient History*, ed. Roger Bagnall et al. (Malden, MA: Wiley-Blackwell, 2012), with bibliography.
56. Chris Epplett, 'Roman Beast Hunts', in Christesen and Kyle, *A Companion to Sport*, 505-19; Jacopo de Grossi Mazzorin, 'The Exploitation and Mobility of Exotic Animals: Zooarchaeological Evidence from Rome', in *The Role of Zooarchaeology in the Study of the Western Roman Empire*, Martyn G. Allen, ed., Journal of Roman Archaeology Supplementary Series 107 (Portsmouth, RI: Journal of Roman Archaeology, 2019), 85-100.
57. Anne Berlan-Bajard, *Les spectacles aquatiques romains*, Collection de l'École française de Rome 360 (Rome: l'École française de Rome, 2006); Gérald Cariou, *La naumachie: morituri te salutant* (Paris: Presses de l'Université Paris-Sorbonne, 2009) (my thanks to Sylvain Forichon for the latter reference).
58. Chris Epplett, 'Spectacular Executions in the Roman World, in Christesen and Kyle, *A Companion to Sport*, 520-32.
59. Sylvain Forichon, 'Sesostris's Chariot in a Roman Circus? A New Interpretation of a Scene Depicted on an Imperial Oil Lamp', *Memoirs of the American Academy in Rome* 63-64 (2018-2019): 237-52.
60. 'Il est donc tout à fait erroné de parler du cirque romain comme d'un simple avatar de l'hippodrome grec, et il est au contraire nécessaire d'insister sur son caractère décidément italique': Thuillier, 'Vingt ans au cirque', 327. On the categories of Roman circus vs. the Greek hippodrome, see Zanovello, 'Il ruolo storico', 840-42. On the question of Etruscan influence, see further Humphrey, *Roman Circuses*, 16-7; Jean-Paul Thuillier, *Le sport dans la Rome antique* (Paris: Editions Errance, 1996), 25-9, 95 ff.; Maurizio Sannibale, 'I giochi e l'agonismo in Etruria', in *Etruschi. L'ideale eroico e il vino lucente, catalogo della mostra (Asti, Palazzo Mazzetti, 17 marzo-15 luglio 2012)*, ed. A. Mandolesi and Maurizio Sannibale (Milan: Electa, 2012), 123-37; Jean-Paul Thuillier, 'L'organisation des *ludi circenses*: les quatre factions (République, Haut-Empire)', in *L'organisation des spectacles dans le monde romain*, Entretiens sur l'Antiquité classique 58, ed. Kathleen Coleman and Jocelyne Nelis-Clément (Geneva: Fondation Hardt, 2012), 173-220, esp. 184-88; and Ibid, *Allez les rouges!*, especially 'Le programme hippique des jeux romains: une curieuse absence' (65-85) and 'L'organisation et le financement des ludi circenses au début de la République: modèle grec ou modèle étrusque?' (86-98).
61. Livy, *History of Rome* 1.9; Cicero, *On the Republic* 2.7.12; and Dionysius of Halicarnassus, *The Roman Antiquities*, 2.30.
62. Marcattili, *Circo Massimo*, 108-22.
63. Francesco Marcattili, '*Ara Consi* in Circo Maximo', *Mélanges de l'Ecole Française de Rome. Antiquité* 118 (2006), 621-51.
    Marcattili, *Circo Massimo*, 18-36.
64. Commonly but less accurately referred to as the *spina*: see Jean-Paul Thuillier, 'Circensia. Des noms, des choses et des hommes', in *Antike Lebenswelten: Konstanz, Wandel, Wirkungsmacht: Festschrift für Ingomar Weiler zum 70. Geburtstag*, ed. Peter Mauritsch et al. (Wiesbaden: Harrassowitz, 2008), 129-33, esp. 130-32 (reprinted as Ibid, *Allez les Rouges!*, 149-54).
65. See also Francesco Marcattili, 'Cerere e il "mundus" del Circo Massimo', in *Le perle e il filo. A Mario Torelli per i suoi settanta anni* (Venosa: Osanna, 2008), 195-223; Carin Green, 'The Gods in the Circus', in *New Perspectives on Etruria and Early Rome*, ed. Sinclair Bell and Helen Nagy (Madison: The University of Wisconsin Press, 2009), 65-78. More broadly, see John Zaleski, 'Religion and Roman Spectacle', in Christesen and Kyle, *A Companion to Sport*, 590-602.
66. For other examples of this coin type and discussion, see Annalisa Marzano, 'Trajanic Building Projects on Base-metal Denominations and Audience Targeting', *Papers of the British School at Rome* 77 (2009): 125-58, esp. 130, 132, 134 fig. 1.1.
67. Zanker, 'By the emperor', 70.

68. Jean-Claude Golvin, 'Réflexion relative aux questions soulevées par l'étude du puluinar et de la spina du Circus Maximus', in Nelis-Clément and Roddaz, *Le cirque romain*, 79–87; Christopher van den Berg, 'The Pulvinar in Roman Culture', *Transactions of the American Philological Association* 138 (2008): 239–74; Marcattili, *Circo Massimo*, 205–10.
69. Alessandro Barchiesi, 'Phaethon and the Monsters', in *Paradox and the Marvellous in Augustan Literature and Culture*, ed. Philip Hardie (New York: Oxford University Press, 2009), 186 (emphasis original). On the study of Rome's 'processional culture' in broader perspective, see Tonio Hölscher, 'Macht, Raum und visuelle Wirkung: Auftritte römischer Kaiser in der Staatsarchitektur von Rom', in *Constructing Power: Architecture, Ideology, and Social Practice*, ed. Joseph Maran, Carsten Juwig, and Hermann Schwengel (Hamburg: LIT, 2006), 185–201, esp. 190 and fig. 29.1; Karl-Joachim Hölkeskamp, 'Raum – Präsenz – Performanz. Prozessionen in politischen Kulturen der Vormoderne – Forschungen und Fortschritte', in *Medien der Geschichte – Antikes Griechenland und Rom*, ed. Ortwin Dally, Tonio Hölscher, Susanne Muth, and Rolf Michael Schneider (Berlin: de Gruyter 2014), 359–95; Idem, '"Performative Turn" meets "Spatial Turn". Prozessionen und andere Rituale in der neueren Forschung', in *Raum und Performanz. Rituale in Residenzen von der Antike bis 1815*, ed. Dietrich Boschung, Karl-Joachim Hölkeskamp, and Claudia Sode (Stuttgart: Franz Steiner, 2015), 15–74; and Tonio Hölscher, *Visual Power in Ancient Greece and Rome. Between Art and Social Reality* (Oakland: University of California Press, 2018), esp. chap. one.
70. See Ludivine Beaurin, Simon Girond, and Matthieu Soler, 'Introduction. Communautés et individus au spectacle de la religion. Dispositifs, stratégies, modalités d'action', *Pallas* 107 (2018): 15–34.
71. Cicero, *On Divination* 1.132; Horace, *Satires* 1.6.111.
72. Tertullian, *On the Spectacles* 8; Cassiodorus, *Variae* 3.51. See also Alessandro Barchiesi, 'Le Cirque du Soleil', in Nelis-Clément and Roddaz, *Le cirque romain*, 521–37; Marcattili, *Circo Massimo*, esp. 135–54.
73. Andrew Feldherr, 'Ships of State: *Aeneid* 5 and Augustan Circus Spectacle', *Classical Antiquity* 14, no. 2 (1995): 245–65; at 248. See Björn Ewald and Carlos Noreña, 'Introduction', in Ewald and Noreña, *The Emperor and Rome*, 1–43, for their highly useful discussion of four themes only briefly glossed here: emperor, mass, and elite in imperial Rome; space; representation; and ritual; Sylvain Forichon, 'Le comportement du prince lors des spectacles de la Rome impériale', in *Le costume de Prince. Regards sur une figure politique de la Rome antique d'Auguste à Constantin*, ed. Philippe Le Doze (forthcoming).
74. Pliny the Younger, *Panegyric* 51.
75. On clothing in the circus (especially in the context of Ovid's *Amores*), see Caroline A. Perkins, 'Ovid breaks the Law: *Amores* 3, 2 and the *Edictum de Adtemptata Pudicitia*', *Paideia* 70 (2015): 137–53, esp. 141–42. More generally, consult Jonathan Edmonson, 'Public Dress and Social Control in Late Republican and Early Imperial Rome', in *Roman Dress and the Fabrics of Roman Culture*, ed. Jonathan C. Edmondson and Alison M. Keith (Toronto: University of Toronto Press, 2010), 21–46.
76. Suetonius, *Augustus* 44.2; Calpurnius Siculus, *Eclogues* 7; the *Lex Ursonensis* (*CIL* 2.5439 = *ILS* 6087, chapter 66 on reserved seating for *decuriones*); and Patrizia Arena, 'Il circo Massimo come microcosmo dell'impero attraverso la ripartizione dei posti,' in *Forme di aggregazione nel mondo romano*, ed. Elio Lo Cascio and Giovanna Daniela Merola (Bari: Edipuglia, 2007), 31–48. It is worth noting that since visiting the games in a specific *municipium* defined the residency (*domicilium*) of a citizen, there was a legal underpinning to one's socialization into the games: see *Digest* 50.1.27, and discussion in Richard Gamauf, '*Pro virtute certamen*: Zur Bedeutung des Sports und von Wettkämpfen im klassischen römischen Recht', in Kaja Harter-Uibopuu and Thomas Kruse, ed., *Sport und Recht in der Antike* (Vienna: Holzhausen, 2014), 275–308, at 296 n. 96, 97 (my thanks for Frederik Grosser for emphasizing this point).

77. Patrizia Arena, *Feste e rituali a Roma: il principe incontra il popolo nel Circo Massimo* (Bari: Edipuglia, 2010).
78. Latham, *Performance, Memory, and Processions*, chapter four; Sylvain Forichon, 'Empereur au spectacle, empereur en spectacle: degrés de visibilité, régimes d'attention et modes de communication du prince au Circus Maximus sous le Haut-Empire', in *Spectateurs grecs et romains: corps, modalités de présence et régimes d'attention (journées d'étude internationales, Paris, les 4 et 5 novembre 2016)*, ed. Emmanuelle Valette and Stephanie Wyler (forthcoming).
79. Paul Zanker, 'Domitian's Palace on the Palatine and the Imperial Image', in *Representations of Empire: Rome and the Mediterranean World*, Proceedings of the British Academy 114, ed. Alan K. Bowman et al., (London: Oxford University Press for the British Academy, 2002), 105–30, esp. 109, figs. 6, 7; Manuel Royo, 'De la *Domus Gelotiana* aux *Horti Spei Veteris*: retour sur la question de l'association entre cirque et palais à Rome', in Nelis-Clément and Roddaz, *Le cirque romain*, 481–95; Barchiesi, 'Phaethon', esp. 170–87 with figs. 14, 15; and for its later development, Clemens Heucke, *Circus und Hippodrom als politischer Raum. Untersuchungen zum großen Hippodrom von Konstantinopel und zu entsprechenden Anlagen in spätantiken Kaiserresidenzen*, Altertumswissenschaftliche Texte und Studien 28 (Hildesheim: Olms-Weidmann, 1994).
80. Josephus, *Jewish Antiquities* 19.24–7. For horse racing as a mechanism for political contestation, see Sylvain Forichon, 'Manifestations à caractère politique et troubles à l'ordre public lors des spectacles à Rome (Ier siècle a.C. - IVe siècle p.C.): étude chronologique et typologique', *Nikephoros* 28 (2015/forthcoming); compare also Richard Nash's essay in this collection.
81. ILS 286, the dedicatory inscription recognizing Trajan as an *optimus princeps* for his generosity in expanding the seating at the Circus Maximus by 5000 places. See further Tamara Jones, 'Seating and Spectacle in the Graeco-Roman World' (Ph.D. diss., McMaster University, 2008).
82. Dionysius of Halicarnassus 3.68.
83. Obelisks: Brian A. Curran, Anthony Grafton, Pamela O. Long, and Benjamin Weiss, *Obelisk: A History* (Cambridge, MA: MIT Press, 2009), chapter two; Molly Swetnam-Burland, '*Aegyptus Redacta*: The Egyptian Obelisk in the Augustan Campus Martius', *Art Bulletin* 92, no. 3 (2010): 135–53. See also Sylvain Forichon, 'L'Égypte, le Nil et les Égyptiens dans les spectacles de la Rome ancienne (I$^{er}$ siècle a.C. - V$^e$ siècle p.C.)', *Latomus* 77, no. 1 (2018): 99–129.
84. See Livy 1.56.2, where he speaks of the *magnificentia* of the Circus Maximus (as well as the Cloaca Maxima) in relation to other present-day architecture. On euergetism, see the classic study by Paul Veyne, *Bread and Circuses: Historical Sociology and Political Pluralism* (London: Penguin Press, 1990); see also Michael J. Carter and Jonathan Edmondson, 'Spectacle in Rome, Italy, and the Provinces', in *The Oxford Handbook of Roman Epigraphy*, ed. Christer Bruun and Jonathan Edmondson (Oxford: Oxford University Press, 2015), 535–56, esp. 544–47 on benefaction; Alberto Ceballos Hornero and David Ceballos Hornero, 'La nominación de los espectáculos romanos en la epigrafía provincial del Occidente latino', *Emerita* 79, no. 1 (2011), 105–30; Kathleen Coleman and Jocelyne Nelis-Clément, 'Introduction', in Coleman and Nelis-Clément, *L'organisation*, xi–xxvii; and Diana Ng, 'Commemoration and Elite Benefaction of Buildings and Spectacles in the Roman World', *Journal of Roman Studies* 105 (2015): 1–23.
85. Jean-Michel Carrié et Christian Landes, ed., *Jeux et spectacles dans l'Antiquité tardive* (Turnhout: Brepols, 2007); Emmanuel Soler and Françoise Thelamon, ed., *Les jeux et les spectacles dans l'Empire romain tardif et dans les royaumes barbares* (Mont-Saint-Aignan: Publications des universités de Rouen et du Havre, 2008); Alexander Puk, *Das Römische Spielewesen in der Spätantike*, Millennium-Studien 48 (Berlin: de Gruyter, 2014), with the important review of the latter by Katherine Dunbabin, 'The Games in

Late Antiquity', *Journal of Roman Archaeology* 30 (2017), 904–12; and, with a focus on theater (despite its title), Gennaro Tedeschi, 'Spettacoli tardoantichi: documenti noti e recenti', *AION: Annali dell'Università degli Studi di Napoli "L'Orientale"*, 41, no. 1 (2019): 81–98.

86. Richard Lim, 'Inventing Secular Space in the Late Antique City: Reading the Circus Maximus', in *Rom in der Spätantike: Historische Erinnerung im Städtischen Raum*, ed. R. Behrwald and C. Witschel (Stuttgart: Franz Steiner, 2012), 61–81; Jean-Paul Thuillier, 'Les jeux romains: Des origines sacrées au sport-business', in *Theaterbauten als Teil monumentaler Heiligtümer in den nordwestlichen Provinzen des Imperium Romanum: Architektur-Organisation-Nutzung, Internationales Kolloquium in Augusta Raurica, 18.–21. September 2013 Auditorium Römerstiftung Dr. René Clavel, Augst-Kastelen*, Forschungen in Augst 50, ed. Thomas Hufschmid (Augst: Augusta Raurica, 2016), 13–23; and more broadly, see Jacob Latham, 'Battling Bishops, the Roman Aristocracy, and the Contestation of Space in Late Antique Rome', in *Religious Competition in the Third Century CE: Jews, Christians, and the Greco-Roman World*, ed. Nathaniel DesRosiers, Jordan D. Rosenblum, and Lily Vuong (Göttingen: Vandenhoeck and Ruprecht, 2014), 126–37; Idem, 'Ritual and the Christianization of Urban Space', in *The Oxford Handbook of Early Christian Ritual*, ed. Risto Uro, Juliette Day, Richard DeMaris, and Rikard Roitto (Oxford: Oxford University Press, 2018), 684–702.

87. Jacob Latham, 'Representing Ritual, Christianizing the *Pompa Circensis*: Imperial Spectacle at Rome in a Christianizing Empire', in *The Art of Empire: Christian Art in Its Imperial Context*, ed. Robin Jensen and Lee Jefferson (Minneapolis: Fortress Press, 2015), 197–224; Latham, *Performance, Memory, and Processions*, esp. chapter six; Natan Henrique Taveira Baptista, 'O circo como templo idolátrico em Tertuliano (*Spect.*, 8.4; 13.4)', *Romanitas-Revista de Estudos Grecolatinos* 5 (2015): 147–67; Fabio Guidetti, 'La riscoperta della concorrenza: Immagini di rituali e cerimonie nei sarcofagi urbani tardoantichi', *Studi Classici e Orientali* 63 (2017): 407–45.

88. For the body of the charioteer as a contested space in late antique Roman North Africa, see Natan Henrique Taveira Baptista, 'A glória atlética entre o desejo e a censura: *spectāculum*, conflito urbano e representação corporal do auriga na África Romana (Séc. III-IV)' (Ph.D. diss., Universidade Federal do Espírito Santo (Brazil), 2015).

89. See the lucid summary of this debate by Olof Brandt, 'The Archaeology of Roman Ecclesial Architecture and the Study of Early Christian Liturgy', *Studia Patristica* 71 (2014): 21–52, at 33–40, figs. 9–11. In addition to the literature listed in Brandt, note the arguments against the influence of the circus form on the basilica made by Tomas Lehmann, 'Circus oder Basilica? Zu einem Grund(riß)problem in der Archäologie', in *Munus. Festschrfit für Hans Wiegartz*, ed. Torstern Mattern and Dieter Korol (Münster: Scriptorium, 2000), 163–69; see also Steffen Diefenbach, *Römische Erinnerungsräume: Heiligenmemoria und kollektive Identitäten im Rom des 3. bis 5. Jahrhunderts n. Chr.*, Millennium-Studien 11 (Berlin: de Gruyter, 2007), esp. 191 with n. 424. For the argument in favor of the circus form's influence, see now Lynda L. Coon and Kim Sexton, 'Racetrack to Salvation: The Circus, the Basilica, and the Martyr', *Gesta* 59 (2020), 1–42.

90. Paraphrasing Ammianus Marcellinus 28.4.29. The interrelationship between imperial and ecclesiastical authority goes beyond the scope of this essay; see now several chapters in Erika Manders and Daniëlle Slootjes, ed., *Leadership, Ideology and Crowds in the Roman Empire of the Fourth Century AD*, Heidelberger althistorische Beiträge und epigraphische Studien Bd. 62 (Stuttgart: Franz Steiner Verlag, 2020).

91. John Chrysostom, *Homilies* 48. See also Nicola Denzey Lewis, 'Popular Christianity and Lived Religion in Late Antique Rome: Seeing Magic in the Catacombs', in *Popular Culture in the Ancient World*, ed. Lucy Grig (Cambridge: Cambridge University Press, 2017), 257–76, at 267 for discussion of the (re)use of the letters E, F, L, and P—symbols of local chariot teams—as monograms on *loculus* enclosures (c. 350 A.D.); and Cristian Mondello, 'Using and Reusing Tokens: Some Remarks about Christian Graffiti on

92. See Gilbert Dagron, *L'hippodrome de Constantinople. Jeux, peuple et politique* (Paris: Gallimard, 2011), and David Parnell's essay in this collection.
93. This section updates, corrects, and expands my discussion of the races in Bell, 'Roman Chariot Racing.'
94. Thuillier, 'L'organisation des *ludi circenses*', 204–8. My thanks to Frederik Grosser for reminding me about this important point and for the reference.
95. Greens: Cassius Dio 59.14.6, 63.6.3, 72.17.1, 73.4.1, 79.14.1; Suetonius, *Caligula* 55.2, and *Nero* 22; SHA, *Lucius Verus* 4.7, 6.3; Petronius, *Satyricon* 70. Blues: Suetonius, *Vitellius* 7.1, 14.3; Cassius Dio 77.10.1; Martial, *Epigrams* 6.46. The introduction of two other factions, the Gold (*Aurea*) and Purple (*Purpurea*), during the reign of Domitian was short-lived and ended with the death of the emperor. Suetonius, *Domitian* 7.1; compare Martial, *Epigrams* 14.55.
96. See Cassius Dio 61.6.1–2, with the famous story of the *praetor* who refused to meet the financial demands of the Blues and Greens and instead threatened to run dogs until Nero intervened by providing the victory prizes; see also Horsmann, *Die Wagenlenker*, 85 with n. 28; regarding the differences between factions and the *praetor* see also Suetonius, *Nero* 22.2. My thanks for Frederik Grosser for emphasizing this point, with references.
97. On the archaeological record of the factions: Humphrey, *Roman Circuses*, 558–60; S. Evangelisti, 'PRASINAE FACTIONIS MONUMENTUM', *Lexicon Topographicum Urbis Romae: Suburbium, Vol. 4: M-Q* (Rome: Quasar, 2006), 261; Lothar Haselberger, *Mapping Augustan Rome, Journal of Roman Archaeology* Supplement 50, rev. edn. (Portsmouth: Journal of Roman Archaeology, 2008), 234 (s.v. stabula factionum); Massimo Pentiricci, 'Il settore occidentale del Campo Marzio tra l'età antica e l'altomedioevo', in *L'Antica basilica di San Lorenzo in Damaso. Indagini archeologiche nel Palazzo della Cancelleria (1988–1993)*, 2 vols., ed. Christoph Frommel and Massimo Pentiricci (Rome: De Luca, 2009), 1: 15–72; and Gian Luca Gregori, 'Documenti epigrafici dal contesto di largo Perosi in Campo Marzio: due nuovi *termini* del Tevere e altri reperti', in *Campo Marzio. Nuove Richerche. Atti del Seminario di Studi sul Campo Marzio. Roma, Museo Nazionale Romano a Palazzo Altemps, 18-19 marzo 2013*, ed. Fedora Filippi (Rome: Quasar, 2015), 443–51.
98. On horse racing in the Campus Martius generally, see Paul W. Jacobs, II and Diane A. Conlin, *Campus Martius. The Field of Mars in the Life of Ancient Rome* (Cambridge: Cambridge University Press, 2015), 66–7. On the *Trigarium*, see most recently Jon Albers, *Campus Martius: die urbane Entwicklung des Marsfeldes von der Republik bis zur mittleren Kaiserzeit*, Studien zur Antiken Stadt 11 (Wiesbaden: Reichert Verlag, 2013), with earlier literature.
99. See *CIL* 6.10046 = *ILS* 5313. David S. Potter, 'Entertainers in the Roman Empire', in *Life, Death, and Entertainment in the Roman Empire*, ed. David S. Potter and David J. Mattingly (Ann Arbor: University of Michigan Press, 1999), 280–350, esp. 299–301.
100. On the specialized range of positions held by these personnel, see further Potter, 'Entertainers'; Jocelyne Nelis-Clément, 'Les métiers du cirque, de Rome à Byzance: Entre texte et image', *Cahiers du Centre Gustave-Glotz* 13 (2002), 265–309 (an exhaustive study with comprehensive bibliography); Sinclair Bell, 'Zirkussklaven', in *Handwörterbuch der antiken Sklaverei* I, Forschungen zur antiken Sklaverei 5, ed. Heinz Heinen et al. (Stuttgart: Steiner Verlag, 2006); Rose MacLean, 'People of the Margins of Roman Spectacle', in Christesen and Kyle, *A Companion to Sport*, 578–89; and Thuillier, 'L'organisation des *ludi circenses*', esp. 177–84.
101. Carolyn Willekes, 'Breeding Success: The Creation of the Racehorse in Antiquity,' *Mouseion* 16.3 (2020), 453–69; at 455, my emphasis.
102. For instance, Silius Italicus, *Punica*, ll. 303–456.

103. A sixth-century program from Oxyrhynchus, Egypt: *POxy.* 2707.
104. On imagery as evidence, see *inter alia* Humphrey, *Roman Circuses*, passim; Zanovello, 'Il ruolo storico', 858–61; Jean-Claude Golvin, 'L'exploitation des images antiques: problèmes de méthodologie', in Nelis-Clément and Roddaz, *Le cirque romain*, 243–59; Marcattili, *Circo Massimo*, esp. 241–79; Forichon, *Les spectateurs des jeux du cirque à Rome*, passim; and Grosser, *Darstellungen von Wagenlenkern*, passim.
105. For lengthier reconstructions, see Meijer, *Chariot Racing*, 65–81; Thuillier, 'Une journée particulière dans la Rome antique. Pour une topographie sportive de l'Vrbs', in *Allez les rouges!*, 155–65.
106. On the *pompa*, see Ovid, *Amores* 3.2.43–58; and see most comprehensively Latham, *Performance, Memory, and Processions*, with full literature but to which should be added: Zanovello, 'Il ruolo storico', 862–64, and Sylvia Estienne, 'Aurea pompa venit: Présences divines dans les processions romaines', in *Figures de dieux: Construire le divin en images*, ed. Sylvia Estienne et al. (Rennes: Presses Universitaires de Rennes, 2014), 337–49.
107. Dionysius Halicarnassus, *Roman Antiquities* 7.70–3.
108. Hölscher, *Visual Power*, 76. On this interplay of 'stability and movement', see now the contributions in *The Moving City: Processions, Passages and Promenades in Ancient Rome*, ed. Ida Ostenberg, Simon Malmberg, and Jonas Bjørnebye (London: Bloomsbury Academic, 2015).
109. Humphrey, *Roman Circuses*, 84.
110. Siliva Saronni, '*L'editor ludi*, il fornitore di cavalli e l'auriga: variazioni d'immagine dei *ludi circenses*', *Annali della Facoltá di Lettere e Filosofia* 61, no. 2 (2008): 291–301.
111. Gwénaëlle Marchet, '*Mittere mappam* (Mart. 12.28.9): du signal de départ à la théologie impériale (I$^{er}$ a.C.-VII$^{e}$ p.C.)', in Nelis-Clément and Roddaz, *Le cirque romain*, 291–317.
112. See further Fabricia Fauquet, 'Le fonctionnement du cirque romain. Déroulement d'une course de chars', in Nelis-Clément and Roddaz, *Le cirque romain*, 261–89.
113. 28.4.30; transl. John C. Rolfe.
114. Ovid, *Art of Love* 1.167–8, in which a spectator requests to see a program (*libellum*) before placing a bet (though as Sylvain Forichon reminds me, there is ambiguity about the type of performance).
115. On these devices, see now Carina Weiß and Sebastien Aubry, 'Gemmen mit Circusrennen. Neue Beobachtungen zu den Zählsystemen der *spina* (*septem ova, delphini*) und eine Preisinschrift auf die *factio der prasini*', *Numismatica e Antichità Classiche* 38 (2009), 227–58.
116. See further now Nathan T. Elkins, *A Monument to Dynasty and Death: The Story of Rome's Colosseum and the Emperors Who Built It* (Baltimore, MD: Johns Hopkins University Press, 2019).
117. J. Nelis-Clément, 'Le cirque et son paysage sonore' in Nelis-Clément and Roddaz, *Le cirque romain*, 431–57. More generally, see now Jeremy Hartnett, 'Sound as a Roman Urban Social Phenomenon', in Annette Haug and Patric-Alexander Kreuz, ed., *Stadterfahrung als Sinneserfahrung in der römischen Kaiserzeit*, Studies in Classical Archaeology 2 (Turnhout: Brepols, 2016), 159–78.
118. Cassiodorus, *Variae* 3.51
119. Marcus Junkelmann, 'On the Starting Line with Ben Hur: Chariot-Racing in the Circus Maximus', in *Gladiators and Caesars. The Power of Spectacle in Ancient Rome*, ed. Eckhart Köhne and Cornelia Ewigleben (London: British Museum Press, 2000) 86–102, at 100. As Carolyn Willekes informs me, however, Junkelmann's suggestion that speeds as high as 75 kmh (cited in Bell, 'Roman Chariot-Racing', 495) could have been achieved in the straightaways is highly unlikely based on precedents in modern horse racing. Also in contrast to Junkelmann's estimates, Sylvain Forichon ('*Furor circensis*', 174) suggests a race duration of 13 minutes at 25 kmh, based upon the unpublished work of Fabricia Fauquet, 'Le cirque romain. Essai de théorisation de sa forme et de ses

fonctions' (Ph.D. diss., Archéologie et Préhistoire, Université de Bordeaux Montaigne, 2002).
120. See Bela Sandor, 'The Genesis and Performance Characteristics of Roman Chariots,' *Journal of Roman Archaeology* 25 (2012): 475–85; Idem, 'Tire Choices in Roman Chariot Racing', *Journal of Roman Archaeology* 29 (2016): 438–42.
121. Silius Italicus, *Punica*, 303–456.
122. Licia Luschi, 'L'omaggio al vincitore. A proposito del rilievo con desultores del Musée Royal di Mariemont', *Studi Classici e Orientali* 65 (2019): 361–410.
123. As suggested for a large cylindrical vase from the circus at Arles: Danièle Foy and Jean Piton, 'La Coupe de l'aurige du cirque d'Arles', *Journal of Glass Studies* 39 (1997): 11–22. See also now Jacques Chamay, Martin Guggisberg, and Kilian Anheuser, *L'aurige et les chasseurs: Chef d'oeuvre d'ofrévrerie antique* (Neuchâtel: Chaman, 2007).
124. See further Meijer, *Chariot Racing*, 76–78.
125. *Nero* 22.
126. *CIL* 6.10048 = *ILS* 5287. The meaning of *eripuit et vicit* glossed here is likely, but not entirely certain; N.B. not '*erupit*' as in Meijer, *Chariot Racing*, 171.
127. Sidonius Apollinaris, *To Consentius* 23.307–427; *Greek Anthology* 15.47, 16.337, 340, and 374.
128. Epictetus 1.9.27.
129. Sidonius Apollinaris, *To Consentius* 23.323–424.
130. This section updates, corrects, and expands my discussion on charioteers in Bell, 'Roman Chariot Racing.'
131. Martial, *Epigrams* 10.53; transl. David Roy Shackleton Bailey. On this passage, see further Mario Ciappi, '*Ille ego sum Scorpus*. Il ciclo funerario dell'auriga Scorpo in Marziale (X 50 e 53)', *Maia* 53, no. 3 (2001): 587–610; Alessandra Tafaro, 'Cross-references between Epitaphs and Funerary Epigrams: A Case-study of Scorpus the Charioteer in Martial 10.50-10.53', *Appunti Romani di Filologia* 18 (2016): 61–76.
132. Horsmann, *Die Wagenlenker*, 78–90.
133. Catalogued in Gerhard Horsmann, *Die Wagenlenker der römischen Kaiserzeit: Untersuchungen zu ihrer sozialen Stellung*, Forschungen zur antiken Sklaverei 29 (Stuttgart: Franz Steiner, 1998).
134. Ingomar Weiler, 'Zur Rolle des Sklaven im Sport des griechisch-römischen Altertums', *Jahrbuch 2009 der Deutschen Gesellschaft für Geschichte der Sportwissenschaft e. V.*, (2009), 8–38, esp. 28–33; Ibid, 'Sport', in *Handwörterbuch der antiken Sklaverei. I–IV*, ed. Heinz Heinen et al. (Stuttgart: Franz Steiner, 2012), s.v. 'Sport' (Ingomar Weiler), esp. section IV ('Die römischen *spectacula*'); Claudio Parisi Presicce and Orietta Rossini, ed., *Spartaco: Schiavi e padroni a Roma. Catalogo* (Rome: De Luca Editori D'arte, 2017), 218–27 cat. nos. 29–37 ('arena e circo'), 227–9 cat. nos. 38–40 ('attori e mimi').
135. Dio Chrysostom, *Discourse* 32.75.
136. Juvenal, *Satires* 7.105–14; Martial, *Epigrams* 10.74; see Horsmann, *Die Wagenlenker*, 287.
137. Pliny, *Natural History*, 29.10.
138. Galen, *De praenotione ad Posthumum (Epigenem)* Kühn 14.604. See further Sinclair W. Bell, 'A Roman Bust of a Charioteer in the Musée des Beaux-Arts in Budapest and Related Representations: A Forgotten Genre of Ancient Art', *Bulletin du Musée Hongrois des Beaux-Arts* (2020), 35–66.
139. Gifts: Suetonius, Caligula 55.2f. Political appointment: Historia Augusta, *Elagabalus* 6, 12.
140. *Annals* 14.14.1. On the practice of emperors as charioteers, see the symbolic interpretation of Giorgio Vespignani, 'L'imperatore dei Romani auriga: una questione di regalità sacra, da Nerone al secolo X', *Mythos: Rivista di storia delle religioni* 6 (2012): 41–50.
141. Parshia Lee-Stecum, 'Dangerous Reputations: Charioteers and Magic in Fourth-Century Rome', *Greece and Rome* 53 (2006): 224–34.

142. As seen by the *Vita Hilarionis*, for instance; see Susan Weingarten, *The Saint's Saints: Hagiography and Geography in Jerome* (Leiden: Brill, 2005), 132–37; Eleonora Bilancia, 'Il significato storico e politico della polemica contro la magia nella Vita Hilarionis di Girolamo', *Sanctorum* 7 (2010), 155–71.
143. On public performers and social disrepute generally, see Catherine Edwards, 'Unspeakable Professions: Public Performance and Prostitution in Ancient Rome', in *Roman Sexualities*, ed. Judith P. Hallett and Marilyn Skinner (Princeton, NJ: Princeton University Press, 1997), 66–95; Hartmut Leppin, 'Between Marginality and Celebrity: Entertainers and Entertainments in Roman Society', in *The Oxford Handbook of Social Relations in the Roman World*, ed. Michael Peachin (Oxford: Oxford University Press, 2011), 660–78.
144. Leppin, 'Between Marginality', 661.
145. *panem et circenses*: Juvenal, *Satires* 10.75–81. See further Zara Martirosova Torlone, 'Writing Arenas. Roman Authors and Their Games', in Christesen and Kyle, *A Companion to Sport*, 412–21; Kathryn Mammel, 'Ancient Critics of Roman Spectacle and Sport', in Christesen and Kyle, *A Companion to Sport*, 603–16.
146. Tertullian, *On the Spectacles* 22.3–4.
147. For instance, Leppin, 'Between Marginality', 664; Bell, 'Roman Chariot-Racing', 496; Sophie M.J. Remijsen, '"Blushing in Such Company"? The Social Status of Athletes in Late Antiquity', in *Shifting Cultural Frontiers in Late Antiquity*, ed. David Brakke, Deborah Deliyannis, and Edward Watts (Farnham, VT: Ashgate, 2012), 199–209; at 206.
148. Horsmann, *Die Wagenlenker*, esp. 46–7, 55–6. See also the important review of Horsmann's work by Wolfgang Decker in *Nikephoros* 14 (2001), 287–311 (reprinted in part as '*Furor Circensis*', *Journal of Roman Archaeology* 14 (2001), 499–510).
149. Andreas Wacke, '*Gloria* and *virtus* als Ziel athletischer Wettkämpfe und die Unbescholtenheit der Athleten sowie die erlaubten Sportwetten nach römischen Rechtsquellen', in *Kultur(en) Formen des Alltäglichen in der Antike*, Nummi et Litterae 7, ed. Peter Mauritsch and Christoph Ulf (Graz: Grazer Universitätsverlag, 2013), 193–236; Gamauf, '*Pro virtute certamen*'.
150. The suitability of the elite appearing or performing in public in a circus is, of course, a different matter, on which see Gerhard Horsmann, 'Augustus als Sittenverderber? Zur Rolle des princeps bei den standeswidrigen Auftritten von Rittern und Senatoren in der frühen Kaiserzeit', in *Gesellschaft und Sport als Feld wissenschaftlichen Handelns: Festschrift für Manfred Messing*, Mainzer Studien zur Sportwissenschaft 25, ed. Norbert Müller and Dieter Voigt (Niedernhausen: Schors, 2007), 121–39; Ibid, 'Public Performances by Senators and Knights and the Moral Legislation of Augustus', in Nelis-Clément and Roddaz, *Le cirque romain*, 475–79.
151. Sinclair W. Bell, Jean-Charles Balty, and Frederik Grosser, 'Charioteer Statues, Public Performance, and Social Infamy in Imperial Rome', forthcoming. I am grateful to my co-authors for permission to summarize parts of our forthcoming paper here.
152. See further Wolfgang Decker, 'Beinamen antiker Athleten,' in Mauritsch et al., *Antike Lebenswelten*, 161–73.
153. Together with other inscribed objects, these inscriptions provide the names of 229 drivers. While the legal status of more than half of these is uncertain, the onomastic evidence confirms that 66 were *servi* (slaves), 14 were *liberti* (freedmen), 13 were *servi* or *liberti*, and that only one was an *ingenuus* (a freeborn citizen).
154. *CIL* 6.37836 = *ILS* 9349. DRVSO CAESAR[E] / C(AIO) NORBANO FLACCO C[O](N)S(VLIBVS) / MENANDER, C(AI) COMINI MACRI / ET C(AI) CORNELI CRISPI BIGARIVS VINCIT / LVDIS MART(IIS), Q(VOS) F(ECERVNT) CO(N)S(VLES), EQ(VIS) BASILISCO, RVSTICO; / LVDIS VICTOR(IAE) CAESAR(IS), Q(VOS) F(ECERUNT) C(AIVS) CORNELIVS SCIP(IO), / Q(VINTVS) POMPEIVS MACER, PR(AETORES), EQ(VIS) HISTRO, CORACE. Given its format, I presume this to be a victory tablet, probably set up in a faction house. See further Horsmann, *Die Wagenlenker*, 252 f. no. 133; Charles L. Babcock, '4.1. The Inscriptions,' in Larissa

Bonfante, Helen Nagy, and Jacquelyn Collins-Clinton, ed., *The Collection of Antiquities of the American Academy in Rome*, Memoirs of the American Academy in Rome. Supplementary Volumes Vol. 11 (Ann Arbor: University of Michigan Press, 2015), 90–104; at 241–42 no. 172 (with earlier literature), fig. 169.

155. That is, if he is the same Menander mentioned in *CIL* 6.10046, the Augustan *tabella columbarii* which describes the *familia quadrigaria* of T. Ateius Capito, then he would have been a member of their *factio prasina*.

156. As Jean-Paul Thuillier has thoroughly demonstrated: '*Auriga/Agitator*: de simples synonymes?', *Revue de philologie, de littérature et d'histoire* 61, 1987, 233–7; reprinted in Thuillier, *Allez les rouges!*, 107–11, and discussed further in Thuillier, 'Circensia', 129–30.

157. See further Horsmann, *Die Wagenlenker*, nos. 30–3, 158–60, 243–46, 271, 275, 294.

158. Eutyches: *CIL* 6.10065a; Helenus: *CIL* 2.4314 = *ILS* 5299.

159. Gian Luca Gregori, ed., *La collezione epigrafica dell'Antiquarium Comunale del Celio*, Tituli 8 (Rome: Quasar, 2001), 147–50 no. 52 = *AE* 2001, 268 (S. Evangelisti); Jean-Paul Thuillier, 'Du cocher à l'âne', *Revue Philologique* 78 (2004) 311–4, and Idem, 'L'organisation des *ludi circenses*', 178, 181.

160. Nigel B. Crowther, 'Observations on Boys, Girls, Youths and Age Categories in Roman Sports and Spectacles', *The International Journal of the History of Sport* 26, no. 2 (2009): 343–64, at 356; reprinted in Zinon Papakonstantinou, ed., *Sport in the Cultures of the Ancient World. New Perspectives* (London: Routledge, 2009), 195–216. Compare also Meijer, *Chariot Racing*, 145.

161. Crowther, 'Observations on Boys', 353. For further considerations on children and athletic competition, see Mark Golden, 'The Second Childhood of Mark Golden', *Childhood in the Past* 9, no. 1 (2016), 4–18.

162. See further Laura Banducci, 'Mourning Deaths and Endangering Lives: Etruscan Chariot Racing between Symbol and Reality', *Papers of the British School at Rome* 82 (2004): 1–39; also the section on 'horse racing' in Jean-Paul Thuillier, 'Etruscan Spectacles: Theater and Sport', in *The Etruscan World*, ed. Jean MacIntosh Turfa (Abingdon: Routledge, 2013), 831–40; and, more broadly, the section 'Le sport en Étrurie' (13–62) in Thuillier, *Allez les rouges!*.

163. Knife handles: Christian Landes, 'Le Circus Maximus et ses produits dérivés', in Nelis-Clément and Roddaz, *Le cirque romain*, 413–30.

164. Based on surviving representations, these helmets fit tightly around their heads and were designed for significant impact; thus, for this and other reasons, a marble head now in the Louvre does not represent the 'head of a charioteer', despite its identification as such by Jean-Paul Thuillier, *Sport im antiken Rom* (Darmstadt: Primus, 1999), fig. 106; Meijer, *Chariot Racing*, fig. on p. 87. See further Sinclair Bell, 'The Face of Victory? A Misidentified Head in Rome and the "Problem" of Charioteer Portraits', in Nelis-Clément and Roddaz, *Le cirque romain*, 393–411.

165. See further Jean-Paul Thuillier, 'Le cocher romain, son habit et son couteau', *Nikephoros* 12 (1999), 205–11; and now Sinclair W. Bell, 'The Costume of the Roman Charioteer: New Insights from a Statue Fragment in Hadrumentum (Sousse) and Related Sources', *Boreas. Münstersche Beiträge zur Archäologie* (2020/in press).

166. *Contra* Cristiana Zaccagnino, who argues that: 'Numeroso stele funerarie ci informano che il defunto era un auriga che trovò la morte in un incidente incorso durante una competizione'; see '*Totam hodie Romam circus capit*: le corse dei carri e i suoi protagonist nell'antica Roma', in Lorenza Camin and Fabrizio Paolucci, ed., *A cavallo del tempo: L'arte di calvalcare dall'Antichità al Medioevo, Catalogo mostra Firenze, Galleri degli Uffizi, Giardino di Boboli, Limonaia, 26 giugno–14 ottobre 2018* (Livorno: Sillabe, 2018), 126–37, at 133. In fact, this is very rarely stated, and the only funerary inscription (*CIL* 2.4314 = *ILS* 5299) that she cites as evidence specifically states that he died of an incurable *intestinal illness*; see below.

In this context, three inscriptions for charioteers are exceptional: (1) the metrical epitaph for C. Iulius Camma[rus?], who is said to have perished in a race: *CIL* 8.16566; Horsmann, *Die Wagenlenker*, 188–89 nr. 27; (2) a short poem in Greek beneath the Latin inscriptions for two brothers M. Aurelius Polynices Macarius and M. Aurelius Mollicius Tatianus speaks of how '… took them, glorying in the circuses, too fast to fate': *CIL* 6.10049 = *ILS* 5286; Horsmann, *Die Wagenlenker*, 253–55 (Tatianus), 269–70 nr. 162 (Macarius); 'M. AURELII POLYNICIS ET M. AURELII MOLLICII TATIANI SEPULCRA', in Adriano La Regina, ed., *Lexicon Topographicum Urbis Romae: Suburbium, Vol. 1: A-B* (Rome: Quasar, 2001), 190–91 (Gabriella Bevilacqua).

167. For instance: (1) M. Aurelius Mollicius Tatianus, age 20: *CIL* 6.10049 b.c; (2) Aelius Hermeros, age 23: *CIL* 2.3181; (3) Crescens, age 23: *CIL* 6.10050 = *ILS* 5285; (4) Hyla, age 25: *CIL* 6 37835; (5) Anonymous, age 25: *CIL* 6.10055 [= *CIL* 6.33938 = *ILS* 5284]; (6) Flavius Scorpus, age 27: *CIL* 6.10048 (7); M. Aurelius Polynices Macarius, age 29: *CIL* 6.10049 a.c; (8) M. Nutius Aquilius, age 35: *CIL* 6.10065a.
168. Pliny, *Natural History* 28.237.
169. *ut auriga indoctus e curru trahitur opteritur laniatur eliditur*: a fragment preserved by Nonius and attributed to Cicero, *On the Republic* 2.68.
170. *ussere ardentes intus mea viscera morbi*: *CIL* 2.4314. See further Horsmann, *Die Wagenlenker*, 215 nr. 74.
171. Martial, *Epigrams* 7.7.9: *magni turba … Circi*.
172. See further Siri Sande, 'Famous Persons as Bringers of Good Luck', in *The World of Ancient Magic: Papers From the First International Samson Eitrem Seminar at the Norwegian Institute at Athens 4–8 May 1997*, ed. David Jordan, Hugo Montgomery, and Einar Thomasse, Papers From the Norwegian Institute at Athens 4 (Bergen: The Norwegian Institute at Athens, 1999), 227–38.
173. Hugues Savay-Guerraz and Kathy Sas, 'Les couleurs du cirque', in *Schone schijn: Brillance et prestige. Romeinse juweelkunst in West-Europa. La joaillerie romaine en Europe occidentale*, ed. Kathy Sas and Hugo Thoen (Leuven: Peeters, 2002), 66–70. On circus gems see now Sébastien Aubry, 'Les courses de chars sur les intailles romaines: inscriptions, variantes et diffusion', in N. Badoud, ed., *Philologos Dionysios. Mélanges offerts au professeur Denis Knoepfler, Recueil de travaux publiés par la Faculté des Lettres et sciences humaines de l'Université de Neuchâtel 56* (Geneva: Librairie Droz, 2011), 639–71.
174. For instance, Jutta Ronke, 'Ein Wagenfahrer-Ring aus Nürtingen. Glücksbringer oder Fanartikel?' *Denkmalpflege in Baden-Württemberg* 29 (2000): 271–75; Paul Fontaine, 'La voix des supporters. Une relecture du gobelet inscrit de Couvin à décor de course de chars, seconde moitié du Ier siècle apr. J.-C.', in *D'Ennion au Val Saint-Lambert. Le verre soufflé-moulé. Actes des 23e Rencontres de l'Association française pour l'archéologie du verre, colloque international, Bruxelles-Namur, 17–19 octobre 2008, Scientia Artis 5*, ed. Chantal Fontaine-Hodiamont, Catherine Bourguignon, and Simon Laevers (Brussels: Institut Royal du Patrimoine Artistique, 2010), 113–18.
175. Richard L. Gordon, 'Fixing the Race: Managing Risks in the North African Circus', in *Contesti magici = Contextos màgicos*, ed. Marina Piranomonte and Francisco Marco Simón (Rome: De Luca Editori D'Arte, 2012), 47–74, with full literature; Jean-Paul Thuillier, 'Factions du cirque et propriétaires de haras dans l'Espagne romaine', *Nikephoros* 26 (2013), 207–25; more broadly see Daniela Urbanová, *Latin Curse Tablets of the Roman Empire*, Innsbrucker Beiträge zur Kulturwissenschaft (Innsbruck: Institut für Sprachen und Literaturen der Universität Innsbruck, 2018). Consult Peter Mitchell's essay in this collection for discussion of the use of protective medicines for enhancing equine performance and combating oppositional interference in the context of Native North America.
176. Betting was rife: Epictetus 1.9.27; Martial, *Epigrams* 11.1.15; Petronius, *Satyricon* 70.13; Tertullian, *On the Spectacles* 16.1. For betting on horse racing in other contexts, see Christiane Eisenberg's and Peter Mitchell's essays in this collection.

177. For example, *CIL* 6.10057: 'Aurelius Heraclides, charioteer for the Blues and trainer for the Blues and Greens.'
178. On this moneybox, see Giulia Baratta, '*De brevissimis loculis patrimonium grande profertur* (Tert. *cult. fem.* 1, 91, 19): i salvadanai', *Sylloge Epigraphica Barcinonensis* 10 (2012): 169–93, especially 180–81 nr. 1, figs. 8a-b.
179. Juvenal, *Satires* 7.112–14; 7.243. However, since most charioteers were probably slaves or former slaves (freedmen) and since slaves could not *de iure* accumulate property, their owners would have received the entirety of the prize money, of which the slave would have received a portion in the form of a *peculium* until their manumission. See further Anne Kolb and Joachim Fugmann, *Tod in Rom. Grabinschriften als Spiegel römischen Lebens* (Mainz: Philipp von Zabern, 2008), 180–4 no. 8, at 182 (discussing the charioteer Crescens: *CIL* 6.10050). On the *peculium* generally, see Heinz Heinen et al., ed., *Handwörterbuch der antiken Sklaverei* (Stuttgart: Steiner Verlag, 2012), s.v. 'Peculium' (Richard Gamauf).
180. As David Matz suggests, the Red faction likely paid for the plaque; see *Greek and Roman Sport: A Dictionary of Athletes and Events from the Eighth Century B.C. to the Third Century A.D.* (Jefferson, NC: McFarland, 1991), 120.
181. *CIL* 6.10048 = *ILS* 5287. See recently Robert Sablayrolles, 'Un "pro" chez les Rouges: le fabuleux destin du cocher Dioclès', in *D'Orient et d'Occident: mélanges offerts à Pierre Aupert*, Mémoires 19, ed. A. Bouet (Bordeaux: Ausonius, 2008), 295–304; Jean-Paul Thuillier, 'Sur le lexique des jeux du cirque', in *Polyphonia Romana: Hommages à Frédérique Biville*, Série Spudasmata 155, 2 vols., ed. Alessandro Garcea, Marie-Karine Lhommé, and Daniel Vallat (Hildesheim: Olms, 2013), vol. 1: 219–27.
182. Peter Struck, 'Greatest of All Time', *Lapham's Quarterly: Blog* (August 2, 2010) https://www.laphamsquarterly.org/roundtable/greatest-all-time (last accessed March 30, 2020).
183. *CIL* 6.10047 = *ILS* 5285.
184. Diocles, Scorpus, and Musclosus in *CIL* 6.10048 = *ILS* 5287.
185. Though not a *milliarius*, the charioteer Fuscus (*CIL* 6.33950) calls attention to the fact that '[h]e was the first of all the drivers to win on the first day he raced', showing that such distinctions were widely prized.
186. *CIL* 6.10047, where Calpurnianus refers to his participation in the 'quinquennial sacred games', the *Agon Capitolinus* instituted by Domitian in 86 A.D.
187. See Mark Golden, *Greek Sport and Social Status* (Austin: University of Texas Press, 2008), esp. 74–9 ('Gladiators' Claims'); Kathleen M. Coleman, 'Defeat in the Arena', *Greece & Rome* 66, no. 1 (2019): 1–36.
188. Seneca, *Epistles* 30.13; Sidonius Apollinaris, *To Consentius* 23.371f. Unskillful turn: Ovid, *Amores* 3.2.69 f.
189. *Letter to Nigrinus*, 29.1, transl. A.M. Harmon.
190. For instance, Statius, *Thebaid* 6; Vergil, *Aeneid* 2.476–77 and *Georgics* 1.272–73. See further Alberto Pavan, 'Consenzio o le virtù dell'auriga. Una rielaborazione della gara delle quadrighe di Stat. *Theb.* VI in Sid. Ap. *carm.* 23 *ad Consentium* 307–427', *Aevum Antiquum* 5 (2005), 227–50; Giuseppe Aricò, 'Pulchrae certent de laude coronae: alcune note sull'episodio dei ludi in Silio Italico XVI 303 ss', *Aevum Antiquum* 6 (2006), 133–46; Leandro Polverini, 'La corsa dei carri *nell'Eneide*', in Mauritsch et al., *Antike Lebenswelten*, 121–27; Jean-Paul Thuillier, 'Manilius (*Astronomica*, 5.67 sq.): le cocher et les agitateurs', in Nelis-Clément and Roddaz, *Le cirque romain*, 459–67; Stefano Rebeggiani, 'The Chariot Race and the Destiny of Empire in Statius' *Thebaid*', *Illinois Classical Studies* 38 (2013): 187–206.
191. Galen, *On the Causes of Respiration* (Kühn) 6.469.
192. Ammianus Marcellinus 28.4.28.
193. Suetonius, *Nero* 22.1.
194. Langner, *Antike Graffitizeichnungen*; Peter Keegan, 'Reading the "Pages" of the *Domus Caesaris: Pueri Delicati*, Slave Education, and the Graffiti of the Palatine Paedagogium',

in *Roman Slavery and Roman Material Culture*, ed. Michele George (Toronto: University of Toronto Press, 2013), 69–98, esp. 89–91.
195. Petronius, *Satyricon*, 70.13.
196. As Kimberly Cassibry argues, the shortened forms of the exclamations on glass cups likely encouraged their consumers to 'participate actively in the creation of the cups' verbal component' and in this way to channel and perpetuate their experience of the games into contexts outside the arenas themselves. See further Kimberly Cassibry, 'Spectacular Translucence: The Games in Glass', *Theoretical Roman Archaeology Journal* 1.1, no. 5 (2018): 1–20; at 7. See also Giulia Baratta, 'Non solo immagini: didascalie e testi epigrafici nelle serie ceramiche di Gaivs Valerivs Verdvllvs con scene di gare circensi e combattimenti gladiatori', in *Le iscrizioni con funzione didascalico-esplicativa. Committente, destinatario, contenuto e descrizione dell'oggetto nell'instrumentum inscriptum. Atti del VI incontro instrumenta inscripta, Aquileia (26-28 marzo 2015)*, ed. Maurizio Buora and Stefano Magnani (Trieste: Editreg di Fabio Prenc, 2016), 425–38; and Kimberly Cassibry, *Destinations in Mind: Portraying Places in the Roman Empire's Souvenirs* (Oxford: Oxford University Press, 2020/forthcoming).
197. Günther Thüry, 'Ein Fund von Rhônekeramik aus Xanten', in *Grabung - Forschung - Präsentation*, Xantener Berichte 30, ed. Martin Müller (Darmstadt: Philipp von Zabern 2017), 155–67.
198. For images of spectacles as social historical evidence, see Steven L. Tuck, 'Representations of Spectacle and Sport in Roman Art', in Christesen and Kyle, *A Companion to Sport*, 432–37; Zahra Newby, 'Roman art and Spectacle', in *Blackwell Companion to Roman Art*, ed. Barbara Borg (Malden, MA: Wiley-Blackwell, 2015), 552–68. On circus scenes specifically, see Bettina Bergmann, 'Pictorial Narratives of the Roman Circus', in Nelis-Clément and Roddaz, *Le cirque romain*, 497–519; Dunbabin, *Theater and Spectacle*, chapter six; Grosser, *Darstellungen*; Bell, *Chariot Racing*.
199. For recent discoveries and discussions of souvenirs and other small finds, see Yvan Barat and Valerian Venet, 'Epaphrodite et sa "gazelle": un souvenir du *Circus Maximus* aux confins de l'Ile-de-France', *Revue Archéoligue d'Ile-de-France* 1 (2008): 209–14; Franziska Dövener, 'Bronzestatuette eines Wagenlenkers aus Altrier', *Empreintes: Annuaire du Musée national d'histoire et d'art, Luxembourg* 1 (2008): 65–7; Landes, 'Le Circus Maximus et ses produits dérivés'; Erwin Pochmarski and Barbara Porod, 'The Silver *Scyphos* of the Roman Villa of Grünau (Gross St. Florian, Styria, Austria) – Expression of the *Otium* of the Roman Owner of a Villa', *Histria Antiqua* 16 (2008): 23–33; Hugues Savay-Guerraz, 'Les couleurs du cirque', in Armand Desbat and Hugues Savay-Guerraz, ed., *Images d'argile. Les vases gallo-romains à médaillons d'applique de la vallée du Rhône: [exposition, Saint-Romain-en-Gal, Vienne, 2004]* (Vicenza: Graphicom, 2010), 104–15; Constanze Höpken, '*Ludi circensis* auf dem Spielbrett: zu Spielsteinen und Spielbrettern eines römischen Zirkusspiels', *Archäologisches Korrespondenzblatt* 41 (2011): 65–71; Norbert Hanel and Ángel Morillo, 'Kunstreiter (*cursores, desultores*) in der römischen Kleinplastik: zur Identifizierung eines Statuettentyps', *Römische Mitteilungen* 118 (2012): 339–353; Germana Vatta, 'Su una statuetta di auriga già nella collezione Gaspary', *Rivista di Archeologia e Storia dell'Arte* 67, s. III (2012) [2015], 75–93; Markus Strauthaus, 'Die merkwürdige Wagenfahrt. Überlegungen zu einem besonderen Gemmen-Motiv', in *"Man kann es sich nicht prächtig genug vorstellen!" Festschrift für Dieter Salzmann zum 65. Geburtstag*, 2 vols., ed. Holger Schwarzer und H.-Helge Nieswandt (Marsberg: Scriptorium, 2016), 1: 433–41, pl. 54; Giulia Baratta, 'Il circo di terracotta: gli aurighi di Gaius Valerius Verdullus', *Epigraphica* 79 (2017): 207–51; Peter Rothenhöfer, Norbert Hanel, and Michael Bode, 'Blei*cistae* mit Produzenteninschriften aus dem römischen Schiffswrack von Rena Maiore (Sardinien): Arelate/Arles (dép. Beuches-du-Rhône/F) als Umschlagplatz im überregionalen Metallhandel?', *Archäologisches Korrespondenzblatt* 47 (2017): 217–29, esp. 219 fig. 4; Cassibry, 'Spectacular Translucence'; Cassibry, *Destinations in Mind*; Sinclair W. Bell, 'The Social Lives of Circus Statuettes: Spectacular Miniatures in Imperial Rome', in *Toys*

*as Cultural Artefacts in Ancient Greek and Roman Cultures: Anthropological and Material Approaches*, ed. Véronique Dasen (forthcoming); and Sinclair W. Bell and Nathan T. Elkins, ed., *The Spectacle of Everyday Life: Sport and* Spectacula *in Roman Social Practice and Material Culture* (in preparation).

200. Holt Parker, 'Toward a Definition of Popular Culture', *History and Theory* 50 (2011): 147–70; at 153.
201. Pliny the Younger's well-known letter (9.6) is representative of this genre of criticism. On 'hippodrome gardens', see Humphrey, *Roman Circuses*, 568–71; Indra Kagis McEwen, 'Housing Fame: In the Tuscan Villa of Pliny the Younger', *Res: Anthropology and Aesthetics* 27 (1995): 11–24; Ann Kuttner, 'Delight and Danger: Motion in the Roman Water Garden at Sperlonga and Tivoli', in *Landscape Design and the Experience of Motion*, ed. Michel Conan (Washington, DC: Dumbarton Oaks Research Library and Collection, 2003), 103–56, esp. 145–46. Note also Paola Ciancio Rossetto, 'Strutture per gli spettacoli in villa: un "teatro" nella villa c.d. *ad duas lauros* nel suburbio romano', *Orizzonti. Rassegna di archeologia* 19 (2018): 77–83.
202. For ancient athletic crowds generally, see Werner Petermandl, 'Geht ihr aber ins Stadion … Ein althistorischer Blick auf das Sportpublikum wie es war, wie es ist und wie es immer sein wird', in *Das Stadion. Geschichte, Architektur, Politik, Ökonomie*, ed. Matthias Marschik, Rudolf Müllner, Georg Spitaler, and Michael Zinganel (Vienna: Turia and Kant, 2005), 127–52; Bettina Kratzmüller, '"Show Yourself to the People!" Ancient Stadia, Politics and Society', in *Stadium Worlds: Football, Space and the Built Environment*, ed. Sybille Frank and Silke Steets (London: Routledge, 2010), 36–55; Michael Krüger, 'Ein kurze Kulturgeschichte der Sportzuschauer', in *Sportzuschauer*, ed. Bern Strauß (Göttingen: Hogrefe, 2012), 19–39, esp. 24–8 (my thanks to Frederik Grosser for this reference); and Peter J. Miller, 'Segregation, Inclusion, and Exclusion', in Christesen and Stocking, *A Cultural History of Sport*.
203. Juvenal, *Satires* 5.142 ff. On the socialization of children and youth into the Roman culture of leisure and games, see Fanny Dolansky, 'Roman Boys and Girls at Play. Realities and Representations', in *Children and Everyday Life in the Roman and Late Antique World*, ed. Christian Laes and Ville Vuolanto (London and New York: Routledge, 2017) 116–36, esp. 122 on horse riding; Michael Carter, '*Armorum studium*: Gladiatorial Training and the Gladiatorial Ludus', in Bell and Ripat, *Sport and Social Identity*, 119–31.
204. Circus sarcophagi: Eve D'Ambra, 'Racing with Death: Circus Sarcophagi and the Commemoration of Children in Roman Italy', in *Constructions of Childhood in Ancient Greece and Italy*, *Hesperia* Supplements 41, ed. Ada Cohen and Jeremy Rutter (Princeton, NJ: The American School of Classical Studies at Athens, 2007), 339–51; Sinclair Bell, 'Roman Circus Sarcophagi: New, Lost and Rediscovered Finds', *Boreas. Münstersche Beiträge zur Archäologie* 30 (2009): 127–40, John H. Oakley, 'Roman Sarcophagi in the Toledo Museum of Art', in *Approaching the Ancient Artifact: Representation, Narrative, and Function*, ed. Amalia Avramidou and Denise Demetriou (Berlin: De Gruyter, 2014), 197–208; and Bell, *Chariot Racing*.
205. *CIL* 6.8628 = *ILS* 1679. DIIS MANIBVS / T(ITI) FLAVI, AVG(VSTI) LIB(ERTI), / ABASCANTI / A COGNITIONIBVS. / FLAVIA HESPERIS / CONIVGIS SVO / BENE MERENTI / FECIT / CVIVS DOLORE NIHIL / HABVI NISI MORTIS. / SCORPVS INGENVO ADMETO PASSERINO ATMETO. See further Horsmann, *Die Wagenlenker*, 286–88 no. 189; D'Ambra, 'Racing with Death', at 350 with fig. 18.5.
206. His horses are also mentioned at *CIL* 6.10052 (*ILS* 5289): VICIT SCORPVS EQVIS HIS. / PEGASVS, ELATES, ANDRAEMO, COTYNVS.
207. While such tombs and artefacts have long explained by scholars in terms of mechanistic, one-size-fits-all interpretations (such as symbolism or metaphor: for instance, Rebeggiani, 'The Chariot Race', at 191), their diversity of imagery and patrons, disparate contexts, and use over several centuries defies any single explanation; see further Dunbabin, *Theater and Spectacle*, esp. 273, and Bell, *Chariot Racing*.

208. This idea of 'basking in reflected glory', known as BIRG theory in sport sociology, is further explored in D'Ambra, 'Racing with Death', 346–47, and Bell, *Chariot Racing*. See also Maria Granino Cecere, 'Scorpus, *clamosi gloria circi*', *Archaeologia Classica* 51 (1999–2000), 411–2. Alternatively, it has been suggested that Abascantus was his patron: Rosario Moreno Soldevila, *Martial. Book IV. A Commentary* (Leiden: Brill, 2006), 465; see, also, Tafaro, 'Cross-reference', 63.
209. Pliny, *Natural History* 7.168.
210. Paul Plass, *The Game of Death in Ancient Rome: Arena Sport and Political Suicide* (Madison: University of Wisconsin Press, 1988), 40–1.
211. This section updates, corrects, and expands my discussion of Roman horses in Bell, 'Horse Racing and Chariot Racing.'
212. See most recently Carolyn Willekes, *The Horse in the Ancient World: From Bucephalus to the Hippodrome* (London: I.B. Tauris, 2016), esp. 211–220; Lorenza Camin and Fabrizio Paolucci, ed., *A cavallo del tempo: L'arte di calvalcare dall'Antichità al Medioevo. Catalogo mostra* (Livorno: Sillabe, 2018). Note also brief discussion in Julia Kindt, 'Capturing the Ancient Animal: Human/Animal Studies and the Classics', *The Journal of Hellenic Studies* 137 (2017): 213-25.
213. Junkelmann, 'On the Starting Line', 98.
214. Patricia Terrado and Ada Lasheras, 'Caballos para el circo: acerca de su transporte en época romana', in López Vilar, *La Glòria del Circ*, 61–6.
215. Ruth Leader-Newby, 'Inscribed Mosaics in the Late Roman Empire: Perspectives from East and West', in *Art and Inscriptions in the Ancient World*, ed. Zahra Newby and Ruth Leader-Newby (Cambridge: Cambridge University Press, 2007), 179–99, with earlier literature.
216. Joaquín Pascual Barea, 'Interpretación de los epígrafes y de la marca del caballo de una jarra de Tamuda', in *Tamuda. Cronosecuencia de la ciudad mauritana y del castellum romano. Resultados arqueológicos del Plan de Investigación del PET (2008-2010)*, Colección de Monografías del Museo Arqueológico de Tetuán (IV), ed. Darío Bernal, Baraka Raissouni, Javier Verdugo, and Mehdi Zouak (Cádiz: Servicio de Publicaciones de la Universidad de Cádiz, 2013), 393–401.
217. Most recently see Michel Matter, 'Des chevaux du cirque: économie et passions à Rome', in *Le cheval, animal de guerre et de loisir dans l'Antiquité et Moyen Âge: Actes des Journées d'étude internationales organisées par l'UMR 7044 (Étude des civilisations de l'Antiquité), Strasbourg, 6-7 novembre 2009*, Bibl. Antiquité Tardive 22, ed. Stavros Lazaris (Turnhout: Brepols, 2012), 61–72; Roger J.A. Wilson, 'Tile-stamps of Philippianus in Late Roman Sicily: A Talking Signum or Evidence for Horse-raising?', *Journal of Roman Archaeology* 27 (2014): 472–86; and Willekes, 'Breeding Success.'
218. Hyland, *Equus*, 210–14.
219. Matter, 'Des chevaux', 63–4; Wilson, 'Tile-stamps', 485.
220. *CIL* 6.37834; Horsmann, *Die Wagenlenker*, 294–96; 'Iscrizione con elogio per l'auriga Avilius Teres', in Camin and Paolucci, *A cavallo del tempo*, 326–27 no. 59 with figure (Cristiana Zaccagnino); and see notes below.
221. For instance, the inscription for the charioteer Avilius Teres (*CIL* 6.37834), which mentions three mares (Pyrallis, Sica, and Melissa) amongst an otherwise male-dominated list.
222. Junkelmann, 'On the Starting Line', 89; see further Cluny Jane Johnstone, 'A Biometric Study of Equids in the Roman World,' (Ph.D. diss., University of York, 2004).
223. *Natural History* 8.162, transl. H. Rackham.
224. Vergil, *Georgics* 3.118–20; see further Ann Hyland, *Equus. The Horse in the Roman World* (New Haven, CT: Yale University Press, 1990), 214–17.
225. Pelagonius, *The Veterinary Art* I.XX.
226. For instance, the inscription for the charioteer Avilius Teres (*CIL* 6.37834), which lists the *introiugis vicit* by the number of victories, the name of the horse, and its provenance (Africa, Hispania, Laconia, and Gaul).

227. For instance, the funerary stele for the race horse '*Aegyptus, intro / iugo / primo*': 'Stele con dedica al cavallo *Aegyptus*,' in Camin and Paolucci, *A cavallo del tempo*, 55 with facing figure (Elena Pettenò).
228. Richard Gordon, 'Imaginative Force and Verbal Energy in Latin Curse-tablets', in Celia Sánchez Natalías, ed., Litterae Magicae. *Studies in Honour of Roger S. O. Tomlin*, 2 vols. (Zaragoza: Libros Pórtico, 2019), vol. 2: 111–30, at 121.
229. See further J. N. Adams, *Pelagonius and Latin Veterinary Terminology in the Roman Empire*, Studies in Ancient Medicine 11 (Leiden: Brill, 1995).
230. Hyland, *Equus*, 204–5, 224–7.
231. Nemanja Markovic et al., 'Palaeopathological Study of Cattle and Horse Bone Remains of the Ancient Roman City of Sirmium (Pannonia/Serbia),' Revue de Médecine Vétérinaire 165, 3:4 (2014), 77–88; see esp. 85 where the authors write that 'exotoses [splints] are the result of external trauma. Injuries that lead to exotosis are mostly likely caused by training and/or horse races at the Hippodrome of Sirmium.'
232. Anne McCabe, 'Julius Africanus and the Horse Doctors', in *Die Kestoi des Julius Africanus und ihre Überlieferung*, Texte und Untersuchungen zur Geschichte der altchristlichen Literatur 165, ed. Martin Wallraff and Laura Mecella (Berlin: De Gruyter, 2009), 345–73. See generally Veronika Goebel and Joris Peters, 'Veterinary Medicine', in Campbell, *Animals*, 589–606.
233. Marta Darder Lissón, *De nominibus equorum circensium pars occidentis* (Barcelona: Reial Acadèmia de Bones Lletres, 1996), with earlier literature.
234. Lissón, *De nominibus*; see also Alison Pollard, 'Gladiators and Circus Horses in the *Iliad* Frieze in Pompeii's Casa di D. Octavius Quartio?,' *Journal of Roman Archaeology* 31 (2018): 285–302.
235. *Epigrams* 10.9.50, transl. David Roy Shackleton Bailey.
236. *Epigrams* 3.63.11. See further Gerardo Bianco, 'Un antico cavallo di razza nella storia delle gare circensi', *Rendiconti dell'Istituto Lombardo de scienze e lettere* 111 (1977): 313–33.
237. Suetonius, *Caligula* 55 (including the emperor's mockery of the Senate through his plan to appoint the horse Incitatus as a senator); *Historia Augusta, Verus* 6.
238. *Nigrinus* 29, transl. A.M. Harmon.
239. Ammianus Marcellinus 14.6.25, transl. John C. Rolfe.
240. Ovid, *The Art of Love* 1.135 ff., transl. J.H. Mozley; see *Amores* 3.2. On this passage and women in the circus generally: Leandro Polverini, 'Donne al circo', in Nelis-Clément and Roddaz, *Le cirque romain*, 469–73; Tara S. Welch, 'Elegy and the Monuments', in *A Companion to Roman Love Elegy*, ed. Barbara K. Gold (Malden, MA: Wiley-Blackwell, 2012), 103–18; and Agathe Migayrou, 'Des femmes sur le devant de la scène: modalités, contextes et enjeux de l'exhibition des femmes dans les spectacles à Rome et dans l'Occident romain, de César aux Sévères', (Ph.D. diss., Université Paris 1 Panthéon-Sorbonne, 2018) (my thanks to Sylvain Forichon for the latter reference).
241. Juvenal, *Satires* 8.57–63, transl. Peter Green. Novatian, *The Spectacle*, 5.3–4, is another (though lesser-known) text that evokes the partisans of the factions, examining the horses and their history; see *Novatian of Rome, The Trinity, The Spectacle, Jewish Foods, In Praise of Purity, Letters*, transl. by Russell J. DeSimone, The Fathers of the Church (Washington, DC: Catholic University of America Press, 1974); Forichon, *Les spectateurs des jeux du cirque à Rome*, 301 (my thanks to Sylvain Forichon for both references).
242. *De methodo medendi libri XIV* [Kühn 10.478].
243. Pliny, *Natural History* 28.257.
244. See further Susanna Sarti, 'Finimenti sonanti. La musica del cavallo nell'Antichità', in Camin and Paolucci, *A cavallo del tempo*, 112–25; generally, see Daniel Ogden, 'Animal Magic', in Campbell, *Animals*, 294–309.
245. Jocelyn M.C. Toynbee, 'Graeco-Roman Neckwear for Animals,' *Latomus* 35 (1976): 269–75, see esp. 270 on race horses; see also Martin Langner, *Antike*

*Graffitizeichnungen: Motive, Gestaltung und Bedeutung*, Palilia 11 (Wiesbaden: Dr. Ludwig Reichert, 2001), esp. nr. 1390 (nrs. 1390–1404: 'Circuspferde mit *palma*, Kranz oder Pferdedecke').

246. Ammianus Marcellinus 28.4.30 (quoted in full above). See also Christopher A. Faraone, 'Cursing Chariot Horses instead of Drivers in the Hippodromes of the Roman Empire', in Sánchez Natalías, Litterae Magicae, vol. 2: 83–101 (*non vidi*).
247. See further Gerhard Horsmann, 'Zur Funktion des *conditor* in den *factiones* des römischen *circus*,' Nikephoros 12 (1999): 213–9.
248. *CIL* 6.10069 = *ILS* 5295. Top left: AQVILO N(IGER) K(ANVS) AQVI / LONIS VICIT C · XXX / SECVND(AS) TVLIT / LXXXVIII / TER(TIAS) TVL(IT) / XXX / VII. Top right: HIRPINVS N(IGER)AQVI / LONIS VICIT CXIIII / SECVNDAS TVLIT / LVI TER(TIAS) TVL(IT) / XXXVI. Base: D(IS) M(ANIBVS) / CLAVDIA HELICE / FEC(IT) L(VCIO) A<V>ILL(IO) DIONYSIO / COND(ITORI) GR(EGIS) RVSSATAE / CONIVG(I) DIGNISSI(MO).
249. *CLE* 1177 = *CIL* 5.4512. See Edward Courtney, Musa Lapidaria. *A Selection of Latin Verse Inscriptions* (Oxford: Oxford University Press, 1995), 194–95 no. 201.
250. On Roman attitudes towards animals generally, see now Ian Ferris, Cave canem: *Animals and Roman Society* (Stroud: Amberley Publishing, 2018), with earlier literature.
251. On this idea see, for instance, Nigel Rothfels, *Savages and Beasts: The Birth of the Modern Zoo* (Baltimore, MD: Johns Hopkins University, 2002). On the changing understanding and representation of animals in broader perspective, see Linda Kalof, *Looking at Animals in Human History* (London: Reaktion Books, 2007).
252. This section updates, corrects, and greatly expands my conclusions to Bell, 'Chariot Racing' and 'Horse Racing and Chariot Racing'.
253. Mark Golden, Greek Sport, 142, with my emphasis.
254. Remijsen, '"Blushing"', 206.
255. Ibid.
256. Compare now Dietrich Ramba, 'Bestimmung der prägenden Wesenszüge im Sport der griechisch-römischen Antike', (Ph.D. diss., Universität Göttingen, 2014), where he argues that Roman chariot racing meets the same seven benchmarks for the definition of 'sport' as Greek athletics. See also Katherine M.D. Dunbabin, 'Athletes, Acclamations, and Imagery from the End of Antiquity', *Journal of Roman Archaeology* 30 (2017): 151–74, esp. 167, where she tempers Remijsen's view of the interaction between athletes in the *agones* and those in the *ludi*, including the role of the factions as sponsors.
257. Kris Rufenacht, David L. Groves, and Mark Foster, 'An Exploration of the Nascar Fanage', *International Review of Modern Sociology* 27, no. 2 (1997): 87–101; at 97. For a more nuanced study of spectator categories (in the context of modern football/soccer), see Richard Giulianotti, 'Supporters, Followers, Fans, and Flaneurs: A Taxonomy of Spectator Identities in Football', *Journal of Sport and Social Issues* 26, no. 1 (2002): 25–46.
258. The sports stadium-as-temple expression endures: the modern football stadium, for instance, has been recently called a 'multimedialer High-tech Tempel': Christoph Rohlwing, *Fußballstadien als Hysterieschüsseln?: Soziologische Studie zum Verhältnis von Architektur, Raum und Gemeinschaft* (Marburg: Tectum, 2015), 101.
259. Pliny, Letters 9.6. Similarly Martial, *Epigrams* 11.1.
260. van den Berg, 'The Pulvinar', 262.
261. Grosser, *Darstellungen*, passim.
262. Lucy Grig, 'Introduction: Approaching Popular Culture in the Ancient World', in Grig, *Popular Culture*, 1–36 on the framing of 'elite culture' and 'popular culture' as opposing constructs, always to the detriment of the latter; quote from 35, my emphasis. More broadly, see the appropriately idiosyncratic collection by Jeffrey T. Schnapp and Matthiew Tiews, ed., *Crowds* (Stanford, CA: Stanford University Press, 2006).
263. Generally, see Eleanor Betts, 'Towards a Multisensory Experience of Movement in the City of Rome', in *Rome, Ostia and Pompeii: Movement and Space*, ed. Ray Laurence and

David J. Newsome (Oxford: Oxford University Press), 118–132; contributions to Eleanor Betts, ed., *Senses of the Empire: Multisensory Approaches to Roman Culture* (Abingdon, UK: Routledge, 2017); Ellen Swift, *Roman Artefacts and Society: Design, Behaviour and Experience* (Oxford: Oxford University Press, 2017); and *A Cultural History of the Senses in Antiquity*, ed. Jerry Toner (London: Bloomsbury, 2014).

264. Sylvain Forichon, 'Essai de restitution des paysages olfactifs dans les édifices de spectacles de la Rome ancienne (théâtres, cirques et amphithéâtres)', in *Paysages sensoriels: approches pluridisciplinaires*, ed. Véronique Mehl and Laura Péaud (Rennes: PUR, 2019), 147–57. Note that an expanded version of this article is expected to be published by the author as 'Reimagining the Olfactory Landscapes of Spectacle Buildings in Imperial Rome', *Memoirs of the American Academy in Rome* 65 (2020/forthcoming).
265. Especially the work of Jerry Toner, *The Day Commodus killed a Rhino. Understanding the Roman Games* (Baltimore, MD: Johns Hopkins University Press, 2014), chapter five ('Win the Crowd').
266. Heike Delitz and Felix Levenson, 'The Social Meaning of Big Architecture, or the Sociology of the Monumental', in *Size Matters. Understanding Monumentality Across Ancient Societies, Histoire 146*, ed. Federico Buccellati, Sebastian Hageneuer, Sylva van der Heyden, and Felix Levenson (Bielefeld: transcript Verlag, 2019), 107–32; at 108.
267. See recently Nathaniel Coleman, *Materials and Meaning in Architecture. Essays on the Bodily Experience of Buildings* (London: Bloomsbury, 2020), which similarly shifts the emphasis away from building typology to the spectator's experience of the built environment, and Rohlwing, *Fußballstadien*, with a focus on modern football/soccer arenas.
268. Thomas A. Markus, *Buildings and Power. Freedom and Control in the Origin of Modern Building Types* (London: Routledge, 1993), 26. See further Joseph Maran, 'Architecture, Power and Social Practice: An Introduction', in Maran, Juwig, and Schwengel, *Constructing* Power, 9–14.
269. See further Forichon, *Les spectateurs des jeux du cirque à Rome*, with my preface.
270. Juvenal, *Satires*, 11.197.

## Acknowledgements

I am grateful to Christian Jaser and Christian Mann for the kind invitation to participate in the Mannheim conference which gave rise to this paper and volume, for their hospitality at the event, for supporting my travel, and for allowing me to join their editorial team; to Gian Luca Gregori, Michael MacKinnon, and Peter J. Miller for kindly sharing their work and references; to Sylvain Forichon, Frederik Grosser, and Carolyn Willekes for generously sharing their unpublished research with me and for their generous and helpful suggestions on this text; to the eagle-eyed Franziska Dövener for commenting on and greatly improving an earlier version of this text; to Quan Pham for his assistance in improving the text's visuals, and for his help with the production of the volume in which this essay appears; and to the following for assistance in procuring images: Claudia Antonelli (Palazzo Trinci, Comune di Foligno), Christiane Backhaus (Stiftung Schloss Friedenstein Gotha), Angela Carbonaro (Sovrintendenza Capitolina ai Beni Culturali), Maria Daniela Donninelli (Museo Nazionale Romano), Nathan T. Elkins (Baylor University), Dr. Fabricia Fauquet, Dr. Valentina Follo (American Academy in Rome), Dr. Jacob Latham (University of Tennessee), Elena Mortelitti (formerly Lion TV), and Dr. Agnese Pergola (Museo Nazionale Romano).

As I was completing this work, my friend and mentor Mark Golden passed away. As this chapter reflects, Mark's scholarship has long been a source of inspiration in my own. I dedicate this work to his memory, with gratitude for his friendship, his kindness and generosity of spirit, and his wisdom and wit. *Precamur, ut iaceas placide. Nemo tui similis.*

## Disclosure Statement

No potential conflict of interest was reported by the author(s).

## Funding

The research for this paper (which originates from my doctoral dissertation) was supported by grants and fellowships from the following institutions, whose generous support the author gratefully acknowledges here: Baldwin Brown Travelling Scholarship for Classical Archaeology, School of History, Classics, & Archaeology, University of Edinburgh, 1999; Postgraduate Research Fellowship (held at the Archaeological Institute, University of Cologne), Deutscher Akademischer Austauschdienst (DAAD), 2001–2002; The Rome Prize (Dorothy & Lewis B. Cullman Pre-Doctoral Fellowship in Ancient Studies), The American Academy in Rome, 2002–2003; Post-Doctoral Fellowship in Roman Archaeology (held at the University of Manitoba), Canada Research Chair in Roman Archaeology, 2007–2008; Summer Research and Artistry Award, Northern Illinois University, 2009; Research Stipend for the 'Memoria Romana' International Research Project, Max Planck Institute/Alexander von Humboldt Foundation, 2010; Fellowship, Loeb Classical Library Foundation, 2010; Fellowship for Study in Berlin, Archaeological Institute of America (AIA)/Deutsches Archäologisches Institut (DAI), 2011; The Howard Fellowship, The George A. and Eliza Gardner Howard Foundation, 2013–14; Margo Tytus Long-term Fellowship, Department of Classics, The University of Cincinnati, 2015; Research Fellowship (held at the University of Mannheim), Re-invitation Programme for Former Scholarship Holders, Deutscher Akademischer Austauschdienst (DAAD), 2017.

# The Emperor and His People at the Chariot Races in Byzantium

David Alan Parnell

**ABSTRACT**
The hippodrome, where Byzantine chariot races took place, was central to the relationship between the emperor and his people. They all watched races and cheered for their favorite racing teams, with both people and emperors sometimes notorious for their rabid fandom. Some of the direct dialogue between emperor and people in the hippodrome also revolved around racing – for example, which racing team might be 'gifted' a particular skilled charioteer. In addition to conversation about the sport, the people expected the emperor to hear their complaints and requests and even exercised their collective power in the hippodrome to try to topple an emperor on occasion. The emperor showed up, despite the potential danger of the peoples' anger, because this dialogue with the spectators was an important part of the legitimization of his power. To refuse to attend the races would have been to cut himself off from the people, which would have been considered unacceptable and caused him even more serious problems. Among many examples of this phenomenon, the dialogue between Emperor Anastasius and the people in the hippodrome in 512 stands out (John Malalas, *Chronographia* 16.19).

One could make a simple observation that the history of chariot racing in the Byzantine Empire is a story of ever-increasing government control and manipulation of the sport for the purpose of advertising the glory of the reigning emperor. Like many one-sentence summaries of significant historical processes, this one contains elements of truth, a great deal of simplification, and leaves out some important caveats. This observation is useful as a starting point for exploring some of the purposes of chariot racing within the Byzantine Empire and explaining the evolution and apparent decline in popularity of the spectacle. The elements of Byzantine chariot racing – from its technical details to the physical space utilized and even the organization of the sport – point to the importance of the relationship between the emperor and the spectators at these events. This relationship remained crucial to the operation of government through centuries of the Byzantine Empire. The core interaction between emperor and spectators becomes clear when examining recent scholarship on the nature of the Byzantine political system alongside what is known of the details of chariot racing. The emperors' primary goal in taking over the administration of the sport was not merely to advertise their glory but to maintain a channel of communication to the Byzantine people that both people and emperor valued.

## Byzantine Chariot Racing

By the fifth century, Roman-style chariot racing was the empire's most popular spectator sport, having eclipsed gladiatorial fights, wild beast hunts, and Greek-style chariot racing.[1] The rules of chariot racing remained essentially the same as in the earlier Roman imperial period.[2] Races were always held on special event days, during which there would be between 8 and 24 separate races. Within each race, four chariots each pulled by a team of four horses would compete. The four teams were delineated by the traditional colors of the sport: Blue, Green, White, and Red. As in modern races, the chariots began in starting boxes whose gates were opened at the same moment. Again, as in modern races, the first chariot to cross the finish line after a lap around the track was crowned the winner. A particular favorite variation was the *diversium*, in which the winning charioteer exchanged horses and chariots with a losing charioteer, and then raced again.[3] Victory in this rematch would prove that the originally-victorious charioteer won because of his skill, not because of his horses and equipment.

While the horses typically stayed with their teams, the charioteers enjoyed both geographic and factional mobility, sometimes moving to a different city or a different team.[4] They could have quite lengthy careers, some spanning 30 years. The most popular charioteers were cheered by their fans, and jeered by the fans of their opponents, by name. They were elements of both cohesion and subversion in Late Roman society.[5] Statues honoring them, and inscribed with a record of their victories, might be raised inside the track. Porphyrius, about whom Alan Cameron has written the most important modern account, was without a doubt the most popular and successful charioteer of the sixth century. Cameron lists at least seven statues that fans of both the Blues and the Greens dedicated to Porphyrius, one of which was made partly of gold.[6]

Byzantine chariot races took place in large arenas known as hippodromes. In the fifth and sixth centuries, the heyday of Byzantine chariot racing, hippodromes dotted the lands around the Eastern Mediterranean. They were to be found at cities ranging from Alexandria, Caesarea, Beirut, Apamea, and Antioch to Nicomedia and Thessaloniki.[7] The vast majority of these arenas were designed based on the largest racing arena of the ancient Roman world, the Circus Maximus in Rome. But by far the most important arena of the Byzantine Empire was the hippodrome of Constantinople. Its history starts with Septimius Severus, who seems to have made it part of his rebuilding of the city in around 200. Constantine I probably completed the structure and built his residence, the Great Palace, alongside it.[8] The hippodrome constructed by Severus and Constantine was a standard Roman circus of the era, built in an elliptical shape and containing a track divided by a longitudinal barrier.

The *Kathisma*, the seating area reserved for the imperial family, was on the east side, and therefore was situated between the track and the Great Palace.[9] The hippodrome was approximately 118 meters wide and 450 meters long and had a capacity of about 100,000 people.[10]

The hippodrome was used for chariot racing for most of a millennium and for much of that time it was one of the most important public spaces in Constantinople. The structure was preserved and remained in use until around 1200, although it was finally dismantled during the construction of the Blue Mosque in the seventeenth century. For a thousand years the hippodrome served not only as a site for chariot racing, but also as the backdrop for major political events such as the celebration of military triumphs and the proclamation of new emperors.[11] Just as the structure was located in the physical heart of Constantinople, so was it also a focus for public life in the city.[12]

In the earlier Roman imperial period, up to perhaps the fourth century, the expenses of mounting chariot races seem to have been borne by individual cities and particularly by wealthy citizens within those cities. Much like sponsoring gladiatorial combats or funding an important public structure, holding chariot races was a form of euergetism: a way for elites to spend private wealth to gain public prestige. However, just like these other expenditures, the considerable costs of chariot racing seem to have been gradually absorbed by the imperial government over the course of the fourth and fifth centuries.[13] The mechanisms by which this took place remain unclear, but by the late fifth century, chariot racing was standardized across the Byzantine Empire and its administration assumed by the imperial government.[14] Government administration of the sport is suggested by the report of John Malalas that the charioteer Porphyrius was 'given' by the administration to the Greens in Antioch.[15] This control is probably also implied by Procopius's complaint that Justinian diverted to the imperial treasury the city revenues that had been raised locally for civic needs and public spectacles.[16] It seems clear, then, that sport and spectacle were bureaucratized in the later Roman Empire during the late fifth century. The state organized and paid for what historians have come to call the four 'factions' – the professional racing teams known as the Blues, Greens, Reds, and Whites.[17] Therefore, although there was athletic competition between these teams on the track, there was no financial or business competition since all were owned, administered, and paid by the government.[18]

## Emperor and Spectators

If the government bureaucratized and paid for athletic teams and chariot races, an obvious line of inquiry is to ask why. What was the relationship between the imperial government, the chariot races, and the spectators at the chariot races? What, in particular, did the emperors get out of this arrangement? For two reasons, it is evident that the emperors considered chariot racing to be of substantial import and worth their attention and money. First, as already addressed, the imperial government assumed the administration and cost of chariot racing. Second, at Constantinople, and at every capital used by the tetrarchs in the earlier period

**Figure 1.** Detail of the pedestal: Theodosius offers victory laurels. Obelisk of Theodosius, Hippodrome, Constantinople. Ca. 390 C.E. Photograph: D. Parnell.

(Antioch, Milan, Thessalonica, Sirmium, and Trier), the hippodrome was located directly adjacent to the imperial palace.[19] At Constantinople, there was even a direct entrance via a spiral staircase from the palace to the *Kathisma*, the imperial box at the hippodrome. This allowed the emperors easy access to the hippodrome. As Hartmut Leppin has argued, for the emperor the *Kathisma* was an interface to the city.[20] The existence of these structures implies that the emperors expected to be regularly present on race days and for other events held in the hippodrome.[21] Art confirms this expectation. The emperor Theodosius I and his court can be seen attending the races on a relief panel on the base of an obelisk in the hippodrome of Constantinople (Figure 1). These observations are an indication that the emperors regarded chariot racing and the opportunity to be with the spectators at chariot races to be of considerable importance to the legitimacy and sustainability of their regimes.

Before moving ahead, a few words should also be said about the nature of the spectators themselves. First and foremost, the spectators at chariot races were overwhelmingly men. Women in general were discouraged from attending these spectacles.[22] These men were also overwhelmingly laypersons, as the clergy generally disapproved of chariot racing. They saw the sport as a powerful rival that lured audiences away from the church and was anyway connected to ancient pagan traditions whose persistence concerned them. As one ecclesiastical author put it, a hippodrome was nothing more than a 'church of Satan'.[23] It is worth noting that this clerical disapproval does not seem to have dampened enthusiasm for chariot racing among the people or its support by the imperial government.

Within the hippodrome, these spectators and the emperor had a complex relationship. Of course, part of this relationship had to do with the chariot races themselves. The spectators seemed to have expected the emperors to both pay attention at the races and even to support a favorite color. This went all the way back to the Late Republic, in which Suetonius records the irritation of the people that Julius Caesar had dealt with correspondence during spectator sports rather than watching and enjoying.[24] Most emperors indeed not only watched but also even declared a preferred color. For instance, Justinian overtly favored the Blues, while Anastasius preferred the Reds. Some emperors even drove chariots themselves, as did Nero in the early Roman Empire and Michael III in the middle Byzantine period.[25]

But because of the nature of the setting – in other words, a large public structure that could seat 100,000 people and give them access to the emperor – the relationship between emperors and spectators was not confined to chariot racing. Instead, both sides took the opportunity to address one another about issues not even remotely related to the races that were going on before them. The emperors expected to be able to make important announcements to the spectators and to bolster their image. Their appearance in the hippodrome amounted at least in part to a chance to show off. For example, in 602 the emperor Maurice used heralds to address the crowd in the hippodrome and assure them that the revolt of Phocas was not serious. He then ordered a series of chariot races to amuse the assembled people. The Blues responded by leading a chant in support of Maurice, assuring him (falsely, as it turned out) that he would overcome his enemies.[26] This sort of behavior on the part of the racing fans was invaluable to the emperor because it could instantly boost his own popularity with the rest of the spectators at the event, or at least the appearance of it.[27] In a similarly dramatic moment a century before, the emperor Anastasius appeared in the hippodrome without his crown and offered to abdicate the throne. This grand public gesture quieted his critics, earned him acclamation, and solidified his grip on the throne.[28] In general, it seems that emperors appearing in the hippodrome had an expectation that they would be cheered or otherwise supported by the spectators gathered there.[29] This is one reason why they attended races so frequently.

Of course, the spectators themselves who attended did not merely show up to support their emperor. They frequently hoped to make requests of the emperor for the improvement of some aspect of their daily lives.[30] These requests could and sometimes did relate to chariot racing itself, as when racing fans of all four colors shouted for the famous charioteer Porphyrius in the hopes that he would be assigned to race for their team.[31] It is likely that emperors were often ready to indulge racing fans in their rivalries over popular charioteers, as this made them appear more interested and involved.[32] Just as frequently, requests might have nothing to do with chariot racing and rather focus on issues of daily life. For example, in the early empire the spectators asked Tiberius to return a particular statue from his private quarters to its original location in the baths of Agrippa.[33] In 507, the Green partisans appealed to Anastasius during the chariot races to release prisoners who had been arrested for throwing stones. When Anastasius refused the request and sent in soldiers to attack the partisans, they proceeded to throw stones themselves at the soldiers and the emperor.[34] There was a genuine expectation on the part of the people that the emperors would respond to the petitions they shouted out in the hippodrome. The emperors of course might refuse but, if refusing, they were expected to give a good reason for doing so.[35] When the spectators presented reasonable petitions, and the emperors responded thoughtfully, the relationship between them went smoothly. However, when the system broke down in one way or another, the result could be frustration and bloodshed, as in the Nika Riot of 532.

## *The Nika Riot*

The Nika Riot is the best-known and most famous popular disturbance of the Byzantine Empire. It is unusual in that it was resolved by a massacre with a relatively high death toll and because it is described in depth by several sources.[36] The riot began, typically for the period, with a request related to chariot racing fandom. The partisans of both the Blue and Green factions petitioned the emperor Justinian for the release of some fellow fans who had managed to survive a botched execution. Although such requests typically came from partisans of just one racing team, it just happened that the surviving prisoners were one fan from each faction. Although the riot started typically, it escalated quickly. When Justinian ignored their request for mercy, the partisans rampaged through the city and burned down a number of important structures, including Hagia Sophia. The name given to the disturbance after the event was inspired by the chant *Nika* ('conquer!') that was taken up by the rioters, and which was typically shouted in favor of their favored racing team in the hippodrome. After initial attempts at repression failed, Justinian took steps to conciliate the rioters, but to no avail, and the disorder continued. Justinian then attempted to negotiate with the rioters from the *Kathisma* in the hippodrome, illustrating the importance of the space as one in which emperor and people routinely met, but the assembled crowd disdained his conciliatory remarks and instead acclaimed a new emperor.

Justinian was allegedly considering flight from Constantinople when the empress Theodora intervened and in a passionate speech urged him to remain and take forceful countermeasures. So Justinian ordered military forces under his most loyal generals to mount an attack on the crowd in the hippodrome. This assault turned into a bloodbath, resulted in the death of approximately thirty thousand people, and effectively crushed the riot. Geoffrey Greatrex argues that the Nika Riot had such a deadly conclusion because of a number of grave misunderstandings between Justinian and the rioting people. Greatrex writes that 'Justinian constantly gave off different signals to the populace, at one moment seeming lenient, at another uncompromising'.[37] Mischa Meier, on the other hand, argues that these miscommunications were not merely misunderstandings, but that Justinian deliberately gave mixed signals to encourage a riot that he could crush. Meier notes that communicating with the people was an integral part of the emperor's job, and that Justinian must have been aware that violence might result from his actions.[38] Regardless of whether Justinian's failure to negotiate consistently with the people was accidental or intentional, it is clear that the populace perceived Justinian's interactions with them as unacceptable. With better communication between emperor and people, it is likely that the Nika Riot would have been both briefer and less bloody in its ultimate conclusion.

Emperors and spectators alike then had certain expectations when they met in the hippodrome for a day of chariot racing, and only some of those expectations related to the races themselves. The races also provided a setting for emperors to impress spectators with their glory and popularity and for spectators to make requests of emperors that they ignored at their own peril.

## The Authority of the Emperor

Most modern Byzantine historians would argue that imperial ideology accepted that the emperor was chosen by God and ruled more or less autocratically. In this view, the empire's political ideology 'revolved around two axes: the imperial power and the Orthodox religion'.[39] In the twentieth century, historians used to take this a step further, arguing that the emperor 'dominated and controlled the entire life of the empire' and that the power he wielded 'was vast, unlimited, and subject to no higher authority'.[40] While recent scholarship has played down some of this absolutism in practice, by insisting that the emperor was not quite as powerful as this in day-to-day life, the ideology of this absolutism has remained relatively intact and historians believe it was the predominant political theory of the empire.[41]

Among historians who have written about the role of chariot racing in Byzantine society, and the exchange between emperor and spectators within the realm of chariot racing, these traditional interpretations of imperial ideology hold sway. Thus Alan Cameron, author of the most important book on Byzantine chariot racing in the last fifty years, states that in Byzantine times an emperor 'owed his throne to God, not men'.[42] In this Cameron was merely following established orthodoxy about Byzantine imperial ideology. He argues that in the period of the principate, the emperors attended chariot races in part to show their similarity to the people (that they were also sports fans) and to engage with the people.[43] But by Byzantine times, because of the rise of the ideology of the *dominus* and, as Cameron describes it, the raising up of the emperor 'far above the level of ordinary mortals', the emperors primarily attended chariot races for their own glorification and the consolidation of their imperial power.[44]

This interpretation has become the standard, which is not surprising. Alan Cameron was a towering figure in the field, and his interpretation of the emperor's goal in attending chariot races worked within well-established orthodoxy about imperial ideology. As a consequence, his interpretation is repeated in reference works throughout the field. For example, the entry for 'Chariot Races' in the *Oxford Dictionary of Byzantium* proclaims that chariot races were 'a traditional and indispensable prop of the monarchy, which continued to use them to celebrate important political events'.[45]

Only much more recently has modern understanding of the importance of imperial ideology in the Byzantine Empire been challenged. That challenge comes from Anthony Kaldellis in his recent book *The Byzantine Republic: People and Power in New Rome*. This volume, which may be fairly described as revolutionary, upends this traditional understanding of Byzantine political theory. Kaldellis does not deny that there is considerable imperial propaganda arguing for the absolute rule of a God-appointed emperor. But he encourages historians to understand it for what it is: propaganda that the imperial court wanted its citizens to believe. Kaldellis neatly unravels an alternative political theory based on the power of the Byzantine people. In this theory, Byzantium was a continuation of the Roman *res publica*: 'and its politics, despite changes in institutions, continued to be dominated by the ideological modes and orders of the republican tradition'.[46]

For Kaldellis, power in the Byzantine Empire may be in the hands of the emperor, but it flows to the emperor through the people rather than coming directly from God as in imperial propaganda.[47] When applying this theoretical construction to the relationship between emperor and spectators in the hippodrome, a rather different explanation of that relationship emerges than the one that Alan Cameron provided. If the Byzantine people and government believed that the emperor ultimately derived his power from the will of the people, as in the Roman Republic of old, this puts the relationship of emperor and spectators in the hippodrome into a rather different perspective. As with Cameron's conclusion that the emperor wanted to use chariot races as an opportunity to advertise his imperial glory, the emperor still has plenty of reason to want to appear in the hippodrome, but the reason shifts. Instead of advertising his God-given glory, the emperor uses appearances at chariot races to maintain the lines of communication with the people who provided him with his claim to sovereignty. In either interpretation, the emperor uses the hippodrome and the spectators to cement his power, but in an interpretation influenced by Kaldellis' argument, the people are active agents in this relationship rather than simply a passive audience there to absorb propaganda. Or, as Peter Bell put it, in the hippodrome 'people and emperor were united in a legitimizing bond'.[48]

This line of reasoning actually fits in better with the available evidence. In most of the cases of interaction between emperor and spectators in the hippodrome, the people are not at all passive but are actively involved in an exchange with the emperor. A critical example demonstrating this vigorous dialogue is the episode involving the emperor Anastasius and the people in the hippodrome mentioned briefly above. In 512, the emperor and his ecclesiastical advisors ordered a Monophysite verse to be added to the chanting of the Trisagion in Hagia Sophia. Most of the people of Constantinople seem to have considered this heretical, so this action caused a protest from the people that spilled out of the church and into the streets. Eventually the people made their way to the hippodrome and Anastasius went to meet them there. Far from assembling passively to await a proclamation of the emperor, the people 'assembled in front of his throne, singing together the hymn of the Trinity [the Trisagion] in the catholic version, carrying a gospel book and a glittering cross of Christ, shouting for the instigators of the heresy, Marinus and Plato, to be thrown to the wild beasts'.[49] Anastasius responded by appearing without his crown, promising to do everything the people asked, and swearing to abdicate if they wished it. This response, which acknowledged the people's sovereignty, pacified them and they 'became quiet and begged him to put on his crown'.[50] Having acclaimed Anastasius, the people ended their protest and the emperor was able to arrest some of the instigators. Thus in this instance, the people did not show up to swallow imperial propaganda, but to make their demands known and to receive satisfaction, and the emperor was not able to achieve control of the situation until he worked with the people.

The hippodrome also played a significant role in the Nika Riot of 532. It was to the hippodrome that the rebellious people led the senator Hypatius in order to acclaim him as emperor in place of Justinian, and it was in the hippodrome where the people were eventually slaughtered in great numbers to bring an end to the revolt.[51]

The hippodrome continued to be the site of complex and weighty interactions between emperor and people after the sixth century. In 695, the people deposed the emperor Justinian II in the hippodrome. Stirred up by the general Leontius and the Patriarch Callinicus, the people 'ran out to the hippodrome' and 'led Justinian into the hippodrome, slit his nose, cut his tongue, and exiled him'. And there they also proclaimed Leontius the new emperor.[52] Clearly the people involved in this rebellion recognized the hippodrome as a location for public gathering and a place for expression of popular will. Possibly there was collective memory of the use of the hippodrome for protests against previous emperors, or perhaps the space was simply recognized as a public place for interaction with the emperor because of its continued use for racing events.

This active relationship between people and emperor continued even into the later Byzantine Empire. In 1197, the emperor Alexius III Angelus sought to impose a 'German tax' on his people. This tax was to pay off western foes to avoid an attack. He assembled the people and the clergy to ask them for contributions. While the source does not say where this assembly took place, historical precedent suggests the hippodrome was the likely site. The assembled people apparently took umbrage at Alexius' request and became loud and seditious, at which point the emperor discarded the proposed tax and insisted it had not even been his idea in the first place.[53]

Taken together, these examples demonstrate that the emperors valued their appearances in the hippodrome not merely to boast of their power but for the opportunity it offered to negotiate directly with the gathered spectators, who represented the people as a whole. This was more than enough reason for the imperial government to take over the financing and administration of chariot racing around the whole empire in the late fifth century and then to preserve chariot racing in Constantinople for centuries. Chariot racing was entertainment to be sure, and it no doubt provided a welcome respite from daily work for the people, but the emperor's primary goal was to maintain an open forum with the people who underwrote his sovereignty and who could make or break him through their collective voice.

## The Long Twilight of Byzantine Chariot Racing

Starting in the seventh century chariot racing declined in the Byzantine world generally, probably mostly because it had become intimately intertwined with government finances. The imperial government experienced significant military setbacks in the seventh century with the back-to-back challenges of the Persian War (602–628) and the Arab invasions (from 634). The resulting financial difficulties likely led to the end of racing in provincial cities, for which evidence ceases in the seventh century. Perhaps in these areas the emperors felt it safe to economize on such public entertainments. On the other hand, chariot racing in general and the racing factions of the colors in particular certainly survived in Constantinople, even if in diminished form, until at least the twelfth century.[54] As has been shown, it is likely that the imperial government made the preservation of chariot racing in Constantinople a priority because of the opportunity the races provided for the emperor to speak directly to the people and to gain public proof of their endorsement of his administration.

## Notes

1. Alan Cameron, *Porphyrius the Charioteer* (Oxford: Oxford University Press, 1973), 228–32. On Late Antique Roman spectacle in general, see the comprehensive Alexander Puk, *Das römische Spielewesen in der Spätantike*, Millennium-Studien 48 (Berlin: De Gruyter, 2014). For Greek-style racing, see Christian Mann and Sebastian Scharff's essay in this volume.
2. For racing in the Roman Empire, see Sinclair Bell's contribution in this volume.
3. Alexander Kazhdan et al., eds., *The Oxford Dictionary of Byzantium*, 3 vols. (New York: Oxford University Press, 1991), 1:412; Cameron, *Porphyrius the Charioteer*, 133.
4. For more on charioteers and fans reactions to them, see David Alan Parnell, 'Spectacle and Sport in Constantinople in the Sixth Century', in *Companion to Sport and Spectacle in Greek and Roman Antiquity*, ed. Paul Christesen and Donald Kyle (Malden, MA: Wiley-Blackwell Press, 2014), 633–45.
5. Giorgio Vespignani, 'La figura dell'auriga nel mondo romano-orientale (secolo IV-VII)', *Porphyra* 19 (2013): 13–28, at 24.
6. Cameron, *Porphyrius the Charioteer*, 221.
7. John Humphrey, *Roman Circuses: Arenas for Chariot Racing* (Berkeley: University of California Press, 1986), 442.
8. Hartmut Leppin, 'Zwischen Kirche und Circus: Der Palast von Konstantinopel und die religiöse Repräsentation Constantins des Großen', in *Hephaistos: Herrschaftsverhältnisse und Herrschaftslegitimation. Bau- und Gartenkultur als historische Quellengattung hinsichtlich Manifestation und Legitimation von Herrschaft*, ed. Joachim Ganzert and Inge Nielsen (Hamburg: Archäologisches Institut der Universität Hamburg, 2015), 129–40, at 132; Giorgio Vespignani, 'Costantinopoli Nuova Roma come modello della *urbs regia* tardoantica', *Reti Medievali Rivista* 11, no. 2 (2010): 117–36, at 118.
9. The *Kathisma* was connected to the Great Palace by a spiral staircase, access to which was controlled by bronze doors that could be securely bolted. This feature was employed during the Nika Riot of 532 to prevent rioters from gaining access to the palace. See *Chronicon Paschale*, ed. Ludwig Dindorf, *Corpus scriptorum historiae Byzantiae* (Bonn:

Weber, 1832); Michael Whitby and Mary Whitby, trans., *Chronicon Paschale 284–628 AD* (Liverpool: Liverpool University Press, 1989), 624.13.
10. Kazhdan et al., *Oxford Dictionary of Byzantium*, vol. 2:934.
11. Ibid. See also Michael McCormick, *Eternal Victory: Triumphal Rulership in Late Antiquity, Byzantium, and the Early Medieval West* (Cambridge: Cambridge University Press, 1986).
12. Giorgio Vespignani, 'Costantinopoli Nuova Roma come modello della *urbs regia* tardoantica', 124–7. The hippodrome might also be considered as belonging to the imperial palace complex; see Franz Alto Bauer, 'Urban Space and Ritual: Constantinople in Late Antiquity', *Acta ad Archaeologiam et Artium Historiam Pertinentia* 15 (2001): 27–61, at 32.
13. Alan Cameron, *Circus Factions: Blues and Greens at Rome and Byzantium* (Oxford: Oxford University Press, 1976), 11–13.
14. This has been the accepted view for years, though recently Alexander Puk has argued that the games during this period were supported by a combination of imperial funding and the maintenance of municipal structures (*Das römische Spielewesen in der Spätantike*, 146–7).
15. John Malalas, *Chronographia*, ed. Ioannes Thurn (Berlin: De Gruyter, 2000); Elizabeth Jeffreys, Michael Jeffreys, and Roger Scott, trans., *The Chronicle of John Malalas* (Melbourne: Australian Association for Byzantine Studies, 1986), 16.6.
16. Procopius of Caesarea, *The Anecdota*, ed. H.B. Dewing (Cambridge, MA: Harvard University Press, 1914); Anthony Kaldellis, trans., *The Secret History with Related Texts* (Indianapolis: Hackett Publishing, 2010), 26.6.
17. The most popular racing teams of the sixth century were the Blues and Greens, and this was apparently a tradition that stretched back to the early Imperial period (31 BC–476 AD). The Whites and Reds were secondary or minor teams, which were managed by and usually paired with the Blues and Greens, respectively. While the Whites and Reds had some adherents, these fans were very much in the minority. See Cameron, *Circus Factions*, 50–6.
18. Cameron, *Circus Factions*, 5–73.
19. Cameron, *Circus Factions*, 181; Bauer, 'Urban Space and Ritual: Constantinople in Late Antiquity', 32.
20. Leppin, 'Zwischen Kirche und Circus', 132.
21. Cameron, *Circus Factions*, 182.
22. Procopius of Caesarea, *The History of the Wars*, 5 vols., ed. and trans. H.B. Dewing (Cambridge, MA: Harvard University Press, 1914–40), 1.24.6.
23. John of Ephesus, *The Third Part of the Ecclesiastical History of John Bishop of Ephesus*, trans. R. Payne Smith (Oxford: Oxford University Press, 1860), 5.17. For additional clerical denunciations of racing and other spectacles, see Cyril Mango, *Byzantium: The Empire of New Rome* (New York: Charles Scribner's, 1980), 63–4; and Puk, *Das römische Spielewesen in der Spätantike*, 21–52.
24. Suetonius, *Life of Augustus*, ed. and trans. J.C. Rolfe (Cambridge, MA: Harvard University Press, 1914), 45.1.
25. Cameron, *Circus Factions*, 179. On emperors as charioteers, see Vespignani, 'La figura dell'auriga nel mondo romano-orientale', 19–20.
26. Theophylact Simocatta, *Historiae*, ed. C. de Boor with corrections by P. Wirth (Stuttgart: Teubner, 1972), trans. Michael Whitby and Mary Whitby, *The History of Theophylact Simocatta* (Oxford: Clarendon Press, 1986), 8.7.8–9.
27. As David Jiménez wrote, 'public entertainments were used by the power to be praised and to spread the propaganda apparatus of the political regime'. See David Álvarez Jiménez, 'The Fanatic is a Fan in a Madhouse: Urban Piracy and the Roman Circus', in *New Perspectives on Late Antiquity in the Eastern Roman Empire*, ed. Ana de Francisco Heredero et al. (Newcastle: Cambridge Scholars Publishing, 2014), 332–45, at 343.

28. Marcellinus Comes, *The Chronicle*; Theodore Mommsen, ed., *MGH: Auctores Antiquissimi*, vol. 11 (Berlin: Apud Weidmannos, 1894); Brian Croke, trans., *The Chronicle of Marcellinus* (Sydney: Australian Association for Byzantine Studies, 1995), a.512; John Malalas, *Chronographia*, 16.19.
29. Cameron, *Circus Factions*, 170.
30. Peter Bell does not go quite so far, but describes these moments in the hippodrome as an opportunity for 'the expression of something approaching ... a popular voice'. See Peter N. Bell, *Social Conflict in the Age of Justinian: Its Nature, Management, and Mediation* (Oxford: Oxford University Press, 2013), 145.
31. This from an epigram found on a statue of Porphyrius ca. 500 (Cameron, *Circus Factions*, 48–50).
32. Cameron, *Circus Factions*, 227.
33. Pliny the Elder, *Natural History*, 10 vols., ed. and trans. H. Rackham (Cambridge, MA: Harvard University Press, 1952), 34.62–3.
34. John Malalas, *Chronographia*, 16.4.
35. Cameron, *Circus Factions*, 165.
36. The key primary sources for the Nika Riot are John Malalas, *Chronographia*, 18.71; Procopius, *History of the Wars*, 1.24.7–54; *Chronicon Paschale*, 620–9; and Marcellinus Comes, *The Chronicle*, a.532. The best modern account of the Nika Riot is Geoffrey Greatrex, 'The Nika Riot: A Reappraisal', *Journal of Hellenic Studies* 117 (1997): 60–86. But see also the revisionist account of Mischa Meier, 'Die Inszenierung einer Katastrophe: Justinian und der Nika-Aufstand', *Zeitschrift für Papyrologie und Epigraphik* 142 (2003): 273–300.
37. Greatrex, 'The Nika Riot', 80.
38. Meier, 'Die Inszenierung einer Katastrophe', 290–1.
39. Averil Cameron, *The Byzantines* (Malden, MA: Wiley-Blackwell, 2009), 12.
40. Milton Anastos, 'Byzantine Political Theory: Its Classical Precedents and Legal Embodiment', in *The Past in Medieval and Modern Greek Culture*, ed. Speros Vryonis (Malibu: Undena Publications, 1978), 13–53, at 13.
41. Judith Herrin, *Byzantium: The Surprising Life of a Medieval Empire* (Princeton, NJ: Princeton University Press, 2007), 174.
42. Cameron, *Circus Factions*, 178. While recent historians may not state it so starkly, this theory is still common today. For example, Peter Bell writes of the emperor's 'charismatic authority', which rests on a claimed special relationship with the divine (Bell, *Social Conflict in the Age of Justinian*, 268).
43. For example, in the way Augustus watched the races intently and said he enjoyed them, as a contrast to the behavior of Julius Caesar (Suetonius, *Life of Augustus*, 45.1).
44. Cameron, *Circus Factions*, 181–2.
45. Kazhdan et al., *The Oxford Dictionary of Byzantium*, vol. 1:412. See also Jiménez, 'The Fanatic is a Fan in a Madhouse', 343.
46. Anthony Kaldellis, *The Byzantine Republic: People and Power in New Rome* (Cambridge, MA: Harvard University Press, 2015), xii.
47. Kaldellis, *The Byzantine Republic*, 19–29.
48. Bell, *Social Conflict in the Age of Justinian*, 291.
49. Marcellinus Comes, *The Chronicle*, a.512.
50. John Malalas, *Chronographia*, 16.19.
51. Procopius, *History of the Wars*, 1.24.31–58.
52. Theophanes Confessor, *Chronographia*, 2 vols., ed. C. de Boor (Leipzig, 1883–5); Cyril Mango, Roger Scott and Geoffrey Greatrex, trans., *The Chronicle of Theophanes Confessor* (Oxford: Clarendon Press, 1997), AM 6187.
53. Nicetas Choniates, *Historia*, ed. John Aloysius Van Dieten (Berlin: De Gruyter, 1975); Harry Magoulias, trans., *O City of Byzantium: Annals of Niketas Choniates* (Detroit: Wayne State University Press, 1984), 478.

54. Cameron, *Circus Factions*, 308. On horse racing around Istanbul in the seventeenth and eighteenth centuries, see Tülay Artan's essay in this collection.

## Acknowledgements

I would like to thank Dr. Christian Mann and Dr. Christian Jaser for their invitation to speak at the Global History of the Horse Racing Conference in Mannheim in June 2017. I also thank the University of Mannheim for the financial support to attend the conference. Finally, I thank Dr. Sinclair Bell for editing this volume.

## Disclosure Statement

No potential conflict of interest was reported by the authors.

# Horse Racing at the Ottoman Court, 1524–1728

Tülay Artan

**ABSTRACT**
This study explores horse races in and around the Ottoman capital city, their occasions, locations or participants before the nineteenth century. The competitions we know to have been organized during the sixteenth and seventeenth century imperial festivals were long-distance endurance races run outside the city walls. Courses corresponding to approximately two, three, four or six hours of racing were set out for specially trained horses, and prizes of cash or fine textiles were awarded to winners. In the course of the early 1700 s, cross-country horse racing evolved into more of a private partying ritual for the sultan and his immediate entourage, coming to be routinely observed at the end of the religious festivities, though the layout then excluded attendance by large crowds. The spatial organization of horse racing evolved from temporary installations to a permanent architecture. All the machinery and pageantry of horse racing, from paddocks through parade rings to the theatrics of the race day, a new stage came to be constructed at the Kağıdhane valley, at the far end of the Golden Horn.

Although Ottoman chronicles frequently mention horse races in and around Istanbul, we do not know much about their specific occasions, locations, or participants before the nineteenth century. When it comes to visual evidence the situation is even more frustrating: there are only two Ottoman paintings showing a horse race (Figures 1 and 2), and they derive from imperial festivals that provided the broader context. One of them relates to 1530, depicting a race organized at the end of festivities held to celebrate the circumcision of the three oldest sons of Süleyman I. The other has to do with the year 1582, when the occasion was Süleyman's great-grandson's, the future Mehmed III's circumcision.

This study explores horse racing in the Ottoman capital, from the time when it acquired regular courses during the sixteenth century, to the early 1700s when cross-country racing was systematized as its most popular form. The competitions we know to have been organized during the 1524, 1530, 1539, and 1582 imperial festivals were long-distance endurance races. Such festivities fell into gradual neglect over the first half of the seventeenth century, completely disappeared until 1675, and were

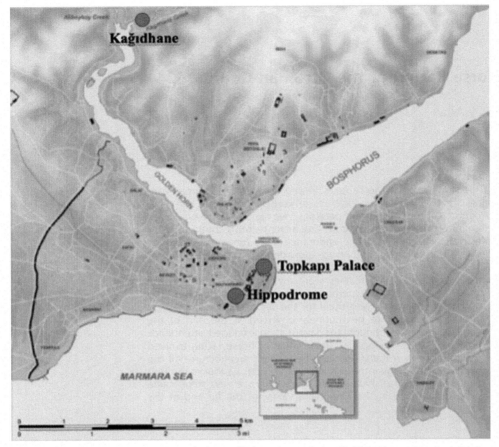

**Figure 1.** Map of the Ottoman capital, the walled-in city and the Golden Horn, showing the location of the Topkapı Palace, the Roman Hippodrome and the Kağıdhane valley. Source: https://www.wikiwand.com/en/Golden_Horn.

then revived after the court returned from Edirne to Istanbul in 1703. Up to that point, this trajectory is very closely parallelled by the history of Ottoman horse racing. Then after the 1720s horse racing in the capital took a new path, and track-based flat racing was introduced. It was also during that time that the spatial organization of horse racing evolved from temporary installations to a permanent architecture. All the machinery and pageantry of horse racing – from paddocks through parade rings to the final theatrics of the race day – a new stage came to be constructed for this drama at Kağıdhane, where a little stream flowed through a valley into the far end of the Golden Horn.

This was where the famous Saʿadâbâd Palace would rise in the first quarter of the eighteenth century, together with all the other dignitaries' kiosks surrounding it.[1] The horn-shaped inlet, the estuary of the Alibeyköy and Kağıdhane streams, geographically separated the historic center of the city (ancient Byzantium, Constantinople and İstanbul) from its parts on both shores of the Bosphorus Strait (Figure 1). The valley lying between two naked ranges of mellow hills along the

Kağıdhane stream was a favourite outing place for the Ottoman sultans. The construction of the new seasonal palace at the mouth of the stream and the numerous festivities, banquets, competitions and races that took place in the palace grounds have been carefully noted by contemporaries, and studied by a number of historians with a focus on new forms of Ottoman sociability and aesthetics. But apart from this sub-urban development, early eighteenth-century chronicles have little to add to our knowledge of the pattern of racing events. They can still be used, however, to tease out the imperial messages that space, scale, and architecture were intended to convey. The first three centuries of a military-charismatic mode of legitimation for Ottoman sultans and the sultanate were accompanied by the prominence of hunting as a prime royal prerogative. The switch, however ragged, from this to horse racing as a public sport can also be read as a reformation in the nature and demonstration of power, as a mirror and model for a new social contract between the court and the people of Istanbul.

## Two Scenes of Sixteenth-Century Horse Racing

The 1530 race was staged in the Kağıdhane valley at the far end of the Golden Horn. The double-folio miniature seen here (Figure 2) presents 'a view of the race held at the time' of the festivities for the late and clearly regretted Mustafa, who would have been sultan if he had not been murdered, as well as his brothers the other princes (*şehzâdeleriyle Sultan Mustafa düğününde vâkî olan koşu teferrücidür*). It is included in the second volume of an illustrated dynastic history titled the *Hünernâme* (Book of Skills), and datable to around 1587–1588.[2] There are no permanent buildings but only makeshift arrangements, reflecting how early this is. The action flows in line with the viewing orientation of Ottoman manuscripts. The riders enter from the right, are attentively watched by two separate groups of mounted men on top of the right folio, with some of the spectators behind them blowing on shrill pipes (*zurna*) to announce the arrival of the contestants. In front of the watching dignitaries are three other mounted men, attending a richly-clad horse without a rider; these are the winners or top finishers of the previous race(s).

Meanwhile the riders continue to race into the left folio and past a magnificent canopy in the upper-left corner, where Süleyman sits on a golden throne, attended by his sword-bearer and water-carrier, his two closest servitors who double as bodyguards. On his right-hand side are his three princes, with a group of youngsters crowding behind them, while on his left-hand side, seated alone, close to but below the sultan is his boon-companion and grand vizier Ibrahim Paşa, with a few officials standing further behind. Five on each page, there are ten contestants in all: beardless young men wearing red or light blue gowns as well as a pointed page-type skull cap. Strikingly, they are riding barefoot, and with neither saddles nor stirrups but only bridles (including headstall, bit, and reins) to control their mounts. Also visible is a turbaned cavalryman, perhaps an umpire, accompanying each group of five on the right and left folios, as well as the unexpected presence of a hound in the lower left foreground,[3] where the race is about to be concluded in front of the sultan's pavilion.

**Figure 2.** *Hünernâme* (Book of Skills). Istanbul, Topkapı Palace Museum Library, inv. nr. H. 1524, 124 b–25 a (1587–1588).

The second painting (Figure 3), on a single folio, was made for another illustrated dynastic history, an account of the reign of Murad III, and is in the second volume of *Şehinşahnâme* (Book of King of Kings), 1592. This sumptuous manuscript has a section on the 1582 circumcision festivities, to which 42 of its 95 surviving

**Figure 3.** Şehinşahnâme (Book of King of Kings). Istanbul, Topkapı Palace Museum Library, inv. nr. B. 200, 85 b (1592).

miniatures are allocated.[4] One of them depicts 'the imperial celebrations race' won by a horse belonging to the vizier Siyavuş Paşa, who, we are told, had been succeded as master of the imperial stables by Hacı (Ahmed) Paşa (*sûr-i hümâyûn koşusunda vezir Siyavuş Paşa kullarının atı geçüb ol hizmete Hacı Paşa varduğudur*). The sultan's tent is pitched in a valley between two hills. Murad III is seated on a stool at the center, with his head turned to two young archers standing on his left-hand side. Also, on that side but outside the tent, there are two other attendants and four more archers bearing lances over their shoulders. On the sultan's right is a dignitary, seated on a stool and attended by two archers.

Mounted men line the hills on both sides. Those on the right include a military band with shrill pipes and drums. More horses are entering the scene from the left; the fact that only their heads appearing from behind the hills suggests that they are coming from afar. In the middle, in front of the sultan's pavilion and right between the two hillocks, are four attendants carrying the prizes – rolls of textiles and purses of coins. Following them is a richly-clad horse, possibly the winner of a previous race. And standing in front of them is an umpire in white carrying a long stick, a symbol of authority.

In the foreground are five contestants, who in this case are racing from left to right. Only half of the leader is pictured, suggesting that he is so fast that the artist could not capture him and his horse in full. All riders are very young and beardless men, their heads shaven except for a scalp-lock. They are wearing sleeveless tunics slit open in front, obviously specially made for riding. Unlike the 1530 painting, their horses are saddled as well as bridled, but they are all barefoot and riding without stirrups.

## No Real Horse Racing at the Hippodrome

These two paintings reflect what should perhaps be considered obvious: urban, track-based flat racing, which hadn't really got going much anywhere else in Europe, was also virtually unknown to the sixteenth-century Ottoman court, whose early preference for long-distance cross-country racing appears to have stood in direct descent from the comparable customs, still prevailing, of the mounted peoples of Central or West Asia. The Hippodrome of Constantinople was built as a typical Roman circus (comparable to the Circus Maximus) under Septimius Severus (193–211), and expanded during the reign of Constantine I (306–337).[5] This was where Byzantine chariot races were staged. Especially after the Nika revolt, the charioteering craze appears to have subsided, so that from the sixth century on the Hippodrome was increasingly given over to other forms of public entertainment and ceremonial. This trend may be said to have continued after 1453, when the Hippodrome became an important ceremonial venue for the Ottomans. Aptly renamed Atmeydanı ('Horse Square'), it kept hosting, and attracting large crowds for, public festivities such as royal weddings or princes' circumcision ceremonies. On such occasions, various equestrian games would be held. But there was no horse racing except for rare and staged demonstrations.[6]

We owe eyewitness accounts of many such events to Celâlzâde Mustafa, a contemporary chronicler. For example, he describes the festivities of 1524, when the marriage of Ibrahim Paşa was celebrated at the Hippodrome and the palace built for the grand vizier on its long north-west side. It was the first of many such grand dynastic festivities to be organized here, right at the center of the historic peninsula.[7] A magnificent throne was set up for the sultan at the new palace palace that rose on the remains of the Hippodrome's western tiers. Field tents captured as war booty in previous battles by Süleyman's ancestors were erected in the Hippodrome across from the sultan's throne. Over June 1–15, jugglers, acrobats and ropewalkers performed; mock battles were staged; every now and then horsemen, too, showed off their skills; music and feasting were virtually continuous. Fireworks were also displayed throughout the last night, after which, significantly for our subject, the partying elite moved from the Hippodrome to the countryside (around two villages named Müderrisköy and Avasköy, in the vicinity of an aqueduct built by Mimar Sinan) to enjoy horse racing and archery.

The following year, the Venetian historian and diarist Marino Sanuto recorded in his diary a conversation between two Ottomans in Venice about the frustration they felt during the Corpus Christi procession. Sanuto quoted one of them as saying that he would prefer tournaments, jousts or races on such festive occasions.[8] Six years later, in Summer 1530 (June 27 to August 25), it was time for the circumcision of the first three sons of Süleyman I – Mustafa (aged 15), Mehmed (9), and Selim (6) – and the Hippodrome was once more the venue for the main body of the festivities.[9] But again, Celâlzâde Mustafa and all other chroniclers note that once the urban celebrations came to an end, the sultan and his retinue moved from the Hippodrome to the countryside, this time to the Kâğıdhane valley, to watch the subsequent horse racing and archery competitions.

When, in Winter 1539, it was the turn of Süleyman's younger son Bayezid to be circumcised, the same pattern of banquets, music and dancing, displays of sugar sculptures and sugar gardens, acrobatic performances, equestrian games, a mock battle, and firework displays was repeated at the Hippodrome. Once more it all lasted two weeks, though unlike the previous summer festivals, it was now over December 6–19. Celâlzâde noted yet again that after the celebrations at the Hippodrome, the sultan moved on horseback to the countryside. However, he made no specific mention of any further races or competitions.[10]

Istanbul had to wait forty-three years for the next imperial festival. In the meantime, Süleyman passed away (in 1566) and was succeeded by Selim II (d.1574), upon whose death Murad III (d.1595) ascended the throne. The circumcision festivities for his son Mehmed (the future Mehmed III, d.1603) were held in Summer 1582, and lasted no less than fifty-two days and nights. Beginning on June 7, they were terminated abruptly on July 24 when a fight broke out between the janissaries and the household cavalry. The sultan and his son quietly returned to the Topkapı Palace; there was no parade, no horse race.[11]

## Kağıdhane: Ottoman Horse Racing Finds its True Home

All this indicates that the sixteenth century court's preferred horse racing venue was moving to the junction of two valleys at the source (or the upper end) of the Golden Horn.[12] The Kağıdhane and Alibeyköy valleys were so named after the two small streams flowing from the north-west and north to the South and into the inlet. Europeans called these two streams the Sweet Waters of Europe. Once known as Barbyses and Cydaris, they had their own place in the mythology of Byzantium. The name Kağıdhane (Paper Mill) is said to have come from Byzantine paper mills that were still visible at the mouth of the stream in the 1550s.[13] Early seventeenth-century travelers noted that the 'little river, formerly Barbyses' was now called 'Chartaricon' by the Greeks (χάρτης, khártēs, papyrus, paper), and 'Chay' (Çay) by the Turks.[14] Here sultans' horses had grazed since the Ottomans' arrival. As stables and paddocks were built and the staff grew, *hara-yı Kağıdhane* (the Kağıdhane stud farm) became the breeding and training centre for imperial horses and horsemen.[15] Archival documents reveal that the sultan's hunting hounds were also kept in the area.[16]

The upper stretches of both valleys were connected to large forested areas. This was a quasi-wilderness frequented by the court for hunting, a sultanic privilege. Hence, parts of both valley were periodically closed to the public.[17] Apart from equestrian sports, there was fresh water for fishing and swimming, while picnicking on the grass was also a favorite court pastime. Since Byzantine and throughout Ottoman times, the Kağıdhane valley constituted a popular excursion spot. Parts of it did not offer much in terms of natural beauty or easy access from the city.[18] Nevertheless, it was these meadows which provided seclusion and refuge from the summer heat for the common people as well as the imperial elite. By the mid-seventeenth century, several such meadows had become individually famous.[19] Evliya Çelebi lauded one in particular, which he referred to by various names, including *çimenzâr* or *Kağıdhane mesiresi*. It was closer to the mouth of the stream (he said) where the water got deeper and wider. When the season permitted, just before the holy month of Ramadan, it was routine for Istanbullus to spend the entire month enjoying themselves in various festivities at Kağıdhane. It also provided shelter and safety for Sufi dervishes and merchants traveling from Asia and Africa, as well as a pleasurable outing for the craft guilds' annual initiation ceremonies. Finally, with rigorous planning, building and planting it was turned into a favorite sultanic garden during the reign of Ahmed III (1703–1730).[20] In a decade over 1720–1730 it was heavily (re)planted with trees transported from the shores of the Bosphorus and the Marmara region.

Every spring, when horses were put out to pasture on Hıdırellez day (May 6), it was here that the master of the imperial stables (*mîrâhûr*) would entertain the sultan to a banquet.[21] On the eastern shore of the Kağıdhane stream, at the entrance of the valley close to the Golden Horn, a decorated wooden kiosk was built and allocated to the *mîrâhûr*.[22] It may have been initially built in the early 1600s – a kiosk depicted during an outing of Osman II (d. 1622), who was a famous *philippa*, has been tentatively identified as Mîrahûr Köşkü.[23] As it came to be frequently visited by later sultans, it was eventually provided with its own landing pier. The sultan and his retinue, departing by boat from the Topkapı Palace or the Karaağaç Garden, would disembark at this point and continue on horseback.

One large stable was situated directly behind Mîrahûr Köşkü. The main buildings of the imperial stables and the stud farm, however, were located on the slopes further up in the direction of the source of the stream.[24] Planted on its shores were cypresses, boxwood, junipers, weeping willows, and eventually enormous plane trees. Meanwhile, a large variety of pasture grass, including some used as remedies for sick horses, have been recorded as growing in the meadows. It was across this whole complex that the Sa'adâbâd Palace was going to be built in the first quarter of the eighteenth century.

From around 1720, Kağıdhane seems to have become the focus of a new interest. First, three marble pools at an excursion spot to the west of the valley, on the hills of Alibeyköy, were repaired and connected to each other; their surroundings were also planted with linden, elm, chestnut, ashwood and more plane trees brought from the shores of the Bosphorus and the Marmara Sea.[25] To the east of Kağıdhane, an imperial kiosk, Hüsrevâbâd (House of the Eternal Hüsrev), was constructed in the Alibeyköy valley. Hüsrevâbâd was not equipped for long stays by the sultan and his *harem*, instead serving as a rest stop for daily excursions and promenades.

In Summer 1722, another imperial kiosk, called Kasr-ı Hümayun or Kasr-ı Sa'adâbâd, was put up on the western shore of the Kağıdhane stream. It was on the southern end of the Cedvel-i Sîm (Silver Canal). This was a newly built waterway that was 1100 m long and 28 m wide, into which a segment of the stream was diverted. Flowing south, the stream was carried first into a trapezoid loop around the three sides of an oval-shaped ring, opening on its longer western side to the village across. From there it continued in that long and straight stretch of the Cedvel-i Sîm directly south to the new kiosk, at which point it rejoined its natural bed and eventually reached the Golden Horn. The canal was lined on both shores with a marble embankment and rounded trees of the same height. The French ambassador is known to have made a gift of forty orange trees for the gardens of the new kiosk.

The following year (1723) yet another kiosk, known as Hürremâbâd (House of Eternal Joy), was erected on the eastern shore of the ring, at the opposite end of the Cedvel-i Sîm and across from the Kağıdhane village. It was here that the stream was first carried into a canal to surround three sides of the oval. In other words, the new kiosk was built on the south-western shore of the canal and was oriented towards the ring, where various games and performances would be held. This kiosk was also called Asafâbâd because it was allocated to the grand vizier and his retinue.

Along the entire western side of the Cedvel-i Sîm, from Hürremâbâd to Sa'adâbâd stretched the *cirid* field, a large rectangular area devoted to a mounted javelin game and other equestrian sports. It was huge, just its shorter side estimated at 200–300 meters. The palace and its gardens were highly visible to the public gaze from the gentle hills surrounding the Kağıdhane valley. Publicly accessible meadows extended along the western side of the waterway and covered the slopes of the hills on the east that formed the natural borders of the valley. Hence it was justly described as an amphitheatre by many European travelers. The term, however, suggests more than just the spatial layout of descending slopes around a narrow riverbed. It seems to refer also to the leisurely activities of the sultan and his court society, watching equestrian games or horse races on the *cirid* field or simply reposing in the small kiosk, Kasr-ı Cînân or Kasr-ı Cenân, as they in turn came to be watched by the commoners.

It has to be noted, however, that this last point is questionable. It is not certain that court society was now visible to a public gathering on the hillside meadows. The festivities organized for the entertainment of the sultan and his retinue were indeed turning public. But other period testimonies insist that the court maintained its control on visibility even in such wide-open areas. There is an engraving by the famous Antoine Ignace-Melling, who served as architect to Selim III, that depicts the *cirid* field and is labelled *Kiad-hané. Lieu de plaisance du Grand-Seigneur*. It was made before the artist's departure from Istanbul in 1802, and published in 1819. The accompanying text claims that the sultan was in the habit of staying at the Sa'adâbâd Palace for as much as a month: 'During that period, it would be prohibited for any man to venture into the area: Bostancıs and black eunuchs stationed upon hillocks would stand guard and send away anyone who approached the grounds. The slightest indiscretion would be punished by death'.[26] The tall, rounded trees that Melling depicted on all four sides of the vast field as well as along the adjoining canal were certainly meant to block the view. Later, these sculpted trees became a place name, 'Topağacı Mevkii', to mark the shores of the canal on nineteenth century maps.[27]

Another problem has to do with the exact location of the race course. Horse races from 1720 to 1728 took their start from Hürremâbâd, and the finishing line was at the imperial kiosk which, as the complex gradually grew, came to be called Sa'adâbâd Palace. But on what side of the Cedvel-i Sîm were they running the west and south-west bank, where the *cirid* field was, or the east and south-east bank, which was where the slopes started? Clearly it had to be the first, and this is further confirmed by the position of the Sultan's Stand, namely the small kiosk adjoining the imperial kiosk at the end of the west bank of the canal.

## Sixteenth-Century Race Field(s) Rather than Genuine Race Courses

In 1524, when the festivities at the Hippodrome came to an end (on June 15), the next day (June 16) horse races and archery competitions were organized outside the city walls (*taşra çıkdılar*).[28] Celalzâde Mustafa says that those horsedealers (*cân-bâz*) who had raised fast horses (*yügrük atlar*), as well as those quick, brave men (*şeh-bâz*) who owned hordes of horses (*hayl ü haşem*), were invited to compete. Rare, beautiful and extremely precious robes of honor were offered as prizes. The sultan rode to the race field in pomp and circumstance, attended by his dignitaries and high-ranking military commanders. 'Post horses' (*menzil atları*) had to ride as far as a station to assume their starting position. As they reached the plain or the race field, they were lined up, and then they started running. They flew as if they were big birds, stretching their wings. The winner, '*rahş* the talented', won a prize and made its owner happy.

Marino Sanuto provides some further details. On June 9, 1524, the Venetian bailo Piero Bragadin wrote to his son that the party gathered somewhere ten miles from the city.[29] There, 250 horses ran for about fifteen miles (roughly 24 kilometers). Fifty won valuable prizes such as cash, robes of honor, slaves, or gold and silver vessels (*vasi*). He also mentions the *gabak* competition where multiple gilded gourds hanging from a pole served as shooting targets. The Venetian bailo noted that there were three poles, each with a *vaso* at the top, and the mounted men who shot arrows at full gallop won prizes of cash or robes of honor. Most importantly, he also added that there were fifty thousand people watching the contests.

While the location of the race field was not mentioned by Sanuto either, Celalzâde Mustafa says that when the horse race was over, they put up a *gabak ağacı* (gourd tree, target tree) in the vicinity of Müderrisköy.[30] This village, later known as Metris Çiftliği, had been given in freehold to Mehmed II's teacher Müderris Alâeddin Tûsî (d. 1482), a scholar from Tus in Khorasan. Müderrisköy is marked neither in modern nor even in nineteenth century maps; however, a water routes and supplies map, dated 1748, marks the village as being near Avasköy. This is an area that is also known as the Shooting Range (*Atışalanı*), which is perfectly consistent with its use as the competition ground for mounted archers shooting at targets on the *gabak* pole.

In Summer 1530, too, as already indicated the festivities came to an end with horse races and archery contests.[31] This time all four period chroniclers – Celalzâde Mustafa, Mustafa 'Âlî, Peçevî İbrahim, and Solakzâde Mehmed – say that these were held outside the city walls at Kağıdhane. The sultan and his entourage arrived on the plain that day, and in Celalzâde's words, the horses, swift as the wind, looked like they were flying over ground. Quick and speedy sorrels (with mane, tail, and legs the same color as the rest of the coat) started from a distance of around a whole stage (or a normal day's journey), and the dust rose to the sky.

Celâlzâde adds that these elite horses were comparable to their superb ancestors. The best and stoutest horse, a fast, unbroken Arab (Bedevî, Bedouin) mare, got the first prize. Its fortunate, prosperous owner received numerous gifts including twenty horses, untold riches, and lavish robes of honor, as well as promotions in rank and status. We have another account of the 1530 race in Mustafa 'Âlî's *Câmi-ü'l-Buhûr Der Mecâlis-i Sûr* [Book of Festivities] of 1582. This was written in verse, and 'Âlî did not elaborate on the horse races organized at that time. But at the end of the *sûrnâme*, as he reverted to prose he summarized the festivities of 1530 day by day, and mentioned that it was on the last day that the court mounted and moved to the open field (*sahra*) at Kağıdhane.[32] The festivities had begun immediately after Ramadan, the holy month of fasting, and lasted 21 days in Şevval. At Kağıdhane, twenty horses competed, and were rewarded in various ways. This information is either confirmed or repeated by other period chroniclers and European eye-witnesses.

In 1539, following the festivities at the Hippodrome, there were races and archery competitions held on 20th December.[33] Celalzâde notes that races being scheduled for 'the next day' (*yarındası koşu olub*), the sultan arrived at the race field on horseback (*koşu yerine vardılar*), but does not mention the exact location. The dignitaries had already prepared their racing horses (*koşu atları hazırlamışlardı*), and they made their way to and ran through the race field (*meydâna koşılub*). Competing horses showed up at the finishing line one by one and collected their prizes. The horse race was followed by an archery competition.

By 1582, a type of manuscript called a *sûrnâme* (Book of Festivities) seems to have attained genre status. There are actually two accounts of the 1582 festival where the poet-authors narrated all daily events, including banquets, performances, competitions, and guild parades and displays: *Sûrnâme-i Hümâyûn* (1583–1588), by an author whose penname was İntizâmî, and the afore-mentioned *Câmi'ü'l-Buhûr Der Mecâlis-i Sûr*, by the renowned historian and statesman Mustafa 'Âlî.[34] The first was illustrated, and lavishly, too, under the direction of the chief court artist Nakkaş Osman, while the second was text only. Furthermore, there is yet another illustrated narrative of these festivities, also prepared under Nakkaş Osman's supervision.[35] This is the court poet Seyyid Lokman's *Şehinşahnâme*, which among its many miniatures devoted to the 1582 festivities also includes our second painting (Figure 2 above). İntizâmî has nothing comparable, while Lokman for his part notes all too briefly that the sultan and his entourage had left the city and arrived at the race field, though even this is valuable because it implies or confirms that there was only one such venue involved.

Meanwhile, however, there are two other episodes during the 1582 festivities which involve horses and deserve attention. First, İntizâmî gives an account of top cavalrymen (*cündi* or *silahşör*) displaying their skills on horseback, including shooting arrows and hitting *gabak* targets, or changing the reins and saddles of their mounts, or even changing horses – all at full gallop. They were masters at fighting in the saddle with swords, lances, javelins or maces. Their almost daily performances generally took place after the guild processions. After they had finished showing off, they sometimes raced (or made as if to race) against each other in what was called a *sipâhi koşusu*.[36] İntizâmî first mention of a *sipâhi koşusu* comes after his description of the achievements of talented cavalrymen from Damascus, Cairo, and even India. Subsequently, a race, he says, took place at the Hippodrome (which İntizâmî refers to as Meydan-ı Esb or Meydan-ı 'Âlî). From his multiple references (including how it was run in pairs), it seems as if this was more of a staged demonstration especially on the part of Egyptian *furusiyya* experts rathen than a genuine race. Nevertheless, his comments on the riders' agility are striking: these cavalrymen, he says, were greedier than burghers who jump from one thing to another (*nev-heves şehirlü*).

Secondly, Venetian agents in the Ottoman capital report that on 30th June the sultan had planned to go to Edirnekapı in order to sacrifice some animals and to watch a cross-country horse race which would be run from Çatalca to Edirnekapı. However, Murad III was warned about the state of unrest among the janissaries because they had not been allowed to participate in the festivities, and he postponed his trip to Edirnekapı.[37] It was only on July 13, the day of the circumcision, that an approximately 30-kilometer horse race could finally take place from Çatalca to Edirnekapı, with the winner receiving a huge prize money of 1000 gold coins.[38] Simultaneously, a great number of sheep were slaughtered and distributed to the populace.

## An Episode of Horse Racing in Edirne

For a multiplicity of reasons that are too complicated to set out here, from 1658 on the sultan and his court took refuge in Edirne, and Mehmed IV visited the capital only sporadically. His sobriquet 'the Hunter' (*Avcı*) reflects a passion for hunting that he developed at a young age. It is possible that he stuck to this arduous pursuit not for pure pleasure but as a kind of substitute for warfare (as by that time it had become too risky for sultans to lead their armies on campaign). Nevertheless, when he was deposed in 1687 by a joint decision of the ruling and religious establishments, among other things he was accused for his indulgence in extended hunting trips and consequent neglect of state affairs.

Mehmed IV's interest in equestrianism was reflected in the 1675 circumcision festival for his two sons, Mustafa (the future Mustafa II) and Ahmed (the future Ahmed III). Simultaneously, his daughter Hadice was married off to his boon-companion Mustafa. There are two major Ottoman accounts of the festivities that lasted nearly forty days. One is the poet Nabî's *Vakāyi-i Hitân-ı Şehzâdegân-ı Hazret-i Sultan Mehmed Gazi*, and the other a *Sûrnâme* by Abdi, who at the time was the scribe to the festival treasurer.[39] Later Râşid, the official court chronicler, noted that upon a *ferman* by the sultan the dignitaries made their own horses available for the race.[40] Four other chroniclers (Abdurrahman Abdi, Hezârfen Hüseyin Ağa, Sarı Mehmed Paşa, and Fındıklılı Mehmed Ağa) also refer to this event at least in passing.[41]

But there is also an eyewitness account by Dr. John Covel, a British clergyman and classicist.[42] First and foremost, Covel was struck by the length of these races: 25 to 30 miles (which, indeed, was extreme by even Kağıdhane cross-country standards). Nevertheless, they drew fields of thirty to thirty-five horses, though Covel also reported that only four horses did the distance in two and a half hours. Significantly, this foreigner operating outside Ottoman cultural norms was able to come up with much fresher observations than the repetitive formulas served up by natives who could not be bothered to provide their future readers with a comparable degree of precision. Instead of just waxing lyrical about speed and stamina, Covel also revolted against the degree of physical cruelty that these races entailed for the horses. These races were 'more to prove the utmost yt a horse can doe, rather then for any pleasure ye spectators can take', he vouched, lamenting that although 'there were very excellent horse indeed amongst them', some were run off their legs and 'were bastionadoe'd in by footmen'. By the end of the race, he wrote, 'some few had so much mettle and strength left as to offer at something which you might call a gallop', and he added that 'it would have greived your soul to have seen them so miserably hackney'd of of their legs'.[43]

Covel also described the court society that he witnessed at the site:

> I have seen them and the rest at Adrianople and at Maidan here several times. He hath but onely the three; the rest are little tents for his servants kitching. I saw the G. SRs. tent at the shew at Adrianople, which was much the same in make and dimentions, but this at Maidan being most perfectly set out with all its appertenances, take its description … This Kiosk, or stand, they remove upon many occasions; he had a farre greater at Demirdesh – to see the horse races. This stood next the outward door of the tents, looking towards the place of execution, as likewise to the plain where the Janissaryes are pay'd, etc., and he is there present himself. At the sights at Adrianople there was another for the young prince.[44]

Both festival books agree that two groups of horse races were organized in Summer 1675, and that the first was on June 15, 1675. Among the chroniclers, Fındıklılı, Sarı Mehmed Paşa and Râşid identify the race field as *Timurtaş Sahrâsı*, also called *Sarây-ı Hümâyûn Sahrâsı*, while Abdi and Nâbî refer to *Hıdırlık* as the site for the spectators.[45] The second group of races was on July 11 or 12, also at Timurtaş (Covel's Demirdesh).[46] Covel's sketch of Edirne's landmarks shows that Timurtaş and Hıdırlık were to the west of the city center. The latter, the only relatively high ground in a generally flat city, had a magnificent view of the Thracian plain.[47] It is a generic place name originating from Khidr (also Hızır), a mystical figure portrayed as possessing great wisdom.[48] As Hıdır means 'Green Man' in Arabic, the Hıdırlık plain in Edirne appears tied to Middle Eastern legends of spring, the renewal of warmth, the reflowering of plants, and the growth of new crops.

## *The First Group of Races*

On June 14, 1675, a message from the Defterdar Paşa, head of the Finance Bureau, was sent to all dignitaries as well as to those who owned the fastest horses (*atları yügrük olanlar*), telling all those who were willing to get ready for the race. The poll tax collector (*Ermeni cizyedarı*) Şeyhzâde Ahmed Ağa was in overall charge of the proceedings (*koşubaşı*). Three categories were planned: a three-hour, a four-hour, and a six-hour long distance race. Nâbî does not mention the starting points. Abdi, however, lists three 'starting points': (1) *menzil-i evvel*, Mustafa Paşa Bridge, six hours; (2) *menzil-i sânî*, Mustafa Paşa's grave, four hours; (3) *menzil-i sâlis*, Tekye, three hours. Just where the second and third points (Mustafa Paşa's grave and Tekye) might be, we don't know. As for the first, today Mustafa Paşa Bridge is in the city of Svilengrad in Bulgaria, which is 33 kilometres from Hıdırlık.

Was this really a starting point or was it instead a turning point after a Hıdırlık start? It is difficult to see how there could have been three different and staggered starting points given the communications technology available at the time, and also how the horses entered could so quickly be taken to these different starting points without exhausting them prior to the race. So while Abdi says that those who were found worthy to compete arrived at the three 'starting points' during the night, this is dubious; what is more likely is for the umpires to have moved overnight to their assigned turning points. If this is the case, in the first six-hour category horses might have made not a one-way trip of 33 but a round trip of 66 kilometres.

But in any case, after the Defterdar Paşa's message the race was set for the next day (June 15), and it was also the Defterdar who recorded the owners, the characteristic signs of the horses, and which race they were chosen for. On June 15, competition began with the three-hour distance race. Abdi elaborates on the Sultan's Stand. He notes that a *sâyeban* had been erected in the lower part of Hıdırlık, on the road connecting the city to the distant, unseen bridge (*köpri yolı*).[49] The grand vizier, his deputy Mustafa Paşa, the dignitaries, and all high-ranking palace personnel were settled at the base of the hill, while a military band was positioned further up the hill to announce the arrival of the horses at the finishing line. Mehmed IV arrived with his son around mid-morning. The sultan and his subjects, rich and poor, on horseback or on foot, gathered around Hıdırlık to watch the road between the Cisr-i Mustafa Paşa bridge and Edirne. When the time came, the big drums and horns (*kûs u nefîr*) were played; then came the clamor of the tympani and trumpets (*tabl u zûrnâ*).

Nabî's account is all in verse, and therefore overloaded with poetic clichés, images or metaphors. Nevertheless, it is mostly borne out by Abdi, who predictably goes into greater detail, including the competing horses, the winners, and their prizes. Thus in the first round, he says, seventeen horses competed, and only eight completed the race of three hours. The one that came first, 'with feet not touching the earth' (to quote Nâbî) received 20,000 akçes. Abdi carefully notes that in the first race, the winner was a pure silver, white or grey horse (*kır at*). 'He' (presumably the owner and not the rider) received his prize money directly from the sultan. The second (also a grey) received 10,000 akçes; the third, a sorrel (*dorı at*) 6,000 akçes; the fourth, a chestnut (*al at*) 5,000 akçes, while the fifth, sixth and seventh each got 3,000 akçes.

Then after an hour the next round of races began. Nâbî once more highlights the clamor of tympani and trumpets, and goes on to describe the first horse to appear as 'going at the pace of an arrow ... so that not even a glance would have been able to get ahead'. Abdi notes that while there were sixteen contestants, only ten completed the race. As in the first race, a white or grey (*kır at*) was the winner, and was awarded 20,000 akçes, while the second, third and fourth were awarded 10,000, 7,000, and 4,000 akçes respectively. The next five horses each won 3,000 akçes for their owners.

After another interval of two hours, the third and final race was run. The road was covered in dust. Fifty horses competed, and only thirteen were able to make it to the finishing line. Once more, Nâbî is not lacking in rhetoric. A magnificent horse, with whom the wind would have to gallop to compete, he says, arrived speedily. These horses, he goes on, were synonymous with a flash of lightning. Could there be anything as fast as this? How could they traverse a space of five hours in a single moment? Abdi, meanwhile, drily notes that the winner, a chestnut mare (*al kısrak*) received 40,000 akçes; the second, a sorrel, 15,000; the third, another sorrel, 10,000; the fourth, a chestnut, 7,000; and the fifth 6,000 akçes.

## The Second Group of Races

Beyond the circumcision ceremonies, the wedding festival began a few days after the races at Timurtaş/Hıdırlık, and lasted for another fifteen days.[50] Râşid, the official court chronicler, says that more races took place on July 11 at Timurtaş Meydânı.[51] Abdi gives the date as July 12.[52] These races also find mention in three other chroniclers (Abdurrahman Abdi Paşa, Sarı Mehmed Paşa, and Silahdar Fındıklılı Mehmed).[53] This open field, also called *Timurtaş Sahrâsı* as previously indicated, was two to three miles from Edirne.[54] There were two races; thirty horses took part in the first, and thirty-five in the second. They competed over a distance of 25–30 miles.[55] Covel says that the two races together took eight hours. Some horses made one or the other race in two and a half hours, and they were utterly exhausted when they reached the finishing line. (This is consistent with my estimate above that the six-hour race must have covered a round trip of 66 kilometers.) Covel adds that he saw some wonderful horses, and takes note of the generous prizes.

Mehmed IV was dethroned in 1687. The immediate cause was the disastrous defeat suffered outside Vienna in 1683. This was part of a more general charge of neglecting the state and military affairs because of his zeal for hunting. Under the newly emerging rule of seniority, he was initially followed to the throne by his two brothers, Süleyman II (1687–1691) and Ahmed II (1691–1695). They were not interested in sports. But when they died after brief four-year reigns and his older son Mustafa II (1695–1703) came on the throne, equestrian sports were revived in Edirne. Thus on April 14, 1698, the last day the Feast of Ramadan, the sultan entertained the grand vizier at a banquet at Timurtaş Sahrâsı. Afterwards, two groups of horses competed over a two-hour distance, and the winner was rewarded with gold coins and precious textiles.[56] This was repeated the following year in the days following the Ramadan Feast, at which time a prince also happened to be born. On April 17, 1699, the sultan once more entertained the grand vizier at a banquet at Timurtaş. Horse races were also held on the same day. Over a two-hour distance, starting from a location known as Kuşöyüğü, five groups of nearly seventy horses competed. Three horses belonging to the Chief Black Enununch won their respective races, and were duly rewarded.[57]

## Horse Racing and Sa'dâbâd Palace in the 1720s

After a long sojourn in Edirne, Mustafa II was overthrown, his brother Ahmed III (r. 1703–1730) was put on the throne, the Edirne interlude came to an end, and the court returned to Istanbul. As part of the court's desperate need to enhance the visibility of the sultan in the capital and to re-establish dynastic legitimacy, various rites and rituals immediately began to be revitalized. Still, over 1710–1720 imperial festivities were limited to processions through the Hippodrome.[58] The court visited Kağıdhane mostly for shooting contests. Nevertheless, on March 1, 1710 and March 29, 1712, the grand vizier of the time entertained the sultan over a banquet and horse races at Kağıdhane.[59]

The breakthrough came in Spring 1719, after Nevşehirli İbrahim Paşa had first married the sultan's daughter (the recently widowed Fatma Sultan), and then become grand vizier in 1718. Râşid narrates in detail how the grand vizier organized a banquet to be followed by entertainments at Kağıdhane. Grandees were given five days to provide horses for the races. On the banks of the Kağıdhane stream and facing the kiosk (Mîrahûr Köşkü?) a pavilion was erected for the sultan; clustered next to it were many more tents for his retinue. They were likened to 'flowers growing in the field', indicating that there were no permanent premises in the area to provide adequate shelter for events on this scale. The sultan arrived on April 15, 1719. Horses had already been gathered at the Kağıdhane village; they were sent off in groups of five, and the winners were rewarded.[60] The chronicler Fındıklılı further notes that on April 23, 1719 the grand vizier once more invited the sultan to Kağıdhane, when, after another banquet, the royal party watched games of *cirid* as well as horse races.[61] In both cases, no specific location was given for the race course.

The last Ottoman imperial festival to fall in the Early Modern Era was celebrated in Fall 1720. Over September 18 to October 2, Istanbul was once more the stage for a major organization. But curiously, it was not the Hippodrome but the Golden Horn that became the venue for the circumcision festivities of Ahmed III's four sons: Süleyman, Mustafa, Mehmed, and Bayezid. Two copies of a *sûrnâme* by the court poet Seyyid Vehbî, sumptuously illustrated by the artists Abdülcelil Levni and Nakkaş Ibrahim, testify to a number of other novelties introduced on this occasion. Furthermore, there is a second *sûrnâme* by Mehmed Hazin, who was in the retinue of the Treasurer of the Festival.[62]

Vehbî, Mehmed Hazin and Râşid all confirm that among various other entertainments, a tournament of Egyptian riders took place on the fifth day of the festivities, which fell on September 22.[63] The venue must have been Kağıdhane, where we know another imperial tent to have been pitched. So Ahmed III has to have moved from the Tersane Garden to Kağıdhane to watch this performance. Some thirty or forty were rewarded, after which these riders moved to another location and raced in groups of four.[64] Although the new location is not given, the small number of the riders suggests a narrow track, perhaps even a short and flat one. Also given that it was the Egyptian *cündîs*, a superior class of cavalrymen, racing among themselves, all this is reminiscent of the *sipâhi koşusu* first mentioned in 1582.

However, it was on the last day of the festivities that a major horse race was organized at Kağıdhane. Vehbî states, in flowery language, that this was dictated by established custom and tradition.[65] Mısırlı Mustafa, the Gedikler Emini (treasurer of state monopolies), was appointed to select the horses to compete and the prizes to be distributed. In turn, around sixty horses were nominated by the grand vizier, other grandees of the imperial council, and the military corps. On October 2, these horses raced in groups of six from a point an hour away to the imperial tent where the sultan sat watching. The course was carefully prepared, manicured so that there was no mud or dust. Horses that made it to the finish were covered in sumptuous textiles according to the rank and status of the owners. Each rider was awarded 10 guruş.[66]

In Fındıklılı's chronicle, all this is only briefly mentioned. In contrast, Mehmed Hazin, the second *sûrnâme* author mentioned above, provides much greater detail.[67] After a game of *cirid*, he says, horses provided by the grandees started out from a location that was three quarters of an hour away, and near the end of the slope heading toward the Kağıdhane village. This appears reliable, especially given that just across the village was the grand vizier's Hürremâbâd kiosk. Meanwhile, Hazin does not give us the exact location of finishing line, though he too notes that the horses were sent out in groups, and adds that his boss (the Festival Treasurer) covered the winning horses in textiles while the riders were given 10 guruş each. Finally, Hazin lists eleven horses which he says came first in their respective groups. Putting this information side by side with Seyyid Vehbî's account confirms the following conclusions: sixty-six horses took part, which were sent off in groups of six, so that there were eleven groups in all. These were the group winners: (1) A chestnut, owned by the *defterdar efendi*; (2) a sorrel, owned by the grand vizier; (3) a sorrel with a star on its forehead (*çakal toru at*), owned by the *reis efendi*; (4) a chestnut, owned by the grand vizier; (5) a sorrel, owned by the *reis efendi*; (6) a chestnut, owned by the grand vizier; (7) a sorrel, owned by the *yeniçeri efendi*; (8) a sorrel, owned by the *yeniçeri ağası*; (9) a sorrel, owned by the *matbah emini efendi*; (10) a sorrel, owned by the *defter emini*; and (11) a grey, owned by the *sipâhiler ağası*.

## Banquets, Equestrian Sports, and Horse Races: A Substitute for Royal Hunting Parties

This 1720 event was still a cross-country race. But in contrast to the excruciating Edirne races of three, four or six hours, it was a shorter course of one hour. Moreover, unlike Edirne, the spatial layout at Kağıdhane must have excluded attendance by large crowds.

Over the next decade, horse racing in the Ottoman capital began to change. First, track-based flat racing was introduced. As, now, it was one side of Cedvel-i Sîm that was used for short-distance races, more than a race course it was an actual race track that came to be incorporated into the architectural program of Sa'adâbâd Palace. It also became routine for the grand vizier and royal groom, Nevşehirli İbrahim Paşa, to entertain Ahmed III over a banquet and festivities at Sa'adâbâd Palace immediately after the holiest days of Islam. Hence a specific time came to be set for the major race of the year – it was always scheduled for the early days of the month of Şevval, after the three-day feast that is celebrated every year at the end of the fasting month of Ramadan.[68] The terminology, too, shifted from 'horse race' (*at koşusu*) to 'competition' (*müsâbakât*). This is evidenced by a number of period chronicles as well as an official code of protocol. Over the next decade, first Râşid and then Çelebizâde İsmâil Asım (who followed Râşid as the official chronicler) dutifully recorded all the horse races that followed the banquets given by the grand vizier in honor of the sultan.

Inevitably, this makes for some tedious reading in purssuit of completeness. On August 10, 1722, when Sa'adâbâd Palace had been completed in just two months, first there was a game of mounted *cirid* and a competition of foot-runners. Râşid says that after lunch, horses provided by dignitaries raced in fifteen groups. Those who entered the competition (*meydân-ı müsâbakat olanlar*) were rewarded with precious textiles, and their riders were each given a piece of gold. The next year, on July 8, 1723 the grand vizier threw yet another banquet at Sa'adâbâd, when those attending toured the just completed harem apartments at Hürremâbâd as well as the then-brand new Cedvel-i Sîm canal. The court then settled down at Mîrâhûr Köşkü where they watched various shows by musketeers and bombardiers.[69] When they returned to Sa'adâbâd on July 15, 1723, they were treated to horse races in addition to other performances.[70] While we are not given location details, it seems as if that summer's races all took place in the *cirid* field.

In 1724, it was on June 27, two days after the Ramadan Feast, that a banquet and a horse race were organized by the grand vizier. Then on September 1, following the year's second Islamic festival, the Feast of Sacrifice (*Eid al-Adha*), the grand vizier once again entertained the sultan over a banquet at Sa'adâbâd Palace.[71] On this occasion horses provided by grandees were sent off in groups of five from Hürremâbâd, the abode of the grand vizier (possibly to that of the sultan, Kasr-ı Sa'adâbâd?), and as usual the winners were covered with textiles.[72] This constitutes a milestone in the history of Ottoman horse racing, for it was no longer an endurance race; instead, the horses appear to have run on a flat track along the Cedvel-i Sîm over a distance of 1,000 meters (which today takes slightly under a minute).

On June 17, 1725, immediately after the Ramadan Feast and on the 5th of Şevval, horses provided by grandees were once more sent off from Hürremâbâd in fives.[73] All these events were termed *müsâbakat*. On June 7, 1726, too (or on the 6th of Şevval), the court had moved to Sa'adâbâd when news arrived of a fire in the city, all further plans were cancelled, and the sultan and his retinue promptly returned to Istanbul. But on June 16 they returned to Kağıdhane and Sa'adâbâd Palace. Our chroniclers keep using the same formulas over and over again to report that they enjoyed the spectacle of horses provided by grandees racing in groups of five.[74] On May 25, 1727 (or the 4th of Şevval), dignitaries and their racing horses gathered at Mîrâhûr Köşkü. The sultan arrived by boat after 2 pm, passed by Mîrâhûr Köşkü, and made his way to Sa'adâbâd. The banquet was followed by a shooting contest between 1500 musketeers, plus performances by gunners and bombardiers, singers and dancers, as well as bears and two hunting dogs. Later, horses provided by grandees were sent off in fives from Hürremâbâd (to Sa'adâbâd?). Before the day ended, members of the court moved to Mîrâhûr Köşkü while the sultan returned to Topkapı Palace.[75] The following year (1728), on May 14 (4th Şevval) there was yet another race between horses provided by grandees. And, yes, they were sent off in groups of five from Hürremâbâd (to Kasr-ı Sa'adâbâd).[76]

Our last record in this series is from 1729. For some reason, after a banquet thrown by the janissary commander (*yeniçeri ağası*) on May 2, the last day of the feast, there is no mention of further celebrations for more than two weeks. Then on May 20 they went to Sa'adâbâd, we are told, for banqueting, enjoying the light shows, and sightseeing.[77]

## Postscript: From Traditional Seclusion to a More Public Life

Ahmed III's (or rather his grand vizier's) deliberate efforts to erase the ill memories of his father, Mehmed IV, by replacing hunting with equestrian sports and horse racing and opening up the whole spectacle to the public, was not pursued by his immediate successors on the Ottoman throne. While Kağıdhane continued to host some stately events, such as ambassadorial receptions, horse racing appears to have fallen into neglect until the last decade of the eighteenth century. Then under Selim III (r. 1789–1807), the search for a location for new war industries turned to the valleys at the far end of the Golden Horn while the inlet's shores, too, began to be lined with industrial buildings. The artillery, bombardier, and sappers corps of Selim's New Model (*Nizâm-ı Cedid*) army, a new body of regular infantry trained and drilled and disciplined on Western lines, too, also conducted military exercises at Kağıdhane.[78]

In the late nineteenth century, while the palatial complex went through a complete remodelling, a new kiosk, the last to be built in the direction of the head of the stream, became the new Sultan's Stand.[79] Long-distance races continued to be run at Kağıdhane, but while they had at least three different starting points, they all ended at the hunting-lodge-turned-viewing-kiosk, Koşu Köşkü. Moreover, it came to be annexed to a long oval racing track, the first visual record of which is from the second half of the nineteenth century. From the 1860s onward, races used to be run around the meadow known as İskender Paşa Çayırı, on the eastern shore of the stream and further north of Hürremâbâd.[80] On a nineteenth century map, an oval race course (*koşu yolu*) is marked among the hills surrounding the meadow on all sides.[81] The Sultan's Stand (the aforementioned Koşu Köşkü), the location of the race committeee, and the spectators' stands are all clearly indicated. Also on the map is the information that 'the overall length of the race course is 1300m'. An engraving from 1863, titled 'Races at Constantinople in the Valley of Djendereh Boghaz, Near the Sweet Waters Of Europe', closely matches the map in question. It too depicts a more regular and permanent race course, including the sultan's and foreign diplomats' viewing kiosks as well as tents for (privileged?) spectators on one side.[82] Across and up on the hill, commoners are shown watching at the foot of a windmill. The title of the accompanying article, published in the November 1863 issue of the *Illustrated London News*, refers to Cendere Passage, literally a narrow mountain pass, which was going to be used alternately with the Kağıdhane valley. The article goes on to explain:

> The valley chosen for the day's sport is a beautiful amphitheatre, hill-locked on every side but that which opens on the village to the west. From the southern end of the course, the inclosing line of high ground suddenly rises first to a short plateau, on which stands an old dismantled windmill, and then into a long waving ridge of a much higher elevation, that winds round the valley back to the very bank of the now dry riverbed. The ground within this long oval is as flat as a bowling-green, and without the expenditure of a shilling furnished a racecourse which no amount of artificial labour could have materially improved.

By the late-nineteenth century, horse racing had become a fully public entertainment in Istanbul. Away from the Imperial Kiosk[83] and the Grand Stand,[84] 'at the southern end of the valley, thousands of native spectators dotted the whole slope of the curving hill-line as thick as locusts – some on horseback, a few in the old bullock arabas, but the large majority squatted on the parched sward, from the edge of the course up to the very brow of the plateau'.[85]

It is this image of a public outing which has stuck in the memory of historians. It is part of a general pattern of how nineteenth century outdoor entertainment in the Ottoman capital came to be romanticized in painting and prose.[86] In sharp and realistic contrast, the Istanbuliote İnciciyan (1758–1833) notes that after 1722, narrow passages for boats going upstream to the village were closed for Istanbullus.[87] The history of horse racing promises to help revisit the always-incomplete representation provided by age-old Orientalist images.

## Notes

1. Sedat H. Eldem, *Sa'dabad* (İstanbul: Milli Eğitim Basımevi, 1977).
2. *Hünernâme*: Topkapı Palace Museum Library, H. 1524, 124b–25a. The manuscript was presented to Murad III in July 1589. There is no information about the artists other than a note on the last folio which praises Nakkaş Osman, then the chief of the royal painting workshop: Serpil Bağcı, Filiz Çağman, Günsel Renda and Zeren Tanındı, eds., *Osmanlı Resim Sanatı* (İstanbul: Kültür ve Turizm Bakanlığı Yayınları, 2006).
3. A century later the chronicler İbrahim Peçevî (d. 1649) relayed that a female hound had passed them all: Bihter Gürışık, Peçevî Tarihi (46b–80a Metin, Dizin, Özel Adlar Sözlüğü) (M.A. Thesis, Marmara Üniversitesi, 2005), 67: TSM B. 206, 62b.
4. *Şehinşahnâme*: Topkapı Palace Museum Library, B. 200, 85b. In addition to several scenes depicting equestrian games, there are other references to makeshift arrangements, horses, and races: 52b, 84a ('der hayme efrâhten-i fârisân-ı rab? ve tırâz-ı râst u râhat'; 'reften-i Hacı Ahmed Paşa be-temâşâ-yı devende-hâ-yı bâd-pâ'; 'der tünd ü tizî-i semendân ve ri'âyet-i çabuk-süvârân'). It was completed in 1592 and presented to Mehmed III in 1597.
5. On horse racing in the Roman imperial period, see Sinclair Bell's chapter in this volume; on racing in the Byzantine empire, see David Parnell's chapter.
6. Brigitte Pitarakis and Ekrem Işın, eds., *Hippodrome/Atmeydanı: A Stage for Istanbul's History*, 2 vols. (İstanbul: Pera Müzesi, 2010).
7. Celâlzâde Mustafa, *Tabakatü'l-Memâlik ve Derecâtü'l-Mesâlik*, İstanbul University Library (hereafter Tabakat, İÜ) T.5997, 90b–94b; Celâlzâde Mustafa, *Geschichte Sultan Süleymān Kānūnīs von 1520 bis 1557, oder Ṭabaḳat ül-Memālik ve Derecāt ül-Mesālik, von Celālzāde Muṣṭafā, gennant Koca Nişāncı*, ed. Petra Kappert (Wiesbaden: Franz Steiner Verlag, 1981), 115b–21a; Funda Demirtaş, *Celâl-zâde Mustafa Çelebi, Tabakâtü'l-Memâlik ve Derecâtü'l-Mesâlik* (Ph.D. diss., Erciyes Üniversitesi, 2009), 155–61.
8. Marino Sanuto, *I diarii di Marino Sanuto*, ed. Rinaldo Fulin, Federico Stefani, Nicolò Barozzi, Guglielmo Berchet, and Marco Allegri, 58 vols. (Venice: A spese degli editori, 1879–1903), vol. 39, 77–8.
9. Celâlzâde, *Tabakat*, İÜ Library T.5997, 153a–9a; Kappert, *Geschichte*, 194a–202a; Demirtaş, *Celâl-zâde*, 265–79.
10. Celâlzâde, *Tabakat*, İÜ Library T.5997, 269a–72a; Kappert, *Geschichte*, 337a–40b; Demirtaş, *Celâl-zâde*, 459–64.
11. See footnote 31 below.
12. Süheyl Ünver, 'Her Devirde Kâğıthane', *Vakıflar Dergisi* 10 (1973): 435–60; Münir A. Aktepe, 'Kâğıthane'ye Dair Bazı Bilgiler', *Ord. Prof. İsmail Hakkı Uzunçarşılı'ya Armağan* (Ankara: Türk Tarih Kurumu, 1976), 335–63; Semavi Eyice, 'Kâğıthane-Sâdâbâd-Çağlayan', *Taç* 1, no. 1 (1986): 29–36; Orhan Şaik Gökyay, 'Bahçeler', *Topkapı Sarayı Müzesi Yıllık* 4 (1990): 7–20; Kağıthane Belediye Başkanlığı, *Osmanlı Belgelerinde Kâğıthane* (İstanbul: Kağıthane Belediyesi, 2007); Hüseyin Irmak, ed., *Kağıdhane Historical Inventory* (İstanbul: Kağıthane Belediyesi Kültür yayınları, 2011).
13. Petrus Gyllius, *İstanbul Boğazı* (İstanbul: Eren Yayıncılık, 2000), 74.

14. George Sandys, *A Relation of a Journey Begun An: Dom: 1610: Fovre Bookes. Containing a Description of the Turkish Empire, of AEgypt, of the Holy Land, of the Remote Parts of Italy, and Ilands Adioyning* (Printed for W. Barren, 1621 [1615]), 37.
15. There were a number of royal stables around the capital (called 'ıstabl-ı hümâyun', 'ıstabl-ı şehinşâhî', 'ıstabl-ı has', 'ıstabl-ı âmire'), where together with horses campaign camels and mules were kept: Abdülkadir Özcan, 'Istabl', TDV *İslâm Ansiklopedisi* 19, 203–6.
16. See note 12 above: '… much frequented by fowle, and rigorously preserved for the Grand Signiors pleasure; who ordinarily hawks thereon …'
17. Writing intermittently between 1662–1684, Eremya Çelebi claimed that Kağıdhane and other excursion spots were closed to public during Mehmed IV's reign: Eremya Çelebi Kömürcüyan, *İstanbul Tarihi. XVII. Asırda*, tr. Hrand D. Andreasyan (İstanbul: İÜ Edebiyat Fakültesi, 1952), 34–5. In 1530, Peçevî refers to the area as *Kağıdhane Sahrası*, an open space. In a 1614 document, Kağıdhane and places in close proximity were noted as hunting grounds (*şikar-gâh olan Kağıdhane*): Ahmed Refik, *On Birinci Asr-ı Hicrî'de İstanbul Hayatı (1592–1688)*, (İstanbul: Enderun, 1988 [1931]), 48.
18. Nineteenth-century photographs and engravings attest to barren hills and meadows at Kağıdhane. The travellers, too, were not thrilled with what they saw: 'the whole extremity of the Byzantine bay was antiently, as is now, notorious for the mephitic exhalations of the marshes near the embouchures of the Cydaris and Barbyses, owing to the quantity of mud they deposit at their junction; whence it bore the expressive appellation of the PUTRID SEA: and so ambiguous was the nature of the territory, that it pastured, at the same time, quadrupeds and fishes; the cattle and the deer of THRACE, and the Pelamides of the EUXINE': Edward Daniel Clarke, *Travels in Various Countries of Europe, Asia and Africa. Part the Second. Greece Egypt and the Holy Land. Section the Third. To Which is Added a Supplement Respecting the Author's Journey from Constantinople to Vienna.* Volume 8, London: T. Cadell and W. Davies, 1818, 184–5.
    However, in his *Hevesnâme* (1499), Tacizade Cafer Çelebi praised the natural beauty of the area and praised cypress, boxwood, juniper, weeping willow trees. Likewise, in his 'Essay in Description of İstanbul', the sixteenth-century poet Latifi extols the natural beauties of Kağıdhane, using common tropes of Ottoman poetry—gardens, gazelles, musks. Poetic desciptions such as his led to an ascription of lush vegetation, extensive forests to the 'sweet waters' of Kağıthane. For a criticism of nineteenth century 'subjective imagination and objectifying observation' and depiction of quays, landings, meadows, groves, rills, streams, curled bridges, fountains and kiosks serving to evoke a timeless, unchanging Orient, see: Reinhold Schiffer, *Oriental Panorama: British Travellers in the 19th Century Turkey* (Amsterdam: Rodopi, 1999), 82; Frederick N. Bohrer, 'The Sweet Waters of Asia: Representing Difference/Differencing Representation in 19th. C. Istanbul', in *Edges of Empire: Orientalism and Visual Culture*, ed. Jocelyn Hackforth-Jones and Mary Roberts (London: Blackwell, 2005), 121–38.
    Curiously, Kağıdhane is not included in two major study on the sixteenth-century gardens: Muzaffer Erdoğan, 'Osmanlı Devrinde İstanbul Bahçeleri', *Vakıflar Dergisi* IV (1958), 149–82; Gülru Necipoğlu, 'The Suburban Landscape of Sixteenth-Century Istanbul as a Mirror of Classical Ottoman Garden Culture', in *Gardens in the Time of the Great Muslim Empires: Theory and Design*, ed. A. Petruccioli (Leiden: Brill, 1997), 32–71. For a literature review: Nurhan Atasoy, *Hasbahçe. Osmanlı Kültüründe Bahçe ve Çiçek* (İstanbul: Aygaz, 2002), 276–85.
19. The celebrated traveler Evliya Çelebi, when he revisited the city in 1653, mentions a number of mesires in the vicinity: Lâlezâr, İmrahor Kasrı, Kuyumcular, Emirgüne, Cendereci Köyü, Çaybaşı, Su Kemerleri, Sultan Osman Havuzu and Kızlarağası çayırı. Evliya Çelebi b. Derviş Mehemmed Zıllı, *Evliya Çelebi Seyahatnâmesi, Topkapı Sarayı*

*Bağdat 304 Yazmasının Transkripsiyonu-Dizini*, vol. 1, ed. Robert Dankoff, Seyit Ali Kahraman, and Yücel Dağlı (İstanbul: YKY, 2006 [1995]), 237–9.
20. Numerous documents attest to plantation of trees in the area. In 1735 and 1745, linden, elm, oak, madrone apple (strawberry tree), boxwood, alder tree, plane tree, laurel tree, judas, wild pear and others were ordered from İznikmid, Karamürsel and Yalakâbâd to İstanbul: Ahmed Refik, *On İkinci Asr-ı Hicrî'de İstanbul Hayatı (1689-1785)* (İstanbul: Enderun, 1988), 133, 160.
21. Hıdırellez, which is known as Ruz-ı Hızır (day of Hızır), is celebrated as the day on which Prophets Hızır and İlyas met with each other on the earth. The words Hızır and İlyas have since fused together pronounced as Hıdrellez. Hıdrellez Day falls on May 6 in the Gregorian calendar and April 23 in the Julian calendar, also known as the Rumi' calendar. In the folk calendar, the year used to be divided into two: The period between May 6 and November 8 was summer, called the 'Days of Hızır', and the period between November 8 and May 6 was winter, called the 'Days of Kasım.' May 6 thus represents the end of winter and the start of the warm days of summer, a cause for celebration.
22. *Evliya Çelebi Seyahatnâmesi*, 145a. For photographs and maps: Irmak, *Kağıdhane Historical Inventory*, 92–100. Mouradgea d'Ohsson, *Tableau General d'Empire Ottoman* vol. 1 (Paris: Imp. de monsieur [Firmin Didot]) 1787–1820), plate 84 (Keaghid-Khané, Promenade publique aux environs de Constantinople).
23. Franz Taeschner, *Alt-Stambuler Hof- und Volksleben, Ein türkisches Miniaturen-Album aus dem 17. Jahrhundert* (Hannover: Orient-buchhandlung Heinz Lafaire, 1925), lv. 22; Eldem, *Sa'dabad*, 117.
24. For photographs and maps: Irmak, *Kağıdhane Historical Inventory*, 178–208.
25. Ottoman State Archives, İstanbul: BOA. C. BLD 1018 (26 S 1135).
26. Antoine-Ignace Melling, *Voyage pittoresque de Constantinople et des rives du Bosphore, D'Après Les Dessins De M. Melling Architecte De L'Empereur Selim III, et Dessinateur De La Sultane Hadidge Sa Soeur* (Paris: Treuttel et Würtz, 1819). For the translation into English: Irvin Cemil Schick, A Picturesque Voyage to Constantinople and the Shores of the Bosphorus (İstanbul: Denizler Kitabevi, 2012), 117.
27. Irmak, *Kağıthane Historical Inventory*, 622.
28. Celâlzâde, *Tabakat*, İÜ Library T.5997, 94b ( ... meydân atları bir menzil yer uzayub gitmislerdi. Meydân basına vardıkları gibi berâber safflar baglayub, bir ugurdan bosanub, kosdılar ... ); Kappert, *Geschichte*, 121a; Demirtaş, Celâl-zâde, 161.
29. Sanuto, *I diarii di Marino Sanuto*, 36.505–7.
30. Müderris köyü, marked by a crowd of houses and trees on the map in question, has been identified as Metris Çiftliği: Kâzım Çeçen, 'Avasköy Kemeri', *Dünden Bugüne İstanbul Ansiklopedisi*. vol. 1 (İstanbul: Tarih Vakfı, 1993), 425.
31. Celâlzâde, *Tabakat*, İÜ Library T.5997, 159a ( ... ve kosu için mukaddemâ yarar ve güzîde atlar yarak olmısdı ... ve kunt bir yügrük 'Arabî-bedevî yunt idi ... ); Kappert, *Geschichte*, 202a; Demirtaş, Celâl-zâde, 277. See also: Sanuto, *I diarii di Marino Sanuto*, 53.443–58.
32. Gelibolulu Mustafa 'Âlî, *Câmi'u'l-Buhûr Der Mecâlis-i Sûr. Edisyon Kritik ve Tahlil*, ed. Ali Öztekin (Ankara: TTK, 1996), 281 (106b); Mehmet Arslan, *Osmanlı Saray Düğünleri ve Şenlikleri I. Manzum Sûrnâmeler*, İstanbul: Sarayburnu Kitaplığı, 2008, 617.
33. Celâlzâde, *Tabakat*, İÜ Library T.5997, 272a ( ... sebük-pâ, nesîm-revân kosu atları hazırlamıslardı. Meydâna kosılub, pey-â-pey yügrükler zâhir olub ... ); Kappert, 340b; Demirtaş, Celâl-zâde, 464.
34. Gelibolulu Mustafa 'Âlî, *Câmi'u'l-Buhûr Der Mecâlis-i Sûr*, 281 (106b); Arslan, *Osmanlı Saray Düğünleri ve Şenlikleri I*, 671; Mehmet Arslan, *Osmanlı Saray Düğünleri ve Şenlikleri 2. İntizâmî Sûrnâmesi* (İstanbul: Sarayburnu Kitaplığı, 2008). For İntizâmî's Vienna copy: Gisela Procházka-Eisl, ed., *Das Surname-i Hümayun: Die Wiener Handschrift in Transkription mit Kommentar und Indices versehen* (İstanbul: Isis, 1995). There is no mention of Çatalca or Edirnekapı in both works.
35. *Sûrnâme-i Hümâyûn*: Topkapı Palace Museum Library, H. 1344.

36. Arslan, *Osmanlı Saray Düğünleri ve Şenlikleri 2*, 156–7, 269, 283, 396, 418, 466 [24a–25a, 90a, 97b–8a, 166a, 180b–81a, 209a]. For references for the cündiyan only: 38a (missing the latter part where there might have been another account of sipâhi koşusu), 38b, 124b–25a, 138a, 160b, 161b–62a, 177b–78a, 184b, 196b, 197b, 201b, 217a. In the Süleymaniye Library copy of İntizâmî's *Sûrnâme*, the cündiyân was mentioned only as 206th group that participated in the festivities: Arslan, *Osmanlı Saray Düğünleri ve Şenlikleri 2*, 618.
37. ASVe, Senato, Dispacci Ambasciatori, Costantinopoli, filza 16, July 2, 1582, c. 112 after: Levent Kaya Ocakaçan, 'Festivities of Curfew Centralization and Mechanisms of Opposition in Ottoman Politics, 1582–1583', *Venetians and Ottomans in the Early Modern Age Essays on Economic and Social Connected History*, ed. Anna Valerio (Venice: Edizioni Ca' Foscari, 2018), 57–72.
38. Derin Terzioğlu, 'The Imperial Circumcision Festival of 1582: An Interpretation', *Muqarnas*, no. 12 (1995): 84–100; Mehmet Arslan, 'Osmanlı'da Bir Muhteşem Şenlik: Şehzade Sultan Mehmet'in (III. Mehmet) Sünnet Düğünü', *Türkler Ansiklopedisi* I (2002): 871–86. Both authors did not cite their reference.
39. For Abdi who had previously served as Chief Black Eunuch's scribe: Mehmet Arslan, *Osmanlı Saray Düğünleri ve Şenlikleri 4-5: Lebib Sûrnâmesi, Hâfız Mehmed Efendi (Hazin) Sûrnâmesi, Abdi Sûrnâmesi, Telhîsü'l-Beyân'ın Sûrnâme Kısmı* (Istanbul: Sarayburnu Kitaplığı, 2011), 511–3; for Nâbî: Arslan, *Osmanlı Saray Düğünleri ve Şenlikleri I*, 688–91. Twelve days after the completion of the circumcision festivities was the weeding of Hadice Sultan to Musahib Mustafa. That round of celebrations also lasted for 15 days. So after six months of preparations, there was two months of festivities.
40. Râşid Mehmed Efendi ve Çelebizâde İsmaîl Âsım Efendi, *Tarîh-i Râşid ve Zeyli I. 1071-1114/1660-1703*, ed. Abdülkadir Özcan, Yunus Uğur, Baki Çakır, and Ahmet Zeki İzgöer (Istanbul: Klasik Yayınları, 2013), 189.
41. Abdurrahman Abdi, *Abdurrahman Abdi Paşa Vekâyi'-nâmesi: Osmanlı Tarihi (1648-1682)*, ed. Fahri Ç. Derin (İstanbul: Çamlıca, 2008), 443. For Hezârfen: Hezarfen Hüseyin, *Telhîsü'l-beyân fi kavânîn-i Âl-i Osmân*, ed. Sevim İlgürel (İstanbul: TTK, 1998), 237; Arslan, *Osmanlı Saray Düğünleri ve Şenlikleri 4-5*, 622; Defterdar Sarı Mehmed Paşa, *Zübde-i Vekayiât. Tahlil ve Metin (1066-1116/1656-1704)*, ed. Abdülkadir Özcan (Ankara: TTK, 1995), 65 and 68; Silahdar Fındıklılı Mehmed Ağa, Nazire Karaçay Türkal, Silahdar Fındıklılı Mehmed Ağa, *Zeyl-i Fezleke (1065-22 Ca. 1106/1654-7 Şubat 1695)* (Ph.D. diss., Marmara Üniversitesi, 2012), 668–72; Râşid Mehmed Efendi ve Çelebizâde İsmaîl Âsım Efendi, *Tarîh-i Râşid ve Zeyli I*, 187–190.
42. Journal of Dr Covel's Travels, 1670–1678, B.L. Add.Mss. 22912, 217a, 220a–20b, after: Özdemir Nutku, *IV. Mehmet'in Edirne Şenliği (1675)* (Ankara: Türk Tarih Kurumu,1972), 105–7. See also: John Covel, *Early Voyages and Travels in the Levant. The Diary of Master Thomas Dallam, 1599–1600; Extracts from the Diaries of Dr John Covel, 1670–1679. With Some Account of the Levant Company of Turkey Merchants*, ed. J. Theodore Bent (New York: Burt Franklin, n.d.), 171–241. Unfortunately, Bent omitted the section on the horse races.
43. Journal of Dr Covel's Travels, 217a, after: Donna Landry, *Noble Brutes: How Eastern Horses Transformed English Culture* (Baltimore: The John Hopkins University Press, 2009), 8.
44. Covel, *Extracts from the Diaries*, 163.
45. (Abdi), *Osmanlı Saray Düğünleri ve Şenlikleri 4-5*, 512; (Nâbî:) Arslan, *Osmanlı Saray Düğünleri ve Şenlikleri I*, 689; Fındıklılı, *Zeyl-i Fezleke*, 670; Râşid Mehmed Efendi ve Çelebizâde İsmaîl Âsım Efendi, *Tarîh-i Râşid ve Zeyli I*, 189.
46. Fındıklılı, *Zeyl-i Fezleke*, 672; Râşid Mehmed Efendi ve Çelebizâde İsmaîl Âsım Efendi, *Tarîh-i Râşid ve Zeyli I*, 190.
47. Fig.6 in Nutku, *IV. Mehmet'in Edirne Şenliği (1675)*.
48. In various Islamic and non-Islamic traditions, Khidr is described as a messenger, prophet, wali, slave and angel, who guards the sea, teaches secret knowledge and aids

those in distress. The night of May 5 and day of May 6 are known as Hıdırellez, a festival that marks the beginning of spring and summer in parts of the Middle East. Hızır is sometimes identified with St. George, whose feast day is May 6 in the Greek Orthodox Church; to Sorūsh in Iran, Saint Sarkis the Warrior, Saint George in Asia Minor and the Levant, and John the Baptist in Armenia.

49. Mehmet Arslan, *Osmanlı Saray Düğünleri ve Şenlikleri 4-5*, 511–2.
50. Covel, *Extracts from the Diaries*, 208ff.
51. Râşid Mehmed Efendi ve Çelebizâde İsmaîl Âsım Efendi, *Târîh-i Râşid ve Zeyli I*, 190.
52. Arslan, *Osmanlı Saray Düğünleri ve Şenlikleri 4-5*, 531.
53. Abdurrahman Abdi Paşa, *Abdurrahman Abdi Paşa Vekayi'-Nâmesi*, ed. Fahri Ç. Derin (İstanbul: Çalıca, 2008), 443–6; Sarı Mehmed Paşa, *Zübde-i Vekayiât*, 68; Fındıklılı, *Zeyl-i Fezleke*, 668–72.
54. Today, the mosque of *Timurtaş* stands in an open field near the city. It was built in the first quarter of fifteen-century by the military officer *Subaşı Timurtaş Paşa*.
55. B.L. Add. Mss. 22912, 220a–20b, after Nutku, *IV. Mehmet'in Edirne Şenliği (1675)*, 105–7.
56. Silahdar Fındıklılı Mehmed Ağa, *Nusretnâme*, 476.
57. Silahdar Fındıklılı Mehmed Ağa, *Nusretnâme*, 547.
58. Tülay Artan, 'Royal Weddings and the Grand Vezirate: Institutional and Symbolic Change in the Early 18th Century', in *Royal Courts in Dynastic States and Empires. A Global Perspective*, ed. Tülay Artan, Jeroen Duindam, and Metin Kunt (Leiden: Brill, 2011), 339–99.
59. Uşşâkî-zâde es-Seyyid İbrâhîm Hasîb Efendi, *Uşşâkîzâde Târihi 2* (İstanbul: Çamlıca, 2005), 1008, 1096.
60. Râşid Mehmed Efendi ve Çelebizâde İsmaîl Âsım Efendi, *Târîh-i Râşid ve Zeyli II. 1115-1134/1704-1722*, ed. Abdülkadir Özcan, Yunus Uğur, Baki Çakır, and Ahmet Zeki İzgöer (İstanbul: Klasik Yayınları, 2013), 1157.
61. Silahdar Fındıklılı Mehmed Ağa, *Nusretnâme*, 1100.
62. Arslan, *Osmanlı Saray Düğünleri ve Şenlikleri 4-5*, 350–427.
63. Arslan, *Osmanlı Saray Düğünleri ve Şenlikleri 3. Vehbî Sûrnâmesi* (İstanbul: Sarayburnu Kitaplığı, 2008), 223.
64. Râşid Mehmed Efendi ve Çelebizâde İsmaîl Âsım Efendi, *Târîh-i Râşid ve Zeyli II*, 1200.
65. Arslan, *Osmanlı Saray Düğünleri ve Şenlikleri 3*, 8, 357, 359–60.
66. Arslan, *Osmanlı Saray Düğünleri ve Şenlikleri 3*, 359–60.
67. Silahdar Fındıklılı Mehmed Ağa, *Nusretnâme*, 1124; For Hazin: Arslan, *Osmanlı Saray Düğünleri ve Şenlikleri 4-5*, 2008, 411–2.
68. Eid al-Fitr, also called the 'Festival of Breaking the Fast', is a religious holiday celebrated by Muslims worldwide that marks the end of Ramadan, the Islamic holy month of fasting, in the first three days of the month of Şevval.
69. Râşid Mehmed Efendi ve Çelebizâde İsmaîl Âsım Efendi, *Târîh-i Râşid ve Zeyli II*, 1322.
70. Râşid Mehmed Efendi ve Çelebizâde İsmaîl Âsım Efendi, *Târîh-i Râşid ve Zeyli II*, 1322.
71. Eid al-Adha is considered the holier of the two. It honours the willingness of Abraham to sacrifice his son as an act of obedience to God's command.
72. Then came the race of the foot runners, also indicating the location and the distance of the horse race: Râşid Mehmed Efendi ve Çelebizâde İsmaîl Âsım Efendi, *Târîh-i Râşid ve Zeyli II*, 1388-1389.
73. Râşid Mehmed Efendi ve Çelebizâde İsmaîl Âsım Efendi, *Târîh-i Râşid ve Zeyli II*, 1433.
74. Râşid Mehmed Efendi ve Çelebizâde İsmaîl Âsım Efendi, *Târîh-i Râşid ve Zeyli II*, 1495 and 1507.
75. Râşid Mehmed Efendi ve Çelebizâde İsmaîl Âsım Efendi, *Târîh-i Râşid ve Zeyli III*, 2013, 1543; compare with 1367. For the Book of Protocol: Hayriye Büşra Uslu, *III. Ahmed Devri Teşrîfâtı (A.D. 347: 1718-1725* (MA Thesis, Mimar Sinan Güzel Sanatlar Üniversitesi, 2017), 153–4 (fol. 131).
76. Râşid Mehmed Efendi ve Çelebizâde İsmaîl Âsım Efendi, *Târîh-i Râşid ve Zeyli II*, 1595.

77. Râşid Mehmed Efendi ve Çelebizâde İsmail Âsım Efendi, *Târîh-i Râşid ve Zeyli II*, 1622–3.
78. Câbî Ömer Efendi, *Câbî Tarihi. (Tarih-i Sultan Selim-i Salis ve Mahmud-ı Sani ) Tahlil ve Tenkidli Metin I*, ed. Mehmet Ali Beyhan (Ankara: TTK, 2003), 4–7: In the summer of 1780, an envoy from the Tipu Sultan arrived asking for help with weapons, fighting techniques as well as drills. After some demonstrations at Kağıthane, the Indian envoy was told that the Ottoman soldiers do not conduct drills in peacetime. In 1794, the new army was moved to Levend Çiftliği.
79. Its origin is not known; it must have been rebuilt several times, possibly on the same location. In the nineteenth-century documents, it was referred as 'yarış köşkü', 'yarış köşk-ü hümayunu', 'yarış kasr-ı hümayunu', or 'koşu sarayı'. Adjoining was a sizeable English garden and a pool. Earliest photographs show a single-storey structure built during the reign of Abdülaziz, where the sultan and his entourage rested. See further Güler Yarcı, 'Kâğıthane Koşu Köşk-i Hümâyunu ve Sâdâbâd'da At Yarışları', *Türk Dünyası Araştırmaları Dergisi* 225 (2016): 97–120; Eldem, *Sa'dabad*, 128.
*Illustrated London News*, vol. 43, no. 1232 (November 21), 525: 'Though little more three weeks had been available for the whole of the preparations, an elegant kiosk for the reception of the sultan – designed by Mr Hutchinson and built by Messrs. Burness and Duff; a smaller pavillion for the Imperial Princes, and a commodious and strongly-built "Grand Stand," had all been constructed in that time, exclusive of the staking and roping-in of the course, and the pitching of a small encampment of tents for the accommodation of the committee, naval and military officers of rank and the refreshment purveyors'.
80. İskender Paşa's (d. 1506) garden and the meadow used to be the pasture ground of the Kağıdhane village. Also known as Mihaloğlu, he was a high-ranking military bureaucrat during the reigns of Mehmed II and Bayezid II. He seems to have had numerous freehold properties in and around the capital: Mehmed Süreyya, *Sicill-i Osmanî*. vol. 3 (İstanbul: Tarih Vakfı, 1996), 808.
81. For a map showing the kiosk and the race field (BOA, Y. PRK. HH. 6/29): Irmak, *Kağıthane Historical Inventory*, 633. For a list of archival documents on horses and horse races at Kağıdhane: *Osmanlı Belgelerinde Kağıthane*, 448–82.
82. *Illustrated London News*, 525.
83. '… Right in front, across the narrow course, along line of gaudy Turkish carriages, emblazoned with all the colours in the rainbow, and filled with yashmacked houris nearly as chromatically gorgeous as their locomotive cages, was drawn up close to the ropes. Slightly behind these were pitched the committee's marque and weighing-tent; and beyond these again – till close to the course fence – were ranged the scores of multiform vehicles which represented the whole available Frank accommodation of this kind that Pera and the Bosphorus villages could muster …'
84. '… The "Grand Stand," adjoining the Imperial kiosk, was well but not inconveniently filled with Porte functionaries, members of the diplomatic and consular bodies, and the invited spectators, of whom, as was proper, a full half were apparently Stamboulees …'
85. '… The first run was for the Esnaf Stakes, which was won by Mr. W. F. Fergusson's Black Prince; the Military Prize was taken by Velly Bey's Rusghier; The Sultan's Cup, the great contest of the day, by Sefer Pacha's Phoenix; the Ladies Cup, by Mr. F. Guarracino's Jeannot; and the day's proceedings were wound up by a hurdle race, in which Emin Bey's Chapkin came first. His Majesty the Sultan was present also on the second day, when the following running took place: The Roumelian Stakes, won by Mehemet Aga's Funduk; the Selling Stakes, by Mr. F. Guarracino's Jeannot; the Ministers' Plate, by Sefer Pacha's Phoenix; the Rahvan Stakes, by Rifart Bey's Bosna; the Committee's Cup, by M. Van Lennop's Shannon; the Consolation Sweepstakes, by Mr. Rayadjan's Ottos; and the Surudji Scurry, by Mehemet Aga's Funduk. With this last run the Constantinople races of 1863 closed. The above account is abridged from a full

description of the races in the *Levant Herald*; and our view of the racecourse is from a sketch by Mr. Hingston Harvey, of Constantinople. We have also received a photograph of the race course from Mr. Derein, photographer, of Constantinople ...'

86. Tülay Artan, 'Contemplation or Amusement? The Light Shed by *Ruznames* on an Ottoman Spectacle of 1740–1750', in *The Ottomans and Entertainment*, ed. Kate Fleet and Ebru Boyar (Leiden: Brill, 2019), 22–42.
87. P. Ğ. İnciciyan, *XVIII. Asırda İstanbul*, tr. Hrand D. Andreasyan (İstanbul: İstanbul Fetih Derneği, 1976), 95.

## Disclosure Statement

No potential conflict of interest was reported by the author(s).

ə OPEN ACCESS

# Urban *Palio* and *Scharlach* Races in Fifteenth- and Early Sixteenth-Century Italy and Germany

Christian Jaser

**ABSTRACT**
For the first time since antiquity, the Italian and German urban horse races for the prize of a precious piece of cloth called *palio* or *scharlach* could be studied as a fully-developed competitive 'sport culture' in all its dimensions, from planning and organization to the competitive performance itself through to the discursive perception and symbolic communication of victories and defeats. On both sides of the Alps, this communal tradition of horse racing experienced its heyday in the later fifteenth and early sixteenth centuries. Notwithstanding this contemporaneity and a bunch of organizational similarities, the Northern and Southern racing phenomena did not form a specific field of transalpine entanglement, but rather unconnected parallel worlds. In this essay, I will present some key comparative aspects of the transalpine field of urban horse racing: organizational structures, spatial arrangements, social range of the participants, the central role of equine agency for the success or failure of racing performances, and different media representations of victories.

In July 1502 the margrave of Mantua, Francesco II Gonzaga, received a letter from the Swabian city Böblingen, signed by his aunt Barbara, who had been married to the duke of Württemberg. In this letter duke Ulrich of Württemberg asked whether Francesco would sell one or two of his calm gaited Barb stallions to him. He claimed it was impossible to get hold of such horses north of the Alps – neither for money nor by any other means. By contrast, he knew that in the princely studs of Mantua a large number of *barbarici* were available. In his letter of reply to the Württemberger, Gonzaga recommended Turkish horses (*turci*) instead, on account of their being both fast and pleasant to ride. His Barb horses on the other hand did not have a slow gait and were only able to run – *[i]psi equi barbarici currere tantum sciant*.[1]

This misunderstanding about the degree of specialization of the horses from the North African Barbary Coast, which in Italy were indeed trained only to take part in

---

This is an Open Access article distributed under the terms of the Creative Commons Attribution-NonCommercial-NoDerivatives License (http://creativecommons.org/licenses/by-nc-nd/4.0/), which permits non-commercial re-use, distribution, and reproduction in any medium, provided the original work is properly cited, and is not altered, transformed, or built upon in any way.

races, appears to be symptomatic of the lack of connection between two series of horse races with the prize being a valuable piece of cloth – in Latin *bravium*, in Italian *palio*, in German *scharlach*. They both had their heyday in the fifteenth and early sixteenth century, and yet they were two separate worlds. On the one hand, we have the dense network of urban *palio* races in Northern and Central Italy – from provincial races in small towns to the main Florentine race of the *Palio di San Giovanni* – whose tradition reaches back to the thirteenth century.[2] On the other hand, we have the Upper German *Scharlach* races in cities such as Vienna, Munich, Nördlingen, Augsburg, Ulm and Strasbourg, for which documentation starts between 1382 and 1473.[3] Based on the interplay of communal and courtly records and of local and translocal spheres of communication, these urban horse races emerge as a fully-developed competitive 'sport culture'[4] that could be studied in all its dimensions – organization, performance, perception – for the first time since antiquity. And yet these races have so far been neglected by general historians and have neither been the object of systematic analysis nor of transalpine comparison.

In the following, the field of *palio* and *scharlach* races will be highlighted with regard to some of its key aspects.[5] First of all, general organizational structures will be addressed, in particular with regards to frequency, finance logics and practices of regulating the competition (I). Secondly, the focus will shift to the spatial arrangements of the races, i.e. the condition and preparation of racetracks as well as the placement of spectators (II). Thirdly, it is important to discuss the social outreach of the horse races and therefore look at the backgrounds of race patrons and jockeys and their interests in participation (III). Fourthly, I will deal with the exposed role of the racehorse as performer of these high-speed-contests, that, especially in Italy, is accredited with the decisive performative agency[6] in the *palio* races. Here, the key lies in the competitive terms *virtù* and *velocità* (IV). Lastly, I want to concentrate on the different media representations of competitive achievement as we encounter them mainly south of the Alps: political readings of race results in diplomatic correspondence, acclamations on the part of the spectators and followers directly after the race, the ostentatious display of the prize and the commemoration of victories in textual, visual and musical form (V).

## Organizational Structures: Frequency, Financing, and Competition Management

On both sides of the Alps, *palio* and *scharlach* races consistently took place annually. For the host cities they were central events in the festival calendar and at the same time a much-noticed occasion for communal self-representation. South of the Alps *palio* races were mostly linked to the anniversaries of the cities' patron saints – for example, the Florentine Palio di San Giovanni or the Ferrarese Palio di San Giorgio – or to *lieux de mémoire* of civic military successes against external and internal enemies.[7] The Upper German *scharlach* races on the other hand, were usually organized on the occasion of annual trade fairs during high church feasts and on patrons' days – such as the Pentecost fair in Nördlingen,[8] the *Jacobidult* in Munich,[9] the Michael fair in Augsburg[10] and the fairs in Vienna on Ascension Day and on

Catharine's Day[11] – or at shooting festivals, which were also attended by visitors from outside the region. Here, the large spectator turnout promised an increase in tax revenue and level of consumption for the city. Consequently, the communal envoy Jakob Protzer presented the prospect of *nutz mit ungelt zern und in ander weg* ('benefit through tax, consumption and other ways') to the council of Nördlingen as an economic effect of the local *scharlach* race.[12]

It was the duty of the city authorities to plan and carry out these racing events. They referred to communal norms and rules that were drafted to help ensure a smooth event and fair competition. Numerous Italian cities had sets of rules in their statutes that were sometimes as in Florence emended and updated through regulations called *provvisioni*. For example, in the statutes of Verona it says

> ... we decide and order that on the first Sunday of Lent each year the *podestà* of the commune of Verona may put up two *palio* banners – *bravia* – at a suitable location. One of the banners is earmarked for a horse race, the other for a foot race. (...) The winner of the horse race is presented with a *palio* banner as prize, the loser with a piece of ham (*baffa*) that is to be hung around the horse's neck after the race and from which everyone can cut a slice.[13]

Even more clearly than the Italian tradition of statutes, the Upper German *Rennordnungen* ('race rules') provide a set of rules for the organization of the competition. For example, the Nördlingen regulations from 1463 concern a range of topics from written registration, inspection and sealing of the participating race horses, to weight checks of the riders and their behaviour during the race and possible manipulation through *zabern vnd andern sachen* ('spells and other things'), as well as safety aspects and the placement of guards around the racetrack. The latter happened not without reason: the Nördlingen *scharlach* race had been raided by knight Anselm of Yberg (Eiberg) in 1442.[14]

The statutes also provide us with more details on the cost of the *palio* banners made out of several meters of damask, velvet or gold brocade[15] and often adorned with the host city's coat of arms. Florence, for example, planned for substantial expenses up to a maximum of 200 florins in 1415.[16] Annual expenses for this purpose are fully documented for both Florence in the fifteenth century city accounts and Munich from 1451 until far into Early Modern times.[17] At this time, the cost of the prizes – a *scharlach* cloth for the winner and a sow for the loser – was split between the city of Munich and the duke's court – a particularity of a residential city. An entry in the chamberlain's accounts from 1454 states: *Item X lb. IIII ß. XIII d. haben wir zalt für halben scharlach halb parchant ain saw der stat tail* ('we have paid ten pounds, four shillings and thirteen denars for half of the scharlach, half of the piece of fustian, half of the sow, the part of the city').[18]

It was part of the standard administrative duties to register the participating horses, riders and patrons, i.e. usually people of high rank who had signed up their horses for the race. The purpose of these procedures was to fix and precisely identify the starting field, especially by means of a detailed description of the race horses including characteristics and colours that is comparable to contemporary horse examination lists.[19] In the register of the Augsburg *scharlach* race in 1476, it states: *H[erzog] Cristoffs von Baiern erst Renner: (...) Item ain raut praun reuß haut ain pläßlin und 4 weiß füß. (...) H[erzog] Jörgen von Baiern Renner. Item ain prauner Türgk mit aim pläßlin der lingk fuoß weiß* ('Duke Christoph of Bavaria's first racehorse: ... Item a bay horse with a blaze and 4 white feet. ... Duke George of Bavaria's racehorse. A brown Turk with a blaze, the left foot white').[20] On the occasion of the Palio di San Donato in Arezzo in 1481 'a chestnut horse with a star on the face and marked white on both hind legs, belonging to Clarice Orsini, wife of said Lorenzo' was among others registered with the rider Fantaguzo.[21]

Registering the jockeys in writing served the purpose of fulfilling the imperative of identifiability and equal competitive opportunities. In order to be able to identify them better during the dynamic race they wore differently coloured robes. In 1559 scribes from Augsburg noted: *der bueb zu Klaidung Gelb, Praun und weiß, aber zwarch auf der ainen seitten, der bueb gar weiß unnd mit ain rotten kreutz, der bueb chrau und leip farb* ('The boy in yellow, brown and white clothes, but black on one side, the completely white boy with a red cross, the grey and skin coloured boy').[22] According to the Upper German race rules jockeys had to weigh a minimum of 120 or 125 pounds. According to a letter from King Maximilian to the town of Nördlingen from 1493, if a rider who was too light, a compensation weight should be attached to the horse *an ziemliche Enden und Stätten* ('on all proper ends and places').[23] In 1476 in Augsburg, the jockeys were weighed on the episcopal scales and the findings were meticulously documented[24]: the jockey Albin Pfaffer weighed the required 125 pounds,[25] his colleague Bartolin Wappner hundred and 22 ½ pounds and *sol II ½ lib. zuo im nehmen* ('is supposed to take 2½ pounds with him'), Leonhard Madowa undercut the minimum weight by two pounds and was also instructed to attach a compensation weight.[26] Presumably, there are few other people in the 15th century of whom we have such precise weight indications.[27]

## Spatial Arrangements: Quality and Preparation of Racetracks

The Italian *palio* races were mostly urban race courses that crossed the urban space from city gate to city gate in a straight track. They manifested an anything but natural, even for premodern times, communal spatial sovereignty.[28] The Florentine Palio di San Giovanni, for example, is of this nature: from the Porta al Prato right across the oldest parts of the city over the Via del Corso, which has its name from the race, to the end at the nun's convent San Pier Maggiore.[29] The key feature of this two kilometer race course was its straightness, which demanded mainly high speed endurance from the race horses.[30]

With respect to the spatial dimension, by contrast, the Upper German *Scharlach* races were suburban events. In Nördlingen, the annual *scharlach* race on the Monday after Corpus Christi took place on the so called *Reichswiese* or *Kaiserwiese* ('Imperial' or 'Emperor's meadow'), the *pratum imperiale* in front of the Baldinger Gate, northeast of the wall on a straight track. This was certainly motivated by pragmatic reasons, since the inner-city area was occupied by market stalls, so that racehorses could not run there.[31] Indeed, even in 1549, Hans Deutsch's view of the city prominently associated the suburban meadow with galloping horses in his cityscape.[32] In Munich, too, the horses raced on a straight track in front of the walls on the so called *Rennweg* ('racetrack') in front of the western Neuhauser gate. This track is basically identical with today's Schleißheimer Straße and is also illustrated with a small race scene on the oldest preserved city map of Munich by Tobias Volckmer from 1613.[33]

Before the racing events the *palio* and racetracks had to be prepared by the officials of the host cities in a way that ensured a smooth event and fair competition. Thus, according to the statutes from 1322–1325 and 1415 the Florentine Capitano del Popolo had to provide 'an unscathed, hard covered, unobstructed' racetrack and remove benches, porches and other obstacles that protruded more than a *braccio*, i.e. half a meter, into the street.[34] In Nördlingen the race commission, which comprised the two mayors and five councilmen, had to repair the entrances to the *Reichswiese*, mend railings and bridges or, if necessary, rebuild them and cover the main bridge with straw and grass. Fishermen were placed nearby this bridge to rescue jockeys who fell into the water.[35]

The strong focus on spectators of these racing events can also be retraced in the temporary building activities of the host cities. In the run-up of Ferrara's Palio di San Giorgio, viewpoints were prepared in different buildings for the duke's family and high-ranking guests.[36] In Florence, too, *magnifici palchetti*, 'magnificent stands', were erected (most probably made out of wood), which afforded the letter writer Marco Parenti and his Venetian guests, who were greatly interested in *palio* races, a view of the contest.[37] We can gain a good impression of the spectators' perspective through a wedding chest (*cassone*)[38] that shows the dramatic scene of horses reaching the finishing line in the Palio di San Giovanni in front of San Pier Maggiore, painted by Giovanni Toscani between 1425 and 1430. There are spectators everywhere – on the struts of houses, at windows and especially many along the edge of the racetrack. With regards to the mass of spectators, the historian Gregorio Dati refers to this event as a *cosa mirabile*, 'wonderful thing'.[39] The same applies to the Upper German races in the suburban space. An anonymous poem on the *scharlach* race in Nördlingen 1442 reports on *ein grosse meng* ('many people') and *ein hubsch gedreng* ('a pretty dense crowd').[40]

## Social Outreach – Backgrounds and Interests in Participation of Race Patrons and Jockeys

On the basis of the lists of participants mentioned above, diplomatic correspondence and historiographic as well as diary documentation, the social outreach of the starting field can be identified relatively accurately. On both sides of the Alps the *palio* and *scharlach* races were a field of interaction between urban and courtly protagonists. Ownership of a competitive race horse undoubtedly required significant financial strength with regards to both purchase and care. Therefore, the victory of a Florentine butcher's son in the Palio di San Giovanni in Florence 1405 was a rare exception.[41] Unlike tournaments, which were open exclusively to nobility, urban horse races on both sides of the Alps attracted participants of heterogenous backgrounds; we find peasants, burghers and patricians as well as lesser noblemen and members of the gentry, princes, high church dignitaries and even kings. The most important and most lucrative *palio* race of Renaissance Italy, the Florentine

Palio di San Giovanni, brought together an elite of race horse owners with studs that were famous throughout Europe – the Gonzaga from Mantua, the Margraves of Este from Ferrara, the Bentivoglio from Bologna, the Baglioni from Perugia, the lords of Mirandola. However, among the winning patrons we also find citizens from Siena, Rome and Lucca as well as the Florentine patrician family of the Benci.[42] Compared to this dominance of princes and *signori* south of the Alps, the lesser remunerated *scharlach* races in Nördlingen attracted participants more from the patrician and lesser noble class, apart from the presence of Albert III, Duke of Bavaria-Munich as race patron in 1449.[43]

The race patrons were able to increase their social capital and demonstrate their social status and financial wealth in front of the urban public through mere participation, but even more so through competitive success. South of the Alps, for example, the presence of princely *signori* of a middle rank who often offered their services as *condottieri* is anything but a coincidence. The urban *palio* races in front of a large number of spectators – i.e. in front of their potential employers – provided them with a welcome opportunity to display the quality of their studs in order to land lucrative future contracts.[44] The spice dealer Gostanzo Landucci's success in the *palio* races – between 1481 and 1485 he won no fewer than 20 races[45] – reflected not only his financial power but also the extent of his business activities that allowed him to import a winning horse like the stallion *Draghetto* from the Barbary coast.[46] At times the starting field turned into pure demonstration of power as it was the case with the 1486 *Scharlach* race in Vienna. Here, the new city ruler, the Hungarian King Matthias Corvinus, ordered an entire phalanx of his entourage to compete in the race and excluded other participants. The king himself put forward four horses, his cousin and military leader Peter Gereb three, the wealthy Hungarian merchant Hans Pempflinger two, whilst the captain Nikolasch Cropez and two scribes registered one horse each.[47]

We know very little about the social background of the riders called *rennbuben* or *ragazzi* on either side of the Alps. Regarding their professional background, we can assume that they worked as grooms or stable boys in the studs of the race patrons or as *barbareschatori*, i.e. specialists on race horses, which often originally came from the Barbary coast.[48] In Upper Germany the jockeys were supposed to be *mannbar lüt*, i.e. sexually mature men, as it is stated for example in the Nördlingen race rule from 1459.[49] Jockeys and *barbareschatori* like Bartolomeo de' Barbari from the Gonzaga stud in Mantua, who was murdered in 1496, were often – despite their expertise in racing – dubious characters and their choleric temperament occasionally led to diplomatic complications.[50] At the beginning of the sixteenth century in Siena jockeys were registered with very striking nicknames that definitely have an ironic undertone and suggest a certain degree of fame: *Spera in dio* – 'he places his hope in God', *Ha paura di esser l'ultimo* – 'he is afraid to be last', *Porta el palio a casa* – 'he takes the *palio* home'.[51]

## The Race Horse as Performer – Agency, *Virtù* and *Velocità*

For the audience the horses' competition was a rather brief event. Montaigne comments on his experience of the Florentine *palio* in 1581 rather unenthusiastically:

'You stood on the street and did not see anything but the horses flashing by'. Likewise, Goethe only states the limits of visibility in light of the kinetic energy on the Roman course: 'You have hardly caught sight of them and they are already gone'.[52] In the same spirit, the Florentine poet and humanist Angelo Poliziano portraits one of the race horses of Lorenzo de' Medici as an invisible kinetic phenomenon: 'At best, you can see it at the beginning and at the end but by no means during the course of the race!'[53] Nobody captivated the agonal excitement and fascinating experience of speed at the finishing line better than Toscani in his painting *cassone*. The galloping horses' bodies stretching towards the finishing line, leaping forward, can remind us of Théodore Géricault's painting *Le derby de 1821 à Epsom* from 1821, whose almost flying horses represent the nineteenth century experience of speed.[54] The corpus of *palio* correspondence around 1500 – from Mantua alone we have hundreds of letters – almost overflows with comparative speed semantics. We often find statements of distances between winning and losing horses by means of horse lengths or well-known milestones[55] as well as dromological superlatives: the horse galloped 'with such speed – *cum tanta velocità* – that it was equal to an arrow'. The author explicitly states this to be *publica fama* ('public opinion').[56]

Assessing the speed performance, the contemporary observers had no doubt that in a *palio* race the horse, and not the rider, had the performative agency. The remark of the Mantuan Angelo de Maximis on the 'cleverness and courage of the rider' (*per astutia et virtù del regazo*) being the decisive element for the positive outcome of the Roman carnival race in 1514 is a rare exception.[57] It is much more common that reports on the races grant a performance monopoly to the horses, which were known by name. In a report on the Florentine Palio di San Pietro from 1509 it says 'The horse of the cardinal of Mantua was the first to enter the Porta del Prato. All the other horses were really close to each other as far as the Borgo d'Ognissanti except your *Renegato Giovine*, who passed all the others on this street and extended his lead up to the *palio* such that the other horses were still at the house of the Duke of Ferrara when he finished'.[58] These ascriptions of equine agency correspond to the specific regulations for Italian *palio* races that took a horse finishing the race *scosso*, i.e. without its rider, to be a valid result.[59] Thus, what we can see on the *cassone* painting mentioned above, namely horses with riders alongside several riderless ones breaking up the competitive unit of horse and rider, was indeed consistent with the rules. If we then take into account the fact that some cities also held races entirely without jockeys, the contemporary focus on the animal's performance becomes even more apparent. Therefore, it seems only natural if a successful race patron like Francesco II accredits his greatest results to the *virtù* of his horses.[60] *Virtù*, a key concept of the Italian Renaissance, expresses the demonstration of superiority of one person over another with its semantic content ranging from 'virtue' and 'talent' to 'merit' and 'strength'.[61] *Virtù* has a highly agonal connotation and with regards to the race horses has to be translated as 'performance tested through competition'.

Accordingly, breeding, grooming, veterinary care and feeding of Italian race horses were subject to a strict regime whose sole purpose was to increase the horses' speed. Even in fifteenth century Upper Germany, where the record on princely and civil studs is anything but satisfying, special formulas for race horses circulated under the title *Hertzog Albrechts Rennen*. The powder made of herbs, roots, mistletoe and wine was supposed to have both a strengthening and relaxing effect: 'And if you want to race, you add one lot of powder to the horse's fodder over four days. Afterwards you can ride cheerfully whenever you want. Nobody will be able to reach you. You will experience a miracle'. It is impossible to ignore the objective of a guaranteed performance improvement in this quote.[62]

## The Meaning of Winning – Political Readings and Media Representation

North of the Alps the scarce media representation of the *scharlach* races consists of brief entries in city chronicles. Princely correspondence was almost entirely restricted to reflections on tournaments and hardly ever mentions horse races. This contrasts strongly with the *palio* races in Italy, which were the subject not only of daily reporting but also of textual, visual and acoustic representation. In the case of winning, the *virtù* and *velocità* of race horses could be converted into *onore*, honor, of the race patrons. The basis for the transformation of equine *virtù* to patronal honor was the 'centaurian pact' between patron and race horse.[63] The role of the horse as representative and equine *alter ego* of its patron or owner was indicated through clear assignments in the lists of participants and was then made visible during the race through heraldic symbols. Referring back to ancient narratives – for example Plutarch's and Curtius Rufus' depiction of the relationship between Alexander the Great and his horse Bukephalos[64] – contemporary anecdotes indicate similar special relationships. Lorenzo de' Medici's biographer Niccolò Valori writes that his race horse Morello, which was so fast that it won all of the races it participated in, would only let Lorenzo feed it when it was ill or exhausted. Whenever Lorenzo approached it, it neighed happily and lay down on the floor.[65]

Reducing social complexity to evident victory, ranking and defeat in race competition allowed the transformation of every success or failure into social value and the demonstration of political status and rank. The *honor de la nostra vittoria* ('honor of our victory'), as Francesco Gonzaga puts it, lay in the symbolic conquest of the respective host city.[66] With tongue in cheek he attested to his Medici rivals in 1513 that due to his *palio* successes the *Excellentissima Repubblica di Fiorenza* had to be counted among his subjects almost every year.[67] Equally, rankings were politically interpreted in diplomatic correspondence, as we can see in different letters by Gian Filippo Salarolo on the performance of the Barb stallion *Fulgore* from the racing stable of the Bolognese ruler Giovanni Bentivoglio. Salarolo reports that *Fulgore* only achieved third place in the Ferrarese *palio* in May 1481, but to the satisfaction of Bentivoglio that meant he was still ranked higher than the horse of the Malvezzi, a rival familiy of the Bentivoglio in Bologna, which came fourth.[68] After the victory of Fulgore in the Bolognese *palio* of San Ruffillo the same year, the superiority of the Bentivoglio could be proclaimed triumphantly again: 'The Malvezzi's horse achieved second place; nevertheless, ten horse lengths behind Fulgore'.[69]

After the *palio* victory, 'acoustic communities'[70] formed *in situ*, consisting of followers and supporters who vociferously acclaimed the victorious patron – *Mantua*,

*Mantua, Gonzaga, Gonzaga*[71] – and who thereby multiplied the symbolic capital in the echo chamber of the urban face-to-face society. According to a poem of praise by Filippo Lapacini on one of the Gonzaga horses, patrons earned the reputation of *virtú* through *palio* successes, so that 'the whole of Italy shouted *Turcho Turcho*', the battle cry of the Mantuan margraves.[72] On top of momentary acclamation, the serial nature of the *palio* races taking place annually in many cities facilitated forms of diachronic memory of performance. The Este and Gonzaga, for instance, established special *guardarobe*[73] for storing the *palio* banners they had won and the offensive self-promotion of the Sienese painter and race patron Sodoma points in the same direction: 'Over many years, he himself had won a great number of *palio* trophies with his horses in this way, and in his vanity, he showed them to anyone who entered his house and often even presented them in the window', as Sodoma's biographer Giorgio Vasari smugly remarks.[74]

Commemoration of *palio* victories was taken to extremes by the Mantuan margraves who created a new media format with the *Libro dei palii vinti*,[75] commissioned in 1512, which was supposed to immortalize the success story of the Gonzaga race horses in text and image.[76] This elaborately designed codex contains 34 race horses, each portrayed as racing sports celebrity. In it we find the name of each horse in golden letters above a picture of it *dal naturale* in front of a fantasy landscape. At the bottom of the page there is a list of the *palio* victories of each race horse, again in coloured letters. In total, the codex accounts for 197 *palio* victories between 1499 and 1518.[77]

This textual and visual commemoration of Italian *palio* races mirrors an intensive political competition between princes, signori and local elites that was accompanied by increasing communicative networking and an 'intensifying use of propaganda and "media"'.[78] It imprinted itself in manifold ways into the sports culture of the Italian Renaissance. Through the competitive leitmotiv of race patronage, opportunities of representation opened up to horse owners that had an effect far beyond the actual racing event. Contrary to that, in Upper Germany the winner's representation was limited to the short-termed surplus of attention in the urban face-to-face society. Immediately after the race, the participants of *scharlach* races were scheduled to enter the city in a procession according to their ranking. The victorious horse and its patron were supposed to get special attention as we can see in the Munich race rules from 1448: *Item wie die phärdt herein lauffen, ains nach dem anndern. Also sollen sie nacheinander herein geen, bis für die Herberg, da das phärt stet, das das tuech gewonnen hat* ('Item, as the horses ride in, one after the other: They shall thus go in one after the other up to the lodging where the horse stands that has won the cloth').[79]

In sum, Italian palio and German scharlach races of the fifteenth and early century share, on the one hand, many similarities: the role of city governments in planning, managing and financing urban horse races; their communal staging as spectator events and annual frequency; the textile quality and hierarchy of prizes; and finally, the fundamental significance of racing patronage by local and foreign racehorse owners. On the other hand, the comparative perspective also shows a strikingly different approach of host cities and race patrons alike on both sides of the Alps.

Whereas Italian palio races were mostly held on religious feast days as inner-city contests, their German counterparts took place during annual trade fairs on suburban racetracks. Strictly speaking, these sport cultures south and north of the Alps operated on different levels, in particular with regard to their scale and scope: in Florence and other Italian cities, there were much richer prizes on offer than in any German race venue. As a consequence, many palio races were run by horses of princes, *signori* and *condottieri*, while the scharlach races had a rather less illustrious starting field from the patriciate and lower nobility down to the citizenry and peasantry.

By the identification of the racehorses as symbolic proxies of their patrons, urban palio races were an occasion for signorile competition, the transformation of equine speed in patronal honor and different media representations of victories. North of the Alps, the decisive agency of individual racehorses and their representative value were neither perceived nor exploited, not even by the sporadic race patronage of German princes. This particular idea of the racehorse as key performer and medium for political and social messages never reached the German racing tradition, at least on the basis of the existing source material. As the letter exchange cited at the beginning of the essay shows, the otherwise manifoldly-permeable Alps were a natural barrier for racehorses, regarding their concrete transport as well as the transfer of their performative and symbolic perceptions. In this respect, Italian and German urban racing cultures during the Renaissance did not form a specific field of transalpine entanglement, but rather unconnected parallel worlds.

## Notes

1. Barbara Gonzaga to Francesco II Gonzaga, [Böblingen], June 25, 1502, in Christina Antenhofer, Axel Behne, Daniela Ferrari, Jürgen Herold, and Peter Rückert, eds., *Barbara Gonzaga: Die Briefe / Le Lettere (1455-1508)* (Stuttgart: Kohlhammer, 2013), 311, 449–50; Francesco II Gonzaga to Barbara Gonzaga, Mantua, July 10, 1502, in: ibid., 312, 450–1.
2. Michael Mallett, 'Horse-Racing and Politics in Lorenzo's Florence', in *Lorenzo the Magnificent: Culture and Politics*, ed. Michael Mallett and Michael Mann (London: Warburg Institute, 1996), 253–62, here 254; Elizabeth Tobey, 'The Palio-Horse in Renaissance and Early Modern Italy', in *Culture of the Horse: Status, Discipline and Identity in the Early Modern World*, ed. Karen Raber and Treva J. Tucker (Basingstoke: Palgrave Macmillian, 2005), 63–90, here 64; Elizabeth MacKenzie Tobey, 'The Palio in Italian Renaissance Art, Thought, and Culture' (Ph.D. diss., University of Maryland-College Park, 2005), 45–49.
3. Miriam Hall Kirch, '"For Amusement, Merrymaking, and Good Company": Horse Racing at a German Princely Court', in *Animals and Early Modern Identity*, ed. Pia F. Cuneo (Farnham: Routledge, 2014), 89–107; Annelie Kalb, 'Beiträge zur geschichtlichen Entwicklung der Pferderennen in Bayern unter besonderer Berücksichtigung der Vollblutrennen (bis 1933)' (Vet. Med. Diss., Munich, 1958), 8–11.
4. For the concept of premodern urban sport cultures in general, see Christian Jaser, 'Agonale Ökonomien. Städtische Sportkulturen des 15. Jahrhunderts am Beispiel der Florentiner Palio-Pferderennen', *Historische Zeitschrift* 298 (2014): 593–624.
5. The only exceptions are the rather descriptive approaches by Galeazzo Nosari and Franco Canova, *Il Palio nel Rinascimento. I cavalli di razza dei Gonzaga nell'età di Francesco II*

*Gonzaga 1484–1519* (Reggiolo: E. Lui, 2003), and Kalb, 'Beiträge zur geschichtlichen Entwicklung der Pferderennen'.
6. Gesine Krüger, Aline Steinbrecher, and Clemens Wischermann, 'Animate History. Zugänge und Konzepte einer Geschichte zwischen Menschen und Tieren', in *Tiere und Geschichte. Konturen einer Animate History*, ed. Gesine Krüger, Aline Steinbrecher, and Clemens Wischermann (Stuttgart: Franz Steiner, 2014), 9–33, here 14–15. See also Mieke Roscher, 'Human-Animal Studies, Version 1.0', in: *Docupedia-Zeitgeschichte*, January 25, 2012, https://docupedia.de/zg/Human-Animal_Studies (accessed August 9, 2015).
7. Richard C. Trexler, *Public Life in Renaissance Florence* (Ithaca: Cornell University Press), 262; Paola Ventrone, 'La festa di San Giovanni: costruzione di un'identità civica fra rituale e spettacolo (secoli XIV-XVI)', *Annali di Storia di Firenze* 2 (2007): 49–76, here 49, 55.
8. Heinrich Steinmeyer, *Die Entstehung und Entwicklung der Nördlinger Pfingstmesse im Spätmittelalter mit einem Ausblick bis ins 19. Jahrhundert* (Nördlingen: Wagner, 1960), esp. 66–70; Hektor Ammann, 'Die Nördlinger Messe im Mittelalter', in *Aus Verfassungs- und Landesgeschichte. Festschrift zum 70. Geburtstag von Theodor Mayer*, vol. 2 (Lindau and Konstanz: Thorbecke, 1955), 283–315; Rudolf Endres, *Die Nürnberg-Nördlinger Wirtschaftsbeziehungen im Mittelalter bis zur Schlacht von Nördlingen. Ihre rechtlich-politischen Voraussetzungen und ihre tatsächlichen Auswirkungen* (Neustadt a.d. Aisch: Degener, 1964), 122–204; Rolf Kießling, *Die Stadt und ihr Land. Umlandpolitik, Bürgerbesitz und Wirtschaftsgefüge in Ostschwaben vom 14. bis ins 16. Jahrhundert* (Cologne, Vienna: Böhlau, 1989), 158–79; Dietmar-H. Voges, *Die Reichsstadt Nördlingen. 12 Kapitel aus ihrer Geschichte* (Munich: Beck, 1988), 47–69; Ingrid Batóri, 'Ratsräson und Bürgersinn: Zur Führungsschicht der Reichsstadt Nördlingen im 15. und 16. Jahrhundert', in *Politics and Reformations: Communities, Polities, Nations and Empires. Essays in Honor of Thomas A. Brady, Jr.*, ed. Christopher Ocker, Michael Printy, Peter Starenko, and Peter Wallace (Leiden: Brill, 2007), 85–119, here 86.
9. Kalb, 'Beiträge zur geschichtlichen Entwicklung der Pferderennen', 9; Michael Schattenhofer, *Von Kirchen, Kurfürsten & Kaffeesiedern etcetera. Aus Münchens Vergangenheit* (Munich: Süddeutscher Verlag, 1974), 265–97, esp. 290; id., 'Beiträge zur Geschichte der Stadt München', *Oberbayerisches Archiv* 109, no. 1 (1984): 9–223, here 66–8; Fridolin Solleder, *München im Mittelalter* (Munich and Berlin: Oldenburg, 1938), 418–9.
10. Max Radlkofer, 'Die Schützengesellschaften und Schützenfeste Augsburgs im 15. und 16. Jahrhundert', *Zeitschrift des Historischen Vereins für Schwaben* 21 (1894): 87–138, here 95; Ludwig Mußgnug, 'Das Augsburger Scharlachrennen von 1454', *Zeitschrift des Historischen Vereins für Schwaben* 46 (1926): 141–2; Franz Häußler, *Marktstadt Augsburg. Von der Römerzeit bis zur Gegenwart* (Augsburg: Wißner, 1998), 129–37; Rolf Kießling, 'Marktrecht', in *Augsburger Stadtlexikon. Geschichte, Gesellschaft, Kultur, Recht, Wissenschaft* (Augsburg: Perlach, 1985), 241–2.
11. Charter of Duke Albrecht III of Austria, September 29, 1382: Vienna, Stadt- und Landesarchiv, Privileg 23, printed in *Die Rechtsquellen der Stadt Wien*, ed. Peter Csendes (Vienna: Böhlau, 1986), 43, 195. See also Kalb, 'Beiträge zur geschichtlichen Entwicklung der Pferderennen', 8.
12. Jakob Protzer to the burgomaster and the council of Nördlingen, Vienna, May 9, 1459, Nördlingen, Stadtarchiv, Missiven 1459, fol. 138v. See also Steinmeyer, *Pfingstmesse*, 40, note 48; Kalb, 'Beiträge zur geschichtlichen Entwicklung der Pferderennen', 16; Rudolf Holbach, 'Feste in spätmittelalterlichen Städten des Hanseraums', in *Il tempo libero: economia e società (loisirs, leisure, tiempo libre, Freizeit), secc. XIII-XVIII*, ed. Simonetta Cavaciocchi (Prato: Le Monnier, 1995), 213–32, here 218.
13. Statutes of Verona, before 1271, lib. I, c. LXVII, printed in Gaetano Da Re, 'I tre primi statuti sulle corse de' palii di Verona', *Rivista critica della letteratura italiana* 7 (1891): 80–7, here 81.

14. Nördlingen race rules from 1463, printed in Gerhard Eis, 'Zu den zeitgenössischen Aufzeichnungen über die süddeutschen Pferderennen im 15. Jahrhundert', *Tierärztliche Umschau* 16 (1961): 353–6, here 354. For the raid in 1442, see Aneta Bialecka, 'Der Überfall auf das Nördlinger Scharlachrennen. Gewalt als symbolische Ordnung der Gesellschaft in der urbanen Festkultur', in *Rules and Violence. Regeln und Gewalt. On the Cultural History of Collective Violence from Late Antiquity to the Confessional Age. Zur Kulturgeschichte der kollektiven Gewalt von der Spätantike bis zum Konfessionellen Zeitalter*, ed. Cora Dietl and Titus Knäpper (Berlin: De Gruyter, 2014), 193–208; Hanns Fischer, 'Der Überfall beim Nördlinger Scharlachrennen. Bemerkungen zu einem vergessenen Zeitspruch aus dem Jahre 1442', in *Festschrift für Klaus Ziegler*, ed. Eckehard Catholy and Winfried Hellmann (Tübingen: Niemeyer, 1968), 61–76.
15. Luciano Artusi, Silvano Gabbrielli, *Feste e giochi a Firenze* (Florence: Becocci, 1976), 58; Tobey, 'Palio', 146–81, 189–90; Duccio Balestracci, 'Alle origini del Palio. Da festa come tante altre a festa come nessun'altra', in *Pallium – Evoluzione del drappelone dalle origini ad oggi: dalle origini ai moti risorgimentali*, ed. Luca Betti (Siena: Betti, 1993), 9–14, here 9–11.
16. *Statuta populi et communis Florentiae publica auctoritate collecta, castigata et praeposia anno salutis MCCCCXV*, 3 vols. (Freiburg: Kluch, 1778–1783), vol. 3, 314, tract. III, lib. V, rubr. XIII (*De bravio currendo in festo beati sancti Iohannis Baptistae*). See also Gregorio Dati, *L'istoria di Firenze dal 1380 al 1405*, ed. Luigi Pratesi (Norcia: C. Tonti, 1902), c. 131, 95.
17. Florence, Archivio di Stato, Camera del Comune, Provveditori, Entrata e Uscita, 16, 342v (June 1401); ibid., 17, 343r (July, 31, 1402); Munich, Stadtarchiv, Kammerrechnungen 60, 1451, 61v.
18. Munich, Stadtarchiv, Kammerrechnungen 63, 1454, 80r.
19. Stephan Selzer, 'Reitende Macht. Italienische Condottiere und ihre Pferde im 14. und 15. Jahrhundert', in *Praemium Virtutis III. Reiterstandbilder von der Antike bis zum Klassizismus*, ed. Joachim Poeschke, Thomas Weigel, and Britta Kusch-Arnhold (Münster: Rhema, 2008), 75–93, here 79–81; Andrea da Mosto, 'Ordinamenti militari delle soldatesche dello stato romano dal 1430 al 1470', *Quellen und Forschungen aus italienischen Archiven und Bibliotheken* 5 (1902): 19–34, here 24 note 4. See, in general, Umberto Eco, *Die unendliche Liste* (Munich: Deutscher Taschenbuchverlag, 2011).
20. List of participants to the *scharlach* race during the Augsburg shooting festival: Juy 19, 1476, Augsburg, Stadtarchiv, Schützenakten 1, Fasz. 1, unpag.
21. List of participants to the Aretine palio di San Donato, August 6, 1480: Arezzo, Archivio di Stato, Deliberazioni del Magistrato dei Priori e del Consiglio Generale, 13, 60v.
22. Augsburg race rules, 1559, Augsburg, Stadtarchiv, Verschiedene Provenienzen – Polizeiwesen, sign. 3, no. 39, 3r.
23. Emperor Maximilian I to the city of Nördlingen, Augsburg, May 9, 1493, Nördlingen, Stadtarchiv, Messe, R 38 F 9, no. 13: Akten zum Scharlachrennen, printed in Ludwig Mußgnug, 'Das Nördlinger Scharlachrennen', *Jahrbuch des Historischen Vereins für Nördlingen und das Ries* 9 (1922/1924): 113–31, here 116. See also Kalb, 'Beiträge zur geschichtlichen Entwicklung der Pferderennen', 17.
24. Invitation to the *scharlach* race during the Augsburg shooting festival, July 20, 1476: Augsburg, Stadtarchiv, Schützenakten 1, fasc. 1, unpag. See also the Nördlingen race rules from 1463 printed in Eis, 'Zu den zeitgenössischen Aufzeichnungen', 354. For the episcopal scales in Augsburg, see Petra Ostenrieder, 'Waagen', in *Augsburger Stadtlexikon*, 397.
25. Invitation letter of the council and the rifle shooters of Augsburg to the Nurembergers, Augsburg, April 20, 1476, printed in Radlkofer, 'Schützengesellschaften', 132.
26. List of participants to the scharlach race during the Augsburg shooting festival, July 19, 1476, Augsburg, Stadtarchiv, Schützenakten 1, fasc. 1, unpag. For contemporary weight measurements in Augsburg, see Rainer Beck, 'Maß und Gewicht in vormoderner Zeit.

Das Beispiel Augsburg', *Zeitschrift des Historischen Vereins für Schwaben* 91 (1998): 169–98, esp. 196–7.
27. For one of the rare reflections on the rider's body weight south of the Alps, see Mallett, 'Horse-Racing', 260.
28. John M. Najemy, 'Florentine Politics and Urban Spaces', in *Renaissance Florence. A Social History*, ed. Roger J. Crum and John T. Paoletti (Cambridge: Cambridge University Press, 2006), 19–54.
29. Mark Christopher Rogers, 'Art and Public Festival in Renaissance Florence. Studies in Relationships' (Ph.D. diss., University of Texas-Austin, 1996), 212–3; Artusi, Gabbrielli, *Feste e giochi*, 59; Heidi L. Chrétien, *The Festival of San Giovanni. Imagery and Political Power in Renaissance Florence* (New York: Lang, 1994), 41.
30. Nicole Carew-Reid, *Les fêtes florentines au temps de Lorenzo il Magnifico* (Florence: Olschki, 1995), 72.
31. Steinmeyer, *Pfingstmesse*, 34; Voges, *Reichsstadt Nördlingen*, 59.
32. Kalb, 'Beiträge zur geschichtlichen Entwicklung der Pferderennen', 16, 19; Fischer, 'Überfall beim Nördlinger Scharlachrennen', 68; Steinmeyer, *Pfingstmesse*, 70.
33. Helmuth Stahleder, *Chronik der Stadt München, vol. 1: Herzogs- und Bürgerstadt. Die Jahre 1157–1505* (Munich: Hugendubel, 1995), 144; Solleder, *München im Mittelalter*, 418; Kalb, 'Beiträge zur geschichtlichen Entwicklung der Pferderennen', 11, 15–16.
34. *Statuta populi et communis Florentiae*, vol. 2, 473–4, lib. IV, rubr. CXXIII. See also *Statuti della Repubblica Fiorentina, 1322–1325*, ed. Romolo Caggese, and the new edition: *Statuti della Repubblica Fiorentina, vol. 1: Statuto del Capitano del Popolo degli anni 1322–1325*, ed. Giuliano Pinto, Francesco Salvestrini, and Andrea Zorzi, 2 vols. (Florence: Olschki, 1999), 164, lib. IV, rubr. XI. See also Yvonne Elet, 'Seats of Power: The Outdoor Benches of Early Modern Florence', *Journal of the Society of Architectural Historians* 61, no. 4 (2002): 444–69, here 451–3.
35. Mußgnug, 'Nördlinger Scharlachrennen', 118, 123; Kalb, 'Beiträge zur geschichtlichen Entwicklung der Pferderennen', 18.
36. Thomas Tuohy, *Herculean Ferrara. Ercole d'Este, 1471–1505, and the Invention of a Ducal Capital* (Cambridge: Cambridge University Press, 1996), 240.
37. Marco Parenti, *Lettere*, ed. Maria Marrese (Florence: Olschki, 1996), 80.
38. See, in general, Jacqueline Marie Musacchio, *Art, Marriage, and Family in the Florentine Renaissance Palace* (New Haven: Yale University Press, 2008); Caroline Campbell, *Love and Marriage in Renaissance Florence. The Courtauld Wedding Chests* (London: Weidenfeld & Nicolson, 2009); Paul Schubring, *Cassoni. Truhen und Truhenbilder der italienischen Frührenaissance. Ein Beitrag zur Profanmalerei im Quattrocento* (Leipzig: Hiersemann, 1915).
39. *Le feste di San Giovanni Batista in Firenze. Descritte in prosa e in rima da contemporanei*, ed. Cesare Guasti (Florence, 1908), 14. See also 'I Giornali di Ser Giusto Giusti d'Anghiari (1437–1482)', ed. Nerida Newbigin, *Letteratura Italiana Antica* 3 (2002): 41–246, here 104 (1451.10) (June 24, 1451). See also Carew-Reid, *Les fêtes florentines*, 42, 76; Artusi, Gabbrielli, *Feste e giochi*, 57.
40. Anonymous poem on the raid against the scharlach race in Nördlingen 1442: Wolfenbüttel, Herzog-August-Bibliothek, Cod. 18.12. Aug. 4° (1494), 258r; printed in Fischer, 'Überfall beim Nördlinger Scharlachrennen', 63. See also Hektor Mülich, 'Chronik 1348–1487', in *Chroniken der schwäbischen Städte: Augsburg*, ed. Ferdinand Frensdorff, Matthias Lexer, and Friedrich Roth, vol. 3 (Leipzig: Hirzel, 1892), 1–440, here 80 (relating to the year 1442).
41. *Diario Fiorentino di Bartolomeo di Michele del Corazza Anni 1405–1438*, ed. G. O. Corazzini, *Archivio Storico Italiano*, 5th series, 14 (1894): 233–98, here 240 (relating to July 28, 1405).
42. 'I Giornali di Ser Giusto Giusti d'Anghiari', 58 (1439.8) (June 24, 1439); ibid., 100, (1449.7–8) (June 24, 1449); ibid., 104 (1451.10) (June 24, 1451); ibid., 122 (1459.24) (June

24, 1459); ibid., 201 (1478.61-62) (July 5, 1478); ibid. 220 (1482.3) (June 24, 1482). See also Nosari, Canova, *Il Palio nel Rinascimento*, 314-27.
43. Nördlingen, Stadtarchiv, Messestandregister 1445, 1468-1470, 1475-1477, 1519, 1522-1527: Messestandregister 1445-1449, 7r-7v, 8r (1445?); 33r (1446?); 48r (1447?); 62v (1448); 78r (1449). See also Mußgnug, 'Nördlinger Scharlachrennen', 118; Fischer, 'Überfall beim Nördlinger Scharlachrennen', 68; Kalb, 'Beiträge zur geschichtlichen Entwicklung der Pferderennen', 16.
44. Selzer, 'Reitende Macht'. See Randolph Starn, 'Heroes in Renaissance Italy', *The Journal of Interdisciplinary History* 17, no. 1 (1986): 67-84, here 77-84; Carlo Marco Belfanti, 'I Gonzaga signori della guerra (1410-1530)', in *La Corte di Mantova nell'età di Andrea Mantegna 1450-1550 / The Court of the Gonzaga in the Age of Mantegna, 1450-1550. Atti del convegno (Londra, 6-8 marzo 1992 / Mantova, 28 marzo 1992)*, ed. Cesare Mozzarelli, Robert Oresko, and Leandro Ventura (Rome: Bulzoni, 1997), 61-8; Anthony B. Cashman III, 'Performance Anxiety: Federico Gonzaga at the Court of Francis I and the Uncertainty of Ritual Action', *Sixteenth Century Journal* 33, no. 2 (2002): 333-52, here 340.
45. *Diario Fiorentino dal 1450 al 1516 di Luca Landucci continuato da un anonimo fino al 1542*, ed. Iodoco del Badia (Florence: Sansoni, 1883), 50 (relating to July 17, 1485).
46. Ibid., 39 (relating to October 8, 1481). In general, see Tobey, 'Palio-Horse', 71; Louis de Mas Latrie, *Relations et commerce de l'Afrique septentrionale ou Magreb avec les nations chrétiens au moyen âge* (Paris: Firmin-Didot, 1886), 443-8, 482-5, 516-23; Richard A. Goldthwaite, *The Economy of Renaissance Florence* (Baltimore: John Hopkins University Press, 2011), 151; Michael Mallett, *The Florentine Galleys in the Fifteenth Century* (Oxford: Clarendon, 1967), 72-82.
47. Wien, Stadt- und Landesarchiv, Oberkammeramtsrechnungen 1486, 9r. For the background, see Aneta Bialecka, 'Spectaculum scarlaci. Ritualität zwischen Integration und politischer Usurpation', in *Grenzen des Rituals: Wirkreichweiten - Geltungsbereiche - Forschungsperspektiven*, ed. Andreas Büttner (Cologne: Böhlau, 2014), 49-72, here 56-58.
48. Mallett, 'Horse-Racing', 260.
49. Mußgnug, 'Nördlinger Scharlachrennen', 115; Tobey, 'Palio-Horse', 66.
50. Nosari, Canova, *Il Palio nel Rinascimento*, 178, 183, 283.
51. List of participants to the palio of the saint Ambrogio Sansedoni, March 10, 1513: Siena, Archivio di Stato, Biccherna 972, 28v, printed in *Giovanni Antonio Bazzi, il Sodoma. Fonti documentarie e letterarie*, ed. Roberto Bartalini, Alessia Zombardo (Vercelli: Società Storica Vercellese, 2012), no. 15, 44; list of participants to the palio of the saint Ambrogio Sansedoni, March 30, 1513: printed in *Nuovi Documenti per la Storia dell'Arte Senese*, ed. S. Borghesi and L. Banchi (Siena: E. Torrini, 1898), 207, 409; list of participants of the palio of S. Maria Magdalena, July 22, 1513, printed in ibid., 207, 409.
52. Michel de Montaigne, *Journal de voyage*, ed. Fausta Garavini (Paris: Gallimard, 2007), 308; Johann Wolfgang von Goethe, *Die Italienische Reise. Hamburger Ausgabe*, ed. Herbert von Einem (München: Deutscher Taschenbuchverlag, 1988), 507.
53. Angelo Poliziano, *In equum Laurentii Medicis*, 1487, in: *Prose volgari inedite e poesie latine e greche edite e inedite di Angelo Ambrogini Poliziano*, ed. Isidoro del Lungo (Florence: Barbèra, 1867), 130.
54. Théodore Géricault, 'Le derby de 1821 à Epsom', Paris, Louvre, M.I. 708. For the speed experience of the nineteenth century as context of this painting, see Geoffrey S. Mac Adam, 'The Pursuit of Presence: Speed and the Transformation of Early-Nineteenth French Culture' (Ph.D. diss., Columbia University, 2006), 99-103; Andreas Braun, *Tempo, Tempo! Eine Kunst- und Kulturgeschichte der Geschwindigkeit im 19. Jahrhundert* (Frankfurt: Anabas, 2001), 14-16; Christophe Studeny, *L'invention de la vitesse. France, XVIIIe-XXe siècle* (Paris: Gallimard, 1995).
55. Gianfrancesco da Crema to Francesco II Gonzaga, Mantua, June 30, 1509: Mantua, Archivio di Stato, Archivio Gonzaga, busta 2475, 393r; Francesco Malatesta to Francesco II Gonzaga, Florence, June 14, 1500, ibid., busta 1103, 72v-73r. See also Bartolomeo de'

Barbari to Francesco II Gonzaga, April 26, 1496, ibid., busta 2450, 61r. See also Nosari, Canova, *Il Palio nel Rinascimento*, 172.
56. Alessandro Gabbioneta to Francesco II Gonzaga, Rome, February 19, 1515: Mantua, Archivio di Stato, Archivio Gonzaga, busta 876, 121r; Giovanfrancesco da Crema to Francesco II Gonzaga, Florence, June 30, 1509, ibid., busta 2475, 393r.
57. Angelo de Maximis to Federico Gonzaga, Rome, March 4, 1514, Mantua, Archivio di Stato, Archivio Gonzaga, busta 862, fasc. VI, 270r.
58. Giovanfrancesco da Crema to Francesco II. Gonzaga, Florence, June 30, 1509, Mantua, Archivio di Stato, Archivio Gonzaga, busta 2475, 393r.
59. Maurizio Gattoni, *Palio e contrade nel Rinascimento. I cavalli dei Gonzaga marchesi di Mantova al Palio di Siena* (Siena: Betti, 2010), 50–7; Marino Zampieri, *Il palio, il porco e il gallo. La corsa e il rito del "drappo verde" tra Duecento e Settecento* (Verona: Sierre, 2008), 62–5.
60. Francesco II Gonzaga to Giuliano di Lorenzo de' Medici, July 31, 1513, Mantua, Archivio di Stato, Archivio Gonzaga, busta 2921, libro 231, 4v. See also Giancarlo Malacarne, *Il mito dei cavalli gonzagheschi. Alle origini del purosangue* (Verona: Promoprint, 1995), 78–9, 238; Francesco II Gonzaga to Alessandro Gabbioneta, Mantua, March 5, 1514, Mantua, Archivio di Stato, Archivio Gonzaga, busta 2921, libro 231, 80v–81r.
61. Guido Ruggiero, *The Renaissance in Italy. A Social and Cultural History of the Rinascimento* (Cambridge: Cambridge University Press, 2015), 16, 446; id., 'Mean Streets, Familiar Streets, or the Fat Woodcarver and the Masculine Spaces of Renaissance Florence', in *Renaissance Florence. A Social History*, ed. Roger J. Crum, John T. Paoletti (Cambridge: Cambridge University Press, 2006), 293–10, here 294. See also Jana Graul, '"Tanto lontano da ogni virtù". Zu Konkurrenz, Neid und falscher Freundschaft in Vasaris Vita des Andrea del Castagno und Domenico Veneziano', *kunsttexte.de* 1 (2012), 1–40, here 2.
62. Eis, 'Zu den zeitgenössischen Aufzeichnungen', 355. Duke Albrecht III is documented as winner of the Augsburg scharlach race in 1448 (Mülich, 'Chronik', at 91 [relating to the year 1448]).
63. Ulrich Raulff, *Farewell to the Horse: A Cultural History* (New York: Liveright, 2018), For the 'continuous tendency to anthropomorphize race horses' in modern times, see Simone Derix, 'Das Rennpferd. Historische Perspektiven auf Zucht und Führung seit dem 18. Jahrhundert', *Body Politics* 2/4 (2014): 397–429.
64. Quintus Curtius Rufus, *Geschichte Alexanders des Großen*, vol. 1, ed. and trans. Holger Koch (Darmstadt: Wissenschaftliche Buchgesellschaft, 2007), 6.5.18, 266; Plutarch, *Alexander / Caesar*, ed. and trans. Marion Giebel (Stuttgart: Reclam, 2007), 8–9.
65. Niccolò Valori, *Laurentii Medicei Vita* (Florence: Giovannelli, 1749), 49. See also Mallett, 'Horse-Racing', 260.
66. Francesco II Gonzaga to Alessandro Gabbioneta, Mantua, March 4, 1514, Mantua, Archivio di Stato, Archivio Gonzaga, busta 2921, libro 231, 78v.
67. Francesco II Gonzaga to Giuliano II. de' Medici, Mantua, July 31, 1513, Mantua, Archivio di Stato, Archivio Gonzaga, busta 2921, libro 231, 4v. See also Malacarne, *Il mito dei cavalli gonzagheschi*, 78–9.
68. Gian Filippo Salarolo to Lorenzo de' Medici, Bologna, May 16, 1481, Florence, Archivio di Stato, Mediceo avanti il Principato, XXXVIII, 182. See also Mallett, 'Horse-Racing', 261.
69. Gian Filippo Salarolo to Lorenzo de' Medici, Bologna, June 20, 1481, Florence, Archivio di Stato, Mediceo avanti il Principato, XXXVIII, 226. See also Mallett, 'Horse-Racing', 261.
70. Jan-Friedrich Missfelder, 'Period Ear. Perspektiven einer Klanggeschichte der Neuzeit', *Geschichte und Gesellschaft* 38 (2012): 21–47, here 37; R. Murray Schafer, *Die Ordnung der Klänge. Eine Kulturgeschichte des Hörens* (Mainz: Schott, 2010), 350–1.
71. Alessandro Gabbioneta to Francesco II Gonzaga, Rome, February 26, 1514: Mantua, Archivio di Stato, Archivio Gonzaga, busta 862, fasc. I.1., 35r–36r, printed in Malacarne,

72. Filippo Lapacini, In laudem Sauri, in Libro dei palii vinti, 1512–1518, Milan, Collezione Giustiniani-Falck, 6v. See also Malacarne, *Il mito dei cavalli gonzagheschi*, 229; Cesare Campana, *Arbori delle famiglie le quali hanno signoreggiato con diversi titoli in Mantua ...* (Mantua: Osanna, 1590), 25; Dolfo, *Lettere ai Gonzaga*, 243; Alessandro Luzio, 'Isabella d'Este e i Borgia', *Archivio Storico Lombardo*, ser. 5, 42 (1915): 115–67, 412–64, here 126; Hans Joachim Kissling, *Sultan Bâjezîds II. Beziehungen zu Markgraf Francesco II. von Gonzaga* (Munich: Hueber, 1965), 57.

Il mito dei cavalli gonzagheschi, 195–6. See also Alessandro del Cardinale to Francesco II Gonzaga, Rome, February 15, 1510, Mantua, Archivio di Stato, Archivio Gonzaga, busta 858, 534r–v; Floriano Dolfo to Francesco II. Gonzaga, Bologna, October 4, 1493, ibid., busta 1143, printed in Floriano Dolfo, *Lettere ai Gonzaga*, ed. Marzia Minutelli (Rome: Edizioni di storia e di letteratura, 2002), I, 3.

73. Francesco II Gonzaga to Giuliano II de' Medici, Mantua, July 31, 1513, Mantua, Archivio di Stato, Archivio Gonzaga, busta 2921, libro 231, 4v. See also Malacarne, *Il mito dei cavalli gonzagheschi*, 78–9.
74. Giorgio Vasari, *Sodoma und Beccafumi*, trans. Victoria Lorini (Berlin: Wagenbach, 2006), 24.
75. For a codicological description, see Malacarne, *Il mito dei cavalli gonzagheschi*, 88–95. See also Nosari, Canova, *Il Palio nel Rinascimento*, 209–16; David Sanderson Chambers and Jane T. Martineau, eds., *Splendours of the Gonzaga: Catalogue* (London: Victoria & Albert Museum, 1981), 147.
76. Malacarne, *Il mito dei cavalli gonzagheschi*, 87–8.
77. Ibid, 93.
78. Volker Reinhardt, *Die Renaissance in Italien. Geschichte und Kultur*, 2nd ed. (Munich: Beck, 2007), 14. See also Mallett, 'Horse-Racing', 257.
79. Munich race rule from 1448, Munich, Stadtarchiv, Zimelien, no. 11, 44v, printed in Ernst von Destouches, 'Die Münchener Jakobi- oder Scharlachrennen, die Vorläufer des Münchener Oktoberfestes', in id., *Säkular-Chronik des Münchener Oktoberfestes (Zentral-Landwirtschafts-Festes) 1810–1910. Festschrift zur Hundertjahrfeier* (Munich: Lindauer, 1910), 3–11, here 4.

## Disclosure Statement

No potential conflict of interest was reported by the author(s).

# Spectacular Spanish Horses in New Spain

Isabelle Schürch

**ABSTRACT**
The essay suggests a two-fold approach to the role of horse-racing during the period of the Spanish transatlantic expansion. First, I will discuss the dominant values and practices in late medieval Spanish equestrianism in order to understand the conquistadors' framework of perceiving and evaluating their own equestrianism. On the Iberian Peninsula, the prevalent public demonstration of equestrian prowess, agility, and speed did not take the form of competitive racing but of collective spectacular performances. One of the most prominent examples are the 'juegos de cañas'. The Iberian cultural setting is important to understand how specific forms of equestrianism were introduced into the 'New World' and how they were transformed. In a second step, I will argue for a conceptual framework based on conquest and competition that integrates Spanish equestrianism, public spectacle, and conquistadorial motives. The Spanish equestrian games offer a special case in point: I would like to suggest that a dissecting look at the dominant elements and functional unities which constitute horse races (such as audience, area, or competition) but also other forms of competitive equestrianism could help broaden our understanding of horse racing culture in general.

When it comes to the story of the Spanish conquest from a Spanish perspective, Bernal Díaz' eyewitness account is not only one of the most popular versions, but it is also an intriguing one, not least because of his detailed description of the equine conquest companions.[1] So, according to Bernal Díaz, when in 1519 he and the other Spanish conquistadors led by Hernán Cortés had finally found a suitable landing place at the shores of today's Mexico, not only humans disembarked, but also several horses. The Spanish activities and their treaty of alliance with the local rulers against the Mexica Triple Alliance did not go by unnoticed by the latter and Moctezuma sent envoys: two young *caciques*[2] and four distinguished elderly dignitaries. For the Spanish it was quite clear that this delegation had to be impressed, and the blue and green beads they wanted to present the Mexica envoys with certainly did not do the trick. And so, the eye-witness Bernal Díaz reported in his *historia*: 'He [Hernán Cortés, IS] paid them every sign of honor and, as there were some good fields nearby, he ordered Pedro de Alvarado, on his fine and well-trained sorrel mare (*una buena yegua alazana que era muy rebuelta*), and some other horsemen (*cavalleros*) to gallop and skirmish (*corriesen y escaramuçeasen*) in front of them, a spectacle which gave the Caciques much pleasure'.[3]

In this perspective, the horses of the Spanish conquest played a significant role. Interestingly enough, though, it is not the often-told story of indigenous leaders being awe-struck by God-like Spanish centaurs. Instead, the Mexica officials are described as pleased consumers of an equestrian spectacle. The study of horses and spectacle might therefore offer another narrative to the still prevalent *imaginaire* of the dominant Spaniards on their fear-inducing quadrupeds.

Not only has Bernal Díaz commented prominently on the importance of the Spanish horses in the so-called conquest of *Las Indias* and the *Tierra Firme*, but he has also proved to be a good source for later studies on the 'exceptional success' of the Spanish. It seems that the heroic conquest-stories of the prominent conquistadorial leaders were more or less explicitly linked up with the exceptional status of the few horses that accompanied them. One of the most curious studies on the Spanish horses in the conquest was written in the 1920s by the very famous adventurer, social celebrity and political figure R. B. Cunninghame Graham.[4] His nostalgic *hommage* to the equine conquistadors is still the most cited book on the role of horses in the Spanish conquest, albeit for want of alternative studies.[5] In more recent research on the Spanish expansion into the Caribbean isles and Mesoamerican mainland, on the other hand, horses are usually listed among steel, guns and germs as one of the decisive factors of the Spanish 'success'.[6] One of the pitfalls of evaluating the role of horses in the Early Modern Americas is thus the tendency to either repeat an over-stated superiority or to simply state a generic 'factoriality' of horses.

In what follows, I would like to suggest a two-fold approach to the role of horse-racing during the period of what is generally termed the Spanish transatlantic expansion into the Caribbean and the American mainland (1490s to 1600s). First, I will discuss the dominant values and practices in late medieval Spanish equestrianism in order to understand the conquistadorial framework of perceiving and evaluating their own equestrianism. On the Iberian Peninsula, the prevalent public demonstration of equestrian prowess, agility and speed did not take the form of competitive racing but of collective spectacular performances. One of the most prominent forms are the so-called games of canes, the *juegos de cañas*. The Iberian cultural setting and its corresponding cultural and social values are important to understand how specific forms of equestrianism were introduced into the 'New World'[7] and how they were transformed in the new transatlantic environment. In a second step, I will argue for a conceptual framework based on conquest and competition that integrates Spanish equestrianism, public spectacle and conquistadorial motives. Unlike other articles in this volume, which deal with well-established and socially pervasive horse racing traditions in ancient Greece, Roman Rome, medieval Siena or early modern England, Spanish equestrianism offers a special case in point: on the one hand, we cannot confirm an equivalent of horse racing in medieval Spain or the early modern Americas. On the other hand, I would like to suggest that a dissecting look at the dominant elements and functional unities such as the range of the public (exclusive/inclusive), the racing area (urban/rural, closed/open) or the goal of competition (win/lose), which constitute horse races but also—as in the Spanish case—other forms of competitive equestrianism, could help broaden our understanding of horse racing culture in general.

## Spanish Horse Riding

The practice of equestrian skills and its ostentatious display has formed an essential part of Iberian cultural and social life at least since the Middle Ages.[8] The popular 'Running of the Wine Horses' (*Los Caballos del Vino*) still takes place annually in Caravaca de la Cruz, in southeast Spain. It takes places around the general festivities commemorating—according to the legend—the apparition of the Holy Cross in 1231. It is quite telling for the Iberian horse-racing case, though, that there are no riders in this race. Instead, there are racing teams, each consisting of a richly decorated horse and four human co-runners, who usually cling quite desperately to the much faster horse. To be announced the victorious team, the horse and all four co-runners have to make it to the finish line at the castle of the Knights Templar. Legend has it that the race commemorates the Templars' alleged breaking of a Muslim siege by bringing in provisions.

For medieval and early modern times, there are numerous equine fiestas. Festive activities such as royal entries, annual calendrical festivals such as the celebratory cycles around Christmas and Easter and local re-enactments of battles between 'Moors' and Christians (so-called *moros y cristianos*) included various equestrian displays: *juegos de cañas* (game of canes), *sortijas* (running of the ring), *bohordos* (martial reed lance games) or bull-runs.[9] In 1585, for example, well-documented *juegos* took place during Philipp II's stay in Tortosa during the festive period between December 25 (the birth of Jesus) and January 6 (Epiphany). The highlight was the elaborate *juego de cañas* on 31 December, which commemorated the 437th anniversary of the town's 'liberation' of Muslim rule.[10] Another preferred occasion for equestrian games was, of course, the Feast of St. James. The cult and role of this apostle transformed significantly over the course of the centuries and he eventually became 'Santiago Matamoros', the Moor-slayer who had famously fought with his white horse in the legendary Battle of Clavijo.[11] The late medieval and early modern equestrian spectacles differed in their social function. Unlike *bohordos* and similar artful martial games, *juegos de cañas*, for example, were almost always exclusively performed by grandees, noblemen and local elites to display skillful, athletic and intricately orchestrated equestrianism in specific, often clearly defined public settings.[12] The central plaza of a town and urban squares in general were the main public areas of such ludic events (Figure 1).[13] As far as the general arrangement of these festivities were concerned, it has to be stressed that they often formed an ensemble of different games, races and sceneries. For instance, the *juegos de cañas* were often preceded or followed by bull-runs.[14]

In Juan de la Corte's painting (Figure 1), the Plaza Mayor in Madrid is set as the visual frame of the *juego de cañas* and the players are depicted in full action

Figure 1. Juan de la Corte, *Fiestas en la Plaza Mayor de Madrid* (1623). Museo de Historia de Madrid. Photo © Asqueladd, Wikimedia Commons, licensed under the Creative Commons Attribution 1.0 Universal Public Domain Dedication (URL: https://creativecommons.org/publicdomain/zero/1.0/deed.en).

performing an attack scene in its center. This seventeenth-century painting dynamically juxtaposes the mounted spectators and their individual features (and horses) with the perfectly and symmetrically orchestrated rows of players. By doing so, Juan de la Corte does not render the actual *juego* visible, but the very idea of the game: perfect control of the fast and quick attack.

Although there seem to be clear connections between these games and medieval competitive equestrian events such as *mêlées*, jousts or other tournaments, several recent studies have come to the conclusion that the Iberian urban ludic traditions and especially the *moros y cristianos* re-enactments and equestrian show spectacles were autochthonous.[15] The urban space was used by local elites to display their skills, competence and power, and to re-enact their social group's meritorious service during the so-called *Reconquista*. The regular re-enactment of the local elites, noble and non-noble *caballeros*, not only shaped the strong narrative of what is today so clearly conceived as the *Reconquista*,[16] but it also formed the basis for local civic identity.[17]

The riding style displayed in, for instance, the *juegos de cañas*, was widely known as *a la gineta*.[18] Although this jennet riding style was considered to be of Moorish origin, it was probably adapted from cross-cultural frontiersmen's raid and skirmish practices. The jennet riding style differed from other riding styles like *a la brida* in many ways. First of all, the rider's position allowed for more dynamic athleticism because of the short stirrups. Whereas other tournament-oriented riding styles favored long stirrups with straight legs and an almost backward-leaning position of the rider, the center of gravity in riding *a la gineta* was placed more forward on the horse and allowed for more dynamic adjustment during quick starts, turns and stops. In this sense, riding *a la gineta* was ideal to perform the high speed and athleticism required for the games of canes. This riding style has, of course, to be put in its cultural context: As a riding practice it required and promoted different athletic competences in riders, but also in horses. The 'jennets' even developed into a specific Iberian horse type and these small but agile horses were praised throughout Europe.[19]

In the late fifteenth century, the jennet riding style became one of the honed riding styles of Iberian noblemen and was refined—in practice and written theory— for artistic equestrian display. In short, in late medieval Spain, urban equestrian games became important events where riding *a la gineta* and the immediately visible display of the riders' skills were judged by the civic public (and peers) and the performances allowed not only for the display but also for the perception, communication and consolidation of values such as nobility, elegance and prowess.

Whereas equestrian spectacles were characterized through their situational and momentous performance, the written evidence in treatises on horsemanship de- and prescribes the ideas, standards and values of the equestrian games. As Joel Fallows has put it, late medieval Iberian jousting and martial games transformed from 'sport to spectacle'.[20] This transition has to be seen in a broader context of the demise of the importance of the military knight in the course of the thirteenth and fourteenth century and the rise of chivalric performance of knightly values in the fifteenth century.[21]

The *juegos de cañas* are an interesting case in point. The idea of the game is the re-enactment of battles or combat actions. It consisted of rows of men riding horses throwing canes (by way of spears) at the opposing parties and blocking them with the shield. Intricately orchestrated, the combat charges were executed really fast by riding forward and escaping in circles or semicircles, but always keeping the row formation (Figure 1). Teofilo F. Ruiz has analyzed these games of canes and re-enactments of battles between Moors and Spanish Christians as a late medieval and early modern phenomenon of fictional warfare.[22] They became highly popular after 1492, after the surrender of the kingdom of Granada, the last Muslim stronghold on the Peninsula, to the Spanish crown. Although the re-enacting split the social elites in two opposing groups (*moros* and *cristianos*), it is important to stress that these *juegos* were 'above all an aesthetic performance featuring elaborate maneuvers on horseback and involving little actual violence'.[23] It seems that the riders had to display remarkable skills: fast starts, sudden turns, collectively performed complicated maneuvers and so on. In general, not the individual accomplishments were honored, but the collective performance. There was no fixed scoring system.[24]

It is therefore not surprising that most of the treatises on the jennet riding style, such as the *Tractado de la cavallería de la gineta* by Hernán Chacón (printed in 1551), center on the *juegos de cañas*.[25] They give advice, for example, on how the horse has to be trained at least two to three times a week for this athletic challenge, how the *plaza mayor* has to be freed from any stones or other obstacles, it has to be sprinkled with water to avoid dust clouds and they even go into costume details and gestural specifics such as the right moment and gesture to throw the right flap of the rider's cape over which shoulder.[26] What counted was the public perception and judgment: The victorious party of a game of canes had to follow all the rules of noble performance, from individual posture to costume, gear and, of course, to the horse's own natural expression of nobility. The game could be lost if one of the players, for example, lost his hat.[27]

In Hernán Chacóns *Tractado*, we find the first elaborate treatise on the *juego de cañas*, which by the mid-sixteenth century, was played in almost all Spanish towns,[28] and also in some of the newly founded Spanish towns on the other side of the Atlantic. Chacón describes how the *caballeros* of a town should gather to organize the teams, each team of at least five riders, and each team should wear its own color. Then they parade in pairs to the town's main square where they are going to play. At the entrance to the square, trumpeters and drummers are placed to mark the beginning of the game. A lot of attention is given to the fact that the fake spears (the *cañas*) are held in exactly the same position, for 'otherwise they look bad' (*parecen mal*).[29] And again in Chacón's words: 'And once they have all entered two at a time, they shall all turn at the same time to charge through the square after the fashion of a battle; they shall do two or three sudden starts and, having done this, they shall ride a lap around the square together, slowly, so as to look at the ladies and knights who are at the windows'.[30]

Then the actual game started. The throwing of the canes at each other was highly orchestrated and individual lone fighters were strictly forbidden. Chacón's treatise clearly confirms that the *juegos de cañas* centered on cultural and social values that were not aimed at single heroism, but at the disciplined and skilled coordination of social formation. Not the individual actions were judged, but the group performance and its aesthetics according to standards of elegance and nobility, *naturalezza* and *gallantería*. Accordingly, the audience was usually not allowed to shout or acoustically support their favorite team. Only remarks such as 'Make way!' (when the teams entered the plaza} or the battle cry 'Santiago!' were considered appropriate. The visual and acoustic regime was strictly focused on the intricate display of swift and elegant equestrianism and the human and equine players were not to be distracted.

And so, it might come as a bit of surprise that the *juegos de cañas* could be used to challenge communal parties or to display political positions. In his study on Spanish festive culture, Teofilo F. Ruiz gives various examples of how games of canes, especially during a royal visit, were used to challenge and negotiate power positions or—quite literally—to fight for privileges.[31] Some of the articles on horse racing in this volume show how these races were almost often performed in a clearly defined setting and location, which allowed for and actually created a specific, situational presence in which both the ruler and his subjects participated. Yet, different local social factions could split up this duality or, at least, added a dynamic dimension to it: families, confraternities or neighborhoods competed against each other. The *juegos the cañas* forced individual riders, for example a participating prince or other prominent members, to keep quite literally in line. Unlike horse racing, which is traditionally laid out as a competitive contest with regard to speed and skill, the Iberian equestrian spectacles focused on riding skills and equine swiftness within the general social framework of *gallardía*, a mixture of elegance, nobility and gracefulness. This equestrian *gallardía*—especially in its most noble form of *juegos de cañas*—served in the sixteenth century as a distinctive signature of Spanishness even far beyond the borders of the Iberian Peninsula.[32]

## Conquest and Competition

It is therefore not surprising that *juegos de cañas* appear in various narrative texts of the early conquest. Antonio de Herrera y Tordesillas (1549–1626) explicitly states in his *Historia general* that in 1503, in the province of Xaragua on Hispaniola, the visiting new governor Nicolás de Ovando observed that the conquistadors started to play *juegos de cañas*. One of them even showed off difficult dressage exercises with his mare (*hazia baylar su yegua, saltar y hazer corbetas*).[33]

The *juegos de cañas* were thus not only brought to the newly 'discovered' Caribbean islands, but they were reconfigured in a new social setting. On the one hand, they were moved from their traditional urban space to a context of conquest. And yet, they are closely associated with the first steps of Spanish settlement and the setting up of new hierarchies in the new territories. On the other hand, the conquistadorial leaders were horsemen who started to re-define a game that was rooted—in the collective memory—in the distant frontier battle past, the Reconquista.[34] Yet, this past could now, in the transatlantic context of conquest, be used as a collective point of reference, and the new frontier battle experience was integrated in Reconquista narratives the Spaniards had brought to the New World. The conquistadors re-invented and quite literally inscribed themselves in their *relaciónes de méritos y servicios* as meritocratic nobility.[35] The propagated visual and physical superiority was therefore not just symbolically marked by equestrian displays. Although the sources are quite sparse, we know of some *caciques* who started to appropriate horse riding and there is at least one comment on an 'Indian' game of canes. Only after the early phase of the conquest was the right to possess horses and riding itself regulated and restricted to Spaniards.[36]

If we look at the availability of horses during the early phase of the Spanish conquest of the Caribbean islands and the Mesoamerican mainland, the restrictions of owning a horse are mainly based on the fact that there were simply not enough horses. It is difficult to estimate the exact number of horses on Hispaniola and Cuba before 1519, but Bartolomé de las Casas, for example, reports a mere 20 to 30 horses on Hispaniola in 1501. The shipping of horses across the Atlantic proved to be a major and unprecedented challenge. In the first 20 years of the transatlantic settlement, considerable efforts were taken to set up studs and farms to breed horses locally: first on Hispaniola, then on Cuba.[37] Only in the 1520s and 30s did these efforts finally start to pay off and the ideal climate and environmental conditions in these latitudes led to an astonishing quick rate of reproduction.[38]

So, when Hernán Cortés organised his expedition to Mexico, one of the main problems was to find enough horses to ship from Cuba to the mainland. Bernal Díaz mentions several times that horses were then (in 1519) still not only expensive, but extremely hard to come by. As for Cortés in 1519, he was lucky to be able to recruit 18 horsemen and owners with their riding horses. Often left out in the more popular editions and translations of his *Historia verdadera*, Bernal Díaz actually listed all of the 16 horses that were the first *equidae* to set their hooves on the American mainland, and by doing so he gives us a detailed overview over each horse's characteristics (Figure 2).[39] This exceptional source allows for a glimpse at how conquistadors perceived their accompanying horses and what were the characteristics

| Owner | Horse name | Gender | Horse Colour Spanish | Horse colour (Denhardt) | Characteristics | Characteristics |
|---|---|---|---|---|---|---|
| Hernan Cortés | | m | castaño zaino | dark chestnut | | |
| Pedro de Alvarado and Hernán López de Avila | | f | alazana | sorrel | Very good, for game and racing | muy buena, de juego y de carrera |
| Alonso Hernandez Puertocarrero | | f | ruzia | grey | good racer | de buena carrera |
| Joan Velázqzez de León | La Rabona | f | ruizia | grey | Very powerful, flexible and a good racer | muy poderosa, muy rebuelta y de buena carrera |
| Cristóval de Olí | | m | castaño escuro | dark brown | Not really good | harto bueno |
| Françisco de Montejo and Alonso de Abila | | m | alazán tostado | parched sorrel | not suitable for war | no fue para cosa de guerra |
| Françisco de Morla | | m | castaño escuro | dark brown | great racer and flexible | gran corredor y rebuelto |
| Juan d'Escalante | | m | castaño claro, tresalvo | light bay, three white stockings | not good | no fue bueno |
| Diego de Ordás | | f | ruçia machorra | barren grey | Pacer, but does not race | pasadera, y aunque corría poco |
| Gonçalo Domínguez | | m | castaño escuro | dark brown | Good and great racer | muy bueno e gran corredor |
| Pedro Gonçales de Truxillo | | m | perfeto castaño | perfect chestnut | Races very well | corría muy bien |
| Morón (vezino del Bayamo) | | m | hovero labrado de las manos | pinto horse (with white forefeet) | flexible | era bien rebuelto |
| Baena (vezino de la Trinidad) | | m | hovero algo sabre morzillo | spotted black horse | Does not jump, not good at anything | no salió, bueno para cosa ninguna |
| Lares el muy buen Ginete | | m | castaño algo claro | bay | Good and great racer | muy bueno, buen corredor |
| Ortiz el Músico and Bartolome García | El Harriero | m | escuro | black | Very good, one of the best | muy bien / éste fue uno de los buenos cavallos que pasamos en la armada |
| Juan Sedeño (vezino de La Abana) | | f | castaña | chestnut/brown | (foaled on board) | y esta yegua parió en el navío |

**Figure 2.** Bernal Díaz's list of the 16 horses in Hernán Cortés' campaign to the American mainland in 1519 (Conquest of Mexico).[56]

they valued most (or least). Bernal Díaz classifies each horse according to the following categories: owners and/or riders, gender (*yegua* or *caballo*), the precise coat color and qualities.[40] Two horses, who reappear in Díaz' account, are even mentioned by name: *La Rabona* and *El Harriero*.

The underlying systematic of the horses' qualities is most probably not just Bernal Díaz' idea but corresponds with a widely shared notion of what a good horse is. There is a limited pattern to evaluate equine characteristics: Usually the horses are judged with respect to speed, power and temperament. A closer look at these categories reveals an interesting intertextual reference. Bernal Díaz' categorization echoes one of the most important legal texts in medieval Spain. *Las Siete Partidas*, King Alfonso X.'s major legal compilation project, discusses, among other things, the ideal knight and his necessary competence to select, judge and ride a good horse.[41] *Las Siete Partidas* defined three qualities that horses must be endowed with to be considered 'good': 'First, they should be of good color; second, they should have good dispositions; third, they should have suitable limbs corresponding to these two qualities'.[42] This categorization seems also to be prevalent in Bernal Díaz's list of horses. Yet, his assessment has to be put into a social context to reveal what importance the 16 horses had in the social reconfiguration that the Spanish-Mexican conquest brought about: career opportunities and the chance to obtain privileges, entitlements and titles for lesser noblemen and adventurers who started to self-fashion themselves as noble knights were highly increased.

Although Díaz presents the horses according to their use for the military campaign, he particularly highlights their skills as 'racers'. It seems that at least seven out of 16 horses were considered to be good at running, or indeed racing. Actually, it is important to point out that the semantic field of *correr* includes different forms of fast running and is not restricted to racing. Yet it is an interesting observation that there is no semantic differentiation between running and competitive racing in Old Spanish, which might point towards blurry boundaries between these activities.

Obviously, it was not horse racing that Bernal Díaz or his fellow conquistadors had in mind when they evaluated the qualities of their horses, but speed. Bernal Díaz relates in detail how Hernán Cortés ordered the riders and their horses to charge and return quickly in groups of three and to manoeuvre as a single unit.[43] The ability to charge and retreat swiftly was not only essential for a good jennet or a horse used for performing *juegos de cañas*, but also for the kind of warfare the conquistador practiced against their Mesoamerican opponents.

In addition to equine qualities and traits, the question of personal ownership and training is a second aspect to point out. As already mentioned before, in the early sixteenth century Caribbean territory, there was no actual market for trading horses and there was almost no selection process for well-suited warhorses. During the first 20 years of the Spanish conquest, Spanish noblemen or *caballeros* owned almost all the horses personally, and it was their own responsibility to ship them across the Atlantic. This personal ownership and responsibility for one's companion animal is also reflected in the equestrian possibilities.[44] It might be slightly misleading to speak of a human-equine partnership, but the relationship between owner and horse was, out of necessity, particularly close. Yet, this mutual dependence should not be confused with emotional attachment or care. Not only was the horse of significant economic, social and martial value, but it was almost impossible to replace a horse once it fell ill or was wounded. Hernán Cortés' own horse fell sick and died shortly after landing in Mexico and he had to convince one of his fellow horsemen to give him his. No details are given about this change in ownership, but the price—whether as economic or social value—must have been significant. And of course, Cortés chose the very best horse available: El Harriero (Figure 2).

Bernal Díaz and other accounts of the early Mexican conquest stress the importance of the few horses available at that time. The shortage of horses in general, but also the even more pressing need for good and well-trained horses, sharpened the focus on the 'equine factor' considerably. Yet, it is important to understand the underlying values that corresponded with Spanish horse riding. The Spanish contemporaries more or less explicitly made the connection of re-enactments in *juego de cañas* with Reconquista frontier skirmishes and the use of these trained horsemanship skills in the new frontier warfare in Mesoamerica.[45] Qualities Spanish riders had formerly looked for in horses suited for *juegos de cañas* now proved to be quite useful in actual warfare. Therefore, not only the narrative relationship between Reconquista and the Spanish conquest is important to stress, but also the equestrian relationship.

In order to argue for an increasingly close connection of equestrian spectacle, nobility and the transatlantic reconfiguration of social orders it is necessary to have a look at equestrian reflections made almost one hundred years later. An interesting case in point is Bernardo de Vargas Machuca, who was not only a well-experienced horseman, but also a good example of a conquistador who tried to monetarize his experience.

Bernardo de Vargas Machuca was born in Simancas in 1557 into a lower noble family and he quickly started to build a military career. After service in the Italian wars, he crossed the Atlantic to try his luck in *Las Indias* like so many others. As he was never able to permanently secure a lucrative title or estate for his services in the new frontier warfare, he returned to Spain and published several manuals on the conquest topic. On the one hand, there is his well-known *The Indian Militia and Description of the Indies* from 1599, a 'how-to' manual on frontier counter-insurgence in New Granada. In this treatise he offers a unique viewpoint and expertise on militia life and its hardship. On the other hand, there is his horse-riding manual, published only one year later, in 1600: the *Libro de exercicios de la gineta*. In this *libro* he reflects on meritocratic nobility and the corresponding art of riding *a la gineta*. Bernardo de Vargas Machuca makes an explicit link between the frontier fights on the Iberian Peninsula and the frontier fights in New Spain and New Granada when he states that the art of riding *a la gineta* was introduced from North Africa to Spain and from Spain to the New World. He goes on to emphasize that only here, in *Las Indias*, was it brought to perfection: 'en esta parte se ha perfecionado más que en otra'.[46]

These early modern Spanish discourses on nobility drew much on equestrian comparisons that several medieval authorities had discussed in detail. Ramon Lull in his famous *Llibre de l'Ordre de cavalleria* from 1275 elaborates the close connection between knight and horse, which ultimately led to the social marking and identity of this specific couple: like the knight who is chosen as the most noble from among 1'000 men, so is his horse chosen from all other animals. And it is the public presentation on horse that makes the difference between a knight and other social groups.[47] Residues of these conceptualizations of knighthood and nobility resonate in conquistadors' reports, especially the *relaciones de méritos y servicios*, and in manual literature informed by conquistadorial experience. True nobility and its expression in equestrian skills and games, was directly associated with and linked to the Iberian Reconquista and therefore, also to actual frontier warfare in the contemporary period of Conquest.

Both of Bernardo de Vargas Machuca's books can be seen as pleas to the Spanish Crown to reinvigorate conquest on the wild frontiers of the Indies and to reward its noble fighters. By turning his expertise and practical knowledge of the militia life into book form, Bernardo de Vargas Machuca tried to gain professional status as a distinguished nobleman. In his *Libro de exercicios de la gineta,* he conceived of a new theory and practice of riding, which can, with good reason, be attributed as a *gineta indiana*.[48] His book became quite a success and in 1619 he was able to publish a revised edition. According to him, only by practicing the 'perfecta y verdadera gineta'[49] in the actual conquest setting can the true nobleman show his services and merits and ultimately, his true and worthy nobility.[50]

His efforts finally paid off, but unfortunately for him, not permanently. When he returned to *Las Indias,* he was rewarded with the governorship of the small and very remote *Isla Margarita*, a true frontier region at that time. He re-built the small main settlement on the island as a veritable capital: A cathedral, an aqueduct, a slaughterhouse and of course, for the professional horseman, a *carrera*. Unfortunately, no specific details are given on this course. But it has to be understood as a specific training ground where horses could be raced in a straight line. Iberian horsemanship treatises such as the influential *Tractado* by Hernán Chacón devoted whole chapters on how to run horses on the *carrera*.[51] It is probably more than telling that a lower nobleman who never really made his fortune or career had his own *carrera*, a stone-enclosed racing and parade ground, on one of the remotest islands at the very edge of the Spanish Empire.[52]

## Equestrian Spectacle, Urban Space, and Social Differentiation

If we consider the opening scene of the Spanish landing at the shores of today's Mexico again, specific elements of early conquest equestrianism can be highlighted. First of all, it is not just a spontaneous decision that led to Hernán Cortés' ordering of this equestrian spectacle. Rather, it was a clear tactical maneuver. He seems to have been quick to understand that staged ruses and the spreading of rumors could be used as tactical framework. Well aware that horses were the biggest quadrupeds ever seen in these latitudes and that the concept of riding was entirely novel to Mesoamerican spectators, Cortés and other conquistadors very often used equestrian displays to frame an aura of wonder and potency.[53] Secondly, this spectacle was made possible because of the suitable terrain. More often than not, the underground was not very favorable for horses, and the horsemen in Cortés' entourage had to avoid swamps and thickets. As mentioned in Díaz' *historia*, the open area needed for a *carrera* (a race) was hard to find. Apart from a few open fields, we also know from other accounts that the beach proved to be an important space for equestrianism. The beach was not only a more or less symbolic area of a liminal space, a 'contact zone' as conceptualized by Mary Louise Pratt,[54] but also an area where the horses and their speed could be best presented. Very often, the showing-off of Spanish horses on the beach in front of the local Taino, Tlaxcalan or Mexica elites was used to great effect by the Spaniards. Only after the foundation of New Spanish towns did the equestrian spectacles and games return to the *plazas mayores*, where they became once again sites of contestation for social hierarchies and a new local identity as conquistadorial meritocracy, and later on as *criollos*.

To conclude: it has to be emphasized that the Iberian equestrian culture centered on a variety of competitive and martial displays of speed, competition and power, which were transformed in the transition from the late Middle Ages to the early modern age of territorial expansion. By the time of the conquest of the West Indies and what was later called New Spain, riding and equestrian games were challenged as a cultural, but also as a social practice. Not only the Spanish conquistadores started to comment on the cultural specificity of their own Iberian equestrian culture and its characteristics such swiftness, elegance and nobleness. Horse racing seems simply not to have been the skill or competitive playground for a 'warrior society' where horses were rare, expensive and vulnerable, and personal. In an interesting recourse to history, frontier *caballeros* started to reflect on their riding skills and the performance of equestrian games as highly marked social practices and played *juegos de cañas*, traditionally reserved to the Spanish elites. As far as horse racing is concerned, the Spanish case is indeed revealing.

Although horse races certainly took place, they seem to have been mere situational contests between riders, like the race performed to show off in front of *caciques* on the Mexican beach. Or, as the use of *carreras* suggests, the racing of courses was part of the general training for fast horses. Still, there certainly are elements that horse races and Iberian equestrian spectacles shared, like the public space (major squares and town centers), the public gathering of the urban society, the possibility to deflect social tensions between urban fractions to the site of contestation and the excitement of speed and skill. Yet, the *juego de cañas*, as a case in point for Iberian ludic traditions, has to be seen as a different mode of enacting equestrian contest and, unlike a race, the game enforced the collectively performed competition and the skillful equestrian spectacle. It is thus not at all surprising that martial festivities rooted in a collectively remembered and shared period of the Reconquista were reconfigured in a new frontier and conquest context. This was not only a step towards a global expansion of equestrian spectacles, but the foundation for what Jean-Pierre Digard has dubbed 'la centaurisation du Nouveau Monde'.[55]

## Notes

1. For a popular English edition see Bernal Díaz, *The Conquest of New Spain*, trans. and with an introduction by John M. Cohen (London: Penguin Books, 1963).

2. The Spanish used the generic term 'caciques' to refer to local noblemen, see Matthew Restall and Kris Lane, *Latin America in Colonial Times*. 2nd ed. (Cambridge: Cambridge University Press, 2018), 165.
3. Díaz, *Conquest*, 116. For the Spanish edition see Bernal Diaz del Castillo. *Historia verdadera de la conquista de la Nueva España. Manuscrito Guatemala*, ed. José Antonio Barbón Rodriguez (Mexico: El Colegio de México, 2005), 118.
4. See R.B. Cunninghame Graham, *The Horses of the Conquest*, ed. by Robert Moorman Denhardt (Norman, OK: University of Oklahoma Press, 1949).
5. In general, it has to be stated that an authoritative study does not exist for horses, such as Marion Schwartz's study on dogs in the Conquista or Virginia De John Anderson's book on domestic animals in early (Northern) America: see Marion Schwartz, *A History of Dogs in the Early Americas* (New Haven, CT: Yale University Press, 1997; Virginia De John Anderson, *Creatures of Empire. How Domestic Animals transformed Early America* (Oxford: Oxford University Press, 2004).
John J. Johnson, for example, took up Cunninghame Graham's initiative and reconstructed major steps in the process of introducing the horse in the Americas; see John J. Johnson, 'The Introduction of the Horse into the Western Hemisphere', *Hispanic American Historical Review* 23, no. 4 (1943): 587–610. Starting in the 1930s, Robert M. Denhardt has also published several articles and a book on the importance of the horse in the early Americas and assembled the most important narrative sources on the subject. The overall intention, though, was to explain the origin of today's American horse breeds; see Robert M. Denhardt, 'The Truth about Cortes's Horses', *Hispanic American Historical Review* 17, no. 4 (1937): 525–32; Ibid, *The Horse of the Americas* (Norman: University of Oklahoma Press, 1947). He then continued his research into the origins of American horse breeds: Ibid, 'The Chilean Horse', *Agricultural History* 24, no. 3 (1950): 161–5, and 'The Horse in New Spain and the Borderlands', *Agricultural History* 25, no. 4 (1951): 145–50.
6. See for example the important compendium on Colonial Latin America by Matthew Restall and Kris Lane which reflects current research and the explicit criticism on heroic, individualistic as well as unidimensional technological narratives mainly influenced by contemporary Spanish perspectives and regimes of value; see Restall and Lane, *Latin America*.
7. The term 'New World' is taken up here to denote the sixteenth-century Spanish perspective on the Americas and should by no means imply a generalizing judgmental (European) perspective. For a critical discussion of the use of New World-terminology see Walter D. Mignolo, 'Putting the Americas on the Map (Geography and the Colonization of Space)', *Colonial Latin American Review* 1, nos. 1-2 (1992): 25–63.
8. Teofilo F. Ruiz, 'Festive Traditions in Castile and Aragon in the Late Middle Ages. Ceremonies and Symbols of Power', in *The Routledge Companion to Iberian Studies*, ed. Javier Munoz-Basols et al. (London: Routledge, 2017), 5–15. For a general discussion of Spanish festive culture see Teofilo F. Ruiz, *A King Travels. Festive Traditions in Late Medieval and Early Modern Spain* (Princeton, NJ: Princeton University Press, 2012), here 212–26. On the importance of fictitious re-enactments of Christian and Muslim battles, sieges etc., see Barbara Fuchs, *Exotic Nation. Maurophilia and the Construction of Early Modern Spain* (Philadelphia: University of Pennsylvania Press, 2009).
9. See Max Harris, *Aztecs, Moors, and Christians: Festivals of Reconquest in Mexico and Spain*, (Austin: University of Texas Press, 2010).
10. For the festivities in Tolosa see Ruiz, *King Travels*, here especially 38–46 and 85.
11. On the transformation of St. James as 'Matamoros' see Klaus Herbers, 'Santiago matamoros: ¿mito o realidad de la reconquista?', in *El mundo de los conquistadors*, ed. Martín Federico Ríos Saloma (Rouen: Silex Ediciones 2015).

12. Teofilo F. Ruiz, 'Elite and Popular Culture in Late Fifteenth–Century Castilian Festivals', in *City and Spectacle in Medieval Europe*, ed. Barbara Hanawalt, Medieval Studies at Minnesota vol. 6 (Minneapolis: University of Minnesota Press, 1994), 296–318.
13. Ruiz, *King travels*, 64–5. For an important case study of the importance of plazas mayor see Jesús R. Escobar, *The Plaza Mayor and the Shaping of Baroque Madrid* (Cambridge: Cambridge University Press, 2003).
14. See Noel Fallows, *Jousting in Medieval and Renaissance Iberia* (Woodbridge: Boydell Press, 2010), 284.
15. See Ruiz, *King Travels* and Harris, *Aztecs, Moors, and Christians*.
16. For critical discussions of the so-called Reconquista in historical and historiographical perspective see Adam J. Kosto, 'Reconquest, Renaissance, and the Histories of Iberia (ca. 1000–1200)', in *European Transformations. The Long Twelfth Century*, ed. Thomas F.X. Noble and John Van Engen (Notre Dame, IN: University of Notre Dame Press, 2012), 93–116, and Nikolas Jaspert, '"Reconquista". Interdependenzen und Tragfähigkeit eines wertekategorialen Deutungsmusters', in *Christlicher Norden – muslimischer Süden. Ansprüche und Wirklichkeiten von Christen, Juden und Muslimen auf der Iberischen Halbinsel im Hoch- und Spätmittelalter*, ed. Matthias M. Tischler and Alexander Fidora (Münster: Aschendorff, 2011), 445–65.
17. Ruiz, *King Travels*, 193–209.
18. Juan Carlos Fernandez Truan and Marie-Helene Orthous, 'El Juego de Cañas en España', *Recorde: Revista de Historica do Esporte* 5, no. 1 (2012): 1–23.
19. For a general discussion of the jennet riding style see Kathryn Renton, 'Muy grandes hombres de acaballo. Spanish horsemanship a la jineta and Bernardo de Vargas Machuca's New Science', in *Authority and Spectacle in Medieval and Early Modern Europe. Essays in Honor of Teofilo F. Ruiz*, ed. Jarbel Rodriguez (Abingdon: Routledge, 2017), 217–26.
20. Fallows, *Jousting*, 267.
21. On the effects of the conquest of Seville in 1284 on urban and rural societies and the role of noble and non-noble knights in Castile see Teofilo F. Ruiz, *Crisis and Continuity. Land and Town in Late Medieval Castile* (Philadelphia: University of Pennsylvania Press, 1994). In general, see also Noel Fallows' introduction in Fallows, *Jousting*, 1–27.
22. Ruiz, *King Travels*, here especially 212–20.
23. Ibid., 213.
24. Fallows, *Jousting*, 284.
25. Hernán Chacón himself states that he had organized many games of canes, not only for King Charles V, but also for knights and lords (*cavalleros y señores*) at the Spanish court, see Fallows, *Jousting*, 276.
26. Hernán Chacón, *Tractado de la cavallería de la gineta*, ed. Noel Fallows (Exeter: University of Exeter Press, 1999), 25.
27. Fallows, *Jousting*, 283.
28. Ibid., 504.
29. Hernán Chacón, *Tractado de la cavallería de la gineta. Selected Passages*, in Fallows, *Jousting*, 504–8, here 505.
30. Hernán Chacón, *Tractado*, here 505.
31. Ruiz, *King Travels*.
32. Ibid.
33. Antonio de Herrera y Tordesillas, *Historia general de los hechos de los castellanos en las Islas y Tierra Firme del mar Océano que llaman Indias Occidentales*, Decada I, libro VI, cap. IV (Madrid: Imprenta Real, 1601), 191.
34. Benjamín Flores Hernández, 'La jineta indiana en los textos de Juan Suárez de Peralta y Bernardo de Vargas Machuca', *Estudios Americanos* 54, no. 2 (1997): 639–64.
35. See Robert Folger, *Writing as Poaching. Interpellation and Self-fashioning in Colonial Relaciones de Méritos y Servicios* (Leiden: Brill, 2011), but also, more recently: Vitus

Huber, *Beute und Conquista. Die politische Ökonomie der Eroberung Neuspaniens* (Frankfurt: Campus Verlag, 2018).
36. Bernal Díaz mentions 'caciques' who were so rich that they owned and rode horses, and that bull-runs, *sortijas* and *juegos de cañas* were practiced in several villages; see Barbón Rodriguez, *Bernal Diaz del Castillo*, 806.
37. Robert M. Denhardt, 'The Horse in New Spain and the Borderlands', *Agricultural History* 25, no. 4 (1951): 145–50.
38. John J. Johnson, 'The Introduction of the Horse into the Western Hemisphere', *Hispanic American Historical Review* 23, no. 4 (1943): 588–9, 593.
39. Which is not entirely true. Archaeologists have excavated equine remains of ancestral horses that became extinct on the American continent approx. 10,000 years ago, see Caitlin E. Buck and Edouard Bard, 'A Calendar Chronology for Pleistocene Mammoth and Horse Extinction in North America based on Bayesian Radiocarbon Calibration', *Quaternary Science Reviews* 26, nos. 17–18 (2007): 2031–5.
40. For a more detailed discussion of the coat colors see Robert M. Denhardt, 'The Truth about Cortes's Horses', *Hispanic American Historical Review* 17, no. 4 (1937): 525–32.
41. *Las Siete Partidas, Volume 2: Medieval Government: The World of Kings and Warriors (Partida II)*, trans. Samuel Parsons Scott, ed. Robert I. Burns, S.J. (Philadelphia: University of Pennsylvania Press, 2012), 442.
42. Ibid., 422.
43. Compare e.g. the Tlaxcalan Campaign, in Díaz, *Conquest, 141*.
44. It is therefore not overly surprising that some of the horses were owned by more than one person, see **Figure 2**.
45. For a descriptive first study on the topic see Charles C. Colley, 'La Jineta. The Art of Moorish Horsemanship in the New World', *El Palacio*, 76 (1969): 31–4.
46. De Vargas Machuca, Bernardo, *Libro de exercicios de la gineta* (Madrid: Pedro Madrigal, 1600), fol. 35r.
47. Lull, Ramon, *Llibre de l'orde de cavalleria*, ed. by Soler i Llopart, Albert (Barcelona: Barcino, 1988), 167.
48. For a critical discussion of the *gineta indiana* see Flores Hernández, Benjamín, 'La jineta indiana en los textos de Juan Suárez de Peralta y Bernardo de Vargas Machuca', *Estudios Americanos* 54, no. 2 (1997): 639–64.
49. De Vargas Machuca, Bernardo, *Teorica y Exercicios de La Gineta: Primores, Secretos y Aduertencias Della, Con Las Señales Y Enfrentamientos de Los Cauallos, Su Curacion y Beneficio* (Madrid: Diego Flamenco, 1619), fol. 9r.
50. For a critical analysis of Spanish nobility, la hidalguía and la caballería see Christina H. Lee, *The Anxiety of Sameness in Early Modern Spain* (Manchester: Manchester University Press, 2016), 23–46.
51. In Hernán Chacón's *tractado* there are whole chapters on the use of *carreras* for the training of horses. It becomes also evident that the training on the course is related to tournament-oriented riding practice. Chapter VIII, for example, is on how to run the *carrera* with or without lances, see Chacón, *Tractado*, 8.
52. Kris Lane, *Captain Bernardo de Vargas Machuca. The Indian Militia and Description of the Indies* (Durham: Duke University Press, 2008), LVIII.
53. Bernal Díaz, for example, tells of several such ruses. For example, Cortés ordered Juan Sedeño's mare, which had just foaled, to be tethered to a tree out of sight from any non-Spanish spectators. Then, when Cortés was talking to his indigenous guests, Ortiz' stallion should be brought. Sniffing the mare, the stallion would perform a very impressive show of neighing and prancing around and by doing so impress (or frighten) the clueless spectators, see Díaz, *Conquest*, 78–79.
54. Mary Louise Pratt, 'Arts of the Contact Zone', *Profession* 91 (1991): 33–40.
55. Jean-Pierre Digard, *Une histoire du cheval. Art, techniques, société* (Arles: Actes Sud, 2004), 101, 115–12.

56. According to José Antonio Barbón Rodriguez, *Bernal Diaz del Castillo. Historia verdadera*, 59–60. For the English translation of coat colors see Denhardt, 'Truth about Cortes's Horses', 525–32.

## Disclosure Statement

No potential conflict of interest was reported by the author(s).1

# The Sport of Kingmakers: Horse Racing in Late Stuart England

Richard Nash

**ABSTRACT**
This essay sketches the general outlines of an argument that locates the rise of horse racing as a national sport in England in the context of national political change. In brief, the argument might be summarized as saying that horse racing was as much the sport of kingmakers as of kings, a recreation of martyrs as well as monarchs; and that some of its early participants were associated with breeding rebellion, as well as racehorses. The earliest public mention of a 'Jockey Club' appears to be a newspaper notice in the summer of 1729, and I have argued elsewhere that this club can be seen acting as a quasi-official body as early as 1717, though not necessarily under that name. Here, I want to extend that argument further in suggesting that the Club whose meeting was publicly announced in 1729 coalesced over the course of the preceding half-century. The argument I sketch here identifies how a very specific emergence of a particular organization of the sport served a very specific ideological purpose during a time of considerable tension over the relationship of church and state. The conflict between Protestants and Catholics, and the anxieties about succession and rebellion that these conflicts engendered, were more than just the backdrop to the rise of the sport; and the particular sport that emerged helped celebrate and popularize a Protestant succession settlement that ultimately excluded dozens of Stuart claimants to the throne in favor of the house of Hanover.

While horse racing in one form or another is almost certainly as old as the domestication of the horse, the modern sport of thoroughbred horse racing has long been linked historically in the popular imagination with the reign of Charles II, as the 'sport of kings'. That monarch took great interest in the sport, and has long been identified with patronizing it at Newmarket, where his statue was recently unveiled, commemorating the 350th anniversary of the opening of the Round Course. Articles written in 1665 exist for a plate race to be initiated the following year; and Charles is often credited with establishing a Royal Plate of 100 Guineas, and writing the articles for that event. In fact, while we know that Charles did participate in, preside over, and adjudicate disputed results at Newmarket during his reign, and that he supplemented contribution races, no articles for Royal Plates are known to exist from his reign; and his known supplementing of contributions is well below the 100-Guinea threshold. There is some evidence from his reign that he is responsible for establishing the plate racing that developed into the modern sport, but apparently at a significantly lesser level than became the standard.[1]

A complementary origin story exists for the animals, themselves, who are the athletes at the center of our sport, those horses now known as thoroughbreds. That name emerged slowly in various cognate forms over the course of the eighteenth century, and only came to serve as a breed identity in the nineteenth-century—no use of the term dates back as far as the reign of Charles. That latter fact is hardly surprising, as one widely credited definition of the breed identified as such in the nineteenth century is horses whose pedigree can be traced back in unbroken tail-male descent to one of three so-called foundation sires: the Byerley Turk, the Darley Arabian, and the Godolphin Arabian. All three of these date from after the death of Charles II, with the earliest (the Byerley Turk) foaled no earlier than the final years of his reign. Yet the sport has for over a century now been frequently referred to as 'the sport of Kings'; and Charles II remains the king most closely identified with its origins.[2]

The argument of this essay is that, while the sport may have been encouraged by, and closely associated with, Charles II, its promotion and emergence as something of a national sport was advanced as a form of political theater by those who most actively opposed that monarch at the end of his reign; and who became the leading proponents of the revolution of 1688. Their commitment to insuring both the perpetuation of the monarchy and the guarantee of a Protestant succession led them mobilize popular support through sporting spectacle; and then by linking that pastime directly to the reign of Charles II, they effected a tacit erasure of the brief reign of his brother, James. In doing so, they appropriated a sport patronized not only by Charles II, but by his illegitimate and ill-fated rebellious son, the Duke of Monmouth, who had sought the throne twice: first by political negotiation via an act of exclusion; and after that political gambit failed, through open rebellion that failed even more dramatically. Despite the failure of both of those attempts, Monmouth's ambitions were realized not by himself, but in the person of his uncle, William III, whose path to the throne was paved by the Protestant aristocrats who had earlier balked at supporting Monmouth's rebellion, but now turned out to support the usurpation by William and Mary; and who then pushed forward the Act of Settlement that perpetuated by political means what the earlier Exclusion Bill would have accomplished had Charles II not succeeded in blocking it. The sport of horse racing emerges from this moment of political crisis not merely as a witness to history, but as an integral feature of political performance, serving to mobilize popular support for a national compromise that guaranteed the preservation of both the institutions of monarchy and (by excluding Catholics from the line of succession) the established church.[3]

The importation of eastern horses long antedates the origins of the thoroughbred. It would defy credibility to imagine that Englishmen returning from the crusades did not bring with them the Barbs, Turks, and Arabians they had seized as spoils of war. Recent studies of equine genetics have established that the influence of such bloodlines, particularly the Turcoman strain, long antedates the more modern era of Turkey Merchants and thoroughbreds.[4] In all likelihood, the spread of such genetic material dates to well before the Crusades, but certainly Shakespeare reminds us in *Richard II* of the important role that the 'noble horse tradition' played in the performative display of horsemanship as a manifestation of regal authority. The usurper, Bolingbroke, at his coronation, displays his superior horsemanship by riding Richard's onetime mount, 'Roan Barbary', a 'hot and fiery steed', with such command that 'with slow but stately pace [he] kept [him] on his course'. Responsive to the skill of 'great Bolingbroke', Barbary moves 'So proudly as if he disdain'd the ground', to the mortification of the deposed Richard, unseated by his rival.[5]

This particular manifestation of equestrian prowess as emblematic of monarchic authority has a long tradition throughout Europe, a tradition actively embraced by the cavalier court of Charles II. Cavalier ideology was deeply imbued with the political lexicon of horsemanship: people, as well as horses, might be 'unruly jades', or could equally be 'proud, and high-spirited'; in either case, a proper monarch, like a proper horseman, could command love, respect, and obedience, with a light touch and no visible expenditure of energy. Such idealized display is assigned to Bolingbroke, where his hot and fiery steed goes with slow but stately pace so proudly as if he disdained the ground. The iconic depiction of such equestrian prowess is ubiquitous in royal portraiture, as in the famous Van Dyck portrait of Charles I, but it was nowhere more elaborately staged as political performance than in the coronation procession of Charles II at the restoration of the monarchy.[6]

Soon after that restoration, Charles began actively participating in the sport of horse racing, establishing a palace and stables at Newmarket (now the site of a National Heritage Centre), competing himself. He signed in 1665 a set of articles establishing a plate race, intended to be held the following year, and 'to be rid for yearly, the second Thursday in October, for ever'.[7] This is sometimes identified as a royal plate, and sometimes as the town plate, but the articles themselves make clear that this was to be a contribution plate, in which subscribers contribute to the prize to be run for, and pay an entry fee, rather than a race where the prize is paid for by a sponsor such as the monarch (royal) or the town corporation (town): 'the noblemen and gentlemen which are then present, and being contributors to the said plate'.[8] While the articles for this race exist, no systematic record of results from such an early date does.[9] So, for instance, it is not clear whether or not the initial running went off as intended, or was one of the many events cancelled in consequence of the calamities of plague and fire that visited London the following year. Some sporadic results do, however, exist; and among these are accounts that King Charles himself rode, in 1671, the (unidentified) winner of 'The Plate, being a flagon of 32 price', defeating Mr. Eliot, the Duke of Monmouth and Thomas Thynne.[10] Again, at the spring meeting of 1675, Charles is recorded as winning the plate: 'Sir Robert Car, writing from Newmarket on March 21st, says: 'Yesterday His Majesty rode himself three heates and a course, and won the Plate—all fower were hard and neer ridden, and I doe assure you the King wonn by good horsemanshipp'.[11]

What is not entirely clear is whether this plate was the town plate or a contribution plate or perhaps a royal plate, though the last mentioned seems most likely. What is clear from the results given, and from other similar results given sporadically from this period is that the Newmarket version of the sport with which Charles amused himself was, at this date, very much a court recreation. In 1680, for instance, different news accounts indicate that on Friday, March 19, Mr. Griffins won the town plate (and presented it to the town), two days after 'Wednesday March 17, the Plate Race was run by the King's horse Tankot, Mr. Mayes horse, Dragon, the Duke of Monmouth's horse Spot, and the Topping Horse of Newmarket, Red Rose, the 4 mile course, but who had the best on't we cannot give you an account'.[12] Clearly those were two different races. And as the result from the 1671 and 1680 plates indicate, the participants were members of the Royal Household or the Court (both Elliott and Mayes were pages in the Royal Household). Disputes, when they occurred, whether over the running of the races or the wagers made, were brought before the king, whose judgment was final. In this era, there was no Jockey Club; or, put another way, at this time the court was the club. The Jockey Club was long thought to have taken shape as a governing body of the sport in the mid-eighteenth century, but recent scholarship has shown that it originated and took an active leadership role much earlier, most likely assuming that role in conjunction with the visit of King George to Newmarket in 1717.[13] If that royal visit seems to have spurred the club to coalesce into a more active organizational role, however, it does not preclude the possibility that between the reigns of Charles II and George I, some version of the club existed in a looser confederacy of sporting 'Noblemen and Gentlemen'. And there is some reason to believe not only that such a club did exist, but that when it re-galvanized itself in 1717, it did so in deliberate imitation and continuation of a political role it had played a generation earlier at the end of the reign of Charles II. In what follows, I want to review some of the evidence in support of such a reading.

While documentary evidence, in the form of written records, is both sparse and scattered, as likely to be found in correspondence and diaries as in any published venue, there are other forms of material culture that offer important clues. When the Jockey Club did take on an organizational role in the Hanoverian era, one corollary effect was the promotion of sporting art, particularly the work of equine portraiture by artists such as John Wootton, Peter Tillemans, and James Seymour.[14] We know, for instance, that a painting of James Cavendish, astride the horse on whom he won a race against time (riding from the Jockey Club headquarters at Williams's Coffee House near St. James Palace to Windsor Castle) for a large wager, was to be hung 'in the picture room of the Jockey Club' in that establishment. When Williams died, his will bequeathed his collection of such paintings to Lord Godolphin, by then the *eminence grise* of the club. Alas, it seems likely that most of these paintings were among the many that were discarded at the end of the eighteenth century, when they were discovered in a state of neglect and damaged by moisture in the Jockey Club coffeehouse established at Newmarket.[15] But quite a few of the larger and more valuable portraits commissioned by individual members of the club still survive in private collections and museums, and in some cases pass under the auctioneer's

Benjamin Pyne
British, 1653–1732
Cup: "Saltby Plate", 1710
Gilded silver
Gift of Mrs. Ernest L. Woodward, 54.13

**Figure 1.** Benjamin Pyne, *Saltby Plate* (1710). A gilded silver cup with engraved 'running horse' icon from the reign of Queen Anne.

hammer.[16] Such is also the case with some (though not many) of the racing trophies of these early days. Like the 'flagon of 32 price' mentioned above, these trophies were commissioned from goldsmiths as prizes to be run for. While the earliest known racing trophies were 'bells', 'spoons' and 'tankards' were also frequent prizes in the seventeenth century, and sometime near the end of that century, the most valuable 'plates' tended to take the form of punchbowls, monteiths, tumblers, or cup-and-covers, what were advertised as a 'Gold Cup', a terminology still in use, though no longer having the literal meaning it once had. In the middle of the eighteenth century, fluctuations in the price of gold across Europe made such trophies more valuable melted and sold than they had originally cost to make, so more than a few were, quite literally, liquidated. But those that survive offer us additional evidence to work with about the early history of the sport.

Queen Anne was a notable patron of the turf during her reign, and Royal Ascot was founded under her auspices. Perhaps it is no accident that the first such meeting took place in 1711, during the new Tory administration that held power during the last four years of her reign. It is tempting to see the creation of a royally sanctioned meet at Ascot as something of a slight to the Whig interests at Newmarket (which Anne continued to support assiduously) not unlike the earlier efforts of Charles to shift his sporting interest from Newmarket to Winchester. Those paintings of actual races that survive from this era seem to strive to record accurately historical details (where written records do exist, many of these details corroborate one another), and one can see the trophy for which horses are contending displayed at the finishing post. That practice can be seen depicted in an engraving that dates from as early as the late years of Charles's reign. Walter Gilbey's little book on racing trophies, now roughly a century old, is quite valuable for the information it provides about the actual goldsmiths involved in producing some of these early trophies, but his history of the craftsmanship involved does little to question or advance what was seen at the

**Figure 2.** Johann Klosterman, *Portrait of Racehorse with Jockey, c. 1690 [perhaps Rutland's Blacklegs]*. The trophies displayed in the lower right feature the 'running horse' icon. Image © Palace House, Newmarket, United Kingdom.

time as a settled history of the sport itself. One good illustration of an early racing trophy is the gilded silver cup, made by Benjamin Pyne, and presented to the winner of the Saltby Plate, sponsored by the Duke of Rutland in 1710. This two-handled drinking cup shows a running horse engraved over the inscription 'Saltby Plate' (Figure 1).[17]

An even earlier illustration appears in one of the earliest equine portraits of a racehorse (Figure 2), one that is believed to show the Duke of Rutland's Blacklegs.[18] This painting has been identified with the Duke of Rutland because it seems to show Haddon Hall in the background. There are a number of oddities in the painting, not least of which is the incongruously gigantic hare who can be seen near one of the palings of the racecourse that is set out in the background. In the lower right-hand corner, perhaps added to the original painting, someone (presumably a trainer) displays the various trophies won by the horse in the portrait. Clearly included in the trophies on display are at least two tumblers, a spoon, a monteith and a pitcher or vase. Engraved on the latter two trophies is an image of a running horse, not unlike that engraved on the Saltby Plate tumbler. The figures in the painting may be tentatively identified as Griffin and Rider (trainer and jockey, respectively, for the 9th Earl, later 1st Duke, of Rutland, from a letter of 1687 regarding Blacklegs:

1687. 27th Oct. Newmarket. Being laste night at Jackson's, & haveing an oportunity to match with Mr. Frampton according to your commission you gave me, I matched Blackleggs laste night with Haucker, 10 stone waite each, for 500 guineys, two forfeite; over ye foure mile course here, to runne ye third Wednesday in March nexte: and tho' I doe selldom take notice of what is donn at Plates, yett hereing you were beaten at Luffnum [Luffenham Heath, near Stamford] and not knowing how yt might alter yr mind, I have made itt but 5 guinneys forfeite till this day fortnight; theirefore only desire you wou'd write me word what you will doe; tho' I do not intend to give my answer till the laste day, before whch time Mr. Rider will see you at Belvoire in order to yr going to Lincoln; if yr Lordship has a mind to match Stately, or Belvoire, with horses of theire age, and will send me commission, I believe I cann match them with horses much worse bredd, and not so likely to runn at Linckcolne. And Sir Robert Howard offers to match Cockain's horse agst Castleton, but I wou'd make no more matches till I heard farther from you. Pray my good Ld lett me know how farr I may goe in matching yr horses for what summs, for I doe really believe I cou'd match them well; but when you send me commission lett itt be full, and I traine to ye laste pound you will let your naggs spurr att; and yr commands shall be observed, and obeyed by yr moste obliged humble servt.[19]

In attending to the trophies, we might start with the monteith (a punchbowl with a scalloped rim from which cups for the punch may be hung). When the Exclusion Crisis of the early 1680s gave rise to the political division and partisan alliances of Whig and Tory, even beverage consumption was branded accordingly, with Tories toasting the king with claret, and Whigs toasting the Protestant cause with punch. Whig pubs were often designated as 'The Punchbowl', and for a time these were popular trophies at Whig-affiliated race meets. Of possibly greater significance is the appearance of the engraved running horse on these trophies. In one sense, of course, it makes sense that a racing trophy would have a running horse engraved upon it. There is remarkable uniformity in the depiction of the engraved running horse on these and other trophies, and while that may be an artifact of the relatively crude and simple form of engraving that characterized equine art of the period, it may also be an early instance of branding. One frequently finds later in the century trophies that show the jockey dismounted and holding a standing racehorse (not unlike the posture in the painting of Blacklegs), so there is no necessary reason for these early trophies to display the icon of the running horse.[20]

Such an engraving does, however, literally inscribe the identity of the horse being prized. We are used to thinking of racehorses as 'thoroughbreds', but the earliest direct use we have of that term with respect to a racehorse dates from the Hanoverian era, and does not become fully established until the early nineteenth century. Nor was such a sense of identity even yet available in this early era. Griffith's letter, for instance, calls attention to the quality of breeding, noting that he would be matching horses of Rutland's breeding against others 'worse bredd', but it is notable that the horse in question, Rutland's Blacklegs comes down to posterity as a valuable running horse and a significant sire, but is himself of 'unknown pedigree'. No record of his breeding exists, and his era on the turf pre-dates that of any of the progeny of the three so-called 'foundation stallions' of what we now recognize as constituting a distinct breed. In this era, horses were horses, and were deemed better or worse bred by the effectiveness of those human agents who bred them (the Manners family, to which the Duke of Rutland belongs, had a reputation for

**Figure 3.** Frances Barlow, *The Last Horse Race Run before Charles the Second* (1687). Image Royal Collection Trust/© Her Majesty Queen Elizabeth II 2020.

breeding quality horses). At this time, horses were more likely to be identified by function than by breed identity; and a horse who was bred and kept for racing was identified as 'a running horse.'[21]

The earliest engraving of a horse race in England was one made by Frances Barlow and published in 1687 (Figure 3), depicting the race at Dorset [sic] Ferry in 1684, represented in the print as the 'last horse race run before Charles II of blessed memory'.[22] Charles did actually go to Newmarket later that autumn, but the weather was bad and his health not good, so it is possible that he did not attend the races there. This rapidly became a popular sporting print, and several aspects of it may bear greater significance than has been previously noted. Of immediate concern here is that Barlow's rendering of a running horse and jockey quickly became the standard icon, with that distinctive unrealistic depiction of a 'rockinghorse' gait, leaping off his hindlegs, and the jockey brandishing an upright whip.[23] This is the image one finds engraved on many racing trophies from this late Stuart era. And it is not impossible that the image had emblematic and ideological significance. Barlow is known to have been active in producing Whig prints opposing James II after 1685; and I believe that this print became emblematic for the cause of Protestant succession.

The dozen years that intervened between the marriage of William and Mary in 1677 and the successful revolution that eventually brought them to the throne in 1689 were tumultuous ones indeed, politically: the list of events, trials, executions, and displays are too long to detail in a single paragraph, but are unparalleled in history. And those years are precisely the ones in which the modern sport of horse racing is generally seen to have arisen (the earliest of the foundation stallions of the thoroughbred was ridden by his owner, Robert Byerley, at the Battle of the Boyne). What has until now been too little noted, however, is how closely related these events were. Charles had given his approval to the marriage of James's daughter, Mary, to the Prince of Orange in hopes (destined to be disappointed) that such a marriage would stem the growing anti-Papist sentiment among his subjects. The month preceding the wedding was spent at Newmarket, where William was particularly well-received by the community. The murder of Sir Edmundberry Godfrey and the unfolding of the (fabricated) Popish Plot which occurred during the fall meet a year later, added fuel to the exclusionist movement being fed by those politicians soon denominated Whigs, as the succession crisis gave rise to the partisan divide of Whig and Tory. Newmarket, and the nearby Cambridge University, were both largely Protestant in religion and increasingly supportive of the Whig exclusion policies; so much so that for the last several years of his reign, Charles II lost the enjoyment he had once taken at Newmarket and was actively planning a more elaborate sporting palace at Winchester, near Oxford, where at least the university was solidly Royalist in its Tory inclinations.[24]

As the Exclusion Crisis neared its zenith, the Duke of Monmouth undertook a western progress in the autumn of 1680, supported lavishly by his close friend (who had raced alongside him against Charles II in that 1671 plate race), Thomas Thynne. The progress capitalized on the recent spike in popularity that Monmouth enjoyed following both his victory and his merciful treatment of the defeated at the Battle of Bothwell Bridge the previous summer. And it was an enormous success. All through September, throngs gathered to view him, and there was one instance published of his effecting a miraculous cure by touching for the King's Evil. Outside Exeter, he was greeted by a thousand young men, clad all in white, unarmed marching to greet him, and at once symbolizing their innocent Protestant virtue and the more ominous subtext of their willingness to come out as a band of supporters. The exclusion movement, managed by Shaftesbury in the upper house and William Russell, son of the fifth Earl (subsequently, first Duke) of Bedford, in the Commons, had been careful not to seek to name a successor—its limited scope sought only to prevent a Catholic from sitting on the throne. The most obvious successor, if one were to exclude James, would be his daughter, Mary and her recently-wed consort, William of Orange. But William was a foreign prince without great personal charm or charisma. And Monmouth (and his companions at court) saw an opportunity to leverage his personal charm and popularity. This first western progress of 1680 confirmed that Monmouth's popular appeal could strengthen the Exclusion movement, and gave rise to the idea that Charles could sidestep the issue of who determines succession by recognizing Monmouth (long acknowledged to be his bastard son) as legitimate.[25]

Two years later, Monmouth conducted a second western progress, and this one was clearly planned in advance as a political campaign and a show of potential force. Monmouth's itinerary took him from race meet to race meet. As the progress continued, the throng accompanying Monmouth grew larger and more raucous.

Charles and his supporters monitored the progress from London by correspondence, and they planned to blunt the momentum when Monmouth reached the Wallasey races. Rather than contesting that race, Tories organized a rival race meet for the same day in nearby Delamere Forest. There was some discussion of postponing the Wallasey plate, but it was decided instead that Thomas Wharton would contest it on behalf of Monmouth's supporters. Thus, on the same day, there was a clean sweep for the Exclusion cause with Wharton defeating Tories on their home course in Delamere Forest while Monmouth captured the plate at Wallasey.[26] The ensuing celebrations, as might be expected, included more than a little drinking; and when, a few weeks later, Monmouth was arrested and taken back to London, the charges against him arose from toasts on this occasion that smacked of treason.

The intertwined nature of politics and horse-racing at this moment in English history is underlined by a poem published that year (Figure 4): *The Horsemanship of England, most particularly Relating to the Breeding and Training of the Running Horse. A Poem dedicated to His Grace the Duke of Monmouth* (1682).[27] While the anonymous poet may very well have been simply seizing on current events to market his poem on the breeding and training of horses for racing, his title not only attests to the public perception of the connection between the sport and ongoing political events, it signals the distinctive transition signaled by the Exclusionist party. In the (literally) reigning cavalier tradition, 'horsemanship' signified the ruler's ability to manage his state, as described by the Duke of Newcastle in his writings on 'horsemanship' as *manege,* and the ability to ride the Great Horse. This was the version of horsemanship on display in Charles II's coronation parade. But this new sport, patronized by that monarch, introduced new models of horsemanship, both breeding and training, associated with innovative—and distinctly Protestant— ideologies of modern improvement.[28] Monmouth, in 1682, served as the charismatic face of this modern performance of politics as horsemanship.

Following his arrest, Monmouth was banished by Charles, but the victory at Wallasey was not the end of his racing political campaign. While we are used to thinking of horse racing as an English sport, sponsored by Charles, Louis XIV sponsored what is the earliest recorded modern international invitational horse race at St. Germain the following February. Once again teaming with Thomas Wharton to provide him with a quality running horse, Monmouth rode the Wharton gelding to victory. Reportedly, Louis offered to buy the horse after the race, and Monmouth and Wharton refused payment, offering the horse as a gift instead, which Louis declined.[29] This may have been a diplomatic dance in which offering such a gift would leave Louis indebted, and so his refusal may have confirmed what was, in fact, the case and suspected by William of Orange–that Louis had already entered into a private treaty with Charles against the Netherlands, and in support of the succession by James.

These events mixing racing and politics in 1682–1683, it should be remembered, transpired between the time the Rye House Plot was supposed to occur and when it was discovered after the fact. Planned during the winter of 1681–1682, the plot called to seize and assassinate the king and his brother on their way home from Newmarket after the spring 1682 meeting. Halfway through the meeting, a fire destroyed half the

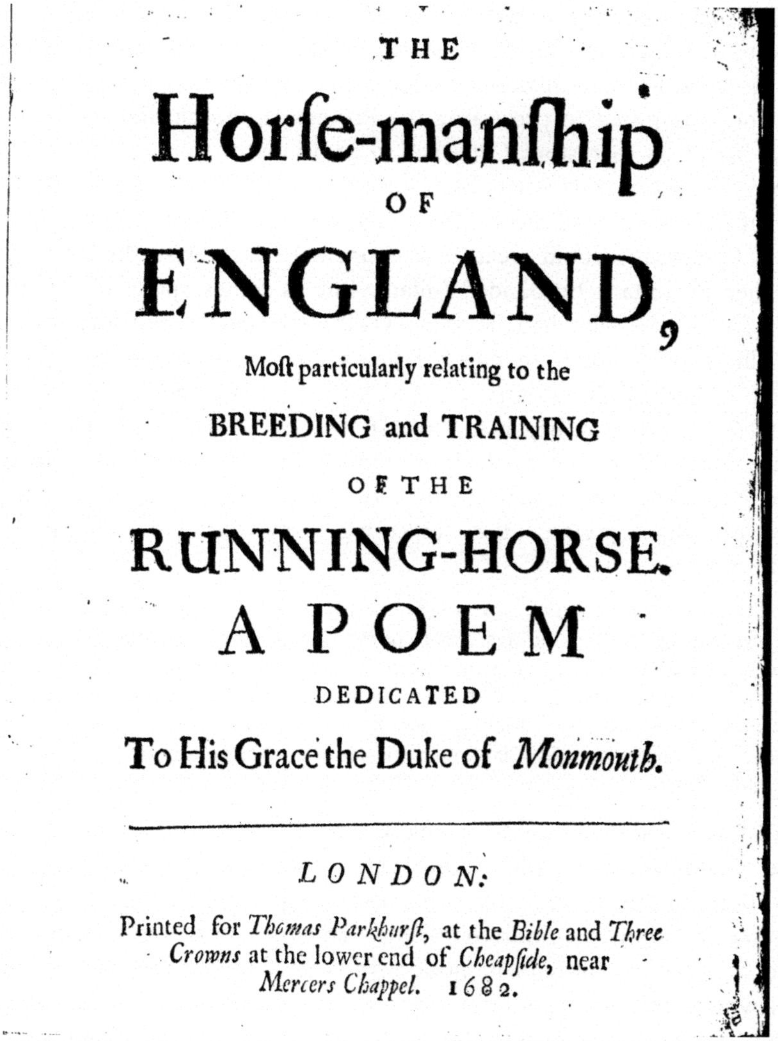

> THE
>
> # Horſe-manſhip
>
> OF
>
> # ENGLAND,
>
> Moſt particularly relating to the
>
> **BREEDING and TRAINING**
>
> OF THE
>
> # RUNNING-HORSE.
>
> # A POEM
>
> DEDICATED
>
> To His Grace the Duke of *Monmouth*.
>
> ---
>
> *LONDON:*
>
> Printed for *Thomas Parkhurſt*, at the *Bible* and *Three Crowns* at the lower end of *Cheapſide*, near *Mercers Chappel*. 1682.

**Figure 4.** Title Page to *The Horsemanship of England, most particularly relating to … the Running Horse. Dedicated to his Grace, the Duke of Monmouth* (1682).

town, sending the royal party home ahead of schedule and foiling the plot. It was only in the summer of 1683 that the plot was discovered, and Algernon Sidney and William, Lord Russell (who had led the exclusion movement in the House of Commons) were tried, convicted, and executed. In the years that followed—and, indeed for at least a century thereafter—Russell, in particular, became identified as Whig martyr who gave his life in the cause of liberty against the absolute authority of the monarch.[30]

Whatever hopes of support the progresses of 1680 and 1682 had led Monmouth to expect were dashed when he launched his ill-fated rebellion against James II in 1685. James was inclined to pursue the plans set by his brother of creating a sporting palace at Winchester, but that was only the least of his many unpopular moves. Lord

Danby, who had been impeached earlier for his role in negotiating a treaty with France (even without knowing that the treaty negotiated had effectively bribed the king) was returned to his ministerial position, but by 1687 was ousted by James when he proved too committed to protecting the Protestant church. James sought to move ahead with his plans to restore Catholics to positions of public trust and authority, intensifying the sentiments that had fueled the Exclusion crisis. But now the pendulum of succession had swung the other way: like Charles, James had no male heir, and if Protestants could weather the storm of his reign, the next in line was Mary and her Protestant husband, William. But as James spoke of the prospect of fathering a son, those who had favored exclusion began to consider seriously what options William might offer to check James's policies of indulgence for Catholics. Charles Talbot, Earl of Shrewsbury, entered into correspondence with William in the autumn of 1687, as rumors began to circulate that the queen might be pregnant. Just before Christmas, the palace formally announce that the queen was pregnant, and proclaimed a national day of thanksgiving for the following month. The week before that day of thanksgiving, the following advertisement appeared in the *London Gazette*:

> At New-Market in Easter Week next 1688, is a Plate of 100 Guineas value to be run for, by Horses, Mares, and Geldings, that never run before; Gentlemen are to ride themselves, Three Heats, Twelve Stone weight: A stranger to put in for his Horse Ten Guineas. The Nobility and Gentry that contribute to this Plate are desired to pay their Contribution-money to Mr. Richard Hoare, Goldsmith at the Golden Bottle in Cheapside, London; or to Mr. Clayton at his House in Newmarket. No Horse can run for this Plate that is not kept one full Month before the day of Running.[31]

Some distinctive features of this advertisement are worth noting. It is, like the town plate whose articles Charles authorized, a contribution plate; and it follows the same conditions as that plate (three heats, twelve stone weight, gentlemen to ride). It restricts entry to 'Noblemen and Gentlemen' and they must be entering horses who have never run before. Subsequent notices indicate that the race is to be subscribed to for five years; and one can infer from similar conditions in later races that the contribution money would likely have been five guineas per horse per year from the line that permitted 'a stranger [non-subscriber] to put in for his horse [for] ten guineas'. If the town plate is the oldest regular fixture at Newmarket, one associated traditionally with the royal plates, the terms of this race identify it with a recurring fixture associated with the early Jockey Club: the Noblemen's and Gentlemen's Contribution Plate/Purse. Moreover, the announced value—100 guineas—is the earliest recorded instance of a plate of this value being contested at Newmarket.[32]

Is the timing of the announcement merely a coincidence of history or something more? Newmarket meeting had been a regular space of recreation for those courtiers close to power in the days of Charles and Monmouth who now found themselves outside the circle of catholic king who no longer patronized the meet. Cromwell had, during the interregnum, suppressed horse racing because meets were seen as providing cover for seditious meetings; and Lord Derwentwater was to launch the Jacobite rebellion of 1715 from a race meet. It is not unlikely that the prospects of William invading to rescue England from his Catholic father-in-law would have been discussed at this meet. William had, both directly and through agents, been engaging in correspondence and conversation with disaffected aristocrats for nearly a year. Bishop Burnet reports that in late April (i.e. soon after this Newmarket meeting), Edward Russell, brother of the martyred William, asked William directly what it would take for him to act, and learned that William wanted a letter of invitation from some of the leading men of the country.[33]

Following the queen giving birth, in June, to a son, such a letter was sent to William, signed by those subsequently termed 'the immortal seven': Lord Danby; Henry Compton, Bishop of London; Richard Lumley, Earl of Scarborough; Charles Talbot, Earl of Shrewsbury; William Cavendish, Earl of Devonshire; Admiral Edward Russell; and Henry Sidney, Earl of Romney who is said to have actually written the letter (in cipher). Of these, the first two (or three) are generally counted as Tories, the remainder Whigs. Lumley and Talbot had been raised as Catholics, and converted to Protestantism, the others born and raised Protestant. The last three, in particular, were all directly related to the Rye House martyrs: Sidney, being brother to Algernon Sidney; Russell brother to Russell; and Cavendish, both brother-in-law and close friend to Russell. No record has yet been found of the subscription list for this 'Noblemen's and Gentlemen's Plate', so whether any or all of these seven were subscribers is a matter of conjecture. There is nothing to suggest participation by Romney, Shrewsbury, or certainly Bp. Compton; but the others range from possible to highly likely. Danby was certainly familiar with Newmarket from his earlier years leading Charles's ministry, and his descendants were certainly active on the turf, so he is possible. Scarborough had been the Queen's Master of the Horse; and had then formed the Queen Dowager's or Ninth Regiment of Horse (originally known as Lord Lumley's Regiment) in which Robert Byerley served and rode his charging horse who became one of the foundation sires of the thoroughbred. Scarborough's son became George II's Master of the Horse and selected Thomas Panton to succeed Tregonwell Frampton as Keeper of the King's Running Horses; He would certainly seem likely to have been included. Lord Orford does not seem himself to have played a significant role in the early history of horse racing, but his siblings and relations were active, and in the next generation particularly many prominent members of the Jockey Club had a direct family tie to the martyred Lord Russell. Devonshire was himself active on the turf, and his son, the second Duke, was widely seen as the leading figure of the early Jockey Club. Tilleman's large painting of 'The Noblemen's and Gentlemen's String of Horses Taking Their Exercise at Warren Hill' was dedicated to the second Duke and featured his string of horses prominently. It is highly likely that he was involved in this subscription.[34]

Beyond that, of course, the subscription almost certainly would have attracted those figures who had most actively supported Monmouth both politically and in his racing activities, in addition to those figures who we know became leading figures both on the turf and at the court of William and Mary. Notable among these would have been the Earl of Godolphin who was one of those in the ministry of James who was charged with negotiating the terms of surrender. He continued to play a leading role in William's ministry and many of the horses who ran as 'the Lord Treasurer's' were, in fact, J. B. Muir has argued a racing confederacy of William and Godolphin, trained by the Tregonwell Frampton.[35] Such confederacies, much like the one which Monmouth enjoyed with Wharton seem to have been not uncommon. Wharton is another who we can safely assume would have participated in the subscription. While he actively supported Monmouth's racing career, he seems to have been at least equally disposed in favor of William as an alternative to James. In his stud book, we find that several of his mares were, in 1684, serviced by 'the Barb brought over by the Prince of Orange'.[36] Presumably, this would allude to a stallion brought by William when he visited Charles in 1681, seeking support in his war with France. Charles, of course, was bound by his secret treaty not to provide such support, and William came away disappointed with only vague rhetoric and no solid commitment; indeed, William is said to have inferred (correctly, as it turns out) that Charles had reached a private accord with Louis.

After the Rye House plot, Wharton's estate was searched for arms, and a cache of weapons seized, but eventually returned. Perhaps Wharton did not come out during Monmouth's rebellion because he knew he was under scrutiny, or perhaps the lesson learned at St. Germain, confirming William's suspicion, led him to think that Monmouth was a poor risk. William's visit in 1681 came in August when Wharton hosted a plate race sometimes referred to as 'the Great Prize' at Quainton Meadow (*Whig's* 155). Daniel Defoe (who did come out for Monmouth's rebellion) wrote in his Tour of the Whole Island of Great Britain many years later, 'It was my hap formerly, to be at Aylesbury, when there was a mighty confluence of noblemen and gentlemen, at a famous horse race at Quainton Meadow, not far off, where was then the late Duke of Monmouth, and a great many persons of the first rank, and a prodigious concourse of people'.[37] Whatever the case, while Wharton did not come out for Monmouth, he was the first to greet William when he arrived on English soil, at the head of a regiment.

By the time Mary died in December 1694, there were signs of stress in the coalition that had welcomed William in 1688. The joint coronation had been a sign from the outset that there was some wariness about placing on the throne the head of state of a country with whom England had recently been at war. In the early years of the reign, while William was often away pursuing Dutch military campaigns, Mary ruled effectively. But Protestant monarchs turn out to be as intent on protecting royal prerogatives as Catholic ones, and even before Mary's death, even some of the original supporters of William's invasion were engaging in correspondence with the Jacobite court in exile. To shore up his support in the elections of 1695, William was advised to follow the path that Monmouth had traveled during the Exclusion Crisis and that George would later be advised to follow after the Jacobite rebellion of 1715: a royal progress.[38]

William was only slightly more open to this practice than George was to prove a generation later, and throughout the summer, notices in the *Gazette* about the contemplated progress varied wildly. In the end, William's progress lasted for roughly three weeks, and began—as George's abruptly curtailed 'progress' would later—with a visit to Newmarket. And in anticipation of that visit, Newmarket hosted 'a Plate of above Sixty Guineas value', according to the same conditions as Wharton's plate at Quainton Meadow. Luttrell's diary records that during the king's visit, Wharton's horses twice proved victorious in matches against horses owned by the Duke of Devonshire, and the king's horse won the town plate. Perhaps as a sign of his pleasure at the event, but perhaps as part of a calculated political campaign, in December of that year, we find the first announcement of what comes to be known as the royal plates, for which Charles receives credit (i.e. those of a value of 100 Guineas):

> These are to give notice that His Majesty is pleased to give two plates yearly, of the value 100 Guineas each, to be run for at Newmarket, on every first Thursday of April and every first Thursday of October, according to the Articles of the Town Plate there.[39]

What royal plates Charles had given seem to have been of lesser value and less regularly given. The only record we have of a plate of 100 Guineas value prior to this is the 'Noblemen's and Gentlemen's Contribution Plate' that immediately preceded William's invasion, a subscription that continued through 1692. The claim to priority of royal patronage in fully funding such a plate not once, but twice, a year seems to belong entirely to William; and yet no attempt is made by him or on his behalf to claim that priority. Instead, this act is publicized almost immediately as continuing the patronage of his royal predecessor, Charles. In doing so, those advancing the sport seek to follow the pattern seen in Barlow's print of 1687, depicting Charles as the patron of the turf.[40] But in doing so, it also serves the political interests of the Williamite succession, by linking William to Charles in his continuing patronage, skipping over notably the intervening gap that marked the reign of James II. Thus, one can see in the events of the late Restoration a coalescing of interests both sporting and political on the part of those courtiers seeking to guarantee a Protestant succession on the throne, and finding in the sport of horse racing an effective way to focus a populist political theater.

The conjunction of horse racing and politics as a form of popular political theater during this period of transition from court-centered monarchy to parliamentary monarchy is underlined in a satire in Charles Leslie's *The Rehearsal* in 1704, following Queen Anne's accession. The Bill of Rights had, at the time of the coronation of William and Mary, settled a line of Protestant succession, through Anne and her heirs. When her son, William, Duke of Gloucester, died in 1700, parliament passed the Act of Settlement the following year, forever excluding Catholic heirs from the throne, and settling the succession, failing heirs of the body of Anne, to pass to Sophia, Electress of Hanover, and her heirs (bypassing dozens of closer, Catholic, claimants). Scotland responded with the Act of Security in 1704, reserving the right to choose its own successor to Anne, and thereby threatening a return to rival monarchs that the Stuart line had joined. Thus, the Act of Union, creating Great Britain became a priority for Anne's administration. Leslie puts in the mouth of John Tutchin's Observator a strategy of political theater linked explicitly to the progresses of Monmouth almost two dozen years earlier and accurately predicting the very actions that would serve as the founding actions a dozen years later of the Jockey Club:

> To get the Young Prince of Hanover over Hither in this Queen's time. That we may Flock about him, as we did about Monmouth; And carry him About to Horse-Races, and such like things, all Round England. And whoever shew not Full Popularity to him,

we'll Mark them as High-Tory-Tantivy-Men; and set the Mobb upon them. We'll have a new List of Worthy Men, and Men-Worthy.[41]

The allusion to 'Worthy Men and Men-Worthy' refers to a list that was kept by the Earl of Shaftesbury, discovered in his papers (and published by Charles) when he fled into exile during the Exclusion Crisis, the former heading describing those he could count on to vote for an Exclusion bill, and the latter describing his opponents as 'Men Worthy [to be hanged]'. The plan to bring over the young prince did not, of course, materialize during Queen Anne's lifetime, but when she died just weeks after the death of the Electress of Hanover, that prince-now Elector-came over to inherit the throne as King George. The Jacobite rebellion that began the following year was put down in 1716, and in 1717, his supporters planned a royal progress. George had little interest, and the original ambitious itinerary kept being shortened, dwindling down in the end to his one and only visit to Newmarket, which in fact, he left early. But the formal organization that had gone into planning that meeting carried over that winter through meetings at what had become the Club headquarters in Williams Coffee Shop across from St. James; and a number of initiatives and recorded procedures ensued, including a regular record of races in the Newmarket Match Book from 1718 forwards.[42]

Many of the leading figures of this more formally constituted club were literal heirs to those supporters of Protestant monarchy who had first mobilized during the Exclusion Crisis and the perceived martyrdom of the Rye House plotters, and then pledged their support, came out for, and served in the ministry of, William and Mary. And one can see in certain actions and traditions of the Hanoverian Jockey Club nods to the revolutionary origins of the sport: a staple of the racing calendar in these early decades was the 'Noblemen's and Gentlemen's Contribution Plate or Purse', which seems to originate with that 1688 subscription; and two events only from the early racing calendar stand out as being for a time relocated to Newmarket for a time, after they seem destined to fail to be renewed: the Quainton Meadow race initiated by Wharton and the Wallasey Stakes at which Monmouth had triumphed during his Western Progress. While Charles was undeniably the royal patron of the turf who set in motion a cultural connection between horse racing and monarchy, the development of that sport, and particularly its cultural and ideological associations were distinctly linked to those who opposed that monarch to the point of open rebellion, and who then subsequently appropriated and extended his sponsorship for a sport of (Protestant) kings.

## Notes

1. In this century there has been a reawakening of academic interest in the history of horse racing in the early modern period. Among the significant contributions to this discussion, one might include the following: Oliver Cox, '"Newmarket, that Infamous Seminary of Iniquity and Ill Manners": Horses and Courts in the Early Years of George III's Reign', *The Court Historian* 24, 3 (2019): 269–81; Mike Huggins, *Horse Racing and British Society in the Long Eighteenth Century* (Woodbridge: Boydell & Brewer, 2018); David Oldrey, Timothy Cox, and Richard Nash, *The Heath and the Horse: A History of Racing and Art on Newmarket Heath* (London: I.B. Tauris, 2016); Rebecca Cassidy, ed.,

*The Cambridge Companion to Horse Racing* (Cambridge: Cambridge University Press, 2013); Donna Landry, *Noble Brutes: How Eastern Horses Transformed English Culture* (Baltimore: Johns Hopkins University Press, 2009); Peter Edwards, *Horse and Man in Early Modern England* (London: Hambledon Continuum, 2007).

2. See further Richard Nash, '"Honest English Breed": The Thoroughbred as Cultural Metaphor', in *The Culture of the Horse: Status, Discipline, and Identity in the Early Modern World*, ed. Karen Raber and Treva Tucker (New York: Palgrave Macmillan, 2005), 245–72.
3. See the extensive historiography already cited, including Cox, '"Newmarket, that Infamous Seminary of Iniquity and Ill Manners": 269–81; Huggins, *Horse Racing and British Society in the Long Eighteenth Century*; Oldrey, Cox, and Nash, *The Heath and the Horse*; Cassidy, *The Cambridge Companion to Horse Racing*; Landry, *Noble Brutes*; Edwards, *Horse and Man in Early Modern England*.
4. Mim A. Bower, Beatrice A. McGivney, Michael G. Campana, Jingjing Gu, Lisa S. Andersson, Elizabeth Barrett, Catherine R. Davis, Sofia Mikko, Frauke Stock, Valery Voronkova, Daniel G. Bradley, Alan G. Fahey, Gabriella Lindgren, David E. MacHugh, Galina Sulimova, and Emmeline W. Hill, 'The Genetic Origin and History of Speed in the Thoroughbred Racehorse, *Nature Communications* 3 (2012), 643; P. Cunningham, 'The Genetics of Thoroughbred Horses', *Scientific American* 264, no. 5 (1991): 92–9; Barbara Wallner, Nicola Palmieri, Claus Vogl, Doris Rigler, Elif Bozlak, Thomas Druml, Vidhya Jagannathan, Tosso Leeb, Ruedi Fries, Jens Tetens, Georg Thaller, Julia Metzger, Ottmar Distl, Gabriella Lindgren, Carl-Johan Rubin, Leif Andersson, Robert Schaefer, Molly McCue, and Gottfried Brem, 'Y Chromosome Uncovers the Recent Oriental Origin of Modern Stallions', *Current Biology* 27, no. 13 (2017): 2029–35.
5. William Shakespeare, *Richard II*, V.v.77–83.
6. I have discussed briefly elsewhere some of the ironies attending the equestrian display of Charles's procession on a horse given to him by Thomas, Lord Fairfax, himself acutely aware of the ideological import of such display: Richard Nash, 'Gentlemen's Recreation and Georgic Improvement: Lord Fairfax on Horse Breeding', in *England's Fortress: New Perspectives on Thomas, 3rd Lord Fairfax*, ed. Andrew Hopper and Philip Major (Farnham: Ashgate, 2014). See also Monica Mattfeld, *Becoming Centaur: Eighteenth-century Masculinity and English Horsemanship* (University Park: Pennsylvania State University Press, 2017).

    There is a considerable body of recent work on early modern horsemanship, particularly with reference to William Cavendish, Duke of Newcastle and cavalier culture. See, among others, Karen Raber and Treva Tucker, eds., *The Culture of the Horse: Status, Discipline, and Identity in the Early Modern World* (London: Palgrave MacMillan, 2005); Peter Edwards and Elspeth Graham, *The Horse as Cultural Icon: The Real and the Symbolic Horse in the Early Modern Period* (Leiden: Brill, 2011); and Peter Edwards and Elspeth Graham, *Authority, Authorship, and Aristocratic Identity* (Leiden: Brill, 2016).
7. J. P. Hore, *The History of Newmarket and the Annals of the Turf* (London: A.H. Baily & Co., 1886), 246.
8. Hore, *The History of Newmarket*, 248.
9. While the record is not entirely clear, I incline to the view that these articles for a contribution plate are the articles for the town plate, though it seems plausible to me that this race was not renewed every year as intended originally until resurrected during William's reign. That would be consistent with evidence discussed below.
10. J. B. Muir, *Ye Olde New-Markitt Calendar* (London: Published by the author at his Sporting Fine Art Gallery, 1892), 18.
11. Hore, *The History of Newmarket*, 326.
12. Ibid., 373.
13. Oldrey, Cox, and Nash, *Heath*, 274–305.

14. Ibid., 286–7. See also David Oldrey, *The Jockey Club Collection: A Catalogue and the Story of Its Creation over Three Centuries* (London: Bloomsbury, 2018).
15. William Sandiver, a surgeon-apothecary at Newmarket, active in racing circles in the latter half of the eighteenth century is the ultimate source for this anecdote, repeated in Frank Siltzer's *Newmarket: Its Sport and Personalities* (London: Cassell & Co., 1923), 214.
16. Sir Walter Gilbey, Bt., *Racing Cups 1595 to 1850* (London: Vinton & Co., 1910). Specific instances of relevant trophies and portraits are cited in the following paragraphs.
17. Benjamin Pyne, *Saltby Plate*, 1710. A gilded silver cup with an engraved 'running horse' icon from the reign of Queen Anne.
18. Johann Klosterman, *Portrait of Racehorse with Jockey, c. 1690* [perhaps Rutland's Blacklegs]. https://commons.wikimedia.org/wiki/File:Portrait_of_a_Racehorse_and_Jockey,_c.1690.jpg (accessed January 5, 2020).
19. *Early Records of the Thoroughbred Horse: Containing Reproductions of Some Original Stud-books, and Other Papers, of the Eighteenth century*, ed. Charles Matthew Prior (London: The Sportsman Office, 1924), 105.
20. See Nathen Amin, *York Pubs* (Amberley, 2016). However, the argument being introduced here about the significance of the emblem of the running horse is my own.
21. Frances Barlow, *The Last Horse Race Run before Charles the Second*, 1687, etching, 36.9 x 51.5 cm. Royal Collection Trust, https://www.rct.uk/collection/602686/the-last-horse-race-run-before-charles-the-second-of-blessed-memory-by-dorsett (accessed January 5, 2020).
22. Oldrey, Cox, and Nash, *Heath*, 29. The location is actually Datchett Ferry, near Windsor Castle.
23. Barlow, *The Last Horse Race Run before Charles the Second* (1687).
24. John Philip Hore, *The History of Newmarket, and the Annals of the Turf*, vol. 2 (1886).
25. Thomas Malthus, *An Historical Account of the Heroick Life and Magnanimous Actions of the Most Illustrious Protestant Prince, James, Duke of Monmouth* (1683).
26. J. Kent Clark, *Whig's Progress* (Madison, NJ: Fairleigh Dickinson University Press, 2004), 164.
27. *The Horse-Manship of England: Most Particularly Relating to the Breeding and Training of the Running-Horse. A Poem Dedicated to his Grace the Duke of Monmouth* (London: Printed for Thomas Parkhurst, at the Bible and Three Crowns at the lower end of Cheapside, near Mercers Chappel, 1682), available at Early English Books online, https://search-proquest-com.ezaccess.libraries.psu.edu/eebo/docview/2248516472/99896425/DBE8306EA5414CCFPQ/1?accountid=13158.
28. See Nash, 'Gentlemen's Recreation', 244–6.
29. Clark, *Whig's Progress*, 164–5.
30. Blair Worden, *Roundhead Reputations: The English Civil Wars and the Passions of Posterity* (London: Allen Lane/Penguin, 2001).
31. *London Gazette*, January 9, 1688.
32. Ibid.
33. Gilbert Burnet, *History of his Own Time*, vol. 3 (Oxford, 1833), 276–84; Nash, 'Sporting with Kings', in Cassidy, *The Cambridge Companion to Horseracing*, 13–25, at 20.
34. Oldrey, Cox, and Nash, 286–7. See also Oldrey, *The Jockey Club Collection*.
35. J. B. Muir, *W.T. Frampton and the Dragon* (Private Printing, 1895).
36. Photocopies of this manuscript volume have been consulted in the Buckinghamshire County Record Office in Aylesbury; the volume itself remains in private hands.
37. Daniel Defoe, *A Tour Through the Whole Island of Great Britain*, rev. edn. (London: Dent, 1974), ii.14.
38. Thomas Babington Macaulay, *The History of England from the Accession of James II*, vol. 4 (Philadelphia: Butler & Co., 1856), 182.
39. *London Gazette*, December 26, 1695.
40. Frances Barlow, *The Last Horse Race Run before Charles the Second* (1687). Image Royal Collection Trust / © Her Majesty Queen Elizabeth II 2020

41. *View of the Times: Their Principles and Practices* (London), October 7, 1704.
42. Oldrey, Cox, and Nash, *The Heath and the Horse*, 277–8.

## Disclosure Statement

No potential conflict of interest was reported by the author.

# Capitalist Horse Sense: Sports Betting and Option Trading during the English Financial Revolution, 1690–1740

Christiane Eisenberg

**ABSTRACT**
The essay explains the rise of horse racing in England around 1700 with reference to the Financial Revolution in the wake of the Glorious Revolution. This period saw a considerable increase in the money supply, without any improved consumption opportunities being opened up to contemporaries. Therefore, the available money was spent on speculative purposes, including option trading in the City of London and horse betting—two commercial activities that were very similar in practice. The essay reconstructs the reciprocal impulses that the two activities gave each other, and analyzes some problematic side effects.

It was a momentous moment in the history of horse racing in England when this sport was linked to the breakthrough of capitalism—which in turn can be traced back to the stimulus of the Glorious Revolution on the further expansion both of the nation state and the Empire. All the parties involved—the state, entrepreneurs and friends of equestrian sports—gave each other impulses for development. However, the resulting elective affinities between sport and economic practices and ways of thinking were not without negative side effects. This provides one explanation why this formative phase of modern horse racing, which lasted until around 1740, has left little trace in the collective memory of the British. Another explanation lies in the fact that many of the economic innovations that were made during this period now appear to us to be self-evident and are no longer questioned.

## The Setting

As far as the economy is concerned, the turn of the eighteenth century was determined by the so-called Financial Revolution.[1] It began in 1689 with the Nine Years War waged by William of Orange against France, which cost much more than previous wars in which the country had been involved. Until then monarchs had filled the gap between government expenditure and income by borrowing money, using their own private assets as security. Not surprisingly, investors were not always eager to take such a risk. This time, as a result of the weakening of the monarchy in the Glorious Revolution, the English elites started to experiment with new forms of financing wars, the specific feature of which was that loans were raised by promising repayment, not from the monarch's private purse, but from parliamentary taxes. To encourage investors to lend the government money, creditors were promised repayment in rotation out of a fund guaranteed by parliament which had the power to tax citizens. What happened was that the king's debts were turned into government debts, the so-called *National Debt*.

In order to carry out these transactions, government bonds were issued, and in 1694 a new joint-stock company was set up as a clearing house: the Bank of England. As part of its own customer business, the bank issued banknotes in Pound Sterling to supplement and replace the previously used promissory notes. This paper money had a new quality. Bank of England notes were not only covered by individual deposits, as in the goldsmiths banks and other financial institutions, but they were also backed up by the deposits of a large number of powerful shareholders. Since the bank also managed funds from a steady flow of tax revenues, Bank of England notes appeared highly attractive to the public. The effect was a significant increase in the demand for such notes, which in turn resulted in a significant increase in money supply and, consequently, an equally marked increase in investment and speculation activity. Public confidence was further strengthened by a promise from the Chief Treasurer of the Bank of England, printed on every note, 'to pay the bearer on demand the sum of ... in £[Sterling]'. True, it would have been easy to interpret this promise as a bluff because the bank had no direct access to the stocks of precious metals in the royal treasury. But in practice this did not matter, because in critical situations the bank's business partners had no interest in taking up the offer inherent in the promise; rather, they did everything they could to keep the money flow moving.[2]

Bank of England bank notes were money of account, i.e. they were also used as a standard for other methods of payment. This was an important precondition for the success of the Great Recoinage, a further measure taken by the English state: this aimed at putting an end to the lack of coins as well as to the practice of clipping coins, which had existed since the Middle Ages. The constant shortage of coinage meant that in everyday business life, even for smaller transactions, bills of exchange had to be regularly put out to tender. This was not only cumbersome, but also a source of numerous conflicts that often ended in court.[3] The solution implemented with the Great Recoinage was to link the new bank notes to the golden Guinea coin in order to subject the whole of England (and, since 1707, of Scotland) to the so-called *cash nexus*. The implementation of the project temporarily brought the economy to the brink of ruin, but in the longer term the hoped-for positive effects became apparent. Deals could now be made anonymously, ad hoc and spontaneously. Business activity was not only boosted by the rise in the money supply, but also by the speed of the flow of money.[4]

This development contributed to the fact that many Britons were faced with a genuinely luxurious problem in the years after 1700. What should, and what could they spend their money on? From a historian's perspective such a question must be taken seriously because in the early eighteenth century, not only was the Industrial

Revolution still a long way off; imperial expansion and imports of colonial goods were also in the early stages.[5] It was therefore almost impossible for Britons to spend money on tangible consumer goods. The breakthrough of the much-quoted eighteenth-century consumer society did indeed not take place until around 1750.[6] Of course, the rich and super-rich could purchase land, build mansions and invest in works of art and new technical innovations. They could also invest in ships and overseas trading activities, although these were extremely risky enterprises. The problem was that there were few other alternatives. Just like their fellow citizens who lived more modest lives, the rich were sooner or later condemned to spend their wealth in the consumption of intangible goods in the sectors of leisure and pleasure, like concerts and operas, the theatre, or other forms of entertainment and sociability.

With regard to spending money, betting was one leisure activity that was particularly effective. This explains the gambling mania that broke out around 1700 and was expressed in the boom of private clubs with betting facilities, and so-called silver and copper hells for the lower echelons which shot out of the ground like mushrooms.[7] Furthermore, contemporaries developed a hitherto unknown preference for betting and wagering—an ancient custom of gambling that could be observed everywhere where sports competitions took place. Typical occasions for this were market days and local fairs, sometimes in connection with a holiday, i.e. with situations where people were only too ready to spend money. In the seventeenth century this specific pattern of sporting behaviour had rarely been widespread among the general population, as historian Emma Griffin has reminded us.[8] The reason may have been the lack of small change, but also the generally lower purchasing power at this time. Not surprisingly, even in the early eighteenth century it was essentially wealthy merchants and tradesmen, members of the liberal professions and, of course, the rich and famous, especially from the aristocracy, who engaged in such betting transactions; the latter not least in order to secure their status in the social hierarchy. The members of these groups knew each other and were willing and able to grant each other credit for such activities of 'conspicuous consumption'–a term coined by the early twentieth-century economist Thorstein Veblen.[9]

The state, too, which relied relentlessly on the National Debt for its wars and undertakings, proved to be a gambler willing to take risks. In any case, it spurred on the general gambling mania considerably by not only bringing government bonds onto the market, but also by selling them in smaller batches, sometimes in the form of lottery tickets, in the street. Furthermore, to create particularly sophisticated speculative opportunities those responsible had some of the schemes conceived by the Groom Porter, the supervisor of the royal gaming tables.[10] All this led to a speculation boom that ended in the breakthrough of the City of London as a site for an utterly new type of business: financial markets or, to use the contemporary technical expression, the stock market.[11] In the second half of the 1690s both Britons and foreigners began briskly trading with large and small sums of money. Even after trading in South Sea stocks—initiated at great expense by the state-owned South Sea Company—created a huge speculative bubble that burst spectacularly in 1720, speculative trading was not permanently affected. As a place where capital was generated for larger enterprises, be it the state or private entrepreneurs, since the mid-1690s the City has been the heart of English or British capitalism, whose breakthrough in Great Britain—and this is explicitly pointed out here—did not take place in the wake of the Industrial Revolution around 1800, but 100 years earlier in the Financial Revolution.

It is hardly surprising that moralizing social critics, satirists, courtesy writers and dramatists regarded the financial bets and other speculations made by and for the political elites in the City of London, as a further form of gambling.[12] Their opinions were not least supported by the fact that orderly investments in shares and government bonds made up only a small proportion of transactions on the financial markets, and the majority fell on 'wild' dealings with derivatives that were driven by so-called stockjobbers. Furthermore, option dealing no longer took place at the well-organized Royal Exchange where stock auctions had been held since the creation of the East India Company in the seventeenth century, since such dealing attracted a mass audience from the outset. Because most participants wanted to carry out such financial transactions personally or with the help of trusted intermediaries, this soon exceeded the capacity of the Royal Exchange to contain their needs. So the relevant trading sites were established in the surrounding alleys and the coffee houses located there, especially in the disreputable Exchange Alley. The transactions carried out there by independent stockjobbers were opaque to the public, and the risk of being cheated by one of these middlemen was compounded by the risks associated with option dealing in general. It was therefore not entirely out of place for critical observers to apply the concept of gambling to such financial activities as well.[13]

## Sporting Impulses on the Financial Markets

The relationship to the world of sport was established by the circumstance that option trading in essence represents a form of time trade: that is to say, speculating on price developments which only took effect after a certain delay in time. Speculators did not buy shares—i.e. property—but only an option—i.e. the right to buy and sell shares. At the end of the agreed period, the option could then either be exercised, or the stake and the rights would lapse. An even more risky form of derivatives trading were the so-called 'forward trades' or—in today's terminology—'futures'. People who entered into such contracts had to meet the agreed date and, if the market did not develop in accordance with their calculations they would be forced to make a substantial cash settlement.

The gambling quality of transactions in the financial markets that arose around 1700 is extremely important for the theme of horse racing, because this feature sheds a light on the structural affinities of betting on horses and options trading. At any rate the reasoning behind the two activities was very similar in both cases. Behind horse-race betting lay the consideration: would a certain horse and rider win or lose a race on a set date? Would it finish the race at the expected time? These were the two questions which dominated sporting activities. The questions which dominated in financial market transactions were: would a share (or other financial security) show a long or short-term profit or would it turn out to show a loss? Would it reach a definite price within the agreed time span? In both cases the expected answers were 'yes' or 'no'.

This binary structure benefited any type of sporting discipline that ended with a clear result—either a win or a loss: hence, it also contributed to the popularity of boxing or cockfighting, for example, or, later in the century, cricket matches. For most early-eighteenth century time traders, however, the analogy of sport and financial transactions was based on the experience of horse races because, at the time, such races were usually organized as matches between two competitors. Tellingly, both in options trading and on the racecourse people put their money on so-called 'light horses' (derivatives), and less on 'heavy horses' (stocks and shares) a preference that was retrospectively explained as follows in the popular guidebook *Every Man his Own Broker* (1761) by Thomas Mortimer, a journalist versed in financial issues:

> The subscription receipts thus paid in full, are called in the Alley, HEAVY-HORSE, because the gentlemen of the Alley can make greater advantage than 3 per Cent. by the LIGHT-HORSE, and therefore will not give near so good a price for the heavy; nay some of them will absolutely have nothing to do with it, for this reason; that they can buy a thousand pounds, LIGHT-HORSE, (with one payment made) for the same money as one hundred pounds heavy, and by buying the light, they have an opportunity of sporting with, and gaining a profit on, a nominal thousand, for the same money, that it would cost to buy an hundred, heavy.[14]

As Mortimer went on to explain, the specific asset of the 'light horses', which, as he added, were also ridden in the lottery ticket trade, lay in the fact that only an initial down payment of 15 percent was required.[15] In other words it was possible to speculate on credit. This had another advantage, as it opened up the opportunity to temporarily use the sums not yet due for other activities: not least for betting on horses. However, betting on the financial market had one particular major disadvantage: it stretched people's patience because the time between the wager and the result could last three and six, and sometimes even twelve months.[16] This was considerably longer than a horse race where the result would be known after around eight to ten minutes (the time it would take for a horse to cover the usual distance of four miles).[17] But if you were a skilful financial gambler, you could combine several *time trades* in order to multiply the chances and the moments of tension.[18] The special challenge here was for speculators to resell the 'light horses'—and by that I mean the options they had bought on credit—at a higher price at the right time before the amount had to be repaid. If they failed to do so they could be ruined for life. But for people with a weakness for gambling the risk factor was what made it so attractive.

One danger was to carelessly assume that both forms of speculation were somehow equal. For on closer inspection they were utterly different. Whereas the number of bets and the size of stakes were of no real consequence in horse racing (as long as the jockey was not himself involved in the result of the race) the success or failure of forward transactions depended on individual speculative behaviour. For every decision made by a market actor influences the general expectations on a speculative market and, precisely because of this mechanism, has the potential to produce a high dynamic of development and set off self-fulfilling prophecies. This difference in categories was clearly still not recognized by inexperienced contemporaries. At least I have as yet been unable to discover any sources to the contrary.

Against this background it may be argued that gambling on horse racing was highly suited to make actors on the financial markets more willing to take risks. Indeed, it even encouraged a degree of recklessness because it seemed to mediate what finance historians generally call financial literacy—in this case a gross misperception.

To support the second aspect of my argument I should like to add a few more observations on parallels in the course of transactions. If the bets were not placed in a coffee house, inn or pub, in both cases, horse betting and option trading, the speculators could wait for opportunities at a betting post in an open area or, in the City of London, in a lane. Here they could meet people to bet against, or brokers who would find the appropriate contacts. Printed forms could be found in these establishments, and the betting partners only needed to enter the place, time and the agreed sum of money, following which the innkeepers acted as stake holders, i.e. for a small fee they would then safeguard the wagers (Figure 1).

Legal assistance seems only to have been called upon in horse-racing circles (and even there only in the case of large sums); however, it seems to have been uncommon with options trading on finance markets. If such *referees* were active— each party had his own—they would also be present at the race to check whether it complied with the agreement. Since it was impossible to exclude the risk that the referees might be biased or corrupt, an umpire was also present on the day of the race to penalize any contraventions of the letter and spirit of the contract and to settle disputes.[19] The origins of the umpire lie in the more recent merchant law.[20] Their function, however, was only publicly visible in sport, where they were also responsible for deciding on the winner. In doing so they simultaneously decided on the outcome of the wager and at the end instructed the stakeholder to hand out the amount deposited to the winner for him to fill his hat with guineas.[21]

Not all horse racing bets were prepared so elaborately. Technically this was almost impossible in the case of spontaneous decisions after the ending of official betting at the posts. Spectators would place such spot bets at any time during the race up until shortly before the winning post. These bigger kicks were one of the main explanations for the nail-biting atmosphere during the races. By firing on the sportsmen, they were also in a way trying to achieve the result they were longing for. Furthermore this passion was one of the reasons— alongside scrutinising and checking the horses and riders—why punters would usually accompany the jockeys during the races (and sometimes they even reached the finishing post ahead of the competitors).[22] In such exciting situations if the betting partners wanted to wager against each other without having to be distracted from the events at hand, they would shake hands briefly or each signal with their hands and call out 'Done!'.[23] On the financial markets anyone who wanted to use the time between making a contract and learning the result of the forward transaction for further trading in options, had to act in a similarly pragmatic manner: and, just as on the racecourse, should he then have made a profit he had to make sure he could take his winnings before his betting partner (whom he had found at short notice), disappeared into thin air.

**Figure 1.** Thomas Rowlandson, *Betting Post* (late eighteenth or early nineteenth century). Water colour. Bequeathed by Rev. Alexander Dyce. London, Victoria and Albert Museum, inv. nr. DYCE 801. © Victoria and Albert Museum, London.

When the winnings had been handed over in the proper fashion each of the parties would go his own way once more. This momentary interaction was much more characteristic in horse racing than in other sporting disciplines, and it is noticeable that the turf has never experienced any collective fan culture to the present day. This specific feature also predestined sportsmen who had been socialized in racing circles for the culture of financial markets. As is clear from the story of the South Sea Company the assembled speculators were not even in crisis situations a community. Their collective behaviour was similar to that of a herd of wild animals that might, under certain circumstances even devastate the market.[24]

## Impulses for Sport from the Financial Markets

I have argued that at the start of the eighteenth century, previous experience in sporting wagers was well suited to raise people's readiness to take risks on the financial markets. If we extend our view beyond the South Sea Bubble crisis, we can see that this connection also worked in the opposite direction, i.e. experience in option business in the finance markets resulted in a preparedness to take greater risks on betting on horse races. It seems worthwhile to examine this aspect more closely.

The first point I would make is that some actors on the financial markets were extraordinarily innovative in inventing ever more refined betting models. Hedging their risks by multiple betting caused a leverage effect. This could be seen, for example, as early as the 1730s at the royal racecourse at Newmarket in the south of England where sweepstakes were introduced.[25] By contrast with traditional matches between two persons whose results were less spectacular, sweepstakes involved groups of three or more persons in which only one person (or a specific section of the group) would 'sweep off' the winnings. The attraction of the new method lay in the fact that the sum of the wagers laid by additional players meant that the winnings paid out were as a result higher than when only two parties were involved. The multiplication of participants also resulted in more variations in the wagers.

The development of hedging, as practised in the Exchange Alley, was another attraction that could prove beneficial to sweepstake participants. In this case they would place parallel bets on several horses and place their money simultaneously on victory and defeat. Some professional gamblers were so proficient in the techniques necessary to calculate the odds that they never incurred any losses.[26]

There was a further impulse from the financial markets that influenced the practice of gambling on horse races. After the first speculation bubble burst in 1720 a whole range of professional gamblers moved to the racecourses. Many of them were amongst the lucky speculators who had sold their shares in the South Sea Company before it collapsed, and their pockets were full of money. A similar wave followed in the mid-1730s when, in the run-up to a proposed law regulating liabilities in loan-financed option trading, a large number of speculators turned their backs on the City of London to look for new opportunities of making money. This invasion into equestrian sports, which, by the way, also led to a boom in professional boxing and the opening of several commercial boxing arenas in London,[27] was a direct consequence of the Sir John Barnard's Act (7 and 8 Geo. II. c. 8), a publicly discussed law 'to prevent the infamous Practice of Stock-Jobbing', which came into force in 1734. It was directed against 'options' and 'forward trades' in their capacity as 'wagers', but did not concern derivative transactions in general, but only those financed by credit. Creditors could no longer bring debtors to court, for brokers were held liable.[28] Although financial experts had expected catastrophic effects from the Barnard's Act, it turned out to have no long-term drastic consequences. Nonetheless, the business basis changed for those who used to buy their 'light horses' on credit, and apparently quite a few looked around for other speculative opportunities, which they then found in horse racing.

Once more it is clear that some of these casual sporting enthusiasts were particularly adept at mental arithmetic as well as probability accounting and used this talent to cream off huge winnings from small stakes by ruthlessly taking their inexperienced betting partners to the cleaners. This fate also befell aristocrats at the very top of society, and in a few cases their families were even drawn into the abyss. We can get an impression of the sums of money that changed hands in this way, when we envisage that the total value of the bets placed at the 1735 Spring Meeting at the royal racecourse in Newmarket, where society's leaders, from the Duke of Devonshire to the current Prime Minister, regularly gathered, was estimated to have amounted to £30,000. This was roughly half the price of a first-class battleship or the equivalent of the annual income of the Royal Household from its estates and other business activities.[29]

## The End of the Story: Measures at Social Disciplining

This example shows that, in the 1730s at the latest, the mutual inspiration of financial market activities and betting on horse races resulted in a dynamic of crisis. Each of the related activities unbalanced the other—in addition to other factors pointing in the same direction. If the trade-offs between both market places resulted in something other than a crisis, I would argue that it was in the rapid spreading of the banknotes and coins, especially the golden Guinea coin, throughout the whole of the British isles. For the City of London was a unique market place, and racecourses were common all over the country.

This offers us an explanation why it took until 1739 for the British state, in the form of Parliament and the Crown, which had continually attempted to introduce regulations on activities on the financial markets, to abandon their utterly indifferent attitude to activities on racecourses and try to intervene by imposing disciplinary measures. Another explanation for the delay might be that government intervention in this area of social life was anything but simple: since *all* contracts agreed in the thoroughly commercialized British society were based on a betting structure it was almost impossible to conceive of imposing a complete ban on racecourse betting. In addition, a freeborn Englishman's idea of ownership and property meant that it was left to his own discretion as to whether he wanted to ruin himself or not. Finally, there were a huge number of sportsmen in both Houses of Parliament and none of them had any interest in spoiling one of their favourite pleasures.

Hence state intervention into horse racing did not take the shape of an anti-betting act. Instead Parliament passed an act to regulate the framework conditions of racing. A Horse Races Act (13 Geo. II. c. 19), was passed in 1739 and came into force in 1740, with the declared aim of 'preventing the excessive increase of Horse Races'. The Act forbade horse races where the prize money was less than 50 pounds and made it compulsory for racecourses to charge an admission price. According to the wording of the Act, the measure was purportedly aimed at race courses attended by the lower classes, that were not patronized by rich aristocrats or the monarchy, and which had to pay out the prize money from subscriptions collected with difficulty from the local inhabitants. But in practice the fixed minimum sum of £50 prize money proved so high that some of the larger racecourses, attended by the rich and the beautiful, were also forced to close—whereupon the whole of horse racing fell into a deep crisis for many years.

Figure 2 shows the rising number of racing venues in the 1720 and 30s in England and Wales and provides an idea of the catastrophic effect of the measure.

In view of the above-mentioned reticence of the entire British establishment towards the prohibition of betting and gambling, it is unlikely that the *Horse Races Act*, passed by parliament in 1739, actually came into being on the initiative of the supporters of the Anti-Gambling League assembled in the House, as was assumed by

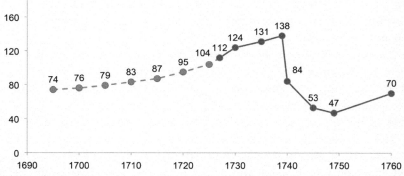

**Figure 2.** Racing venues in England, 1695–1760. The broken line is based on data collected by the historian Peter Borsay, the solid line on the investigations of a contemporary, John Cheny, who had been publishing a racing calendar since 1727. Cheny's data include races for prizes of at least £10 (1727–1739) or at least £50 (1740–1760).[30]

the outside world. Without being able to give an extensive explanation here,[31] there is much to suggest that it was the monarch in person who had become active. George II, who came to the throne in 1727, was probably the only representative of the state who was completely unprejudiced when it came to horse racing practices in his kingdom. He came from the tiny Duchy of Braunschweig-Lüneburg in North Germany, an utterly backward economic region, where he had developed a pronounced interest in breeding horses as part of his efforts to improve agriculture. Firstly, in his capacity as King of England George II had a political interest in the continued existence of the nobility as a coherent social group; and thus also in the continued existence of aristocratic estates. As a father, he had a private interest in the education of his under-aged sons, the Duke of Cumberland and the Prince of Wales, whose interests threatened to drift off into the sport scene. Last but not least, in his capacity as supreme warlord, hence as commander of the cavalry in 1739—the year in which the Horse Races Act was passed—he was planning a colonial war between Great Britain and Spain that would later go down in history as the War of Jenkin's Ear. Cavalry horses were to be used for the first time in joint 'amphibious actions' with the fleet. Hence George II wanted to see the horses in his country used for combative purpose, and not for racing.

The Crown was also co-responsible for the revival of horse racing around 1750; this time, however, not directly through the person of the King himself but via his son, the Duke of Cumberland, who was now not only a grown man but a war hero. In 1745 he had used a cavalry regiment to put down a Jacobite uprising in Scotland. This was the legendary Battle of Culloden, which earned him the name of 'the Butcher', and the horses in his regiment were—*honi soit qui mal y pense*—fast and particularly agile 'light horses'. After his major victory the Duke of Cumberland planned to rest on his laurels in Newmarket where his interest moved to breeding horses, and he was also successful in this field, as his stable included Eclipse, the most famous racehorse of the eighteenth century. The younger generation of sportsmen active there was very conscious of social climbing and knew only too well how to exploit their famous contemporary for propaganda purposes. Thus, horse racing was put back on the agenda.

Figure 2 shows that, after a shock-induced paralysis that lasted about a decade, the curve began to rise once more after 1750. From then on horse racing was radically reformed in the areas of regulation, organisation and management, not only in relation to gambling, but also to breeding as an international business, an activity comparable in its importance for eighteenth-century capitalism to today's motorcar industry. The relationship with capitalism was now put on a new footing, because financial thinking extended to the so-called real economy and economic experts discovered that sport in general and horse racing in particular could be used for further experiments there.

## Notes

1. P.G.M. Dickson, *The Financial Revolution. A Study in the Development of Public Credit 1688–1765* (London: Macmillan, 1967). For a more recent state of research, see Henry Roseveare, *The Financial Revolution 1660–1760* (London: Longman, 1991), 29–60.
2. Geoffrey Ingham, *The Nature of Money* (Cambridge: Polity, 2004), 121–4; Michael Hutter, 'The Emergence of Bank Notes in 17th Century England. A Case Study for a Communication Theory of Evolutionary Economic Change', *Sociologia Internationalis* 21 (1993): 23–39, here 37.
3. Craig Muldrew, *The Economy of Obligation. The Culture of Credit and Social Relations in Early Modern England* (London: Macmillan, 1998).
4. Bruce G. Curruthers, *City of Capital. Politics and Markets in the English Financial Revolution* (Princeton: Princeton University Press, 2009), 161–2; Christine Desan, *Making Money. Coin, Currency and the Coming of Capitalism* (Oxford: Oxford University Press, 2014), 360, 376, 382.
5. Linda Levy Peck, *Consuming Splendor. Society and Culture in Seventeenth-Century England* (Cambridge: Cambridge University Press, 2005); Maxine Berg, *Luxury and Pleasure in Eighteenth-Century Britain* (Oxford: Oxford University Press, 2005).
6. These are the general findings of the contributions in Neil McKendrick, John Brewer and J.H. Plumb, *The Birth of a Consumer Society. The Commercialization of Eighteenth-Century England* (London: Hutchinson, 1982); John Brewer and Roy Porter, eds., *Consumption and the World of Goods* (London: Routledge, 1993).
7. For an overview see Nicholas Barry Tosney, *Gaming in England, c. 1540–1760* (Ph.D. thesis, University of York, 2008), and Jessica Richard, *The Romance of Gambling in the Eighteenth-Century British Novel* (Houndmills/Basingstoke: Macmillan, 2011).
8. Emma Griffin, *England's Revelry: A History of Popular Sports and Pastimes, 1660–1830* (Oxford: Oxford University Press for the British Academy, 2005), 9–11. See also the substantial study by Maria Kloeren, *Sport und Rekord. Kultursoziologische Untersuchungen zum England des sechzehnten bis achtzehnten Jahrhunderts* (Ph.D. Thesis, University of Cologne, 1935, reprint Münster: Lit-Verlag, 1985), 41, 47, 57 f. and passim. The author explicitly states and gives numerous examples that the public's willingness to bet did not begin until the 1690s and 1700s.
9. This is a result of my study in progress *Der Sportsgeist des Kapitalismus. Geld, Markt und Vergnügen im Großbritannien des 18. Jahrhunderts*. For the term cited, see Thorstein Veblen, *Theory of the Leisure Class* (New York: Mentor Edition, 1954).
10. Anne Murphy, *The Origins of Financial Markets. Investment and Speculation before the South Sea Bubble* (Cambridge: Cambridge University Press, 2009), 49 f., 53, 60, 148; Roseveare, *Financial Revolution 1660–1760*, 44.

11. Murphy, *Origins of Financial Markets*. See also Ranald C. Michie, *The London Stock Exchange. A History* (Oxford: Oxford Unversity Press, 1999), 15–36; Edward Chancellor, *Devil Takes the Hindmost. A History of Financial Speculation* (London: Penguin, 2000), 30–95.
12. Silke Stratmann, *Myths of Speculation. The South Sea Bubble and 18$^{th}$-Century English Literature* (Munich: Fink, 2000).
13. Murphy, *Origins of Financial Markets*, 161–92; Chancellor, *Devil Takes the Hindmost*, 30–57; Stuart Banner, *Anglo-American Securities Revolution. Cultural and Political Roots, 1690–1860* (Cambridge: Cambridge University Press, 1998), 14–40.
14. Thomas Mortimer, *Every Man His Own Broker: Or, a Guide to Exchange-Alley. In which the Nature of the Several Funds, Vulgary called Stocks, is clearly explained; and the Mystery and Iniquity of Stock-Jobbing laid before the Public in a New and Impartial Light ( ... )* (London: printed for S. Hooper, at Caesar's Head, the Corner of the New Church in the Strand, 1761), 138. 'Light Horses' are also mentioned in a diatribe (probably from the early 1730s) against the politician John Barnard. The passages quoted by Ludwig Samuel, *Die Effektenspekulation im 17. und 18. Jahrhundert. Ein Beitrag zur Börsengeschichte* (Berlin: Industrieverlag Spaeth & Linde, 1924), 118. A further indication of the equivalence of horse betting and option transactions is the common term 'refusal' for both. The extract from a collection of older racing conventions of the Common Law ('Rules Concerning Racing in General'), quoted by Robert Black, *The Jockey Club and its Founders in Three Periods* (London: Smith, Elder & Co., 1891), 373.
15. Mortimer, *Every Man his Own Broker*, 145, 161. For the meaning of the adjective 'light' in the financial markets of the time see also S. R. Cope, 'The Stock Exchange Revisited: A New Look at the Market in Securities in London in the Eighteenth Century', *Economica* 45, no. 1 (1978): 1–21, here 1: 'a loan on which only one or two instalments have been paid'.
16. According to Samuel, *Effektenspekulation*, 88, there were four settlement dates: mid-February, mid-May, mid-August and mid-November. Even longer periods are mentioned by Anne Murphy, 'Trading Options before Black-Scholes: A Study of the Market in Late Seventeenth-Century London', *Economic History Review* 62, no. s1 (2009): 8–30, here 12.
17. See the chapter on 'Distances', in Wray Vamplew and Joyce Kay, *Encyclopedia of British Horseracing* (London: Routledge, 2005), 99–100, here 99.
18. See the diatribe against the financial politician Barnard from the early 1730s, quoted in Samuel, *Effektenspekulation*, 118.
19. Julia Allen, *Swimming with Dr Johnson and Mrs Thrale. Sport, Health and Exercise in Eighteenth-century England* (Cambridge: The Lutterworth Press, 2012), 51. When using the terms referee and umpire, I have deviated from Julia Allen's description, and oriented myself to the language commonly used in horse racing. See, for instance, John Bee, *Slang. A Dictionary of the Turf, the Ring, the Chase, the Pit, of Bon-ton, and the Varieties of Life ( ... )* (London: Printed for T. Hughes, 1823). In other sports the terms might have been different. See, for instance, the *Oxford English Dictionary* (*OED*) on the 'Referee', paragraph 3: ' ... in certain sports (such as tennis and cricket) this function is performed by an umpire or umpires, while the referee is an off-field official who may arbitrate on specific issues if they arise.' See also the *OED* on the 'Umpire' (paragraph 3). http://www.oed.com/ (accessed February 7, 2016).
20. Wyndham Beawes, Lex mercatoria rediviva: or, *The Merchant's Directory* (Printed for the author, by J. Moore, 1752), 308 f. (available via *The Making of the Modern World*, http://tinyurl.galegroup.com/tinyurl/A9h6K2 (accessed May 29, 2019).
21. Allen, *Swimming with Dr Johnson*, 51; Carl Chinn, *Better Betting with a Decent Feller. Bookmaking, Betting and the British Working Class, 1750–1990* (Hemel Hempstead: Harvester Wheatsheaf, 1991), 17.
22. Allen, *Swimming with Dr Johnson*, 52; Zacharias Conrad von Uffenbach (1710), quoted in *O Britannien, Von deiner Freiheit einen Hut voll. Deutsche Reiseberichte des 18.*

*Jahrhunderts*, ed. Michael Maurer (Munich: Beck, and Leipzig/Weimar: Kiepenheuer, 1992), 43–74, here 60 f.
23. See the detailed description (though on cockfights) ibid., 56 f., and Allen, *Swimming with Dr Johnson*, 51.
24. Wray Vamplew and Joyce Kay, 'Introduction', in Vamplew and Kay, *Encyclopedia*, vi–viii, here vi; Francis E. Merrill and Carrol D. Clark, 'The Money Market as a Special Public', *American Journal of Sociology* 39, no. 5 (1934) 626–36, esp. 627 f.
25. Richard Nash, 'The Newmarket Bank and the Beginnings of Bookmaking', in *The Heath and the Horse. A History of Racing and Art on Newmarket Heath*, ed. David Oldrey, Timothy Cox, and Richard Nash (London: I.B. Tauris, 2016), 292–5, and see also his chapter in this volume. See also Mike Huggins, *Horse Racing and British Society in the Long Eighteenth Century* (Woodbridge: The Boydell Press, 2018), 85 f.
26. Chinn, *Better Betting*, 32–4. Chinn dates the introduction of sweepstakes to the 1750s, which was state of research at the time his book was written, but this can now be considered outdated on the basis of Richard Nash's research findings (see previous note).
27. Dennis Brailsford, *Bareknuckles. A Social History of Prize-Fighting* (Cambridge: Lutterworth Press, 1988), 4–6.
28. 'An Abstract of the Act to Prevent the Infamous Practice of Stock-Jobbing', in *An Abstract of All the Acts passed in the Seventh Session of the Seventh Parliament of Great Britain, and in the Seventh Year of the Reign of our most Gracious Sovereign Lord King George the Second* (London: John Baskett, Printer to the King's most Excellent Majesty, 1734), 27. See also Cope, 'Stock Exchange', 8 f.
29. Richard Nash, 'The Newmarket Bank and the Beginnings of Bookmaking', in Oldrey, Cox, and Nash, *The Heath and the Horse*, 292–5, esp. 294 f. The comparative values according to John Brewer. *The Sinews of Power. War, Money and the English State, 1688–1783* (Cambridge, MA: Harvard University Press, 1990), 34, and Peter Temin and Hans-Joachim Voth, *Prometheus Shackled. Goldsmith Banks and England's Financial Revolution after 1700* (Oxford: Oxford University Press, 2013), 17.
30. Borsay's list shows the first mention of the racetracks. It is based on the relevant racing literature, regional racing calendars and the regional press, while Cheny, who gathered information by riding across country, indicates the total number of racing venues found. Therefore, starting with the year 1712, I adjusted his numbers by subtracting the newly added (and often short-lived) ones. The basis for these calculations was the collection of his annual racing calendars in Gale's Eighteenth Century Collection online. Peter Borsay, *The English Urban Renaissance. Culture and Society in the Provincial Town, 1660–1770* (Oxford: Oxford University Press, 1989), 355–67. The value for 1735 was added on the basis of John Cheny, *An historical list of all horse-matches run, and of all plates and prizes run for in England (of the Value of Ten. Pounds or upwards) in 1735. [ ... ]* (London, 1735). Eighteenth Century Collections Online. Gale. Humboldt Universitaet Berlin (accessed March 28, 2016) [Gale Document Number: CW3304925930 - http://find.galegroup.com/ecco/infomark.do?&source=gale&prodId=ECCO&userGroupName=humboldt&tabID=T001&docId=CW3304925930&type=multipage&contentSet=ECCOArticles&version=1.0&docLevel=FASCIMILE].
31. The following explanations summarize some results of my own research for the manuscript *The Sporting Spirit of Capitalism*.

## Disclosure Statement

No potential conflict of interest was reported by the author(s).

## ORCID

Christiane Eisenberg http://orcid.org/0000-0002-0161-0228

# 'A Horse-Race is the Same All the World Over': The Cultural Context of Horse Racing in Native North America

Peter Mitchell

**ABSTRACT**
Native American horse racing has received little scholarly attention. Focussing on the Great Plains and the Southwest reveals that, far from being a diversion, it was a major focus for male competition for status and prestige. Since these concerns were at least as strong externally as internally, horse racing (and racehorse acquisition) formed part of a continuum of agonistic activities that also encompassed warfare. Moreover, the significance of races for the standing of individuals, men's societies, and tribal groups led to widespread use of protective medicines for enhancing equine performance and combating interference from opponents. Gambling formed part of this set of practices that collectively warrant describing Native American horse racing as a form of what Johan Huizinga termed 'sacred play'. For these reasons it encountered strong opposition from Euro-American authorities during the reservation era. Conversely, the persistence of Native American horse racing traditions via rodeo and Indian Relay racing attests to the enduring importance of the values they express. Opportunities exist for extending this preliminary assessment into a broader comparative study of Indigenous horse racing traditions across the post-1492 world.

## 'One of the Most Exciting Amusements'

In the 1830s one of the great artists of the American West, George Catlin, remarked of the Mandan (Rųwą́ʔka·ki)[1] people of what is now North Dakota that, 'Horse-racing here, as in all more enlightened communities, is one of the most exciting amusements, and one of the most extravagant modes of gambling' (Figure 1).[2] He went on to say that, 'a horse-race is the same all the world over,' a conclusion roundly condemned (though without explanation) as 'erroneous' by the twentieth-century ethnographer John Ewers in his landmark monograph *The Horse in Blackfoot Indian Culture*.[3] That not only the Mandan, but also many other Native Americans, engaged in horse racing is well established. However, with but a few recent exceptions there has been remarkably little discussion of the topic since Ewers wrote about it over 60 years ago.[4] Intended as an initial step toward exploring Indigenous

**Figure 1.** Horse racing on a course behind a Mandan village in what is now Missouri 1832–1833 as depicted by George Catlin. Smithsonian American Art Museum 1985.66.432, Washington, DC (Source: Wikimedia Commons https://commons.wikimedia.org/wiki/File:George_Catlin_-_Horseracing_on_a_Course_Behind_the_Mandan_Village_-_1985.66.432_-_Smithsonian_American_Art_Museum.jpg (accessed January 22, 2019)).

horse racing practices not only in North America but also in other parts of the world to which horses were (re-)introduced as a consequence of the so-called 'Columbian Exchange',[5] this study thus offers a fresh assessment of Catlin's remark.

Its principal focus falls upon two of the historic centres of Native equestrianism in North America, the Great Plains and the Southwest (Figure 2), and it begins by giving a sense of how horse races were organized and the form that they took. Merely to assert, however, that horse racing was something 'learned from the Spanish' is not particularly helpful,[6] even in the unlikely event that it were true. Instead, to understand horse racing's importance for Native American societies it must be situated within the broader context of Indigenous gaming practices. This, in turn, identifies one of the key questions to be addressed: how far was horse racing part of a continuum with other games and contests and to what extent did it therefore involve ritual, ceremonial, and other elements, rather than being simply a diversion or an opportunity to win wagers. In other words, was horse racing an example of what Johan Huizinga termed 'sacred play'?[7]

The essay also explores two related concerns. First, why were attempts made to suppress horse racing in the aftermath of Euro-American conquest of the Plains and the Southwest and the confinement of Native peoples to reservations? Second, how far do nineteenth-century traditions of horse racing still persist in contemporary Native American practice and the broader culture of the North American West? Both

**Figure 2.** Map of the Great Plains, Plateau, and Southwest of Canada and the United States, showing the approximate locations of Native peoples mentioned in the text c. 1870. Note that the Piegan are not shown as they are a sub-division of the Blackfoot.

topics involve placing horse racing within a wider context of resistance to colonization and forced acculturation. On all three counts, Native American racing on horseback is an eminently anthropological topic, one that arguably merits more attention from historians and other social scientists than it has hitherto received.

By way of background recall that while horses evolved in North America they also became extinct there through a combination of the environmental changes marking the transition to post-glacial climates and human hunting at the end of the Pleistocene, some 11,000 years ago.[8] Horses were reintroduced by Cortés in 1519, were in Native hands within a generation, and had spread north of the Río Grande before the Spanish began settling New Mexico in 1598. That spread, it should be noted, had nothing to do with horses left behind by the *entrada* of Francisco Coronado in 1540-42 (they were not, and only two of Coronado's ~600 horses were mares in any event). Nor did it have much to do with the Pueblo Revolt of 1680 that temporarily expelled the Spanish from the Southwest: Utes (Nú·čiu), Navajos (Diné), and Apaches (Ndé) all had horses long before that. Instead, through processes that were almost entirely Native, rather than European, controlled, horses began moving north onto the Plains and into the mountain areas to their west early in the seventeenth century and continued to do so thereafter, transforming the lives of all those who adopted them in ways that were still ongoing in the mid-1800s.[9]

## Racing Horses in Native North America

How did Native Americans race the horses they acquired? One of the earliest references is that of David Thompson, who wrote of the Piegan (Pi-kániwa), a Blackfoot (Niitsítapi) group, around 1800 that they raced horses 'not in the regular manner,' but by betting on who could first run down a deer or kill the most bison at a time.[10] As Ewers notes, however, Thompson probably simply failed to see horse races of a more conventional kind, since oral traditions suggest that they were being practised decades before this, perhaps almost as soon as the Piegan acquired horses around 1725.[11] Races were held between tribal groups, and in at least some cases truces might be arranged between otherwise hostile communities specifically so that they could take place.[12] Additionally, they also took place within the same tribe, with different Blackfoot warrior societies, for example, frequently competing against each other, each society having previously identified its own fastest horses in private trials.[13] Similar practices are recorded among the Gros Ventre or Atsina (Haaninin),[14] as well as other nations. Often, larger camps at which people could aggregate because of seasonal bonanzas from summer bison hunts[15] or, on the Columbia Plateau, salmon runs and camas root harvests[16] provided the context for racing competitions. In one instance in October 1839 as many as 4,000 people from several tribes are said to have converged to race at a location near the modern city of Denver in Colorado.[17]

Most commonly, two horses were raced against each other over a level course measuring some 3–6 km in length.[18] Both Blackfoot races on the Northern Plains and Navajo contests in the Southwest took this form,[19] although races between several competitors at a time were far from unknown. Additionally, among some groups horses were raced over shorter distances of around 500 m,[20] or a longer course might be subdivided so that races of different lengths could be run along it.[21] Navajo, Kiowa (Ka'igwu), and Blackfoot, among others, typically selected horses thought to be closely matched in speed, something that intensified the associated betting.[22] Where there was insufficient level ground, races might be run around a hill, or, among the Northern Shoshone (Nɨmɨ) a stick,[23] and back. A pair of judges, one from each side, was commonly used to ensure fair play among the members of the Blackfoot confederacy and in their competitions with neighbouring peoples,[24] something Catlin himself depicted in a painting of a Mandan horse race now in the Smithsonian American Art Museum (Figure 1).[25] Blackfoot and Comanche (Nɨmɨnɨ) might also station observers along the course to make sure that the race was run fairly and to provide feedback to spectators,[26] while among the Ute races might be repeated to fully establish the superiority of one horse over another.[27] Finishing lines consisted of a furrow scraped in the earth, a pair of piled rocks, or a tree.[28] The latter was a practice of the Comanche, who also engaged in two other kinds of race, both of which emphasized their agility on horseback. In one, riders rushed at a pole set on forks some 1.8 m above the ground, the winner being the first to touch it without stopping too soon, hitting it, or being thrown from his horse as the latter passed below. Alternatively, strips of hide were fastened 2–3 m apart on the ground and riders raced their horses at full speed toward them from some 200 m away, jumping between the strips before turning around and returning to the start: a horse that did not get all its feet beyond the first strip, or that put just one beyond the second, was disqualified even if it had the better time.[29]

To win all these events demanded considerable skill, as well as horses of high quality. Among some Northern Plains groups (the Hidatsa (Hirá·ca), the Blackfoot, and the Lakota) colts intended for use as racehorses might be trained from the age of about one year and were frequently castrated to make them faster or prevent them from tiring easily.[30] The efficacy of slitting a horse's nostrils to make it long-winded while running may be doubted, but was nevertheless widely practised, for example by Navajo, Comanche, and Lakota.[31] Harness equipment was reduced to the bare minimum: along with a whip, a single twist of rawhide rope sufficed as a bridle for Hidatsa, Blackfoot, and Comanche riders, among others.[32] Saddles, if used, were of the same flat type employed when hunting, i.e. pads of soft skin stuffed with antelope hair.[33] However, riding bareback was also common, with jockeys wearing the minimal possible amount of clothing – or none at all, as Catlin discovered to his embarrassment when challenged to take part in a race at one Hidatsa village![34] Riders did not, it should be noted, have to be the horses' owners: among Blackfoot, for instance, they were typically the latter's younger male relatives, while in similar vein Comanche explicitly preferred 'little men'.[35]

Betting was a fundamental part of Native American horse races, their 'principal mode of gambling' as George Catlin described it for the Comanche,[36] who wagered horses, blankets, and cattle.[37] Navajo, on the other hand, bet 'buckskins, saddlebags, blankets, and bundles' (of sacred objects),[38] while at Blackfoot races horses, guns, bison robes, blankets, and food were all common stakes, with men and women typically placing separate wagers among themselves. Saddles, bows and arrows, and even tipi lodges could also be wagered, although contrary to one early report referring to the Blackfoot wives were not.[39] Losers who protested at their loss were likely to be publicly humiliated and might forfeit the trust of their fellows.[40] As well as providing a means by which desirable possessions, including trade goods and booty captured in war, could circulate within the community, betting readily served as an expression of community solidarity in contexts in which riders from one group competed against those of another.[41]

## More than Sport: Ritual and War

What I have described so far is not all that dissimilar to the horse races with which nineteenth-century Euro-American observers might have been familiar. However, in other respects Native American horse races differed considerably from contemporary European norms. Most obvious, perhaps, was the widespread employment of protective medicines believed to enhance a horse's performance or guard against the evil intentions of competitors. Cheyenne (TsisTsisTsas), for example, rubbed the dried leaves of arrowhead (*Sagittaria cuneata*) onto their racehorses as a charm, but also employed skunkbush (*Rhus trilobata*) to prevent them from tiring and to bewitch the horse ahead so that it would exhaust itself. A third but unidentified plant, *vanó?ova*, might be scattered behind the lead jockey to slow down his opponents.[42] Several other botanical stimulants are recorded for a wide range of Plains groups, either to make horses run faster, to increase their stamina, or to revive them after a race (Table 1).[43] Moreover, in at least some instances such stimulants needed to be applied in a ceremonial manner by specialists with appropriate ritual knowledge.[44]

Fearing witchcraft, Navajo and Apache also made extensive use of medicines, including applying 'coyote pollen' (powdered dust from where a coyote had stood) to the base of the horse's tail, sprinkling the horse's body with a solution of *camote-de-monte* (*Peteria scoparia*), providing infusions of spruce (*Picea* sp.), juniper (*Juniperus* sp.), ponderosa pine (*Pinus ponderosa*), or White River coraldrops (*Besseya* (previously *Veronica*) *plantaginea*), and rubbing herbs into the horse's feet.[45] Conversely, they also knew how to make a horse lose a race: whether by applying medicines brewed from sacred datura (*Datura metaloides*), jimsonweed (*D. stramonium*), or poison ivy (*Toxicodendron radicans*) to the legs or via the mouth, or by burying something that had touched the horse (dirt from its tracks, saliva, sweat, hair, manure, urine etc.) in a place where someone had died or been buried and then singing over it for evil to

Table 1. Stimulant and restorative plants administered to Native American Plains horses (after Ewers, *The Horse in the Blackfoot Indian Culture*; Morgan '"Sugar Bowls" (*Clematis hirsutissima*): A Horse Restorative of the Nez Perce).

| Linnaean name | Common English name | Ethnic group[a] | Mode of administration |
| --- | --- | --- | --- |
| *Acorus calamus* | Sweet flag | Oglala Lakota; Yankton Dakota | Infusion offered as a drink |
| *Anaphalis margaritacea* | Western pearly everlasting | Cheyenne | Dried and powdered flowers placed on sole of each hoof and blown between the ears |
| *Clematis douglasii* | Sugar bowls | Nez Perce | Piece of the root placed in the nostrils after scraping off its outer surface |
| *Ionoxalis violacea* | Sheep sorrel | Pawnee | Bulbs pounded and consumed as food |
| *Laciniaria scariosa* | Blazing star | Omaha | Corms blown into the nostrils |
| *Paeonia brownii* | Wild peony | Ute | Root chewed and placed in the mouth |
| *Silphium lacinatum* | Compass plant | Omaha; Ponca | Not specified |
| *Thalictrum dasycarpum* | Meadow rue | Pawnee | Not specified |
| *Thalictrum sparsiflorum* | Fewflower meadow rue | Cheyenne | Dried and ground to a fine powder administered by mouth |
| *Xanthoxalis stricta* | Yellow wood sorrel | Pawnee | Bulbs pounded and consumed as food |

[a]The self-designations for groups not otherwise mentioned in the text are: Nez Perce Nimí'ipuu; Omaha Umáha; Pawnee Ckírihki kuru·riki; Ponca Ppákka; and Yankton Dakota Ihanktonwan Dakota Oyate.

come to the animal. Recovering the items buried by the witch could counteract this, as could the use of other plant-based medicines.[46]

Blackfoot likewise used plant-based ritual medicines to influence races, tying them to a horse's tail, spraying them onto the rider's quirt, or holding them in his mouth to forestall being overtaken by another rider.[47] They also sought to prevent horse medicine men (i.e. individuals with specialist ritual knowledge of horses) from approaching the horses to be raced for fear that they might use their powers to cause an animal to tire or falter.[48] To get round this, Blackfoot horse medicine men could provide a jockey with a willow stick to which horse medicine had been applied with instructions to touch the competing horse with it during the race. Alternatively, they might paint a rock with medicine and then touch a rawhide horse with the rock so that it would leave the course or buck.[49] At least among the Comanche the medicines used to influence a race's outcome were tabooed to women and they had to be removed from the horse by washing it in a creek immediately after the race.[50]

At one level practices such as these might be considered akin to cheating, and certainly the latter was not unknown. One could, for example, enter a horse that looked good, but was actually very slow, wagering against it in order to win the bet, or conversely enter one that looked weak, but was actually very fast.[51] Alternatively, one could run one's own horse (or that of one's opponent if one could gain access to it) all night long so that it would be too tired to compete effectively the following day, or deliberately hold a horse back during the race itself. At least among the Navajo, practices such as these were treated more as a good joke than as a moral issue; being found out merely required one to acknowledge one's actions with good grace so that a rematch could be rearranged or wagers returned.[52]

Nevertheless, attempting to influence the outcome of a horse race by invoking supernatural powers or using what might be called magical aids immediately places Native American horse racing within a much broader context of competitive play. That context was one in which gambling – 'a central aspect of indigenous culture'[53] – constituted another means of trying to predict, and thus control, the future so that creation should continue to unfold as it had previously.[54] Along with warfare, many competitive games and contests on the Plains also formed part of a continuum of agonistic activities in which individuals sought to prove their superiority and excellence vis-à-vis others.[55] While war and raiding provided the most prestigious avenue for securing this (albeit in an external context), games and races offered 'an acceptable substitute for displaying prowess between members of the same tribe',[56] especially for younger males. Pursuing prestige through these means was one of the principal ways by which men sought to maintain and enhance their self-esteem and status while simultaneously striving to make a name for themselves that would long be remembered. 'Game involvement [could thus] serve as a primary means of socialization for engagement in warfare', which was simply an extension of gaming redirected at the extra-tribal level.[57]

Clearly, then, horse racing occupied a more serious position in many Native American societies than might initially seem to be the case. As rule-governed contests emphasizing the display and demonstration of physical prowess and skill, horse races afforded individuals and the men's societies and ethnic groups to which they belonged opportunities for ascertaining, challenging, confirming, and enhancing their social standing.[58] The fact that all possible means, including the manipulation of supernatural powers, should be deployed in pursuit of this is wholly consistent with the general spiritual connections of gambling and gaming across many North American societies.[59] Partaking of the qualities of what Huizinga called 'sacred play',[60] i.e. contests and rituals in which cosmic order is epitomized and maintained, horse racing – like foot races, other games, and counting coup on an enemy – was thus far from being a purely secular activity.[61] Instead, it was both secular *and* sacred,[62] requiring strategies that were themselves both practical and mystical.[63] Moreover, since the stakes involved extended beyond material possessions to include the pride, honour, and status of the individuals and groups competing, it is all the more understandable how disputes over the outcomes of horse races could sometimes precipitate violence of the kind that erupted after a dead heat between Piegan and Kutenai (Ktunaxa) jockeys in 1878,[64] or even the all-out warfare that broke out over the winnings from races between previously co-operating Cree (Ne·hiyawak) and Blackfoot camps in the spring of 1841.[65]

Conceptually, the link between horse racing and warfare is underlined further by the way in which Blackfoot men's societies challenged each other to a horse race: someone who had already been successful in war would dress himself and his horse in exactly the same way as when he had counted coup on an enemy, ride to the lodge of the leader of the rival society, sing his personal war song, shoot at the lodge's poles, and issue his challenge. Hearing this, the other society's leader would rush out and fire his gun in the air, boasting that, 'I killed an enemy, knocked him down and scalped him. You are not going to scalp me'.[66] Men's behaviour immediately before the start of the race reinforced the association: members of the competing societies re-enacted their coups on past enemies against each other, for example by knocking their rivals down and pretending to scalp them.[67]

To win races horses needed both stamina and speed (Figure 3). On the nineteenth-century Plains men sought precisely the same qualities for the 'buffalo runners' they trained to get in close to a running bison so that the rider could shoot to kill at close range after which the horse would swerve away to avoid injury.[68] The swiftness, endurance, courage, and agility that this demanded were precisely the same qualities prized among the horses that a man rode in war. In many instances, indeed, the horses used to race, hunt, and fight were one and the same, just as among the Blackfoot and the Navajo the medicines used to ensure success in all three activities were also frequently identical.[69] In this vein, while recalling a bison hunt in the Yellowstone area around 1869, the Hidatsa elder Buffalo-Bird-Woman remembered that a woman named Otter had once ridden *Ita-takic* (White-Face), a gelding used both in horse races and for hunting bison;[70] her brother, Wolf-Chief, made the same point with respect to another horse.[71] Blackfoot racehorses, on the other hand, were used as buffalo runners after they had reached the age of nine, i.e. when they were no longer considered at their very best for racing. But whether employed sequentially or contemporaneously, such important animals, like a man's favourite war pony, received special treatment from many Plains peoples in so far as they were used minimally, if at all, as pack animals or for ordinary riding.[72]

Being 'the most valuable horse' that a man could own,[73] racehorses were highly desired, and even today may be offered in payment for valued items, such as the

**Figure 3.** Horse racing of the Sioux near Fort Pierre (South Dakota) c. 1836 as depicted by Karl Bodmer (Maximilian von Wied, *Travels in the Interior of North America 1832–1834, Volume 1*, Plate 30 (Köln: Taschen GmbH, 2001) (Source: Wikimedia Commons reproduced under Creative Commons CC0 1.0 Universal Public Domain Declaration (https://commons.wikimedia.org/wiki/File:Karl_Bodmer_-_Horse_Racing_of_the_Sioux_(Source).jpg) (accessed January 22, 2019)).

right to use a particular kind of painted lodge design, among some tribes, for example the Blackfoot.[74] Typically, owners kept them close to home, even picketed at the tipi door.[75] Men might undertake expeditions with the specific intention of trying to acquire such animals[76] and their capture on a raid brought great prestige, something widely recognized in the systems of graded honours accorded successful warrior exploits.[77] The Piegan elder Mountain Chief, for example, used the capture of a sorrel racehorse from the Flathead (Séliš) as a key event to remember the year 1853/54,[78] while another, Saahkómaapi, interviewed by David Thompson late in the eighteenth century, considered horse theft to be far more impressive than actions on the battlefield precisely because of the greater risks that it entailed.[79] Acquiring already trained racehorses by taking them from others was nevertheless itself an act of war, part of a pattern in which enemies made horse raids but horse raids in turn made enemies.[80] In this respect, just as much as because winning races conferred prestige and social standing or because supernatural powers were invoked to achieve both goals, Native American horse racing and horse races were far more than a simple contest of skill between individuals and their mounts.

## 'Pernicious Practices'

With these points in mind it becomes easier to understand why, in the aftermath of the wars, epidemics, and ecological destruction that forced Native Americans onto

**Figure 4.** Indian women racing on horseback at the Pendleton Round-Up, Umatilla County, Oregon, c. 1940, photographed by Ralph I. Gifford. (Source: Oregon Multicultural Archives, Oregon State University Special Collections & Archive Research Center P218-SG2 https://www.flickr.com/photos/osucommons/4987077826/in/photolist-8AG5us-8AG2ys-YGgWdT-8ACYJX-r6xK7G-YMqESu-LgZsTY-Lh8RbB-Lh8G5v (accessed January 22, 2019)).

reservations in the late 1800s, Euro-American authorities took such pains to suppress horse racing and other 'pernicious practices'.[81] Widely recognized as being among 'their chief amusements',[82] Native Americans' love of horse racing was considered by both missionaries and government officials to be heathen, potentially subversive, and inimical to the instillation of the Protestant work ethic that would supposedly transform equestrian hunters into model proto-capitalist, Christianized farmers and ranchers.[83] The traditional emphasis on betting at horse races incurred particular ire,[84] especially where horse races formed part of the fairs promoted by Office of Indian Affairs agents. As early as 1877, for example, gambling and horse racing faced suppression on the Flathead Reservation in Montana,[85] though in what is now western Oklahoma the Southern Arapaho (Inuna-Ina) were able to continue racing by making it an important part of annual Independence Day celebrations at their Fort Reno reservation until this was forcibly ceded away in 1891.[86] Over two decades later, the Indian Office's Commissioner, Cato Sells, could still be found arguing that, 'If, *to the Indians*, the paramount features [of such events] are to dance and wager on horse races, the quicker the fairs are terminated the better'.[87] Unsurprisingly, however, his suggestion that horse races should be replaced by 'slow mule races' met with little enthusiasm, and two years later he was again demanding that horse racing be replaced at Kiowa and Comanche get-togethers by more acceptable athletic contests, foot races, and baseball.[88]

Similar efforts were made on the Northern Plains where, from the late 1890s, the Oglala (Oglála) Lakota living on the Pine Ridge Reservation in South Dakota were encouraged to take part in fairs that were also shared with their Euro-American neighbours. The Office of Indian Affairs promoted these events in order to encourage agricultural production, but for the Oglala their primary function was to emphasize traditional kinship ties and tribal unity. Horse races at such gatherings were initially repressed where possible, but from 1917 increasingly tolerated in the form of relay races within a rodeo format that could provide 'a positive point of contact for whites and Indians'.[89] Indeed, for the Oglala, as for other Native American groups like the Crow,[90] rodeo's attractiveness lay precisely in its being a cultural innovation that allowed them to perpetuate treasured ways of doing things, including coming together 'as a people... in ways that local whites would accept'.[91] So much was this so that when the Office of Indian Affairs lost interest in promoting the Oglala Fair, rodeo (and horse racing) became one of the main emphases of the fairs organized entirely by the Oglala themselves,[92] just as they were at similar events among the Crow and other tribes.[93]

## The Persistence of Native American Horse Racing Traditions

Rodeo's growing popularity in the Inter-War period among both Native Americans and Euro-Americans has been noted by several writers (Figure 4).[94] Ian Dyck, in particular, has emphasized the strength of Indigenous contributions to its development,[95] and at least among Blackfoot competitors these include a continuing belief in the efficacy of traditional medicines for affecting the outcome of competitions.[96] For them, as for the Oglala, the Comanche, and the Kiowa,[97] rodeo has provided one highly effective way of retaining traditionally significant cultural practices in a very different world: 'to gather; to wager; to give away horses, cattle, and other gifts; to reaffirm the status of individual horsemen; and to retain certain elements of their own equestrian heritage'.[98] It is not, however, unique. Horse racing has also survived in other contexts, such as Navajo ceremonial dances (where it is accompanied by much betting) and in annual relay races among the Jicarilla Apache (Haísndayĭn).[99] But it is perhaps the relatively recent rise to prominence of Indian Relay racing that underlines more clearly than anything else the persistence of horse racing patterns inherited from pre-reservation times.

Developing at powwows and county fairs in the 1980s,[100] Indian Relay was originally called 'pony express' after the mid-nineteenth-century United States postal service. It is now restricted to Native American participants, follows standardized rules, and was regulated between 2013 and 2017 by the Professional Indian Horse Racing Association (PIHRA) before coming under the supervision of its successor, the Horse Nations Indian Relay Council (HNIRC).[101] Still considered, with good reason, an extreme sport, Indian Relay involves a team of three horses, a jockey who leaps on to them, a 'mugger' who catches the newly dismounted horse, and two handlers who hold the other animals. An almost exclusively male competition (though women may own, or even train, the horses, and in some instances have now begun to race them),[102] Indian Relay is run on a half-mile (800 m) oval track using specially (re)trained Thoroughbreds or Quarter Horses, often animals with prior experience of conventional flat racing. The jockey starts on or next to the first horse, races round the track, jumps off, and changes on to the second, and then the third, horse, ideally without colliding with the horses or riders of the up to six other teams taking part in the same event. Covering some 2.5 km in total, the whole race lasts just a few minutes.[103]

Today, HNIRC brings together almost 50 relay teams from over 15 Native American nations. Multiple events are held each summer across the Northern Plains and the Plateau, with HNIRC publishing a regular online magazine about its activities, maintaining an informative website, and also organizing more conventional horse races, including events for women and children.[104] Of particular interest in this context is the way in which several features of Indian Relay racing replicate aspects of nineteenth-century Native American horse races. Jockeys use only very simple bridles and ride without saddles and on occasion employ the 'wheel and run' start used in some nineteenth-century races.[105] Additionally, symbolic designs that may bring good luck are often painted on both horses[106] and riders, traditional medicines are used to promote their speed and endurance,[107] and the principal reward for winning a race is not necessarily money, but rather prestige.[108] In at least some cases, moreover, those participating draw explicitly on longstanding family traditions of horse racing.[109] As Amelia-Roisin Seifert perceptively remarks, this is a sport 'based around a modern day "warrior" ethos of masculine bravado, skill and competition, anchored by a love of horses'.[110] In all these respects, as well as in its emphasis on minimizing the use of harness equipment and its invocation of supernatural aid, Indian Relay underlines the enduring nature of Native American horse racing traditions even while its participants employ the resources of Western veterinary and nutritional medicine, sports science, and long-distance transportation and communicate their exploits via social media. Importantly, several documentary films relating to Indian Relay have now started to provide an Indigenous voice on these same traditions and to draw the attention of non-Native audiences to them and to their history.[111]

## Racing Futures

In an initial effort to assess how far George Catlin was correct to write that 'a horse-race is the same all the world over',[112] this study has focussed on two regions of Native North America, the Great Plains and the Southwest. It has argued that rather than being practised simply as a diversion, Native American horse racing in these areas formed part of a cultural context that emphasized and exalted competitions between men for the purpose of asserting, confirming, and enhancing their status and prestige in relation to those of others. Supporting Catlin's comment, and thus taking issue with John Ewers' condemnation of it,[113] the other essays in this issue confirm that such social and political concerns were far from absent in cultural contexts as different as Classical Greece and Rome, the European Renaissance, and early modern Britain.[114] In Native North America, however, those concerns were at least as strong externally as they were internally, meaning that horse racing formed part of a continuum of agonistic activities that encompassed warfare, and could even precipitate it where different tribal groups disputed the outcomes of races. Moreover, because the best racehorses were typically also those preferred for hunting bison or riding into war, there was every incentive to acquire them – pre-trained – by raiding other tribes, an act that itself won honour and encouraged yet further raids. The significance attached to race outcomes in terms of the wagers made on them and their consequences for the standing of the individuals, men's societies, and tribal groups taking part also meant that reliance was frequently placed on supernatural aid: protective medicines for enhancing a horse's performance were widely used, witchcraft and the interference of ritual specialists belonging to the opposite side widely feared. It was for these reasons, and not just because of concerns about Native 'idleness', that horse racing encountered such opposition from colonial authorities during the reservation era. Conversely, the persistence of Native American horse racing traditions, most conspicuously via the development of rodeo and, more recently, Indian Relay racing, attests to their enduring importance for Indigenous people and the continuing significance of the values that they express and celebrate.

Future investigations of the points raised here would certainly benefit from exploring the relevant ethnographic and historical literature in greater depth while simultaneously launching a more detailed investigation of the horse's continuing significance for Native North American communities. This topic continues to remain curiously under-explored by anthropologists, although the work of Amelia-Roisin Seifert and Brandi Bethke, like that of Elizabeth Atwood Lawrence a generation ago, shows that it is not wholly neglected.[115] Attention should be particularly directed toward a more detailed consideration of the diversity of horse racing practices between regions of North America and among different Indigenous groups in order to avoid homogenizing all Native American societies in the image of just a few. Research into differences in the religious and political associations that horse racing held (and still hold) and in the responses made to attempts to suppress races after Euro-American conquest may be especially productive.

At the same time, we must remember that North America was not the only region to which horses returned, or were introduced, as a result of Europe's post-Columbian expansion. There is thus also much scope for a broader comparative study of how Indigenous horse racing traditions emerged in many different parts of the world.[116] Such investigations could, among others, call upon the Mapuche of Chile and Argentina, the Aónik'enk of Patagonia, the Wayúu of Colombia, the Mocoví of northern Argentina, the Māori of New Zealand, and the involvement of Aboriginal Australians in developing an antipodean form of rodeo.[117] In short, just as the horse's encounter with Indigenous peoples post-1492 demands a global approach, so too does any analysis of how, when, why, and under what circumstances Native forms of horse racing emerged, resisted attempts at suppression, and persisted. Collectively, such studies should allow us to understand better how far George Catlin was or was not correct when he asserted that, 'a horse-race is the same all the world over'.[118]

## Notes

1. The commonly accepted English names for the various Native American groups mentioned are employed in the text, but the relevant self-designation follows in brackets after their first usage where this differs.
2. George Catlin, *Letters and Notes on the Manners, Customs and Conditions of North American Indians, Vol. I* (New York: Dover, 1973), 143. Catlin's work, and especially his paintings, provides important documentation of Native American societies on the Great Plains at a time (1830–8) when Native equestrianism was at its height and effective control of the region by the United States had yet to be imposed. Nevertheless, while often sympathetic to those whom he described and depicted, it must be acknowledged that Catlin shared with many of his contemporaries a tendency to idolize those whom he saw as 'noble savages' and – quite wrongly – a 'vanishing race' (Laurence Hauptmann, and George Hamell, 'George Catlin: The Iroquois Origins of his Indian Portrait Gallery,' *New York History: Quarterly Journal of the New York State Historical Association* 84 (2003): 123–51; Robert Lewis, 'Wild American Savages and the Civilized English: Catlin's Indian Gallery and the Shows of London,' *European Journal of American Studies* 3, no. 1 (2008): document 6.
3. John Ewers, *The Horse in the Blackfoot Indian Culture with Comparative Material from Other Western Tribes* (Washington, DC: Smithsonian Institution, 1955), 235.
4. Though for recent efforts to the contrary see, Brandi Bethke, 'Dog Days to Horse Days: Evaluating the Rise of Nomadic Pastoralism among the Blackfoot' (Ph.D. diss., School of Anthropology, University of Arizona, 2016); Amelia-Roisin Seifert, 'An Introduction to Contemporary Native American Horse Culture: Notes from the Northwest Plateau,' in *The Meaning of Horses: Biosocial Encounters*, ed. Dona Lee Davis and Anita Maurstad (London: Routledge, 2016), 147–63.
5. Alfred Crosby, *The Columbian Exchange: Biological and Cultural Consequences of 1492* (Westport, NJ: Greenwood Publishing, 1972).
6. As stated by Alyce Cheska, 'Sport as Ethnic Boundary Maintenance: A Case of the American Indian', *International Review for the Sociology of Sport* 19, nos. 3–4 (1984): 241–57.
7. Johan Huizinga, *Homo Ludens: A Study of the Play-Element in Culture* (London: Routledge and Kegan Paul, 1950).
8. Jack Broughton and Elic Weitzel, 'Population Reconstructions for Humans and Megafauna Suggest Mixed Causes for North American Pleistocene Extinctions', *Nature Communications* 9, no. 1 (2018): 1–12.
9. This process has been most recently reviewed by Peter Mitchell, *Horse Nations: The Worldwide Impact of the Horse on Indigenous Societies Post-1492* (Oxford: Oxford University Press, 2015). New research suggests, however, that horses spread north even faster than previously thought, reaching as far as Wyoming, for example, by the mid-1600s. See, Cassidee Thornhill, '*Equus ferus caballus* during the Protohistoric in Wyoming: Looking for the Horse in the Archaeological Record' (M.A. diss., Department of Anthropology, University of Wyoming, 2016).
10. David Thompson, *David Thompson's Narrative of His Explorations in Western America, 1784-1812*, ed. J.B. Tyrell (Toronto: Champlain Society, 1916), 359.
11. Ewers, *The Horse in the Blackfoot Indian Culture*, 227–8.
12. Philip Stepney, and David Goa, *The Scriver Collection* (Edmonton: Provincial Museum of Alberta, 1990), 39.
13. Ewers, *The Horse in the Blackfoot Indian Culture*, 228, 230.
14. Regina Flannery and John Cooper, 'Social Mechanisms in Gros Ventre Gambling', *Southwestern Journal of Anthropology* 2, no. 4 (1946): 391–419.
15. Ewers, *The Horse in the Blackfoot Indian Culture*, 227–8.
16. Ruthann Knudson, 'Fish, Roots, Game, and Trade in the Columbia Plateau', *Journal of Forestry* 78, no. 8 (1980): 542–56; Helen Schuster, 'Yakima and Neighboring Groups', in

*Handbook of North American Indians Volume 12 Plateau*, ed. Deward Walker (Washington, DC: Smithsonian Institution, 1998), 327–51; Eugene Hunn and David French, 'Western Columbia River Sahaptins', in *Handbook of North American Indians, Volume 12: Plateau*, ed. Deward Walker (Washington, DC: Smithsonian Institution, 1998), 378–94.

17. William Butler, 'Indian Horse Racing in Colorado', *Southwestern Lore* 84, no. 1 (2018): 29–34, who notes the existence of at least two further horse racing locations in Colorado.
18. For example, see the description given by Henry Boller, *Among the Indians: The Far West, 1858–1866* (Philadelphia: T.E. Zell, 1868), 66–7.
19. Janet Cliff, 'Playing with Games: Cheating in Navajo and Euro-American Gambling', *Western Folklore* 49, no. 2 (1990): 221–5; Ewers, *The Horse in the Blackfoot Indian Culture*, 230.
20. For examples of such shorter races see William Hamilton, 'A Trading Expedition Among the Indians in 1858', *Contributions of the Montana Historical Society* 3 (1900): 33–123 for one between Piegan and Crow (Apsáaloke) competitors, and James Schultz, *My Life as an Indian* (Greenwich: Fawcett Publications, 1907), 134–6 for another between Piegan and Kutenai (Ktunaxa) jockeys.
21. Butler, 'Indian Horse Racing in Colorado', 310.
22. Cliff, 'Playing with Games'; Ewers, *The Horse in the Blackfoot Indian Culture*, 229
23. Robert Lowie, 'The Northern Shoshone', *Anthropological Papers of the American Museum of Natural History* 2 (1909): 165–306.
24. Ewers, *The Horse in the Blackfoot Indian Culture*, 229, 231, 233, 235.
25. *Horseracing on a Course Behind the Mandan Village*, 1832–1833, oil on canvas, 49.7 x 70.0 cm, Smithsonian American Art Museum, Washington DC, https://americanart.si.edu/artwork/horseracing-course-behind-mandan-village-4109 (accessed January 22, 2019).
26. Ewers, *The Horse in the Blackfoot Indian Culture*, 231; Thomas Kavanagh, ed., *Comanche Ethnography* (Lincoln: University of Nebraska Press, 2008), 135.
27. James Russell, 'Conditions and Customs of Present-Day Ute in Colorado', *Colorado Magazine* 6, no. 3 (1929): 104–12.
28. Richard Dodge, *Our Wild Indians: Thirty-Three Years' Personal Experience Among the Red Man of the Great West* (Hartford, CT: A.D. Worthington, 1883), 340; Ewers, *The Horse in the Blackfoot Indian Culture*, 230.
29. Dodge, *Our Wild Indians*, 340.
30. Gilbert Wilson, 'The Horse and the Dog in Hidatsa Culture', *Anthropological Papers of the American Museum of Natural History* 15, pt. 2 (1924): 125–311; Ewers, *The Horse in the Blackfoot Indian Culture*, 228; Royal Hassrick, *The Sioux: Life and Customs of a Warrior Society* (Norman: University of Oklahoma Press, 1964).
31. LaVerne Clark, *They Sang for Horses: The Impact of the Horse on Navajo and Apache Folklore* (Boulder: University Press of Colorado, 2001), 184.
32. Wilson, 'The Horse and the Dog in Hidatsa Culture', 183; Ewers, *The Horse in the Blackfoot Indian Culture*, 230; Kavanagh, *Comanche Ethnography*, 135.
33. Wilson, 'The Horse and the Dog in Hidatsa Culture', 190.
34. Demetri Shimkin, 'Introduction of the Horse', in *Handbook of North American Indians. Volume 11: Great Basin*, ed. Warren L. d'Azevedo (Washington, DC: Smithsonian Institution, 1986), 517–24; Catlin, *Letters and Notes*, 197–8.
35. Ewers, *The Horse in the Blackfoot Indian Culture*, 230; Kavanagh, *Comanche Ethnography*, 135.
36. George Catlin, *Letters and Notes on the Manners, Customs and Conditions of North American Indians, Vol. II* (New York: Dover, 1973), 65.
37. Kavanagh, *Comanche Ethnography*, 135.
38. Clyde Kluckholn, Willard Hill, and Lucy Wales Kluckholn, *Navajo Material Culture* (Cambridge, MA: Belknap Press, 1971), 388.

39. Edward Wilson, 'Report on the Blackfoot Tribes', *Report of the British Association for the Advancement of Science* 57 (1887): 183–200. Wilson's report is refuted by Ewers, *The Horse in the Blackfoot Indian Culture*, 230–1.
40. Ewers, *The Horse in the Blackfoot Indian Culture*, 232; Kavanagh, *Comanche Ethnography*, 135.
41. Richard Ford 1983, 'Inter-Indian Exchange in the Southwest', in *Handbook of North American Indians. Volume 10: Southwest*, ed. Alfonso Ortiz (Washington, DC: Smithsonian Institution, 1983), 311–22; Theodore Stern, 'Cayuse, Umatilla and Walla Walla', in *Handbook of North American Indians. Volume 12: Plateau*, ed. Deward Walker (Washington, DC: Smithsonian Institution, 1998), 395–419.
42. Jeffrey Hart, 'The Ethnobotany of the Northern Cheyenne Indians of Montana', *Journal of Ethnopharmacology* 4 (1981): 1–55.
43. For discussion of one such instance, see George Morgan, '"Sugar Bowls" (*Clematis hirsutissima*): A Horse Restorative of the Nez Perce', *Journal of Ethnopharmacology* 4, no. 1 (1981): 117–20.
44. Frank Dobie, 'Indian Horses and Horsemanship,' *Southwest Review* 35, no. 4 (1950): 265–75.
45. Clark, *They Sang for Horses*, 184–5.
46. Ibid., 185–6.
47. John Hellson, and Morgan Gadd, *Ethnobotany of the Blackfoot Indians* (Ottawa: National Museum of Canada, 1974).
48. Ewers, *The Horse in the Blackfoot Indian Culture*, 230.
49. Ibid., 272.
50. Kavanagh, *Comanche Ethnography*, 135.
51. Ewers, *The Horse in the Blackfoot Indian Culture*, 232, provides an example of the latter situation among the Piegan.
52. Cliff, 'Playing with Games'. As she discusses, Euro-American failure to appreciate Native views on cheating was at the root of the massacre at Fort Fauntleroy, New Mexico, in 1861 when at least 12 Navajo were killed. The incident arose after a Navajo rider lost control of his horse because his reins had been cut, leaving his Euro-American competitor the winner. The soldiers present first denied that their compatriot had cheated, then refused to return their ill-gotten winnings, and finally used force to prevent one Navajo from entering the fort to retrieve them.
53. Stewart Culin, *Games of the North American Indians* (Washington, DC: Bureau of American Ethnology, 1907), 14.
54. Yale Belanger, 'Towards an Innovative Understanding of North American Indigenous Gaming in Historical Perspective', in *First Nations Gambling in Canada*, ed. Yale Belanger (Winnipeg: University of Manitoba Press, 2011), 10–34
55. John Loy and Graham Hesketh, 'Competitive Play on the Plains: An Analysis of Games and Warfare among Native American Warrior Societies, 1800–1850, in *The Future of Play Theory: A Multidisciplinary Inquiry*, ed. Anthony Pellegrini (Albany: State University of New York Press, 1995), 73–106.
56. Robert Morford and Stanley Clark, 'The *Agon* Motif', *Exercise and Sport Sciences Reviews* 4 (1976): 164.
57. Loy and Hesketh, 'Competitive Play on the Plains', 78
58. Ibid., 98–9.
59. Belanger, 'Towards an Innovative Understanding of North American Indigenous Gaming in Historical Perspective', 20–2.
60. Huizinga, *Homo Ludens*.
61. As recounted by Clark, *They Sang for Horses*, 31–2, among the Navajo and Apache even the gods raced horses in myths that recounted the creation of horses and other animals. Both peoples, for example, tell how the elder of the Hero Twins borrowed a horse from Father Sun in order to defeat his opponent in a race around the world. In another myth, Clark, *They Sang for Horses*, 23–4, details how a race is held around the horizon

to restore harmony among the animals, but the god Black Begochiddy cheats by changing the appearance of his mount, a donkey, so that with narrower feet and a shorter tail it can run faster than all the others.

62. Virginia McGowan, Lois Frank, Gary Nixon, and Misty Grimshaw, 'Sacred and Secular Play in Gambling among Blackfoot Peoples of Southwest Alberta', in *Culture and the Gambling Phenomenon: Proceedings of the 11th National Association for Gambling Studies Conference, Sydney, Australia, 2001*, ed. Alex Blaszczynski (Alphington: National Association for Gambling Studies, 2001), 241–55.
63. Culin, *Games of the North American Indians*, 807, makes a similar point with reference to the Crow.
64. Schultz, *My Life as an Indian*, 134–6.
65. George Colpitts, 'Peace, War, and Climate Change on the Northern Plains: Bison Hunting in the Neutral Hills During the Mild Winters of 1830–34', *Canadian Journal of History* 50, no. 3 (2015): 420–41.
66. Ewers, *The Horse in the Blackfoot Indian Culture*, 229.
67. Ibid., 231.
68. Mitchell, *Horse Nations*, 156–7.
69. Ewers, *The Horse in the Blackfoot Indian Culture*, 270–5; Clark, *They Sang*, 186
70. Wilson, 'The Horse and the Dog in Hidatsa Culture', 280.
71. Ibid., 299, 305.
72. Ibid., 310; Ewers, *The Horse in the Blackfoot Indian Culture*, 228; Hassrick, *The Sioux*, 162.
73. Ewers, *The Horse in the Blackfoot Indian Culture*, 228.
74. Adolf Hungrywolf, *The Blackfoot Papers. Volume Two: Pikunni Ceremonial Life* (Skookumchuk: The Good Medicine Cultural Foundation, 2006), 352.
75. Thomas Biolsi, 'Ecological and Cultural Factors in Plains Indian Warfare', in *Warfare, Culture and Environment*, ed. R. Brian Ferguson (Orlando: Academic Press, 1988), 141–68.
76. Hassrick, *The Sioux*, 162.
77. Loy and Hesketh, 'Competitive Play on the Plains', 82–3.
78. Adolf Hungrywolf, *The Blackfoot Papers. Volume One: Pikunni History and Culture* (Skookumchuk: The Good Medicine Cultural Foundation, 2006), 16.
79. Anthony McGinnis, *Counting Coup and Cutting Horses: Intertribal Warfare on the Northern Plains, 1738-1889* (Lincoln: University of Nebraska Press, 1990), 11.
80. Biolsi, 'Ecological and Cultural Factors in Plains Indian Warfare'. Additionally, see Ewers, *The Horse in the Blackfoot Indian Culture*, 239, for a further twist to this argument when he notes how 'some young [Blackfoot] men were both luckless and inveterate gamblers, who lost all their horses and were forced to return again and again to enemy camps to recoup their losses. *Their love of gambling kept them poor and at the same time kept them active as horse raiders*' (emphasis added).
81. Captain Lorenzo Cooke, Acting Agent of the Blackfeet Reservation, Montana, as quoted by the United States Commissioner of Indian Affairs, *Annual Report of the Commissioner of Indian Affairs, for the Year 1894* (Washington, DC: Office of Indian Affairs, 1894), 159.
82. Wilson, 'Report on the Blackfoot Tribes', 192.
83. McGowan et al., 'Sacred and Secular Play in Gambling among Blackfoot Peoples of Southwest Alberta'.
84. For example, Ewers, *The Horse in the Blackfoot Indian Culture*, 234.
85. Stephen Dow Beckham, 'History since 1846', in *Handbook of North American Indians. Volume 12: Plateau*, ed. Deward Walker (Washington, DC: Smithsonian Institution, 1998), 149–73.
86. Loretta Fowler, 'Arapaho' in *Handbook of North American Indians. Volume 13: Great Plains, Part 2*, ed. Raymond DeMallie (Washington, DC: Smithsonian Institution, 2001), 840–62.

87. Clyde Ellis, '"There is No Doubt... The Dances Should Be Curtailed": Indian Dances and Federal Policy on the Southern Plains, 1880–1930', *Pacific Historical Review* 70, no. 4 (2001): 557, emphasis in the original text, which was written in 1914.
88. Ibid., 558.
89. Elisabeth Saunders, 'Pine Ridge Reservation Fairs: Building Intercultural Communities Through Play', *James A. Rawley Graduate Conference in the Humanities Paper* 27 (2008): 8. http://digitalcommons.unl.edu/historyrawleyconference/27 (accessed May 30, 2017). The Oglala were not alone: the Gros Ventre likewise made horse races a central part of their annual Hays Fair from the very beginning of the twentieth century, including races against the Assiniboin (Nakota), with whom they shared their small Fort Belknap reservation; see Loretta Fowler and Regina Flannery, 'Gros Ventre', in *Handbook of North American Indians. Volume 13: Great Plains Part 2*, ed. Raymond DeMallie (Washington, DC: Smithsonian Institution, 2001), 677–94.
90. Frederick Hoxie, *Parading Through History: The Making of the Crow Nation in America 1805–1935* (Cambridge: Cambridge University Press, 1995), 363.
91. Saunders, 'Pine Ridge Reservation Fairs', 9.
92. Ibid.
93. Allison Fuss Mellis, *Riding Buffaloes and Broncos: Rodeo and Native Traditions in the Northern Great Plains* (Norman: University of Oklahoma Press, 2003), 49.
94. Allison Fuss, 'Cowboys on the Reservation: The Growth of Rodeo as a Lakota National Pastime', *South Dakota History* 29 (1999): 211–28.
95. Ian Dyck, 'Does Rodeo Have Roots in Ancient Indian Traditions?', *Plains Anthropologist* 41, no. 157 (1996): 205–19.
96. McGowan et al., 'Sacred and Secular Play in Gambling among Blackfoot Peoples of Southwest Alberta', 248.
97. Ellis, 'There is No Doubt... The Dances Should Be Curtailed'; Saunders, 'Pine Ridge Reservation Fairs'.
98. Fuss Mellis, *Riding Buffaloes and Broncos*, 19.
99. Clark, *They Sang for Horses*, 310, who describes the Navajo dances as 'squaw dances', a term now understood by some as derogatory, but likely to be a reference to dances associated with Enemy Way (*Ana'í Ndáá'*) ceremonies that traditionally counter the harmful effects of ghosts; see Clyde Kluckholn, Dorothea Cross Leighton, Lucy Wales, and Richard Kluckholn, *The Navaho* (Cambridge, MA: Harvard University Press, 1974), 228–9.
100. Seifert, 'An Introduction to Contemporary Native American Horse Culture', 157. But see also Bethke, 'Dog Days to Horse Days', for the suggestion that its origins should be placed as early as the 1920s.
101. 'New Council to Oversee Indian Relay Racing', *Seminole Tribune*, March 31, 2017, 3C, http://semtribe.com/STOF/docs/default-source/tribune-archive/2017/seminoletribune_march31_2017.pdf?sfvrsn=b41f96ee_6 (accessed January 22, 2019); PIHRA (Professional Indian Horse Racing Association), https://en-gb.facebook.com/pages/category/Education/Professional-Indian-Horse-Racing-Association-476531622450149/ (accessed January 18, 2019).
102. Jenni Whiteley, 'Eastern Idaho State Fair Adds All-Female Indian Relay Race', *Idaho State Journal* https://www.idahostatejournal.com/members/eastern-idaho-state-fair-adds-all-female-indian-relay-race/article_08eae969-71d2-545e-a5ca-6387e6d6e1b8.html (accessed August 9, 2018).
103. Seifert, 'An Introduction to Contemporary Native American Horse Culture'.
104. HNIRC (Horse Nations Indian Relay Council), http://www.horsenationsrelay.com/blog/ (accessed January 18, 2019).
105. In this kind of start horses are lined up with their tails to the starting line and heads opposite the direction of the race so that they have to wheel around when the race begins. A nineteenth-century account can be found in Butler, 'Indian Horse Racing in Colorado', 31.
106. Bethke, 'Dog Days to Horse Days', 339.

107. Ibid., 344–5; see also the film *Indian Relay*, directed by Charles Dye (2013; Bozeman, MT: KUSM-TV/Montana PBS and ITVS), http://www.pbs.org/independentlens/films/indian-relay/ (accessed January 22, 2019).
108. Seifert, 'An Introduction to Contemporary Native American Horse Culture', 158.
109. Hungrywolf, *The Blackfoot Papers. Volume Two*, 684.
110. Seifert, 'An Introduction to Contemporary Native American Horse Culture', 158. Much the same combination of celebrating an equestrian warrior heritage, including the use of traditional religious practices such as praying in sweat lodges before a race and placing sacred eagle feathers on the horses taking part, marks the famous Suicide Race of the Omak Stampede, held annually in Washington State since 1935. This involves racing down a 70 metre-long steeply (~33°) angled hill and then across the Okanogan River at its base before completing a near 500 m sprint to the local rodeo arena. Unsurprisingly, deaths and injuries to horses, if not to riders, are far from uncommon (Nick Timiraos, 'The Race Where Horses Die', *Wall Street Journal*, August 11, 2007, http://online.wsj.com/public/article/SB118678342614494614-M49PZaSriaBsYASGQhdKeSlj5OU_20080810.html?mod=rss_free The Race Where Horses Die (accessed January 22, 2019).
111. As well as *Indian Relay*, examples include *Fast Horse*, directed by Alexandra Lazarowich (2018; Edmonton, Canada; Handful of Films), https://handfuloffilms.ca/our-films/fast-horse/ (accessed October 28, 2019), and *Equus: Story of the Horse*, directed by Niobe Thompson (2019; Edmonton, Canada; Handful of Films), https://handfuloffilms.ca/our-films/equus-story-horse/ (accessed October 28, 2019).
112. Catlin, *Letters*, 143.
113. Ewers, *The Horse in the Blackfoot Indian Culture*, 235.
114. See also, for example, Mike Huggins, *Flat Racing and British Society, 1790–1914: A Social and Economic History* (London: Frank Cass, 2000); Elizabeth Tobey, 'The Palio in Italian Renaissance Art, Thought, and Culture' (Ph.D. diss., University of Maryland-College Park, 2005). Peter Edwards, Karl Enenkel, and Elspeth Graham, eds., *The Horse as Cultural Icon: The Real and the Symbolic Horse in the Early Modern World* (Leiden: Brill, 2012); 593–624; and Sinclair Bell and Carolyn Willekes, 'Horse Racing and Chariot Racing', in *The Oxford Handbook of Animals in Classical Thought and Life*, ed. Gordon Campbell (Oxford: Oxford University Press, 2014), 478–90.
115. Elizabeth Atwood Lawrence, *Hoofbeats and Society: Studies of Human-Horse Interactions* (Bloomington: Indiana University Press, 1985); Bethke, 'Dog Days to Horse Days'; Seifert, 'An Introduction to Contemporary Native American Horse Culture', 147.
116. Mitchell, *Horse Nations*.
117. John Cooper, 'The Araucanians', in *Handbook of South American Indians, Volume 2: The Andean Civilizations*, ed. Julian Steward (Washington, DC: Smithsonian Institution, 1946), 687–760; George Musters, *At Home with the Patagonians* (London: John Murray, 1871); Alfred Métraux, 'Indians of the Gran Chaco', in *Handbook of South American Indians, Volume 1: The Marginal Tribes*, ed. Julian Steward (Washington, DC: Smithsonian Institution, 1946), 197–370; Kathryn Hunter, 'Rough Riding: Aboriginal Participation in Rodeos and Travelling Shows to the 1950s', *Aboriginal History* 32 (2008): 82–96; Carolyn Mincham, 'A Social and Cultural History of the New Zealand Horse' (Ph.D. diss., Massey University, 2008); Felipe Garay Méndez, 'El hacerse hombre en la Guerra: la construcción de las masculinidades en el caso de Bahía Portete' (Monografía de Grado, Universidad del Rosario, Bogotá, 2014), 73.
118. Catlin, *Letters and Notes on the Manners, Customs and Conditions of North American Indians, Vol. 1*, 143.

## Acknowledgments

I am grateful to Christian Mann and Christian Jaser for inviting me to take part in the meeting that was the genesis of this special issue. I should also like to thank Patrick Alexander for his comments on the essay (though he has, of course, no responsibility for its contents), as well as Britt Bousman for helping to locate some of the more difficult to acquire references, Sam Lunn-Rockliffe for the map, and the referees for their helpful and informative suggestions.

## Disclosure Statement

No potential conflict of interest was reported by the author(s).

# Index

**Note:** *Italic* page numbers refer to figures

African horses 48–9
agones 4, 9–10
agonistic victor monuments 14
Alibeyköy 5, 92, 97, 98
ancient Olympic Games 2
Anne, Queen 153, 164
Anselm of Yberg 119
apobates 10
archery competitions 96, 100–1
art 15–16, 28, 53, 81, 142, 170
Artan, Tülay 5
athletic abilities 42
athletic competition 28, 51–2, 80
athletics 14
athletic victors 29, 40

Bank of England 169
Barlow, Frances *156*
Bell, Sinclair 4
betting 4, 6–7, 38, 168, 170–6, 185–6, 191–2
Blackfoot 182, 185–6, 188–90
Bragadin, Piero 100
breeding horses 14, 177
byzantine chariot races/racing 5, 78–9, 84, 87, 96
Byzantine Empire 78–80, 83, 85–6

Cameron, Alan 79, 84–5
Catholics 5, 150, 157, 160–3
Catlin, George 186
charioteers 3, 5, 11–15, 20, 36–46, 48–53, 79
chariot races/racing 4–5, 8–12, 14, 18, 29, 32, 36–7, 42, 46, 51, 53, 78–87
chariots 9–13, 15, 36, 38–40, 45–6, 49, 79, 82
Charles II of England 5, 149–52, 156–8
Chartaricon 97
circus at Arles 31
circus at Tarragona 31
Circus Maximus 28–32, 34, 36–7, 44, 52–3, 96
City of London 170–1, 173, 175–6

coinage 4, 14, 19–20, 34, 169
Columbian Exchange 183
Comanche 185–6, 188, 192
competitions 2, 4–5, 9, 11, 52, 91, 93, 101, 104, 107, 118–19, 122–3, 134–5, 192–3
conquistadors 139, 141–3
Constantine I 79, 96
Constantinople 5, 13, 36, 79–81, 83, 85–7, 92, 96, 109

Digard, Jean-Pierre 144

economic effect 119
Eisenberg, Christiane 6
emperors 5, 34–7, 41, 53, 78–87
England 5–6, 156, 158, 162, 168–9, 175–6
English Financial Revolution 6, 168
epigrams 17–18
epinician 18
equestrianism 134–5, 143, 183
equestrian spectacles 134, 137, 142–4
equestrian victors 4, 14, 18
Equine Performance 28, 48
euripus 30, 32, 34, 36, 38–9
exclusion crisis 155, 157, 160, 162, 164

factions 11, 29, 36–40, 42–7, 51, 80, 83
Fallows, Joel 137
fastest horses 103, 185
festivals 9–10, 13, 32, 101, 106
festivities 91, 93, 96, 98–102, 106–7, 135
financial markets 6, 170–6
Florence 119, 121, 126
foot races 119, 189, 192
four-horse chariot race 9–11, 17

Gamauf, Richard 42
gambling 170–3, 175–6, 178, 182, 188–9, 191
games of canes 5, 135, 137–9

grandees 106, 108, 135
Greeks 11–13, 29, 32, 44, 51–2, 97

Helenus 43–4, 52
Hidirlik 103–5
hippic disciplines 4, 9–11
hippodrome 5, 9, 11–14, 79–86, 96–7, 100–1, 105–6
horseback race 9–10
horsemanship 151, 158
horse medicine 188
Horse Races Act 176–7
horse racing/races 2–8, 12–13, 29, 50–1, 91–3, 96–7, 99–103, 105–10, 118–19, 124–5, 134–5, 138, 144, 149–51, 156–8, 160–4, 168, 171–8, 182–6, *183*, 188–94; cultures 2, 135; emergence of 5–6; practices 177, 183, 194; traditions 7, 134, 192–4
horse raids 190
Horsmann, Gerhard 42

imperial government 80, 82, 86–7
imperial ideology 84–5
Indian Relay 7, 192–4
infamia 41–2
inscriptions 11, 17, 31, 37, 40, 44, 46, 48–50, 154
Istanbul 91–3, 97, 99, 105–6, 108–9

Jaser, Christian 4–5
Jockey Club 5, 152, 161, 163

Kağidhane 92–3, 97–8, 100–1, 105–9
Klosterman, Johann *154*
Kurke, Leslie 19

late medieval Spain 134–5, 137
Leppin, Hartmut 81
light horses 172, 175, 177
Lull, Ramon 142

Machuca, Bernardo de Vargas 142
Malalas, John 80
Mann, Christian 4
Mantuan margraves 125
Marcellinus, Ammianus 38
Markus, Thomas 53
meadows 97–8, 109
Mitchell, Peter 6
modern races 79
Monmouth 150–1, 157–60, 162–4
*moros y cristianos* 135
Mortimer, Thomas 172
mule-cart race 9
Mustafa, Celâlzâde 96, 100

Nash, Richard 5–6
Newmarket 149–53, 155–8, 160–4, 175, 177
Nika Riot 83–4, 86
nobility 121, 137–8, 142–3, 160, 177
North America 6, 183–4, 194

Olympia 9–13, 18–20
Olympic Games 9, 11–12, 46
Olympic victory 11–12, 20
option trading 6, 168, 171–3
ordlingen 118–22
organizational structures 118
Ottoman Court 91
Ottoman horse racing 92, 97, 108

palio victories 124–5
Parnell, David Alan 5
Pausanias 10, 12–13
Pheidolas, Corinthian 12
pernicious practices 190–1
politics 85, 158, 163
power 5, 11–12, 18, 20, 84–6, 93, 136, 141, 144, 153, 160, 169–70
Pratt, Mary Louise 144
prize money 102, 104, 176
prizes 3–5, 9–11, 13, 39, 42, 95, 100–1, 104, 106, 118–19, 125–6, 151, 153
professional careers 42
Protestants 5, 155, 157–8, 160, 164
Ptolemaic dynasty 17–18

quadrigarius 42–3
qualities 3, 120, 122, 141, 155, 158, 189

racecourses 7, 37, 109, 154, 173, 175–6
race field 100–1, 103
race horses 3–4, 11, 36, 43, 48–9, 51, 118–20, 122–6, 154–5, 186–7, 189
race organization 3–5
race patrons 118, 122, 124–5
racetracks 3–4, 34, 39, 45, 51, 118–21
Remijsen, Sophie 52
Roman Charioteers 40, 42, 44
Roman Circus 2–3, 29, 53, 96
Romans 16, 29, 32, 34, 36, 41–2, 45–8, 52–3, 123
Rowlandson, Thomas *174*
royal plates 149–52, 160, 163

Sanuto, Marino 100
Scharff, Sebastian 4
Scharlach races 5, 117–18, 120–2, 124–6
Schürch, Isabelle 5
self-representation 4, 14, 18, 42
Selim III 99, 109

# INDEX

Septimius Severus 79, 96
shipwrecks 40
social complexity 124
social differentiation 143
social disciplining 176
Spanish conquest 133-4, 139, 141-2
Spanish horse riding 135
Spanish horses 133-4, 142, 144
spatial arrangements 2, 5, 118, 120
spectators 3-4, 13, 29-30, 37-8, 40, 47, 50-1, 53, 78-85, 103, 109, 118, 121-2
sporting impulses 6, 171
sporting victors 19
sport of horse racing 150-1, 163
sport of kings 3-6, 149-50

Tarragona 31, 45
teams 3, 14, 38-40, 45-6, 49, 53, 79-80, 82, 138, 192-3
Thompson, David 185, 190

tribes 185, 188, 190, 192, 194
trophies 153-5
two-horse chariot race 9, 20, 43

umpires 11-13, 93, 95, 104, 173
urban horse races 118, 121, 125
urban space 120, 136, 143
urban spectacle 28

values 40, 42, 137, 142, 160, 163, 194
victories 3, 5, 9, 11-12, 14, 17-20, 36-7, 39-40, 42-3, 46, 50, 53, 79, 124, 157-8
victorious horses 14, 125
victor monuments 14-16
victor statues 14, 16

Wacke, Andreas 42
wagering 170, 188
winnings 11, 13, 46, 52-3, 123-4, 151, 173-5, 189, 193

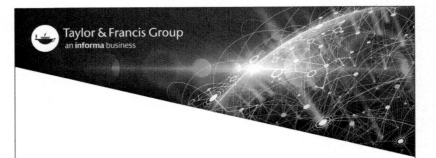